Please Take Me Home

Also by Clare Campbell and Christy Campbell

Bonzo's War: Animals Under Fire
Dogs of Courage: When Britain's Pets Went to War

Please Take Me Home

The Story of the Rescue Cat

Clare Campbell and Christy Campbell

corsair

CORSAIR

First published in Great Britain in 2016 by Corsair

13 5 7 9 10 8 6 4 2

A CIP catalogue record for this book
is available from the British Library.

ISBN: 978-1-4721-1569-0 (hardback)

Typeset by Hewer Text UK Ltd, Edinburgh
Printed and bound in Great Britain by CPI Group (UK) Ltd., Croydon, CR0 4YY

Papers used by Corsair are from well-managed forests
and other responsible sources.

MIX
Paper from
responsible sources
FSC® C104740

Corsair
An imprint of
Little, Brown Book Group
Carmelite House
50 Victoria Embankment
London EC4Y 0DZ

An Hachette UK Company
www.hachette.co.uk

www.littlebrown.co.uk

To all forsaken cats . . .
and those who sought to save them.

Contents

Author's Note

I have loved cats for as long as I can remember. From my earliest years, cats have comforted and reassured me, and occasionally even licked away the tears from my eyes when I was sad. And in return I have loved them, fed them, paid their vets' bills and mourned them with a lasting grief when they eventually died. I have never forgotten a single one of any of the eleven cats I have owned during my lifetime: Frosty, Ginger, Queenie, Lisa, Benny, TC, Heathcliff, Oscar, Ferdy, and our own 'rescue' cats, Fergus and Luis. This feline roll of honour is engraved on my heart.

Cat love runs in the family. My aunt, my namesake Clare, used to collect strays from a very young age in Cork where she grew up, infuriating my Irish grandfather, so I would be told, by feeding them under the table and sneaking them up to her room at night. All three of our children are following in their parents' paw steps and are already firmly committed cat people.

According to the animal behaviour expert, Professor John Bradshaw, one of the distinctions between the way that dogs and cats interact with human beings is that dogs know we are different to them and cats don't. Cats apparently see us as odd-shaped members of their own tribe. Each of the behaviours they display towards us, such as purring, kneading, 'chinning' and sometimes washing our faces or hair with their tongues, is a variant on the mother–kitten relationship. But it's never quite certain in our house who is the mum and who is the kitten.

In evolutionary terms, our 9,000-year love affair with cats is still in its early days. So yes, we sometimes get it wrong – and in the past we often got it *very* wrong, as researching this extraordinary story showed my husband and co-author Christy over and over again. In the comparatively short history of human interaction with cats, we have used them to rid us of rats and mice, then turned them into pets for our amusement – and now here's the shocking part – before killing them, in the name of 'kindness', when we decided that they had too many kittens.

A century ago, many towns and cities had some sort of 'cat rescue league'. What actually happened to the rescuees? Well, we decided to find out.

How could we have mistreated them so – the stray cats, the feral cats? Why were those humans who sought to help them so often derided as mad or just prolonging the animals' misery? Why did it take so long for minds to change?

Eventually, things did get better. Having a rescue cat is now a badge of honour, and those who do the actual rescuing – then *and* now – are worthy of much more honour still. A lot of what follows in this book is as much about those noble pioneers as about cats.

Beyond all this there are many of us who genuinely love cats while at the same time respecting their right to be their own contrary, always independent furry selves. I don't believe I am exploiting the cats sitting in front of my fire on a winter's evening. They clearly have the upper paw in our relationship. And I wouldn't have it any other way.

Interaction between humans and cats, as with all animals, is still on its own trajectory. It is destined to change again, as it has in the generations before us, and will continue to do so after we are gone. All we can hope for is that it will be a change for the better.

Clare Campbell

On Becoming a Cat Rescuer

There are many and varied reasons why cats become rescue cats, as this book shows. Mostly, it is due to some human's fault. How people get hold of rescue cats is more straightforward. You just look on-line and go to an adoption centre (see p. 403). The self-adopting stray is another common way, but make sure you are not snatching someone's lost pet or a neighbour's greedy cat looking for an extra dinner. Do all the right veterinary stuff and be committed long-term if you are going to keep it.

Which leaves the really big question. *How do humans become cat rescuers?*

The key personalities in the story that follows, the mind-changers, the rescuers, the innovators – *not* the killers and the hoarders – are remarkable women: it's an all-female thing. People like Alice Swifte, Anne Mayhew, Alice Gordon, Jessey Wade, Nerea de Clifford, Babette Lewyt, Betsy Saul, Sarah Grove-Grady, Mary, Duchess of Bedford, Ruth Plant, Kate Horne, Jenny Remfry and Celia Hammond will be forever righteous among cats. But so will the many thousands of go-it-alone individuals and volunteers for cat protection groups whose dedication over many years has made things that bit better for the animals we love.

How did they start? What motivates them?

I could do little better than enquire further by following my own cats' stories. Our beloved ginger cat, 'Ferdy', had died. Our twelve-year-old son was grieving and so were we. The house was empty. One day I looked at the internet, tapped in 'rescue kitten south London' and found a cat rescue not far away in Clapham. It was an Edwardian house with a small walled garden, bright and clean and full – but not too full – of cats. We took two, did the vet stuff and never looked back. Several years later, we returned to ask our friend Victoria how she got started. This is her story:

If you are born with compassion towards animals, it is a feeling you cannot ignore, or ever walk away from. From a very young age I found it impossible to pass a stray cat or dog by the roadside without imagining how I would feel if I found myself abandoned, hungry or homeless.

Brought up by my parents in a flat in Prague, in Czechoslovakia, I longed for a dog. When my parents told me they were not allowed to keep pets in our apartment, I used to borrow other people's dogs instead, going to the park and asking if I could walk the dogs I met there, or sometimes even luring cats and dogs back to the flat and feeding them anyway. I remember in particular a large Alsatian I made friends with and used to bring home all the time.

At the age of seven or eight I noticed that a block of flats near our apartment had a cellar with bars across the windows. Peering into this one day I saw a tabby cat at the window and someone moving around in the dark. Wondering to myself, 'Why would anyone be living in a cellar?' I summoned up my courage and knocked on the door.

It was opened by an old lady who told me that her son had escaped from Prague to go and live in the US, leaving her alone to face the confiscation of the family's money and property as a result. So now she lived a beggar's life, sleeping in a cellar and feeding her two cats on whatever scraps she could find.

Moved to tears by her story, I decided to help her. For several years after this I used to take her food from our flat whenever I could, until one day I went to visit her and found the cellar boarded up. After asking the people who lived in the neighbouring apartments if they knew her, I was told that she had died suddenly. No one knew what had happened to her cats but it bothered me all my life that I never discovered what happened to them, and did not get the chance to help them. It was the most traumatic event of my childhood.

Coming to Britain as a young woman in the 1970s, I started living in a house near Clapham Common with my then boyfriend, Joseph, later to become my husband. One day, our black and white cat went missing and I started walking around the roads nearby, calling and searching for him.

Meeting an old woman in her seventies, I asked her if she had seen my cat. She told me her name was Hilda and that she herself had several strays, including a black and white one, at the house she shared with her two sisters in nearby Wakehurst Road. She invited me to come back and see if one of the cats might be mine.

Going into the house was fascinating, and the relationship between the three unmarried sisters positively Chekhovian. Although the cat Hilda told me about turned out not to be mine (ours later returned home safely), Hilda and I quickly became friends – to the extent that following the death of her two sisters several years later, Hilda suggested that Joseph and I move in with her.

Although we initially refused, on the basis that we were young and enjoyed having noisy parties at home that she might not appreciate, Hilda eventually managed to persuade us to come and live in Wakehurst Road. As we were both working as teachers, we raised a mortgage to buy half the house from her, continuing to help her in her cat rescue and re-homing work and now starting to do a lot of our own as well.

The first cat we took in ourselves was a pregnant stray tortoiseshell whom we named 'Rosie'. Within days of finding her, she gave birth to four kittens. Knowing that we could not keep all four we had to have two destroyed (it seemed the right thing to do, but was very upsetting) but kept the remaining two with us. Turning one bedroom upstairs into our 'cat room', we also started looking out for strays on the Common (there had previously been a colony of feral cats in the area) as well as encouraging cats to come into our garden by putting out titbits and leaving the door of the shed ajar so that it was easy for them to come in and shelter. Pretty soon, we had Rosie and a further tabby living with us, to be shortly followed by several new furry residents.

Whenever we could, we found homes for our rescuees, always checking beforehand that the home environment was suited to the cat's needs. Only very rarely would we give a kitten to anyone elderly, although in one case we did where the cat lived very happily until being returned to us as arranged on the eventual death of her lady owner.

During this time, I also met and befriended Kathleen, an Irish cat-lover who used to come and stay in our house and look after our cats whenever Joseph and I went to Prague to visit our families.

One night while we were away we got a call in Prague to say that Kathleen's husband had been killed in a hit-and-run accident while out walking their dog. Joseph and I returned immediately and tried to help Kathleen after that as much as we could. Joseph assisted her in making an insurance claim following the loss of her husband, and Kathleen then asked him to invest the money for her by buying her a retirement property near Waterford in Ireland.

Although Kathleen herself didn't show much interest in looking after the property, both Joseph and I felt it should be kept in good order and used to visit Ireland several times a year to open up the house and maintain it properly.

It was on these visits that we first started to notice how many stray cats and kittens there were in the area. Local people did not seem to allow their cats into their homes, and cats and kittens being killed on the roads was an almost daily occurrence. Often the youngest kittens would crawl under the bonnets of cars to keep warm, only to be killed instantly when the engine was switched on.

At first Joseph and I tried in vain to see if we could persuade their owners to neuter them, even offering to do so at our own expense, but our neighbours appeared outraged by this suggestion and seemed to think it was a sin against nature rather than a way of minimising the massacre of unwanted cats. So instead we began taking them in ourselves, and driving them back to the UK to find homes for them here.

On our next trip to Waterford I was walking along the beach one day when I found an injured seagull. Asking at the local post office if there was a vet in the village, they directed me to the house of an old lady called Mary Galvin, who operated an animal rescue shelter from her small coastguard's cottage nearby. From then on we became friends, helping one another both with homing and caring for any animals we found . . .

Often we would return from our trips to Ireland with as many as three cats and two dogs in the car with us. It wasn't difficult to do this, as animals didn't need pet passports at that time, and as there was no rabies in either Ireland or the UK, the authorities were fairly relaxed.

Then one day Mary took me with her to introduce me to Ann Schunmann, a German-born woman who had left her former home in Kent and gone to live in Ireland at the age of seventy-two in order to buy a cottage near the mountains and start her own animal rescue centre.

Ann was an immensely strong-minded and impressive woman. Her house was surrounded by two acres of land, backing on to woodland at the foot of a mountain range. It was exquisitely beautiful but Ann was more concerned about rescuing animals than admiring the countryside.

From then on, Joseph and I began bringing even more cats back to the UK, on one occasion having twenty-six in the back of the car in a single trip. Meanwhile, back at home we began spreading our net wider to find the most suitable homes. At first we had worked mainly by word of mouth. But now we joined websites, working with cat charities in order to find the best homes for the cats we were bringing here.

Among these charities were Cats Protection in Purley, south London; Romney House Cat Rescue, which is managed by Sylvana, a very good friend of mine who runs a charity from her own home; and finally Happy Endings in Kent, the project of two wonderful young men called Chris and Terry who have frequently helped me to raise money to support Ann now that she is getting older and more frail.

Mary Galvin from the coastguard's cottage has since sadly died, while at ninety-one, Ann too will soon have to hand over the day-to-day running of her shelter. But for now she is still determined to keep going for as long as she can, in spite of her increasing infirmity. That's what loving cats is like. You can't give up even when reason is saying you really should . . .

Our own dear rescue cats, Fergus and Luis, were left in a basket on Ann Schunmann's doorstep in Ireland five years ago. We are forever in her debt for the two dearest felines imaginable.

A Note on the Sources

Cats are not known for writing their memoirs; rescue cats in particular would find it especially difficult. However, those who love cats or work around them professionally as vets, rescuers, advocates, behaviourists – and indeed, persecutors – have left abundant records. Cat ladies of the past, also known as 'auxiliary feeders' or 'care-givers', were, by their nature, highly secretive – until their nocturnal doings turned up in press reports or court cases when things got out of hand. Some of their stories were recorded by Ruth Plant, founder of Cat Action Trust, in an unpublished manuscript kindly made available to the authors by Dr Jenny Remfry, beacon of feral cat research in Britain.

Published sources drawn on for this history include contemporary journals and magazines, especially *Our Cats* for the Edwardian period, the *Animal World* (journal of the RSPCA), which also includes pre-1908 extracts from the Annual Reports of the Battersea Home for Lost and Starving Dogs, *The Cat*, journal of the Cats Protection League (a vital source), the *Veterinary Record*, *Truth*, the *Herald of the Golden Dawn*, the *Animals' Friend*, *Pet Trade News*, *Fur Trade News*, plus many American and UK national and regional newspapers, a substantial proportion of which have been digitised by 2016 and are held on microfilm at the British Library in London.

The story of Mrs Morgan and the Royal Cat Scandal of 1903 is on file at the National Archives – opened after a

100-year closure. The less sensitive, perhaps, wartime records of NARPAC and the later feral colony travails of the British Museum are also there and have long been available. The London Metropolitan Archives have early material gathered by Charity Organisation Society snoopers on cat shelters in the metropolis, and on the notorious 'Cat Contessa', the Countess de la Torre. The conflicts between the US Humane Society, PETA, and the advocates of 'no-kill' are widely recorded on the internet. *Messybeast.com*, curated by hands-on cat rescuer, Sarah Hartwell, is a peerless source of cat-human history. It also succeeds admirably in its founder's aim of providing 'a convenient on-line resource for owners of old or disabled cats, [made] freely available to the smaller, independent cat-rescue groups'.

Some UK animal charities, unfortunately, are historically revisionist about their record, and bar access to their archives by researchers. Nor are they subject to Freedom of Information legislation. Blue Cross (ODFL) and Cats Protection have been admirably open. We are especially grateful to the RSPCA for making available to the authors the records of the Homeless Cats Sub-Committee (1911–14) and the Homeless Animals Sub-Committee (1966–74), both of them at times jaw-dropping reads.

Abbreviations

ADL	Animal Defence League
C4	London Cat Care and Control Consortium
CAT	Action Trust
CHAT	Celia Hammond Action Trust
COS	Charity Organisation Society
CPL	Cats Protection League
EBI	Euthanasia by Injection
FAB	Feline Advisory Bureau
FeLV	Feline Leukaemia
FIV	Feline Immunodeficiency Virus
GCCF	Governing Council of the Cat Fancy
HAS	Human Animal Studies
HSUS	Humane Society of the United States
NARPAC	National Air Raid Precautions Animals Committee
ODFL	Our Dumb Friends' League
PDSA	People's Dispensary for Sick Animals of the Poor
PTS	Put To Sleep
RSPCA	Royal Society for the Prevention of Cruelty to Animals
SBDA	Society to Befriend Domestic Animals
SFSPCA	San Francisco Society for the Prevention of Cruelty to Animals
SNIP	Society for Neutering Islington's Pussies
SPCA	Society for the Prevention of Cruelty to Animals
TAVR	Trap Alter Vaccinate and Return
TNR	Trap Neuter and Return
UFAW	Universities Federation for Animal Welfare

Introduction

Everyone loves hearing a story about a cat that gets lost and finds its way home. It might be the distance travelled, it might be the length of time it was missing – months, years even – that makes the particular story especially worth telling, but there is that wonderful feeling when it turns out well. The cat is back where it belongs, in a home, with a family or loving owner whose human heartbreak at the loss has been healed in a flash. The cat, one feels sure, is also pleased at the outcome.

Lots of us let cats roam at will outside the house – that's why cat flaps were invented – hence we also know the tremulous worry when our friend fails to appear on cue around feeding time, when the snoozing spot on the sofa remains empty for too long, when the call at the back door mysteriously brings no response. And the overwhelming relief when a mysteriously wet and ruffled character does at last reappear. What cat-lover is unmoved by a LOST CAT poster taped to a lamp-post with a plea by some traumatised owner for a sighting? Or excited and relieved by the sadly much rarer CAT FOUND announcement with its promise of joy at cats and humans reunited. It's been going on for ever. Cats Protection has a LOST CAT placard from 1860s London in its archive which was reproduced in one of the early editions of its hugely informative journal, *The Cat*.

Your cat isn't going to tell you where it's been, what sort of secret adventure it found preferable to your company, what type of attention or food it got or what laps it might

have curled up on during its time away . . . but you can fanta-
sise. You might even be cross. *Now don't you dare go straying
again!* But you know too that whatever wild-side excitements
the neighbour's garden may have temporarily provided,
home really is where your cat's heart is.

That's the thing about cats. Why the solitary predator that
came to dinner chose to stay is still an unsolved mystery. Some
say we 'domesticated' cats for own cave-dwelling convenience. Others will tell us that cats adopted us because our cosy
homes represented a (sometimes) benign habitat niche.

All we know is that by 'owning' cats we are obliged to look
after them, to provide food and shelter, veterinary intervention including neutering, spaying and vaccination, and, on a
good day, micro-chipping and insurance. And love. We have
obligations toward our cats which most of us are more than
happy to fulfil in return for what we foolishly (some like to
tell us) regard as their loyalty and affection. Those obligations
continue as we try to contort the cat into an ever more compli-
ant part of our own complex lives.

And cats *are* amazingly loyal – although greedy cats will go
looking for extra treats and a neglected cat will leave if it can.
But in our way of looking at it, and as emerges in this narrative, no cat ever 'escapes' from human company. It *strays*.

That is what makes it so big a deal when a cat goes missing.
Which is why, if a cat stays missing, we comfort ourselves
with myths about strays being adopted by kindly strangers. In
a tradition sadly discontinued, the Edwardian magazine *Our
Cats* and *The Cat*, the now 85-year-old journal of the Cats
Protection League, regularly featured heart-rending poems
ostensibly sent in for publication by stray cats.

Domestic cats never submitted poems about how content
they were. Perhaps they were too lazy or too comfortable to
bother. Versifying cats faded from fashion, but from the 1960s
on, as the era of what would come to be called 're-homing'

dawned, their place would be taken by a new wave of literary felines skilled in writing tear-jerking autobiographies. Sometimes these drama-filled back-stories would be relayed from a human, third-person point of view. Whatever, these mini-memoirs remain a universal means of grabbing the attention of a potential adopter of a cat in trouble. The authors have collected their favourite examples from over the past half-century and reproduced them throughout, in the text and at the beginning of each chapter. Some might come from recent internet posts – although it is to be firmly hoped that by the time this book appears, the cats in question will have long since had their pleas answered; others come from way back. They may seem formulaic: there's a lot of why-you-will-love-me information to get across in a short space, but they are never banal. In fact, we think they are deeply moving.

The emotional power of cats, especially stray cats, was what compelled the human participants in *Please Take Me Home* to make their sometimes extreme interventions in feline affairs. Which is where this story really starts – with the will of a wealthy Victorian woman, Mary Anne Kennett, who wanted to be kind to 'lost and starving' cats in the way she considered best. As it turned out, the money she left to a famous institution would be used for something that was the opposite of benign – but it was the beginning of a moral stampede. Having invited this wild, independent creature into our cities, humans were alarmed when the cat population expanded out of control. It was down to us to make good our terrible mistake – but what to do?

Arguments on that same subject would rage for decades. Was it right to destroy outcast cats and their offspring in acts described as 'care' and 'mercy', or to effect mass sterilisation – or was it better to encourage adoption, the process which would come to be known as 're-homing'?

Huge sums of money left in the wills of wealthy women were fought over, since people really hate it when an aunt

leaves her money to cats! When the concept of animal rights
– as opposed to animal welfare – came along, the arguments
got even more strident. Cat-lovers found themselves derided
as mawkish sentimentalists.

Cats always engender deep passions, cats in trouble especially so. There have always been cats in trouble. There
always will be.

But very slowly, things did get better for cats generally. It
would take over a century – a millennium in cat years – for the
'disreputable stray' to become the twenty-first-century must-
have fashion icon and internet sensation – the rescue cat.

It happened more or less in three waves. At the beginning
there were domestic cats who lived in comfortable cohabita-
tion with humans. Then there was the second estate, of stray
cats: 'friendless', 'forsaken', they had become detached from
humankind, but were still at heart one of us. And because of
that they deserved a special fate – sadly, not necessarily a good
one.

Beyond that was the third feline estate – nobody's cat –
hardly seen, tended by armies of women in the darkness. In
the compass of the authors' own childhood memories, the
winds of war had left such animals stranded in cities as bomb-
site colonists, breeding down the generations as urban wildlife. These were the 'feral' cats. Little by little, they too would
begin to be accepted, as our modern mindset turned from the
mass destruction of the past to the concept of individual
rehabilitation.

Every life worth trying to save. Every cat deserving of a
home. *Please Take Me Home* is the 150-year story of how all
the lost cats came in from the cold.

In the fashionable academic niche of 'Human Animal Studies'
there has been a recent boom over the last three decades in

studies of pets in history, but often these cut-and-paste theory-heavy observations fail to pursue primary sources. Dogs are big. Cats get scant attention. One of the most accessible writers in this field, Erica Fudge, wrote sagely in 2008: 'We can see, I think, that a cat's refusal to conform to human expectations and desires makes it the ideal pet for philosophers to contemplate.'* How true. Cats secretly know this. They especially love being contemplated by philosophers. Dogs, not so much.

Charities do not help when some of them bar access to their archives or dress up their historic record of mass killing as something different. It's sensitive where legacies are involved. And felines are tricky. Are they truly companion animals, or are they what one historian called 'the anti-pet par excellence'? What is their economic function? Where do they fit in, in 'a world liberated from human speciesism', as new wave, post-human studies might phrase it? Are they even worthy of investigation? A recent history of animals in cities ('urb-an-imals') ignored cats entirely. Perhaps they were just too difficult.

What follows, the authors hope, is an entertaining and readable narrative, but one full of challenges. Our researches revealed a catastrophe of biblical proportions, of the industrialised destruction of beautiful, blameless creatures, of a tragic delusion that for so long made that destruction acceptable. It is a story of cruelty and kindness, of casual indifference and

---

* The French philosopher, Jacques Derrida, delivered a to-be famous address, 'The Animal That Therefore I Am (More to Follow)', at a conference in 1997, inspired at the outset by being followed into the bathroom by his loved and securely homed female cat and intensely stared at while he was naked ('there is no nudity in nature'). This prompted a moral meditation, published in book form after his death, on the logic and ethics of distinguishing the human from the animal. 'Derrida's Cat' would become a universal player in first-wave critical animal theory, to the general benefit of all cats – including strays. There's a mug and a T-shirt.

intense, caring energy. And of the flow of legacies to charities which shamelessly pitched for the business.

Above all, it is a story of a great *change of mind* – the dawning realisation that killing 'unwanted' companion animals in their millions for human convenience was a moral outrage – and of the people who brought that about.

The fight continues.

The bravery and loyalty of our cats towards us never falters – however badly we may have treated them. As we researched this story, we often wondered why cats did not simply rise up and overthrow their oppressors long ago. Perhaps one day they will.

Along the way there are the stories of the many people who really cared about cats. Who had to take hard decisions. Who were practical and kind, and did something good for cats in their lives – and were doubtless loved in return. In our own tiny way, as adopters of two rescue cats, we know a little of how that feels.

Clare and Christy Campbell

PART ONE

ONLY A STRAY

1850–1930

1

In the Matter of Cats

'Cats are not born attached to people; they're born ready to learn how to attach themselves to people.'

Dr John Bradshaw, *Cat Sense*, 2014

'I want a cat. I want a cat now. If I can't have . . . any fun, I can have a kitty.'

Ernest Hemingway, *Cat In the Rain*, 1925

'When humans go into space on a permanent basis they will most likely take cats and not dogs.'

pgtruspace, online commentator,
Scientific American, May 2009

Once upon a time, all domestic cats were rescue cats. All cat-persons know that in the great understanding reached between cats and humans countless centuries ago, wild felines were invited into cosy caves and cabins and given a bit of food and shelter in return for doing what came naturally – killing mice.

Those cats who were genetically friendly continued to turn up at the door. Down the generations the snuggle-up gene came out on top and the run-under-the-sofa gene was suppressed, although it's still in there. Cats may, in fact, have domesticated themselves, but it was clear to those they had so purringly beguiled, that they had been rescued from their own brutish condition by being given a purpose in the service of man.

It was up to cats if they broke the bargain by breeding over-enthusiastically, killing birds, getting lost, sharpening their claws on the furniture, making too much noise, spraying, fighting, hissing or generally being difficult. Then they might be cast back into the wild and need rescuing all over again by old ladies who lived in the woods.

But then things got more complicated. Humans moved to cities and took cats with them. As industrial societies grew and prospered, certain animals became 'companions', to be treated as members of the family. However, cats, unlike dogs, had not had to be selectively bred over the preceding centuries to be useful, to hunt things, dig out badgers or herd sheep. In their long relationship with humans, had cats really been domesticated – or had they simply found the best survival niche ever? Some people would come to think they were only pretending to like us all along.

A twenty-first-century animal behaviourist asked: 'Cats contribute virtually nothing in the way of sustenance or work to human endeavour. How, then, did they become commonplace fixtures in our homes?' We all know why. They did so by being cats.

But even after several millennia of hanging round humans, cats still had a long way to go. 'It is the fashion to ascribe to the cat very few good abilities. She is said to be selfish, cruel, greedy and without an atom of affection, indeed in disposition the very reverse of the dog,' said *Beeton's Book of Home Pets*, published in 1861. 'Popular opinion may be summarised in the following effusion of a modern writer – "I do not love the cat. His disposition is mean and suspicious".' Cats might even consider themselves to be the superior in their relationship with a human, unlike dogs with all that boisterously desperate master-adoration.

It had taken a long time, but by the second half of the nineteeth century in Europe and America, cats began to clamber their way, first into respectable family households as the furry essence of happy domesticity, and on into the higher reaches of fashionable society – to come out on top in a fluffy parade of 'pedigree' Persians, Angoras and other much-to-be-brushed exotica beloved of middle- and upper-class ladies. They were indeed 'pets', their primary function to be pampered objects of adoration – which might even give a little affection back in return.

Cats were developing a class structure – posh cats, bourgeois cats and the teeming under-cats, who existed on the fringes of polite society but still within it, expected to earn their keep as mouse-catching militia in humbler but still cat-loving homes.

In the matter of acquiring a cat, 'pedigrees' came from established breeders. Lowlier cats came from family or neighbours, from street markets like Club Row in east London or kittens peddled door to door. Seeking out an adult cat and giving it a home was rare – although several pioneer lost cats' home promoters like Anne Mayhew would try and place their older street-finds with well-wishers. The self-adopting stray was something for mad cat ladies.

A stray cat was a 'disreputable' creature (the word was used by a leading charity), pestiferous, disease-spreading, something from the gutter. One might as well invite a rat into a respectable home.*

---

* For many years from the 1880s onwards, clinical researchers published findings on cats as transmitters of diphtheria to humans, especially children. 'It is a frequent occurrence to see children carrying cats in their arms, and even kissing them. It is obvious that if the cat were ill with diphtheria, the children under such circumstances would almost inevitably contract the disease,' said one such. The supposed connection was sustained by public health and school officials in Britain until disproved in the 1920s, but the prejudice persisted for many decades thereafter – a constant counter to the prospect of adopting a stray into a family.

An urban cat economy was established in parallel in which lowly livings might be made – such as the 'cats'-meat men' who acquired horse-flesh and offal from slaughtered working horses and sold it on skewers for a farthing as food for domestic cats. They would know where kittens were to be had. Veterinary intervention meanwhile was virtually non-existent.

Some grander city cats inhabited a strange halfway world as nursery favourites or inhabitants of the servants' hall, until the time came for the master and mistress to shut up their sumptuous houses to leave for the country in early autumn, when the cats were simply abandoned and left to fend for themselves. This scandal of the 'forsaken cat' would go on for decades.

The forsaken cat was a different creature to the 'lost cat'; different again to the 'wandering cat' and indeed to the 'unwilling stray': the 'unwilling' implied that a stray had been forced off the path of righteousness by being picked up and transplanted by a child, or chased in the street by a dog. Such cats had once in their lives been tame, and sufficiently conditioned to embrace and actually need the company of humans. Indeed, they were only too keen to respond to overtures and 'allorub' – a good word, meaning to rub a part of their body on another individual – usually the person who fed them. Modern cat geneticists have theorised convincingly that an important route to apparent domestication was the persistence into adulthood of juvenile characteristics that made cats playful, antic-prone and generally cute. Even stray cats could be cute.

Strays were the heartbreakingly appealing creatures over which, in the decades to come, an ocean of anguish would be expended. In fact, over a hundred years later, the stray would be the pet of choice for a quarter of cat-owning households. That is how they got in the door in the first place – by simply turning up and asking to be let in. Who could resist? Being one such was the best chance for a cat that had fallen out of someone's favour to find a way back in to someone else's. Kittens fared best, they always did.

At the bottom of the heap was an altogether different feline caste – the cats who knew no human master or mistress. They had been living in cities for ever, hidden, crepuscular, accepting the beneficence of humans when offered (usually by an elderly female hand) with extreme stand-offish reluctance, and, when they showed themselves, prey in turn to every danger and human-inflicted malevolence imaginable. The cruelty of street children towards cats was Hogarthian.

Charles Dickens, a great observer of the feline condition, was more aware than some of the multitudinous cats in the London shadows. His often-quoted 1859 account of a walk through the 'shabby small streets of cats' about 'the Obelisk in Saint George's Fields . . . in the vicinity of Clerkenwell-Green . . . the back settlements of Drury-lane' records:

> [T]he cats of shy [disreputable] neighbourhoods exhibit a strong tendency to relapse into barbarism. Not only are they made selfishly ferocious by ruminating on the surplus population around them, and on the densely crowded state of all the avenues to cat's meat; not only is there a moral and politico-economical haggardness in them . . . but they evince a physical deterioration . . . their black turns rusty, like old mourning; they wear very indifferent fur . . .
>
> In appearance, they are very like the women among whom they live . . . They leave their young families to stagger about the gutters, unassisted, while they frouzily quarrel and swear and scratch and spit, at street corners. In particular, I remark that when they are about to increase their families (an event of frequent recurrence) the resemblance is strongly expressed in a certain dusty dowdiness . . . I cannot honestly report that

I have ever seen a feline matron of this class washing her face when in an interesting condition.

These were the cats which would, in years to come, be talked of as 'feral'* – domesticated cats that through whatever circumstances had indeed relapsed into the barbarism in Mr Dickens's description – and their descendants, born generation after generation into the vagrant underworld from which the only rescue, it would seem for a century, was human-inflicted death.

Cats could survive and reproduce in the crevices in which nineteenth-century cities abounded. Dogs could not – at least, not for long. And they were much more obvious. Packs of dogs in the street simply would not do. As a modern cultural geographer wrote of canines in the later-Victorian metropolis:

The key boundary line lay between the private and public zones of the city. The dog became properly private – as a pet – but only at the expense of being out of place in the public realm – as a stray. The dog was [increasingly] portrayed as an animal that naturally loved the family, and suffered as a 'homeless' vagrant on the streets [and hence had to be removed].

---

* The term was used by Charles Darwin in 1859 to describe pigeons that had returned to a pre-domesticated state. Modern animal behaviourists describe the cat (*Felis catus*) as existing in a spectrum, from: 'feral independent wildlife' (hidden from man with no habituation to human company as kittens); 'feral-interdependent-free-roaming-unowned' (a limited relation with man); 'domes-ticated-interdependent-free-roaming-loosely-owned (abandoned pets or semi-feral, hanging round cafés, tourist sites etc); to 'domesticated owned pets' (dependent on man for food and shelter). Of the two interdependent categories, 'taming and placement in homes of these cats is difficult but possible and their kittens can become household pets, if socialised early enough'.

Just as the rise of the residential suburbs was a miraculous boon for stay-at-home felines, the communal human-made spaces of the city – squares, churchyards, hospitals, lunatic asylums, workhouses, railway arches, markets, subterranean railways, gasworks, board-schools, graveyards, prisons, factories – brought astonishing new territorial opportunities for go-it-aloners.

Their opportunist residents were anthropomorphised in the English-speaking world as 'beggar cats' and 'tramp cats', or, because of their supposed nomadic existence, 'Arab cats'. Whatever they were called, in the second half of the Victorian era, the urban stray cat 'problem' came to dominate the imagination of intensely motivated groups on both sides of the Atlantic. To many enlightened people, the cats' very presence was an affront to the 'sanitary idea' of how modern cities should be – in spite of their evident utility in killing rats. In Britain, the stray cat 'problem' was to be regulated by that municipal novelty and bane of mad cat ladies – the Vestry Inspector of Nuisances.

Some especially 'disreputable' cats were seen somehow to have wilfully chosen their lowly path. The sexuality of female cats, for instance, was always shocking. A promiscuous female human, it might be whispered in polite society, had the 'morals of an alley cat'. The doings of tom cats were less commented upon.

In the minds of some people, beggar cats joined the irredeemable workhouse inmate and the sexually incontinent in the uncompromising political debates of the day, which distinguished between the so-called deserving and undeserving poor. Charity would be wasted on them, it was said.

The plight of all such cats came to be a burning issue – although nobody had taken much notice before. But like souls to be saved by missionaries in darkest Africa, or 'fallen women' closer to home, might they too be rescued?

When an Irish lady, Miss Alice Swifte, of Rathfarnham, Dublin, announced her intention with an appeal for funds in 1881 of founding a home for 'forsaken' cats, the first outside America, there was much guffawing. In fact, it would eventually open in 1885 (see p. 38). But there were those too who saw it as a timely intervention in a gathering moral crisis both for cats and humans generally.

The 'forsaken' cat, 'friendless', 'deserted' – there were lots of ways of saying it – so thoughtlessly abandoned by pleasure-seeking owners, who meanwhile took their dogs to the seaside or their country estates, typified for some people all that was immoral and cruel in the spirit of the age. Cats had been made dependent on man for food and shelter, then they were casually abandoned. If cats could be so treated, where was the human decency in it? 'It's only a cat.'

In answer to those who mocked cat advocates, the *Animal World*, journal of the RSPCA, anthropomorphised the fate of one such 'left-behind', forced to steal from the house next door 'until a boot-jack is thrown at him from an upstairs window':

> He knows now surely that every man's hand is against him, that his is a case of a cat against the world.
>
> Those who deride Miss Swifte's trial home in Dublin should remember that cats have few friends and once they are cast into the streets they are unlikely to find homes for themselves as dogs sometimes do. Nor are they stray animals like dogs; they find their homes easily, being undaunted by distance or physical impediment.
>
> It is only when they return to their homes to be driven away again and again do they become straying animals. Hence, it may be concluded, in respect of those wretched feline creatures we see in the streets so often – careworn, attenuated, dirty, despairing animals – that they are exiles or

street Arabs; forsaken by the human beings who used to fondle them, and who, having grown tired of them, are too weak of resolution to put them out of existence.

To address this tragedy, it was not enough to 'make house-owners and their servants mindful of their duties to cats' – but 'over-propagation' must be addressed. As the *Animal World* put it:

> A prolific cause of cat-suffering is the needless and absurd multiplication of cats. Instead of killing the kittens at birth (save one) . . . they are kept to be the playthings of infants.

So that was the advice for Victorian cat-lovers. Drown the kittens and keep one. Shut up your house and go on holiday, but make sure you kill your cats first. It was not exactly a recipe for feline happiness but it would have to do for now. Sadly, things would get a lot tougher for cats before they got even remotely better.

2

Humblest of Servants

GOOD HOMES WANTED

1. Small strays very fond of each other; they must have lived together. Found wandering on Hampstead Heath, we think they must have been left there and they are very young . . .

2. Mother and child put on the dustman's cart when he was not looking and brought to us by the dustman who has four cats of his own so cannot keep them. He is helping with their boarding to pay for their food till they find new homes.

    Enquiries to Mrs de Clifford, No. 12 the Close, New Malden, Surrey.

                                                    The Cat, 1958

The rise of the domestic cat was set against a big change in human–animal relations generally. Religious in inspiration, but practical in delivery and effect, for all sorts of reasons animals in general got a sliver more consideration every decade that passed during the nineteenth century. This might be expressed by the placing of water troughs for horses or driven cattle in city streets, the encouragement of children to show tenderness to animals (why, then, did they persecute cats so mercilessly?) and by the pro-animal philosophical outpourings that would accompany the shocking proposals of Charles Darwin.

In a tiny, stray-cat-related glimpse of the great moral re-examination, a prominent clergyman could say at the 'annual meeting of subscribers to the Edinburgh Home for Lost and Starving Dogs and Cats' late in the century that although 'he was not an evolutionist', he could thank 'Charles Darwin for having put before them the grand fact of the brotherhood of the animals'. That, at least, was why he seemed to care about cats in trouble.

In much of the discourse of the time, animals were presented as being willingly complicit in subjecting themselves to human mastery. But that implied obligations on our part to treat them well in return. Domesticated cats had had their wild natures brought under control – maybe not entirely. Pussy was a moral lesson on the hearthrug – an exemplar of mankind's own journey from brute beast to civilisation. As a corollary, a profound awakening was around the corner on understanding the 'animal' instincts and senses that drove human behaviour. Forget about hunting mice – look at how cats went about reproducing themselves. For many commentators, then and ever since, the cultural identification of cats with women provided plenty to philosophise about.

The status of animals became a topic of political as well as religious debate. They should come within the law of men. The tormenting of living creatures by the labouring classes for amusement was already abhorrent and would progressively be made illegal. Not so the sports of the rural upper class, but they might be one day. Famously, through the nineteenth century, campaigning societies had been formed for the further 'prevention of cruelty', especially the brutality generally shown towards working animals or hapless cattle on their way to slaughter.

The Society for the Prevention of Cruelty to Animals (it

became 'Royal' in 1840), was founded in 1824: the first animal welfare charity in the world. It attempted both to police mistreatment via its force of 'constables' while at the same time lobbying the British Parliament at a stately pace, advancing legislation by the (all-male) legislature to somehow make things better all round. A Ladies' Committee was founded in 1870. More and more of its income would depend on the legacies of wealthy women.

In 1857 the Society published its first pamphlet on the treatment of domestic animals which, like any faithful servants, were entitled to kindness. Chapters were devoted to the horse, the dog, the hedgehog (useful for devouring cockroaches), and indeed the cat – 'humblest among the servants of man'. 'This animal is wild and fierce in a state of nature and it is only when some of this natural fierceness remains that the cat is useful to us,' said the pioneering RSPCA publication. As 'an indoor companion and plaything' she lost some of her utility as a destroyer of vermin.

Legal protection for felines was slowly improving. Mr John Colam, Secretary of the RSPCA from 1860*, would remind his colleagues some years later (in an oft-repeated anecdote) of his experience as an advocate when an attempt to bring a cruelty prosecution† at the Marlborough Street Magistrates' Court in London was thrown out. The bench chairman, a Mr Mansfield – described in a report as a 'country sportsman' – declared that cats were 'vermin'.

---

* His personal intervention to halt a 'Grand Spanish Entertainment of Bull-fighters', using real bulls, in March 1870 at the Agricultural Hall, Islington while defying the blows of 'hundreds of roughs' in the audience, brought him national fame.

† The Cruelty to Animals Act 1849 prescribed penalties for any 'person [who] shall cruelly beat, ill-treat, over-drive, abuse, or torture any horse, mare . . . dog, cat, or any other "domestic animal" as distinguished from those *feræ naturæ*, of wild nature'.

Mr Colam had worked hard to change the magistrate's mind and a conviction of the cat-abuser eventually resulted. Indeed, so total was the law official's conversion that he 'never hesitated to prosecute in cases of cruelty to cats', Mr Colam would recall. From 1861 cats enjoyed some deterrent protection from being taken without their owners' consent under the Larceny Act. But where did this leave ownerless street cats? Did they have any right to life?

There were, of course, many more urgent issues for campaigners. Although 'food' animals had progressively been vacated from cities, the abuse of horses in the streets by whip-wielding cabmen excited urgent emotions among RSPCA members and others generally. There would be concerns about pit ponies and the export of worn-out horses being turned into sausages by horrid Belgians. But by the third quarter of the nineteenth century, it was vivisection, medical experimentation on living creatures, especially cats and dogs, that was the burning issue for animal advocates.

The Battersea Home for Lost and Starving Dogs (see p. 45) would have to reassure its supporters many times over that it was not secretly selling its strays to the fiends with scalpels who would supplant the horse-beating cabmen and cruel animal-baiters in the demonology of ever more vocal activists. Pets extending the 'paw of trust' to humankind were being sliced up alive. A flogged horse was all too obvious. The vivisectors did their vile deeds in secret. Light must be shed on dark places and where it did not penetrate, baroque fantasies bloomed. The RSPCA seemed woefully supine; indeed, it might be accused of being actively opposed to doing anything to upset the medical and scientific interests within the Society.

Activists demanded action, led by the combustible Miss Frances Power Cobbe, founder in 1875 of the Victoria Street Society, whose campaigning, along with others, led to a

Royal Commission on animal experiments. The press reports of the testimony were horrifically graphic. The suffering of cats at St Bartholomew's Hospital at the hands of Viennese physiologist Dr Emmanuel Klein, a beastly foreigner, as evidenced by his 'wantonly brutal and mischievous' testimony before the commission, caused public horror. Klein admitted that he only anaesthetised his feline subjects to 'protect himself from scratches'. It emerged that experimenters would place a phial of chloroform on a shelf above the dissecting table so as to claim that 'the procedure was performed under anaesthetic'. But the report's eventual conclusions, so it would be said by many, were not nearly tough enough. A dissenting minority report by Klein's chief interrogator, Richard Holt Hutton, joint-editor of *The Spectator*, declared that subjecting these trusting, domesticated creatures to severe pain, even in the advancement of science, was akin to moral treachery. He further referred to the theft from their 'proper owners' of dogs and cats for the purposes of cruel experiments. Pets being stolen for vivisection became a stalking terror for animal-lovers for a century to come.

Cats themselves remained staunchly independent. Nobody was going to shackle them to a cart like a dog – forbidden by the Cruelty to Animals Act, otherwise known as the 'Dog Cart Bill' of 1854. The 'work' they were set to in humbler households, of catching rodents, was altogether agreeable. Nevertheless they might be the victims of fur-trappers or wicked vivisectors, and remained the targets of the universal malevolence of street urchins. Abandonment by thoughtless holiday-making owners became, as ever, a huge issue. Commercial boarding catteries were as yet unknown.

Sections of polite society (overwhelmingly female) became obsessed with animal welfare, to a degree that might seem pathological to later generations. When it came to cats, choices must be made. Were you a cat-lover, who found joy

and fulfilment in the company of cats, their breeding, groom-
ing and showing? In some quarters that was considered
eccentric enough. Or were you ready to plunge into the
feline netherworld with its flashing-eyed excitements in the
dark, and myriad, overwhelming tragedies? These two cat-
worlds, home and astray, existed side by side, and very occasionally, they might come together.

Mrs Alice Fawcett fell into the underworld by accident. As
she told readers of *Our Cats* in a letter, one day her own cat
went missing in a London suburb:

> I used to go out late at night with a bag full of scraps, hoping
> to come across the lost one. Oh! the pitiful sights that I saw.
> Lean, famished, gaunt spectres sitting in doorways, lurking in
> areas, to all I offered a portion of my scraps and they wolfed
> it down. Surely our hearts ought to go out in pity to all such
> . . . Truly indeed is our sympathy with those good kind ladies
> who so patiently and bravely undertake to alleviate the misery
> of their lives.

Readers shuddered, tut-tutted and moved on. But some of
them, clearly, were already secret adepts of the cause. Among
the journal's genteel readership there were some who thought
they might do well by gathering up some meaty titbits and
heading out for an evening stroll in search of cats. It was a
guilty secret, an amiable eccentricity. 'Respectable' home-
making married women did it, as well as the much-
stereotyped spinster cat lady.

One society figure dressed herself 'in rags' to pursue her
passion on the streets of west London. There were rumours
that a royal princess might be smitten with feline mania.
When, a century later, cat-behaviour studies became formal-
ised, such people would be described as 'auxiliary feeders'. In
America they would be called 'care-givers', not to be confused

with 'cat hoarders' who took things into much murkier territory. In this discourse, we shall call them 'cat ladies'. Their
doings would be as mysterious to later researchers as those of
the cats to which they dedicated so much of their lives.

Little by little, felines found their public advocates. Like
former naval surgeon and prolific author of boys' adventure
stories, Dr William Gordon Stables, whose 1873 book, *Cats:
Their Points and Characteristics, with Curiosities of Cat Life*,
pleaded for their parliamentary protection on these grounds:
'First then because she is a pet – a pet in many a nobleman's
and gentleman's family as at any poor man's fireside, because
pussy is so beautiful, so gentle, so loving and so kind, because
she is affectionate to her owner and loves children so . . .
Second because we're Christians and thirdly because she is an
animal of great utility.' He advocated a cat licence of one
shilling and threepence for a 'utility cat', and two shillings for
'valuable cats and household pets'. Collars were to be compulsory, and cruelty to cats to be punishable by fines. Failing to
feed cats would draw a prison sentence on those convicted of
such malign neglect, while Government Cat Inspectors
should generally keep an eye on things. 'This would have a
salutary effect in checking the present trade of cat-skin hunting,' he suggested.

But of the teeming Arab cats – 'thousands on thousands,
who never had a home and never will, preferring a nomadic
life, because they never knew a better' – something must be
done. Just as Parliament had passed a law (the Dogs Act,
1871) for 'the destruction of worthless dogs, found straying
and begging in the streets', so must it be for cats, Dr Stables
insisted. 'How can we get rid of this surplus feline
population?

'A place would be required in every town, or district,
where all cats found straying without a collar could be taken,
and if not claimed within three or four days, to be either

sold, given away, or destroyed,' he argued. He was a little ahead of his time, even if such a state of affairs for dogs was already being worked on by some eccentric enthusiasts. In his plan, fireside cats with identifiable owners would have the extra comfort of the law. But waifs and strays had better watch out. Only a very few cat-lovers of the time would argue with that.

The energetic Dr Gordon Stables was not a cat rescuer. His proposal of mass destruction with a few kind words on the way to a 'painless death' was very much in tune with the times. What else to do? But amid various other eccentricities, such as an enthusiasm for gipsy caravans and the protection of sea birds, his advocacy of cats as generally worthy of respect and protection put him on the side of the righteous. Meanwhile Messrs. Spratt's took out adverts in his pioneering work about cats for their new 'Patent Cat Food', thereby anticipating by many decades a mass, middle-class market for such a thing.

But the time of the cat as a universal and beloved pet was certainly coming, with a growing cult among cat-adepts of near religious worship of their grace and beauty. A tiny 'show' was held at the Crystal Palace, south London, in 1868, featuring twenty-five cats. The great breakthrough came in 1871, the 'year of the cat', when no less than five grand feline competitions were held across Britain, including two at the Crystal Palace, into the second of which 'Cats Belonging to Working Men' would be encouraged. Enormous values were put on cats – even if 'breed' distinctions were inchoate and classification largely done by colour. In the 1883 event, one tortoiseshell was given the 'fancy price' of £10,000. Of that year's show it was reported: 'In the class for black cats, Zulu, 2 years, attracted much attention on account of her two snow-white kittens, but she was not awarded a prize.' Words about cats poured out.

As Miss Frances Simpson,* among other things founder of the Blue Persian Cat Society and the author of the 'Practical Pussyology' advice column in *Our Cats* magazine, was to note in her *Book of the Cat* (1903):

> The cat literature of the present day has been steadily on the increase. The first paper to supply special cat columns was *Fur and Feather* . . . In 1899 *Our Cats* was started, and is widely read by the ever-growing circle of cat lovers, and claims the unique distinction of being 'the only newspaper in the world solely devoted to cats'.

By now, cat shows were regular events. The 'National Cat Club' had been founded in 1887, aiming to promote the breeding of pedigree cats; it held its first show at the Crystal Palace that summer with the general object of boosting cats all round. The Club's first President was the noted illustrator Harrison Weir, but he resigned, significantly, because he felt that members were more interested in prizes than in promoting the welfare of cats and raising their status. A grand cat show organised by pet entrepreneur Mr Charles Cruft at the

---

* Clergyman's daughter Miss Frances Simpson was Britain's most prolific writer and pro-cat propagandist in the early years of the twentieth century. On her death in 1926 it was noted by the editor of *Cat Gossip*: 'We [have] lost the "Fairy Godmother of the Cat Fancy", Miss Frances Simpson, whose tongue and pen for half a century have been placed at the service of Puss.'

As feline historian Sarah Hartwell noted: 'In addition to her writing and editorial roles [Simpson] advertised her services writing out pedigree forms for sixpence each. The sale of pedigree cats was also a source of income, hence the title of one of her books: *Cats for Pleasure and Profit*. She also allowed her name to be used in advertising, endorsing Tinkers Kit-Kat Mixture ("Prevents and Cures Distemper, Fits and Fevers") and Nomis Powders ("Prevent Show Fever!") . . . She also endorsed Wilson's Cat Remedies, and Salvo's various treatments for feline ailments . . . although privately, she confessed to being deeply sceptical about patent cat remedies.' She never married.

Royal Aquarium Westminster in March 1894 was a commercial failure.

The Queen's granddaughter, HH Princess Victoria of Schleswig-Holstein, became the NCC's Patron. In 1898 Lady Marcus Beresford founded the rival 'Cat Club' with another hugely posh roster of presidents and vice-presidents, with the object of promoting the 'true breeding of cats'. The rift would be repaired in 1910 when the two sides formed the 'Governing Council of the Cat Fancy' or 'GCCF'.

Breed-specific cat clubs began to be established. The artist Louis Wain,* his work too anthropomorphically cute for some modern tastes, became the master publicist of the National Cat Club and its sometime Chairman.

When Queen Victoria herself acquired an immensely fashionable Angora, called 'White Heather', it seemed that the social ascent of cats was complete, although it would be noted: 'The Queen and her daughters take a deep interest, not alone in finely bred cats, but in poor and homeless waifs as well.'

Her favourite Prime Minister, Lord Salisbury, had a cat called 'Floss', 'sleek and well bred', who, according to *Our Cats*, reportedly held 'long conversations in murmurs and soft purrs' with the bearded titan of high-Victorian politics.

The same journal would comment in July 1902 on the new social acceptance of cats, especially by the 'smart society woman', who 'knows the value of individuality and generally makes a speciality of some particular breed of cat . . .'

'Half a century ago the unmarried girl valiant enough to avow a liking for that much snubbed animal [the cat] would have written herself down as a spinster for all time,' said *Our*

* When, old and destitute, Wain was admitted to a mental asylum in 1925, an appeal was made, reminding cat-lovers of his work supporting 'innumerable cats' homes and receiving shelters for stray cats'.

Cats. 'A cat would never have been allowed to console the heroine of the early Victorian novel though a dog, whose fidelity rather than his pedigree was insisted upon, was the inevitable accessory . . .'

The higher cats climbed in status, however, the grimmer the life of street cats appeared to be. Nobody had taken much notice before. Thus it was that, just as the plight of street dogs had suddenly become big news, the stray cat slunk slowly out of the shadows to stake its claim to the beneficence of the charitable.

In America the very first 'humane shelters' appeared in the 1870s. Unlike the municipal 'pounds', which rounded up street animals, promptly killed them or sold them to vivisectors, these shelters sought to bring some form of compassion to the process. Two Philadelphia ladies, Elizabeth Morris and Annie Wain, began collecting strays – dogs at first, then theirs would be the first place in the United States to care for cats. They would shelter the animals and seek kindly adopters for them. If enough new homes could be found, mercy killing would be unnecessary.

In May 1874 their establishment would be incorporated as 'The Refuge for Homeless and Suffering Animals' in a basement at South 10th Street. After a few years it moved to 1242 Lombard Street in the city, an address where it could still be found almost a century and a half later. But, as with Battersea, the acceptance of a contract to act as the city's street animal control agency meant the idealistic days would soon be numbered. There were too many strays and not enough homes – the equation that would so vex cat 'welfarists' for ever after. 'Cats of good moral character [how did they know?] are provided with meals and lodging', it would be reported – 'while homeless, sick or suffering felines [up to fifty a day] are put out of the way humanely'. The advent of the electric trolley car on the streets of the city in 1892 had brought a doleful increase in casualties, injured cats routinely being 'put out of the way with a tightly woven bag and a bottle of chloroform by Agent Philip J. Smith, in charge of the refuge'.

About the Philadelphia operation, later to be known as the 'Morris Refuge' after Elizabeth Morris, it would not long afterwards be reported: 'If at [a] fortnight's end, no owner, past or prospective, has appeared and no one cares to prolong poor doggy's life by paying for its keep at the rate of fifty cents per week, its quietus is made . . . with the fumes of burning charcoal or by the inhalation of chloroform, both methods being most merciful.'

Indeed, the Philadelphia rescuers had been among the first to use the still comparatively novel chemical compound for the destruction of injured or sick animals which they judged to be beyond redemption. The volatile liquid had been well known as an anaesthetic in human medicine for some decades, especially in childbirth. It might be seen as controversial, even sinister; its power to render humans senseless meant it was associated with abductions, rapes and murders, but when Queen Victoria was administered chloroform for the birth of two of her children, in 1853 and 1857, it became much more respectable.

In Britain, such use had already been proposed by the eminent anaesthetist, Sir Benjamin Ward Richardson, as, in combination with carbonic acid gas, it was 'a means for the painless destruction of life in the lower creation' as he phrased it. He wrote: 'In 1869 I made a communication to the Royal Society for the Prevention of Cruelty to Animals, and suggested a mode for killing painlessly dogs and cats that were wounded in the streets.' The Society would award him a medal. While rendering humans simply unconscious, chloroform alone in sufficient doses would be fatal for a cat or dog. All it required was an enclosed airtight space.

Where Philadelphia led, Ireland, Britain and continental Europe would soon follow. The trouble for street cats was that, by alerting people to their plight, they invited judgement. Were their miserable lives worth living at all?

Dogs, meanwhile – and we are going to have to mention them because where dogs were heading, cats would soon follow – were even more on the up. 'Pure-bred' dogs, long since ornaments of the aristocracy, now became beloved of the urban middle class. The first 'dog show' in Britain, a small affair, was held in 1859. The Kennel Club was founded in 1873 to regulate breeds and bloodlines. Certain dogs became ragingly fashionable, especially 'ladies' dogs' like the Poodle and the Pomeranian, the latter being helped by the endorsement of Queen Victoria.

The Queen Empress lent royal status to a range of doggy endeavours including Spratt's, the famous makers of dog biscuits – granted the exalted status 'By Special Appointment to Her Majesty'. Enthused by royal patronage, fashionable women took dog exhibiting to their bosom. Soon it would be the turn of cats.

3

Forsaken Cats

LUTHER

Male, age (approx.) 2, DOMESTIC SHORT-HAIR, white, can live with mature family.
Hello, my name is Luther. I came into Cats Protection care because my owner sadly passed away. I am a shy and timid chap at first and will need an owner with an understanding and patient nature so that I can blossom. I would like a house with a secure garden to explore and a calm, quiet house to relax in. Please come and see me.

Cities, of course, teemed with lowlier dogs, just as they had always done. But now it was clear. On one side were the pets of the middle class with loving homes and nursery fires to snooze beside. On the other were the canine wretched of the earth. It was just the same for cats.

Into this ocean of misery stepped the proto-rescuers of mid-Victorian Britain, kindly ladies for the most part, some of them caught by the idea that the abandoned stray had somehow fallen from a one-time state of love and security into its wretched condition. It was the classic 'two-nation' plotline of so much literature of the period – Oliver Twist with a wet nose.

The most famous rescuers thereafter were Mrs Mary Tealby and her well-off friend Mrs Sarah Major, founders in autumn

1860 of what was to become the Battersea Dogs Home. Mrs Tealby, a woman in her late fifties, divorced and of modest means, in her wanderings around lower-middle-class north Islington, had despaired at the sight of dogs dying 'of lingering starvation' in the streets. She was moved to establish her famous canine asylum – 'The Temporary Home for Lost and Starving Dogs' – in a stableyard behind 16–17 Hollingsworth Street, Holloway, where lost dogs might be corralled, cared for and, it was to be hoped, retrieved by their owners. Or even bought for a few pence. 'PERSONS who require DOGS are particularly requested to visit the TEMPORARY HOME for LOST and STARVING DOGS, Hollingsworth St., St. James's Road, Holloway,' said a press notice of 1864. 'Very often handsome dogs, and always useful, are to be found there.'

That was the way to do it. It was a marker for all those who would strive to 're-home' a lost or unwanted animal in the future. If it could be done. The 'Home' was to be neither a permanent residence for 'old, worn-out favourites' nor a hospital, but a 'temporary refuge to which humane persons may send only those lost dogs so constantly seen in the streets'. 'Lost' was a nicety, of course: it implied a temporary fall from human society that might be redeemed. 'Starving' was more to the point.

Charles Dickens – or more likely, as scholars have pointed out, a dog advocate called John Hollingshead, a contributor to *All the Year Round*, the popular weekly periodical that Mr Dickens 'conducted' – was drawn to visit the Home some years after its founding. The investigation was inspired by the 'exhibition of prize dogs' (one of the first) being held at the newly opened Agricultural Hall in Islington, north London, where he was struck by the aloof arrogance of such 'prosperous dogs'. After inspecting the prize dogs, the writer ventured northwards, less than a mile, to Mrs Tealby's Holloway asylum to be confronted by a cage within which:

Twenty or thirty dogs of every conceivable and inconceivable breed, rush towards the bars, and, flattening their poor snouts against the wires, ask in their own peculiar and most forcible language whether you are their master come at last to claim them.

The contrast with the pampered pooches at the canine competition down the road was overwhelming:

For this second dog show is nothing more or less than the show of the Lost Dogs of the Metropolis – the poor, vagrant, homeless curs that one sees looking out for a dinner in the gutter, or curled up in a doorway taking refuge from their troubles in sleep.

And if readers were baffled by what had brought them here, he explained: 'A society has been formed to rescue these miserable animals from slow starvation; to provide an asylum where those who might appear to have a slight value are doctored, fed, and gradually restored to health . . .' Kindly Londoners might assist the good cause thus:

If a well-appointed person should find a miserable dog attempting to attach himself to his boot-heels, he should find a street vagrant or boy and propose to him that for a certain [reward] he shall convey the dog to the asylum at Holloway, where he will be certainly taken in, and a printed receipt handed to the person who delivers him at the gates.

There were two possible fates for a Holloway dog, he noted. Either 'finding a new home with those kindly persons who make their way to Hollingsworth Street in search of a canine companion . . . Or where they are utterly useless and diseased, a cur can be in an instant put out of his misery with a dose of Prussic acid.'*

The Home, the writer noted, also 'employed persons to go about the streets and, in extreme cases, to administer a dose of Prussic acid to such diseased and starving dogs as it has seemed merciful to put a quick end to'.

So there it was – the 'kill/no-kill' dilemma at the heart of all animal 'rescue' – then, and ever since. It was there when Mrs Tealby and her helpers first went on the prowl round Islington looking for Lost Dogs and has never gone away.

There too in the writer's observations was the idea of the 'kindly person' who might, in a different context, offer a home not just to a dog, but perhaps, and very unusually at a time when class barriers were so impregnable, to a foundling child or a workhouse starveling.

Mrs Tealby's Temporary Home for Lost and Starving Dogs was exactly what it said, a place of shelter for a transient population of unfortunates, some of whom might be claimed by those prepared to pay a little – or face death by whatever technical means were then available.

And people did come – the curious, the compassionate and those who saw God's work in rescuing animals. And some took dogs home with them. From the moment of its foundation, the Home embarked on the to-become-familiar animal welfare course of fundraising, bagging aristocratic patrons, fending off the complaints of neighbours (the barking!) – all the while having to endure bucket-loads of ridicule.

The Times, for example, published a mocking letter on 18 October 1860, very soon after the asylum opened: 'When we hear of a "Home for Dogs", we venture to doubt if the originators and supporters of such an institution have not taken

---

* Hydrogen cyanide, a liquid administered by squirting it down the animal's throat. Pharmacists would do it for a few pence.

leave of their senses,' said its correspondent snootily. 'Surely charity can better be bestowed by thinking of homes for starving, and wandering children!'

In fact, the model 'London Children's Home', as an alternative to the workhouse as a refuge for street children, was not founded until nine years later.

Another correspondent was blunter about Mrs Tealby's purpose: 'The appointment of a canine hangman would be of greater service to the public.'

Punch magazine had been especially unfunny, 'to a degree that had threatened to overwhelm the promoters of the new institution with dismay and despair', so it would be recorded much later. 'Mr Dickens was almost alone in giving support.' When, twenty years after its beginnings, the attention of Mrs Tealby's foundation turned to cat rescue, the outpouring of mockery was more restrained. Because by then perhaps, the pioneering work with the dogs had actually seemed to be successful. And Queen Victoria had become the Home's patron.

The ladies of Holloway (plus more and more men) may indeed have gone a bit dotty – but they were soon to be of more apparently practical service. The Metropolitan Police Commissioner, Sir Richard Mayne, moved to contract the Home 'to be a depot for dogs taken up from the street by Act of Parliament'. The Metropolitan Streets Act, 1867, required dogs to be publicly muzzled for fear of rabies. 'The [Home's] Committee deemed it to be right to embrace the opportunity of thus extending their work, though their resources would be sadly taxed,' so it was recorded, fifty years after the event. The Home was now effectively part of the animal-control-public-health apparatus of the metropolis. The 'canine hangman' jibe had come true.

When the complaints about barking became overwhelming, in 1871 the asylum moved to Battersea, south London, to crouch beside an already noisy railway viaduct where it has remained ever since. After her Private Secretary, Sir Henry Ponsonby, had paid two personal visits to the Home at her request, in 1885 Queen Victoria became Patron. She personally subscribed ten pounds a year to its funds, with a proviso that the interval between a dog's arrival and its destruction should be increased from three (as prescribed by the Dogs Act, 1871) to five days – so that lost dogs would have an increased chance 'of being returned to their owners, many of whom fail to enquire about their canine friends'. The Committee could hardly disagree – but it would put an ever-expanding operation under even greater strain.

There was no doubt of the Queen's love of dogs. They had provided her with companionship since childhood. After the death of Albert, the Prince Consort, she retreated into grieving widowhood. A Collie called 'Sharp' relieved some of the mourning gloom at Windsor and Balmoral – while 'frightening most of the royal entourage and regularly fighting with other dogs'.

The *Animal World* told a convoluted story of Sharp entering an old Highland woman's croft with Her Majesty on some benevolently intended visit and frightening a kitten under a table. Queen Victoria was most certainly not amused. '"Bad Sharp! Bad Sharp!" she cried, clapping her hands in disapproval, showing the true instinct of women eagerly interposing to mitigate the suffering of a poor terror-stricken little cat.'

A Pomeranian would curl up on her own deathbed at Osborne House on the Isle of Wight, where she would expire in the arms of her (cat-hating) grandson, Kaiser Wilhelm II.

But cats? After decades of apparent indifference, Victoria would enthusiastically embrace them later in her reign. It is recorded that when the RSPCA presented a sketch by the sculptor George Adams for a proposed Medal for Kindness to be awarded in her name – 'Her Majesty detected the absence of a domestic cat'. She drew one in her own hand, placed in the right foreground, insisting that 'everything should be done to change the general aversion to and contempt for and towards cats' – and formally wrote to the Society thereafter urging them to work for the protection and safety of cats – 'which were generally misunderstood and grossly ill-treated'. John Colam was the medal's first recipient.

On the matter of ill-treatment of cats, Her Majesty surely had in mind those many respectable people, presentees at court many of them, whose attitude to cats so carelessly depended on their own pursuit of pleasure. By the 1880s the 'Forsaken Cat' was a public scandal, as it was in any city of the world with a pet-owning bourgeoisie. London's wealthy families thought nothing, it seemed, once the season of balls and court presentations was over, of departing to their country estates or to disport at continental spas, simply shutting up their oil-painted stucco mansions in the capital or leaving their cats at the mercy of indolent servants. There were heartbreaking reports every summer of 'cats wandering wretched, round the houses that were once their homes, mewing piteously at doors which there is no one left to open, waiting on the window-sills in the same old spirit of patient assurance . . .'

The Queen herself would surely never countenance such heartlessness. When in summer 1888 the 'Animals' Institute', a horse hospital in Knightsbridge run by society ladies, started to protest about Belgravia's homeless felines, Her Majesty was observed taking her pets with her very publicly from Windsor to Osborne on the Isle of Wight in special baskets. The regal point was clearly made. 'She has induced many a lady to do likewise,' it was noted, 'and has thereby not only benefited a large number of domestic pets, but has also given impetus to the wicker-work trade, for pretty wicker cat-baskets are in great request.'

In 1901 it was recorded: '[W]hen the Court moved it was accompanied by what might be called a caravan. The cats were at Balmoral, Osborne, Windsor and Buckingham Palace as regularly as the Queen. Persian cats, Manx cats, Maltese cats, Angora cats, tabby cats and nondescripts . . . all travelled in State. They were placed in wooden boxes with an open wire front, and had plenty of clean straw to lie on,' wrote Louis Wain.

Royal cats travelled in dainty baskets. Lowlier cats did not travel at all. They must stay and fend for themselves.

The abandoned cats of London had been a sad spectacle for years. How could people be so cruel? The universal philanthropist, the extraordinarily wealthy Baroness Angela Burdett-Coutts, President of the RSPCA Ladies' Committee, publicly took up their cause in 1875, writing: 'A very benevolent lady, well known to me, who was detained late in London last autumn, was so pained by the condition of some of these animals in the streets near her house that she collected a good many and distributed them amongst friends.'

It was not just ladies. Cat-loving Captain Arthur Rickard raised the issue on the letters page of *The Times* in September 1877:

> Sir, Grant me space in your columns to point attention to the cruel sufferings of numberless cats now starving in the fashionable streets and squares of the West End. I could show you from almost any standpoint some dozen of these poor domestic animals crawling about the areas and gardens in every state of starvation. Their owners have shut up the princely palaces in which these poor creatures have been reared, and are away enjoying themselves everywhere that enjoyment is to be found.

Street boys persecuted them with the usual stone-pelting cruelty – while the *Animal World* reported the grisly pastime of 'sanguinary swells who perambulate the squares at night with dogs hoping to find sport in hunting down wary or timid cats'. The RSPCA did what it could in the courts, with varied success. Setting dogs on cats in Kensington was seen by some as a public service. They were just vermin, after all.

As in London, so in every town and city. The *Animal World* published a delightfully over-the-top story in 1880 about a Scottish shopkeeper, one Cameron Cordier, who quit the city (one assumes Edinburgh) for the month of August with his wife and family, leaving the cat behind shut in the house with nothing but some milk and chicken bones. Consumed with remorse he returns home after ten days to call, 'Chi-chi, chitty-chitty, puss-puss,' in the hope his forsaken cat may still be there. She is not. After a whisky-induced nightmare about the cat taking its revenge as he sleeps, he wakes up to see a little face appear round a door:

> Now he feels its ragged whisker driven along his skin, then its smooth furred body, and the whisk of its stiffly upright tail; back again, round again . . . purr . . . purr.
>
> 'Man alive, there's nothing wrong with her,' said Cameron . . . 'She has just gone out of her mind for a bit wi' loneliness, and seems to know me better in the dark than the light . . .'
>
> Cameron caressed and fondled her, petting and mutually caressing, but still he could not exhaust that creature's appetite for affection; and all alone in that house, there came a fellowship between the humble animal and the man – the great wide hungering desire of all nature to be loved – and the tears filled Cameron's eyes at witnessing the pent-up feeling that lowly cat had shown.
>
> 'God made us all,' he said. 'I would have gone nearly mad myself if I'd been shut up alone in that dark house for a week. Puir pussy! Puir pussy!'

John Colam, Secretary of the RSPCA, waded in to the grow-ing debate. 'During one evening's walk I encountered twenty-two cats whose appeals for help were very distress-ing,' he wrote in a letter to *The Times*. And further:

> I am sorry to state the evil alluded to is not confined to Belgravia, but extends to all other districts where there are good houses occupied during the summer months, and left empty after July. The complaints received here day-after-day, testify that this is a West-end [wide] scandal . . .

But should not his Society do something to stop such cruel abandonment? It might be possible to prosecute, he said, 'when cats have been purposely left in houses vacated by the occupier . . . but in the protection of stray cats that is impos-sible'. He spelled out the law as it stood:

> Stray dogs are taken possession of and fed by the police in accord-ance with statutory law; but policemen have no powers enabling them legally to remove or kill starved cats; and this remark applies equally to the officers of this Society, and to all private persons not being the owners of such cats, or owners' servants.

There were many who recommended the destruction of animals found starving in the street, said Mr Colam. But such a course would be 'dangerous', he argued. The RSPCA's journal, the *Animal World*, which Mr Colam edited, spelled out the conundrum: 'No relief can be given to terminate the misery . . . the Society cannot feed thousands of homeless cats turned out of luxurious accommodations . . . Nor dare it kill; for power is not given even to magistrates to do this.'*

---

* As even forsaken cats might have owners, this would be an offence against property laws. Meanwhile there were plenty of prosecutions for 'cruelty to cats'

There was a long-rumbling argument meanwhile about the shooting and trapping of rural 'poaching' cats by game-keepers and 'sportsmen' – which was perfectly legal, it seemed, although some cat-lovers tried to make a case. In 1884 a distressed cat owner wrote: 'I have myself lost within the last ten days a favourite cat, which now it is certain has fallen a victim to the gun of a gamekeeper . . . It seems only too true that there is no legal remedy for this wanton destruction of domestic animals . . .' And these were cats with identifiable owners. Street cats had no existential right to life at all. Just kill them without cruelty.

And, so the RSPCA Secretary was further aware, there were those who advocated 'cats' homes', of the sort that Mrs Tealby had established for dogs. Mr Colam had been associated with the Lost Dogs' Home since soon after its founding, but saw grave problems doing the same for cats. As he told *The Times*:

> Probably such provision would encourage the expulsion of cats. Moreover, a home for London cats is impracticable, and if opened would cause terrible sufferings to the refugees it

---

across Britain, as a search of newspapers of the period readily shows. In a prosecution brought by the RSPCA in 1874, a certain Herbert Brooks, a gentleman of south Hackney, was charged with cruelly beating a neighbour's cat because it had 'attacked his pigeons'.

To its owner's horror, the cat had crawled home and died on the doorstep. The police were summoned. The presiding magistrate, Mr Bushby, on the bench at the Worship Street Police Court, doubted that 'someone would not be responsible under the [Cruelty to Animals] Act if he killed a cat which had destroyed his property'. But then the offending creature must be dispatched, 'without cruelty'. Killing cats was not against the law – but being cruel to them was.

The 'horrible brutality' of this case ruling went beyond a mere fine. The sentence for cat-abuse was fourteen days' imprisonment. 'The decision created great surprise.'

endeavoured to succour, for the nature of a cat rebels against
cages . . . Disease quickly follows such confinement. I have
inspected several collections of stray cats [presumably those of
freelance hoarders], in all of which disease and misery
prevailed.

But someone was prepared to act. In Dublin, Ireland, then an
integral part of the United Kingdom, the forsaken cat was
also a phenomenon of the late summer months. As recorded
earlier, in March 1881 Miss Alice Swifte of Whitechurch
Lodge, Rathfarnham, the daughter of a prosperous barrister,
had publicly declared her intention of founding a 'Home for
Deserted Cats' on the lines of the Home for Lost Dogs in
London. It would be the first such dedicated feline shelter
(other than freelance cat collectors) in the British Isles.

She opened a subscription list. Among the first donors named
were 'Jack Cat', 'Pussy', Miss Frances P. Cobbe (the prominent
anti-vivisectionist), Baroness Burdett-Coutts, 'Lover of Cats'
and 'One in Favour of a London Cats' Home'. When enough
funding was in place, she would open her experimental cat
shelter for business. It would take a few years yet.

Was kindly Miss Swifte an amateur, with the kind of dangerously utopian delusions 'that come as a result of sentiment-
gone-mad?' so it was asked by correspondents of the *Animal
World*. Was living alongside multiple felines even possible? The
RSPCA already knew enough about mad cat ladies to be suspicious. For years past it had prosecuted in a string of notorious
cat-hoarder cases. But Miss Swifte was not one of them. Her
proposal invited all sorts of enthusiastic comments, including
this from someone identified only as 'X'.

We once had sixteen rescued cats and they all retired to rest
at night when we did, rising every morning when the fire
was lit; kennelling of cats will present hardly any difficulty.

The *Animal World*, after some correspondence with Miss Swifte, was convinced that 'comforts consistent with economy will be given to the inmates for the preservation of their health until homes are found for them'. The journal further found the Irish pioneer imbued with 'practical common-sense' and urged all cat-lovers to 'back the *movement*' (authors' emphasis). The Cats' Home Movement, for that is exactly what it was, had begun. It would never look back.

The RSPCA journal predicted that the 'novel experiment, if successful, will be copied in London and elsewhere'. Indeed it would be. The Refuge for Homeless and Suffering Animals, that fine establishment in Philadelphia founded not long before, so it was pointed out, had 'taken in 4,406 cats, according to its latest report received in London' but this 'gave no details as to their fate'.

'Most likely they were killed painlessly in the airtight chamber at the Refuge by means of carbonic acid gas – but many hundreds are found owners and homes, no doubt,' the journal noted cheerfully. There were plenty of subsequent suggestions from readers as to how Miss Swifte's project should be conducted and managed, including 'the necessity of an apparatus for killing with chloroform any cats it was decided to destroy'.

In summer 1881 John Colam, having been associated with Mrs Tealby's venture since the start, at last formally joined the Battersea Lost Dogs Home Committee where the new enthusiasm for cats' homes had taken hold. But he was wary of emulating Miss Swifte's feline initiative. He told his fellow Committee members: 'Thousands of poor strays are found in our streets and squares. The police cannot take up cats; neither can private individuals, so there is no legal way of getting a cat into the Home.' There was soon to be a change of mind.

4

Stray Cat Blues

LEWIS NEEDS A LOVING NEW HOME

Hello, my name is Lewis and I'm a gorgeous chocolate spotted silver OCICAT. I am 8 years old, micro-chipped and neutered. I am hoping to find a new home because although I love my present owner very much and she loves me, I am finding it diffi-cult to cope with the stresses and tensions in my present home . . .

I am a gentle, loving soul with plenty of spirit. I like company and enjoy being involved in whatever is going on – unless it is the vacuum cleaner! I also enjoy sitting on my owner's warm lap and getting lots of strokes and cuddles.

It was not the abandonment of cats by wealthy city-dwellers but 'vivisection' that continued to so strongly excite the emotions of late-Victorian animal advocates.

The Royal Commission published its report and the 1876 Cruelty to Animals Act had been the immediate result, but the feebleness of its watered-down provisions as passed by Parliament just accentuated the controversy, stirring deep campaigning passions that would continue for generations to come. Meanwhile animal cruelty in plain sight remained as big a moral challenge as ever.

Two of those deeply affected were Mr Richard Barlow Kennett of Petersfield, Hampshire, and his wife, the philan-throphic Mary Ann Kennett. Both were keen members of the Victoria Street (anti-vivisection) Society. When Mrs Kennett died in July 1882 aged sixty-nine, her will was abundantly generous to animal charities. It said:

> The testatrix leaves all her property upon trust for her husband for life. At his death, she bequeaths £6000 to the Royal Society for the Prevention of Cruelty to Animals; £2000 to the Metropolitan Drinking Fountain and Cattle Trough Association; £1000 to the Temporary Home for Lost and Starving Dogs, established in London in 1860. The ultimate residue she leaves to her husband absolutely.

There was a gothic twist at the end: 'The testatrix desires her husband to kill her favourite black cat with chloroform immediately after her death.'

The discussions Richard Kennett may have had with his wife before her death can only be guessed at. That she wished for her own favourite (and presumably healthy) black cat to be killed at her husband's own hands, gave a clue as to the purpose of the Mary Kennett legacy.

It was to unite them in an affirmation of love for cats – by inflicting a 'merciful' death on a beloved animal, thus symbolically putting the unfortunate pet beyond the reach of experimenters like the abominable Dr Klein. It will seem perverse and cruel to us, but was entirely in tune with the spirit of the age. Time and again in the stray-cat 'rescue' mania that would grip the imaginations of so many (overwhelmingly) women on both sides of the Atlantic, the phantasm of the vivisector lurking in every shadow was the excuse for killing without hope of redemption. Killing and more killing. It would go on for decades, a human–feline tragedy on an epic scale.*

---

* Fifty years later, an elderly anti-vivisectionist, Mrs Clara Edith Dalton, would become embroiled in a bizarre assault case against the Superintendent of the

Mrs Kennett had not specified chloroform idly. It was by now commonplace as an anaesthetic. Its use as a lethal agent in small animal euthanasia had been the special concern of the pioneer anaesthetist, Sir Benjamin Ward Richardson. He experimented with electricity – which turned out to be far too dangerous to the operator – and various narcotic vapours. His work was world-famous. The perfected instrument would be carbonic acid gas and chloroform combined. 'There is no anaesthetic more certain in its action and none more certain to kill if it be administered in a determinate manner,' he wrote. By the time Mary Ann Kennett added her deadly codicil, chloroform was being hailed as the true friend of the wayward cat.

Mr Kennett did not wait for his own demise to dispense his late wife's bounty. In the years to come he would shower money on both the RSPCA and the Victoria Street Society, and endow schemes for cats' homes in Dublin, Notting Hill, Portsmouth, Tunbridge Wells and Birmingham. He discreetly backed the Willesden Home for Lost Cats (the 'Mayhew', see p. 82) from the beginning and in 1889 granted a certain Mrs Walker £1,000 to acquire a leasehold north London property, 37 Richmond Road, Dalston, to be a lost cats' home. There would be trouble ahead. Mr Kennett was the secret millionaire of nineteenth-century cat rescuers. But almost all of the cats would die in the process of being saved. In fact, the Kennett legacy ensured it.

Soon after Mary Ann Kennett's will was proved, Richard Kennett made the Battersea Dogs Home a remarkable offer.

Hastings PDSA clinic (the newly established veterinary charity) , because he had wrenched a cat-basket out of her hands in fury. Mrs Dalton cheerfully confessed that over decades she had killed 'thousands of stray cats' in the seaside town 'before the PDSA has showed up', and spent £1,000 on chloroform. It was, as she explained, 'to spare the cats from vivisection'. Where was the fault in that? There were many like her.

He would make a donation of £500, but only on condition of the 'institution receiving cats as well as dogs to protect them from starvation', as John Colam would explain to a specially called general meeting of the supporters of the Dogs Home gathered at the RSPCA headquarters, 105 Jermyn Street, on 10 November 1882.

Admitting cats was a major change in the way the Home was run. Taking in strays as the Kennett legacy implied, had up to now been considered impractical if not illegal. Or was it? The Executive Committee had already made their decision and now invited wider consent. According to Mr Colam, addressing the meeting:

> It has always struck us as remarkable that the humane impulse that has tended to succour starving dogs should not have been touched into commiseration with starving cats . . . At first it was difficult enough to work against opposition to the Dogs Home without taking on new work . . . The time has now arrived, however, when steps may be taken for the relief of even outcast cats . . .

This meant both 'securing temporary accommodation for hundreds of household favourites, otherwise turned adrift at the commencement of the holiday season', and more to the point, 'providing a readily merciful means to put wretched vagrant cats out of their misery', he said. Indeed, Mr Kennett's donation depended on it. Mr Colam could also reveal that 'a further £1,000 should be forthcoming should his late lamented wife's wishes be fulfilled'. There were loud cheers.

But boarding cats would not be taken in as 'patients', he insisted. There would be no infirmary, no care of sick animals, certainly no medical treatment which might be construed as 'experimentation'. No suspicion of vivisection must taint the proposal.

If there were doubters, Mr Colam referred them to the new refuges for cats in the United States which were doing excellent work. And Mr Thomas F. Brady of the Dublin SPCA, Miss Swifte's associate in her splendid pioneer home across the Irish Sea, was there to add his voice. Dublin in late summer was full of starving cats, carelessly abandoned by their fashionable owners, he said to nobody's surprise. 'At present Miss Swifte has made a temporary home at her father's house where she receives all the homeless cats that are brought to her and disposes of them humanely.'

There was an objection from a certain Mr Cowie. Would there really be no further consultation on the admission of cats – and indeed the disposal of vagrants? There would not. There were details that only the Committee could master, said Mr Colam, and 'practical difficulties in carrying out Mr Kennett's suggestion which have to be resolved first'. A sub-committee would be responsible. A press notice duly appeared:

HOME FOR LOST AND STARVING DOGS

Richard Barlow Kennett, Esq., having generously offered to give the above Institution a donation of £500 conditionally that provision be made for receiving and disposing of (by a merciful death, or otherwise) cats which have been found in the streets in a starving condition, and conditionally also on sums being received from other persons to the amount of £1000 within a limited period of time . . . an APPEAL is now made . . .

So that was it. Mr Colam had got over his legal scruples. He was always aware that cats, even strays, were private property, and people 'should think twice before sending any strange and possibly homeless cat to the Home' as he would tell a later annual meeting, but his fellow council member, a certain Mr Almack, could advise that any 'doubters could chance legal proceedings with safety'. To which Mr Colam jocularly agreed, whatever the Larceny Act might say, that the chance of arrest and prosecution for removing a stray cat from the streets of London was nil.

Thus it was that, although neither the police nor the Home's staff could go out and take cats off the street, if they were brought to the Home's gates by 'kind-hearted persons, chiefly ladies . . . to whose sympathetic natures the sufferings of forsaken cats have specially appealed', as the RSPCA's own journal would put it, that was perfectly acceptable. The law as it stood actively encouraged the private army of bombazined cat-nappers.

What to do with them once they were 'received'? Cats were not happy in communal captivity; they 'soon begin to fret and languish', Mr Colam would tell an annual meeting. 'We cannot fondle or caress them, we cannot keep men to do that or provide soft cushions (laughter), and, finding themselves deserted by those they love, they pine and suffer. Dogs seem to be differently constituted.'

And cats were not easy to kill. According to the Home's own history: '[there was concern] that the arrival of cats would endanger keepers – it would be almost impossible to administer Prussic acid to cats without enduring great risks to the hands and faces of the Home's servants.' These were the practical difficulties the sub-committee was formed to address. There was, however, a deeper and more sensitive agenda.

Battersea had long been seeking a better method of euthanising its temporary canine inmates. The existing process would be described by Sir Benjamin Richardson: 'You doubtless know that the former method of destroying dogs at that institution was by administering doses of Prussic acid to the animals. One of the men would hold the animal while the other poured the poison into its open mouth.'

Sir Benjamin, the grand-master of narcotically induced sleep, had the answer. He was approached by the Committee to devise a 'lethal chamber' capable of euthanising not only cats but, much more directly given the Home's primary function, the many hundreds of stray dogs, ever more of which arrived each day care of the Metropolitan Police. Cats would open the door. The Kennett legacy would pay for it.

5

'Every Cat Wants To Be Personally Useful'

Single London woman with inadequate accommodation for herself and her cat (a rescued stray) seeks to contact any fellow member interested in her problem . . .

Cat Lady in Trouble, *The Cat*, 1968

Early spring 1883 was a busy time at Battersea. Unlike dogs, there was no police contract for bringing in the street cats of London, no clarity as to whether it was even legal. But cat 'boarding' most certainly was legal, and a worthily humane way of easing the West End cat scandal. Preparations must be made.

Two arches of the London, Chatham, and Dover Railway viaduct were rented, one to serve as a projected 'cats' house'. The second would accommodate, when it was completed, Sir Benjamin Ward Richardson's remarkable device, the Lethal Chamber.

The Home's annual meeting in March at the RSPCA's headquarters heard the sub-committee's report on the admission of cats. As soon as there were sufficient funds to match Mr Barlow Kennett's generous offer, the plan would go ahead. The Committee was also 'strongly impressed by the necessity of building a chamber for the destruction of both dogs and cats by means of carbonic oxide gas – as carried out in the United States of America', as the sub-committee's report recommended, read out to rousing cheers. The extemporised cats' house was ready by August. A press notice appeared:

ARRANGEMENTS FOR RECEIVING CATS

[The time has come when many householders] allow their servants to turn adrift domestic cats. In order to abate this evil, the Committee of the Temporary Home for Lost and Starving Dogs have directed provision to be made, which is now ready, for receiving and boarding cats at from 1s 6d a week for each animal. The animals must be delivered at the Home when the bearer will be required to sign a paper on behalf of the owner exonerating the Committee in the event of death etc . . .

The cats' house was configured evidently both as a facility for paying guests and as a pound for strays – although the first inmates that summer of 1883 were forty 'boarders'. By the end of the holiday season, there were twenty-five left in residence. There was concern among some people, however, that these contented holiday-makers might be a front for something else.

A correspondent of the *Animal World* writing as 'Sans Souci' claimed in December to have been told that 'stray cats were being collected and sent to the Home to be destroyed'. If so, it was an outrage. 'Is this all we have to offer to the victims of human caprice and tyranny,' he asked . . . 'to hurry them into death as compensation for the miseries of their own lives?'

He (or perhaps she) suggested acquiring a barn where 'cats could live and no one could make them afraid'. Those cat-lovers who considered giving money to the Home should rather 'set up their own small refuge and rescue a few cats here and there'.

That would not do at all. The allegation of killing all stray cats was dismissed by the editor ('many have been killed with justice and mercy [but] . . . animals may be seen that have been there several months', he wrote) – while the idea of a barn containing thousands of free-living cats was 'little short of craziness', according to Mr Colam. 'Every cat wants to be personally useful and the object of somebody's attention and regard,' he said, with doubtless caring intentions.* No more feline utopias would be promoted in the columns of the RSPCA's journal, although the idea would never go away. Henceforth, attention would be on the all-consuming lethal chamber beneath the railway arch at Battersea Park Road station, so practical, so merciful, its advent now imminent.

The Home's 1884 annual meeting held in March went through a brisk agenda, hearing how a detective had been appointed to follow purchasers of dogs home to ensure anti-vivisection oversight – an announcement greeted by 'cheers'; how thirteen dogs admitted had showed signs of rabies and been destroyed; and that John Colam's son, J. Charles Colam, had been appointed Secretary (his younger brother, Matthias, would shortly supplant him). It also heard that, although subscriptions so far did not match Mr Kennett's, that kind gentleman had handed over £500 for providing 'accommodation for lost and starving cats and for the erection of a lethal chamber'.

---

* Much academic effort has been spent analysing why stray cats and dogs have been such a target for Anglo-Saxon sensibilities, as opposed to street animals in other cultures, Indian village dogs for example. The obsession went way beyond public-health imperatives. In this modern analysis, lack of *ownership* defined the lack of a right to live for an animal and also justified its destruction. The Lost Dogs' Home operated by turning strays taken off the street back into *property* – if only briefly – then applying a stark test. If unclaimed, or if they failed the desirability test with prospective purchasers, they were killed. Whatever the law might say, ownerless cats meanwhile had no utility or right to life whatsoever.

Arrangements for cats were proceeding, 'very tentatively
. . . gathering experience day by day', so the meeting heard.
A permanent house for boarding cats was planned but 'the
Committee could not hold out any hope to reduce the
expense of the cats by payments and purchases to any appre-
ciable extent'. Stray cats, it was reported, would prove 'almost
impossible' to sell.* An appeal was made 'to all cat-lovers' to
fund the boarding department further. At least that might pay
its way.

Then came the real news. The building of the lethal chamber had begun. Indeed, it would be ready in a month. John
Colam got to the point – it was for dogs, not cats. 'Our new
plan will get rid of the necessity of handling dogs and prevent
danger and suffering to the Home's servants,' he said. 'The
process is painless and is simply the negation of life.' He
described the chamber's working until the closing of the
door, 'when in less time than it takes me to tell you, every
animal will pass away from consciousness to absolute death'.
The meeting erupted in cheers.

And so Sir Benjamin Ward Richardson's device was soon
nearing completion in its railway arch. The great anaesthetist
himself would shortly acknowledge the benefactor who had
made it possible:

> Through the generosity of one benevolent man, Mr [Barlow]
> Kennett, I have constructed at the Dogs Home at Battersea a
> large lethal chamber in which from fifty to one hundred dogs

---

* A widely reported cruelty case in February 1886 did not help. When a Mr
Thomas McConnell of Ewhurst, Surrey, 'a young man of independent means',
was prosecuted for setting his dogs on three cats, killing them one after another,
it emerged that he had 'obtained twelve cats from the Battersea Home for Lost
Cats, and they were sent to the Defendant's residence . . . a home had been
found for the other nine'. Offering cats to the public became much more
prescribed after that.

can be narcotized at once and without waking be allowed to pass from sleep to death . . .

I put the process first into operation on Monday, 15 May [1884], by subjecting thirty-eight dogs to the fatal narcotic vapour.

The device itself consisted of a wheeled cage arranged on two levels and capable of holding one hundred dogs at a time. It was pushed into a purpose-built chamber, as Sir Benjamin would write, 'already charged with a mixture of carbonic oxide and ethylated chloroform in vapour, both powerful anaesthetics'. A valve arrangement protected the operators. The insertion process took thirty seconds – death up to five minutes.

Soon after its commissioning trials Sir Benjamin noted: 'Cats lie asleep much longer than dogs before they cease to breathe. They fall into sleep as rapidly as dogs, but do not pass so quickly into the final sleep.' An integral stethoscope allowed the operators to check that signs of life were extinct. The only question left was how to dispose of the bodies.

A visitor to Battersea that summer of 1884 noted the cat boarders were 'plump and well fed . . . [but] the poor found-lings were suffering from colds contracted in their miserable wandering and looked shivering for want of warm nests to creep into'. Where were the cosy blankets and baskets? Where indeed. 'Nearly all the pussies thronged to the bars for notice and the starvies fairly climbed as high as my shoulder to be stroked,' said the anonymous correspondent writing in the *Animal World*, 'excepting one who sat by the contribu-tions box and mewed.'

The writer, signing as 'Ignoramus', added this: 'I make a point of always selecting my cat, when a vacancy occurs, from the homeless vagrants and am bountifully rewarded by the intense gratitude they show me.' Here was a kind and good, early lost-cat adopter – but there were very, very few like him (or her).

There would be no more doubt. On 19 November 1884 Mr Barlow Kennett took up a specially engraved trowel to formally lay the foundation stone for the now fully approved 'House for Starved Cats'. 'It was the happiest day he had ever known,' so it was reported.

The lethal chamber in the adjoining railway arch was proving just as felicitous. The work of small animal destruction had been transformed – but what to do with the bodies? In the first full year of its use, the resulting carcasses, almost twenty thousand of them, were removed by train to 'Mr Mitchell's Farm' at Broadlands near Enfield north of London, where: 'The dogs [referred to with grim humour as 'the Londoners' by railway men] were stacked in layers to the height of 10 ft. by 6ft. square – each stack consisting of about 2000 carcasses – the layers alternating with sphagnum-moss, gypsum and carbolic acid. The process took about ten weeks and left nothing but the fur and the bare bones.'

Local objections to the macabre pyre mounted. Having failed to find 'anyone willing to convey the dead bodies from the Home for any satisfactory use in agriculture or chemistry', the Committee sanctioned the construction of an on-site crematorium. A public appeal for funds was made and lists of donors published. Perhaps the Home's royal patron would contribute? The Queen's Private Secretary was informed by letter that in Germany the hides of stray Berlin dogs were turned into gloves for soldiers and the bodies rendered for medicinal fats.* 'We shall do neither,'

* Publishing the royal correspondence in her revealing history of the Home in 1971, Gloria Cottesloe, wife of the then Battersea Dogs Home Chairman, Lord Cottesloe, confided, 'The carcasses are taken from the Home nowadays and used for purposes of this sort.'

said the Home's Secretary Charles Colam, 'but we are driven to the Crematorium.'

Queen Victoria thought the whole thing ghastly. Could not euthanised dogs be buried in pits under quicklime, she suggested. And although she 'could not object to such an arrangement [so her Private Secretary informed Mr. Colam by letter], she will not contribute to it'.

The crematorium was commissioned in early 1887, when it would be reported: 'The bodies of 200 dogs or cats can be consumed together. The time needed for the cremation lasts about eight hours.' The 'pure white bone ash' was bagged up and sold (to 'soap-makers' according to *The Strand* magazine) and the revenue declared in annual accounts. Such income from rendered carcasses would provide a useful revenue stream for many decades to come – as for almost all the 'welfare' charities.

It would also be the case that respectable south London pet-owners would bring in cats when 'unable to take care of them', to the number of 180 in the year 1895, along with 290 'lost and deserted cats in a distressing condition that had to be destroyed soon after admission', as the annual meeting was told. The ever rising numbers of cats so volunteered showed, so it would be said, 'a growing appreciation on behalf of the public of the most painless and merciful scheme ever devised for the termination of the life of their favourites'.

To aid the 'poorer classes' the price per dog (destroyed) had been lowered to one shilling. The price per cat was sixpence. 'Homeless cats', meanwhile, were 'received without charge, sheltered and fed for a few days and then, if not sold, consigned to the lethal chamber'.

All this was done with an admirable openness. The Home's Annual Reports and formal newspaper announcements would be very clear on the admission and the fate of 'neglected cats' which were either 'found homes or [were] sent to the lethal chamber'. The fabled chamber was even open for the public, provided they were 'not in search of sensational spectacle'. Coyness about destruction would only creep in much later, to the point where the historic record could hardly be admitted to at all.*

Once, attitudes were very different. It was something to be proud of. Inquiries about Battersea's modern methods came from all over the world. The lethal chamber was a wonder of the age – efficient, humane, an adornment of the great modern metropolis – and it would be eagerly replicated.

Meanwhile a visit to Battersea's cats became a staple of summer newspaper reporting, even if the number coming in was a trickle in comparison to dogs. A keeper told a newspaper reporter: 'Cats don't trouble us much. Very few of them come to us, as compared with the dogs.'

The reporter noted the 'stray cats, picked up in West-end areas, and brought to Battersea by benevolent ladies . . . They are fed twice a day. In the morning they get new milk, and a varied diet of the customary horse-flesh and fish. Many parcels of fish are sent as presents for the cats.

'The frolicsome pussies have decidedly comfortable quarters', it was noted, 'and they, too, have a playground, in which are planted tree trunks, of which they freely avail themselves.

'Just now, especially on the days immediately preceding the Bank Holiday and all through August, some lost ones are brought in daily, hungry and thin and very mean and lowly-looking,' it was further reported. Their fate seemed sealed. But there were some happier outcomes:

---

* As part of its September 2013 Cat Takeover campaign, it was announced: 'Battersea has been rehoming cats of all ages and sizes since 1883 and since then we've *found homes for* more than 200,000 fabulous felines.' A Battersea spokesperson told the authors: 'We've taken in 235,715 cats since we opened our doors to them' – a commendably successful re-homing rate.

If they have kittens, not infrequently, a purchaser comes and redeems one of the party. Occasionally, too, a mourning owner, generally female, discovers her own special treasure behind the iron bars, and takes it away with great rejoicing . . .

The fear of rabid dogs gave the lethal chamber extra moral authority. Dissent in the Committee or among the Home's wider subscribers – and there had been misgivings – fell quiet. The destruction rate of dogs climbed to 90 per cent. To allay fears that death might be other than painless, pre- and post-mortem photographs of dogs with a 'peaceful expression on their faces' were made available to those attending the Jermyn Street meeting – along with a 'powerful' viewing glass for those who might still have doubts. The pictures would be published in several illustrated magazines, featuring the 'Herculean' uniformed attendant who was evidently master of the gruesome proceedings. Was this what the charitable Mr and Mrs Kennett had really intended? During one of many rabies scares of the period, the Home Secretary was asked in Parliament if the police had 'instructions to arrest and, if necessary, to destroy all un-muzzled cats'. It was all very amusing. Mr Henry Matthews replied that, although he was 'aware of a large number of homeless cats in London', he had been assured that 'cases of rabies in cats are comparatively rare . . . If I gave the police instructions to arrest cats, I am doubtful if they would find it easy or possible to obey my instructions.'

But cats were indeed being 'arrested'. The summer boarders might be conveyed to Battersea from their grand houses by servants, but the strays got there through the efforts of gaggles of women, going out at night with baskets and improvised traps. Some worked together, some alone. In high summer 1889 the *Pall Mall Gazette* had this warning for cats:

'A band of ladies who are just now very much on the look-out for starving cats will surely claim you as their own, entrap you, and take you down to Battersea, where, after five days' sojourn, there yawns the mouth of what is euphemistically called a lethal chamber . . .'

Irish-born beauty and journalist Lady Colin Campbell also visited the Home not long after her spectacular divorce hearing had transfixed London society. She recorded the experience for the Catholic journal the *Tablet*, whose editor had commissioned her to investigate, following the appearance of a newspaper appeal by a certain 'Miss M – earnestly begging kind homes for poor cats cruelly left to starve by late Christian owners'. The forsaken cat scandal now had a religious imperative.

'No one who has been in London during [late summer] can have failed to notice the number of gaunt, lean, hungry cats that throng the West-end squares during those months', she wrote, 'or the increase of cat-corpses that are then to be found in the gutters of side streets'. But thank goodness for the 'Committee of the Temporary Home for Lost and Starving Dogs – who for the last five years have made provision for receiving and boarding cats during the absence, or otherwise, of their owners'. She was sanguine, however, about the fate of non-boarders:

> Unfortunate stray cats and kittens lost, wilfully or otherwise, in the London streets . . . will find a ready asylum if any kind-hearted Samaritan will pick them up and take them to Battersea. No charge is made for stray cats; they are received with open arms and lodged in the 'waifs and strays depart-ment', a big store-house built up into the arches of the rail-way bridge, which contains not only a couple of big, comfort-able cages for the lost cats, but also what is usually the last asylum of all in their career, the famous 'lethal chamber'.

Was that really all that could be done? In summer 1889 Mrs
Walker's north-east London cats' home had opened for business as a semi-detached out-station of Battersea. However,
within a matter of months, her benefactor Mr Barlow Kennett
was dead, the landlord (an upstanding physician) was outraged,
the neighbours in uproar and the 'sanitary authorities' had
been called in. Lawyers advised that the Home must be closed
at once. The Dalston survivors were evacuated southwards
for destruction.

Some freelance cat collectors meanwhile discovered that
they could do the job of ending feline misery themselves with
a simple box and rag. Readily obtainable, chloroform could
be used to extinguish life in any confined space – as many
thousands of urban cats were about to discover.

But set against the obsessive cat removers were those who
would comfort cats where they found them. Their work was
by its nature more clandestine. The *Pall Mall Gazette* had this
to report during the summer mass-abandonment season: 'The
cats, the starving cats, are left behind in London, and there is
none to look after them, save where here and there a lone old
lady toddles along the streets, basket in hand, and lets pieces
of juicy meat glide down between the area railings.'

Mr William Fotheringham of Southend-on-Sea complained
in a letter to a newspaper that his housekeeper, 'a sympathetic
old lady, cannot bear to see these unfortunate animals in
distress'. For the past fifteen years his residence had 'been
turned into a home for incurables . . . I find myself compelled
to make arrangements with the chemist for their periodical
destruction,' he wrote. 'I love cats – but what is one to do?'

Over and again, in letters to the *Animal World*, the cat feeders were judged to be foolish sentimentalists just prolonging
the misery. There were dark mutterings as rival cat-lady armies
clashed by night in the dimly gas-lit streets. The great rescue
cat war of late-Victorian London was only just beginning.

6

The Case of the Cat Contessa

KARA

Due to unforeseen circumstances Kara our beloved BROWN SPOTTED BENGAL is looking for a new home. Kara is 12 years old, in excellent health and full of energy. She is neutered and micro-chipped and is fully vaccinated. Kara is a bubbly, funny girl who loves to play games with ping pong balls and feathers, and cannot resist cardboard boxes. She likes to go out to play but does not like the cold so prefers to stay in at night and cosy up with her family.

She would prefer a home where she is the only cat . . .

Of course there had always been cat rescuers, kindly people, overwhelmingly women, who would feed and comfort those cats that might cross their path. There was a fine line between the old lady down the lane who looked out for the cats and the 'cat hoarder' – someone who actively acquired multiple felines by whatever means, way beyond their ability to look after them, more and more to the point of madness.*

Several such cat ladies would become infamous over time, like the wealthy Mrs Griggs who had lived in Southampton Row, Bloomsbury, London, in the early nineteenth century.

---

* Twenty-first-century cat behaviourists stress that the cat is a solitary predator. Offering one a niche habitat in your home is fine. Maybe two is one too many.

She was, apparently, 'remarkable for her benevolence to cats'. It was reported at the time of her death:

> Her executors found in her house 86 living and 28 dead cats. Her mode of interring her favourites was, as they died, to place them in different boxes, which were heaped one on another in closets. She had a black female servant; to her she left £150 per annum to keep the favourites whom she left behind.

There were cat collectors and there were street-feeders. Some were rich and some were poor, but the two cat-lady types were different in how they operated. In his epic survey, *London Labour and the London Poor*, published in 1851 by the journalist and social researcher Henry Mayhew, his information-gathering among the capital's 'cats'-meat men', whose lowly trade in skewers of horseflesh kept felines of all degree alive, produced plenty of anecdotal evidence of women, wealthy and otherwise, who purchased large quantities to feed strays:

> There was one woman – a black – who used to have as much as 16 pennyworths each day. This person used to go out on the roof of the house and throw it to the cats on the tiles. By this she brought so many stray cats round about the neighbourhood that the parties in the vicinity complained; it was quite a nuisance . . .
>
> There was also a mad woman in Islington, who used to have 14lbs of meat a day. The party who supplied her had his money often at 2 pounds and 3 pounds at a time. She had as many as thirty cats at times in her house. Every stray one that came she would take in and support.

For some reason the north London district of Islington would prove very popular with cat ladies. Forty years after Henry

Mayhew's survey, the case of Mrs Elizabeth Ann Cottell, widow of an army surgeon, shocked polite society when she turned the former London home of the esteemed historian and philosopher Thomas Carlyle, No. 24 Cheyne Row, Chelsea, into a cat- and dog-filled 'menagerie'. The 'house was now in a most disgusting state, and a scandal to the neighbourhood', a police court was told in 1892 when the Vestry Nuisance Inspector intervened. The RSPCA brought a cruelty prosecution.

The obsessions of Mrs Mary Chantrell of Ivy Cottage, Rottingdean, Sussex, were reported in newspapers for thirty years from 1867; she was constantly in and out of court (again in cases brought by the RSPCA) for 'cruelly starving and neglecting' a shifting population of cats and dogs left supposedly in the 'care of two servant girls who had no money with which to buy the animals food, and the tradesmen had stopped the supplies'.

Mary Chantrell had been an artist, a childhood prodigy who had exhibited at the Royal Academy, until cat collecting claimed her. At the end she was found sleeping on the streets of suburban south London. It was reported: 'When she was brought up at Penge Police Court on a charge of sleeping out of doors without visible means of subsistence, it was plain that she was a woman of refinement and education. She appeared in court with several bundles, a portfolio of her own drawings, and carrying two cats under her cloak. The prisoner pleaded: "Don't take away my little cats from me. They are my models for painting".' The bench sentenced her to four days' imprisonment. The fate of the cats was not reported.

American cat-rescue ladies took a little longer to find their destiny. Mrs Rosalie Goodman was a German immigrant who, for almost a decade from the mid-1870s, offered comfort to the street cats that lived in her Madison Street neighbourhood on the Lower East Side of New York. She was not wealthy but managed somehow to fund her cat-collecting obsession by renting out rooms in her tumbledown house to tenants who did not seem to mind the overwhelming feline company.

It had begun simply enough. One day she came upon 'a little kitten, a homeless street Arab which she nursed and Christianized' and named 'Tiger'.

One day someone stole Tiger and hid him in a basement, where he starved to death. 'I found nothing but his bones, and I buried him,' she would relate, 'and then I made up my mind that I'd take care of all the cats I could when people turned them out in the cold to starve.' And so she did.

After her husband Henry's death in 1871, a more serious cat-collecting habit developed. In February 1875, a reporter from the *New York Sun* paid Rosalie a visit to hear her story. He found that: 'the yard in the rear is a special playground for cats . . . It is spacious, dirty and abounding in sly nooks that are just the thing for cats. At the back are a half-dozen patched wooden buildings similar to the one inhabited by Mrs Goodman, each with an opening upon the enclosure.' Scattered throughout were 'dozens of cats dining on soup and milk in white and yellow earthenware dishes'.

Rosalie Goodman and her four children occupied two small rooms on the second floor; others were rented out. When asked if they got along with the cats, one man said, 'IF any of her tenants interferes with the rights of her cats, or abuses them, he may expect to leave his room at the earliest date . . .'

Mad cat ladies soon became a favourite story for American news editors. A year after Mrs Goodman excited attention, a *New York Times* reporter tracked down Mrs Anna W. Steiner, living on the top floor of a house at No. 306 West 36th Street. He found: 'Four tiger-like tortoise-shell cats eating from a large bowl of bread and milk . . . The walls of her sitting room are covered with pictures of cats, and a large picture of Mr Henry Bergh [who had founded the American Society for the Prevention of Cruelty to Animals in 1866] hangs over the mantel.' Mrs Steiner told him:

> I have tried to do all I can for the poor creatures for the last ten years, for I take a great interest in cats. You see, cats are different from dogs, for dogs can bite and the poor cats can't, and I don't see why folks prefer having a big, ferocious dog to a nice, beautiful cat . . .

Her main concern was those 'horrid boys' who like their London (or any other city) counterparts delighted in tormenting cats with no one to tell them it was wrong. There was also the habit of New Yorkers, as with wealthy Londoners, of simply abandoning their pets for the summer to somehow survive in the sweltering city while they sought cooler climes.

What did Mrs Steiner do with the cats? 'Well, I find good homes for them,' she said. 'There's a dear good butcher on Sixth Avenue, between Thirty-sixth and Thirty-seventh Streets, who had taken care of five or six for me, and ladies who want a nice cat often come to me for one. Now I hope if you hear of any kind person who would like to have a nice cat you will send him to me.' Mrs Steiner seems to have been a rescuer all right, a very practical one and on a good day, might be considered a prototype re-homer.

Victorian London had plenty of such people. Florence Nightingale, the Lady of the Lamp who found fame for her attempts to salve the medical horrors of the Crimean War, teetered on the brink of being a crazy cat lady. She owned over sixty during her long life and at one point was said to have had seventeen scampering round her Mayfair home, No. 10 South Street, 'with a nurse to attend to each'.

According to her, 'cats possess more sympathy and feeling than human beings'.

One special favourite was a large Persian named 'Mr Bismarck', described as 'the most sensitively affectionate of cats'. When another, 'Mr Muff', wandered into the woods at the family country house in Hampshire and was shot by a gamekeeper, Miss Nightingale was 'broken-hearted'.

Living with so many cats was complicated. One called 'Quiz' escaped from its basket at Watford Junction while on a railway journey but was thankfully recovered. Miss Nightingale confessed herself to 'have had quite too much of policemen, and printing handbills, and offering rewards and paying them, for lost or stolen tom cats in London'. Printed handbills! Presumably they were stuck on lamp-posts around her Mayfair home in the great urban tradition of the LOST CAT poster.

Florence Nightingale did not collect street animals. Her cats came from friends or were kittens born below stairs. And she was sufficiently wealthy and enough of a national treasure to get away with her obsession.

Another society figure of the period, the Dowager Countess Mary Della Torre, failed on both those counts. The doings of the notorious Cat Countess were reported in newspapers across the English-speaking world as her battles with neighbours, appearances in police courts and general cat-centred eccentricity spiralled into bonkersness.

Born illegitimately as 'Theresa Reviss' in colonial Calcutta around 1840, according to her account of an Italian father and a Scottish mother, her sultry beauty and flashing wit secured her entry into fashionable European society. 'Tizzie', as she was known, married an Italian aristocrat who installed her in a splendid villa. In spite of his gambling and the political upheavals of the Risorgimento, she managed to hang on to enough money to install herself in west London as Mary,

Countess de la Torre, and take lodgings in four rooms over the basement and ground floors of a house at No. 35 Pembroke Square, Earls Court.

Soon it was filled with cats (and indeed dogs), bringing down the wrath of respectable neighbours. A certain Mr James Wade who lived to the immediate right apparently was the strongest objector to the injurious smells. The landlady did not seem to mind and the Countess somehow managed to retain the loyalty of a servant, an Irish girl called Mary O'Donnell. However, as it was soon to be reported:

At the Hammersmith Police Court, the Countess de la Torre, residing in Pembroke Square, Kensington, was summoned by Mr Harding, clerk of the Kensington Vestry, for keeping a number of cats and dogs in her dwelling rooms, so as to be a nuisance. Thomas Abbott, one of the Inspectors of Nuisances for the parish, said that in consequence of the abominable stench arising from the house where the defendant occupied four rooms, he inspected them, and found in three, eighteen cats and nine dogs kept in the most offensive manner. The animals were running about the stairs and rooms, but were confined to the house . . .

The defendant said that she had six little kittens, which the inspector called cats . . . The defendant, in answer to the complainant, said she was a member of the Royal Society for the Prevention of Cruelty to Animals, and she took care of the cats of people who were away. She did so to prevent them from being starved.

A year later, the *Pall Mall Gazette* reporter found her living in squalor in her shuttered dwelling, doors barred against intruders, without furniture, with bowls of red 'disinfecting powder' dotted around, and with 'a low oak chair, [providing] the only remnant of luxury in the room'.

The floor was carpetless. In one corner was a small heap of blankets; at my feet was a small open hamper half-filled with straw, the bed of one of her cats. Between us stood a deal box, which might be used as a table, but was occupied by various cats during my sitting of two hours. By her side was another box filled to overflowing with letters and papers, to which she constantly referred.

The report continued, crafted in that high Victorian way of writing – sentimental yet full of imagery:

In her chair by the window, in that bare room surrounded by her cats in council, sat the Countess . . . She is apparently about forty-five years old, with a pale, intellectual face, furrowed by much trouble, a broad high forehead, from which her dark grey hair is brushed away.

Her face lightens up when excited, and the wildness of her brown eye softens when her cats jump up on her lap. A grey knitted shawl was fastened round her neck and fell to her waist, where it was joined by a well-worn cotton dress. 'Perhaps,' she began, 'I inherited my fondness for animals from my father. He had a passion for cats. Whenever I take a poor starved creature in I think of my father, and fancy that I am paying a tribute to his memory. I have no other tie in the world but my cats, no one to care for, no one to care for me.'

At the imminent prospect of the court bailiffs pounding on her door, the Countess confided:

At present I am in a state of siege. I am ordered to abate the nuisance, and daily I am subject to a fine of ten shillings until I do so. I keep my doors locked, so that my enemies shall not enter if I can help it. Oh! Will the law allow them to come and kill my cats?

'The Countess then led the way down the steps on to the kitchen floor,' the story continued, 'down a passage which took us to the area. "Here are my dead pets," she cried, as she pulled open the door of the coal-cellar. On the top of an empty hamper lay two fine black-and-white cats, rigid with the cold of a violent death. These were lifted up, and beneath the hamper were three more fine cats, also dead, apparently from strychnine.

A gaggle of street children mocked her and her pets. RSPCA posters pinned to her door invited jeers. According to reports, 'little boys and girls – wicked urchins – called out, "Thou should be drowned as a witch".'

Meanwhile, neighbours were clearly taking more direct action. As she told her interviewer: 'Since the decision of the magistrate on Saturday, poison has made sad havoc among the cats.' It was reported:

> The Countess burst into tears as she told of the death of her red cat 'Ruby', of the tabby Manx 'Rosie', of the decease of 'Jumbo', of 'Bella,' 'Bob' and 'Cobby'. 'I would not have sold them for a hundred pounds apiece,' sobbed the Countess, crying bitterly. 'How can they inflict this agony upon me? My cats are all I have to care for in the whole world. Does the law of England say how many cats or how many dogs I shall keep? No. Then why shouldn't I be allowed to have my cats in peace . . .'

So where had all these cats come from? She claimed that the stray cats of west London somehow knew they would be welcome in her home. They had come over the garden wall or 'hungrily mewed about her hospitable door'.

Others arrived in baskets by parcel post sent by persons unknown, or were placed with her by the desperate, the penniless, 'a seamstress thrown out of her dwellings', or 'by a woman in Brighton who had to go suddenly to India'. Many felines who sought her out were doubtless Belgravia cats abandoned in the summer months by their fashionable owners. Once through the Countess's doors, they bred and multiplied: cats, cats and more cats.

The correspondent found a nursery room on the floor above with cots for kittens arranged around the fireplace. A never-ending parade of strange cats made their own way to her house, according to the Countess. All animals were drawn to her, evidently. 'She has even cherished spiders more for the delicate beauty of their workmanship than for themselves,' said the report. '"I used to bring them to me by a peculiar low hiss", she said.'

After every police case (all lost), after every fresh mention of the Countess and her cats in the press at home and around the world, letters of support and sympathy would arrive, some containing a small donation, allowing her at least to pay the cats'-meat man. The *Pall Mall Gazette* reporter met the lowly tradesman 'with his armful of skewers' on her doorstep. 'The door closed upon him, but I heard the cats chorusing a devouring welcome. Some day they may devour the Countess . . . It would be a sublime ending.'

On one occasion, following yet another visit from the police, the Countess was taken to Holloway Gaol and her suffering cats to Battersea for dispatch in the recently installed lethal chamber.

Her fame crossed the Atlantic. The *New York Times*, carrying the story in June 1885, recognised 'intemperance in cats' as 'a feminine vice and it is very seldom that a man becomes addicted to it'.

The Countess Della Torre [sic], who is frequently brought before the London police courts, sometimes keeps as many as sixty or seventy cats, and other women almost as bad are from time to time mentioned in the English police reports. In some of these cases the thirst for cats is probably inherited, and in others intemperance in cats is due to moral weakness and absence of self-control.

Cat passion was a potentially fatal addiction, so the *New York Times* editorialised in June 1885 about the de la Torre case, with the dire warning that 'whether or not such an unfortunate woman escapes imprisonment as a disorderly cat keeper, she is bound to be finally found dead in the midst of her cats'.

It was an extreme judgement. But in part true, as the grisly circumstances in many cases of cat collectors over the years would prove. But the Countess was not ready for her cat-surrounded exit yet. She moved to humbler lodgings in Fulham but her battles with neighbours, landladies and the council authorities continued. It was reported:

'The Countess de la Torre, who carried a goat in her arms, appeared at Hammersmith Police Court on May 20 to answer an adjourned summons charging her with disobeying an order to abate a nuisance caused by "an accumulation of cats" on her premises at Richmond Gardens, Lillie Road, Fulham.'

Goats became a parallel obsession. After an episode inhabiting a 'sawpit', she retreated to rural Buckinghamshire 'dressed as a herdswoman' with a flock of them, while the number of cats in her ménage reportedly remained undiminished.

Cat collecting was clearly a step towards the insane asylum. And it was no solution to the perceived sufferings of the forsaken urban cat. Even Mr Henry Bergh of New York, the ASPCA founder so revered for his kindness to animals and mentioned by Mrs Steiner, saw that leaving New York's stray cats to the mercy of the streets was no longer enough. In 1880 he prepared an ordinance for the city's Board of Aldermen, 'authorizing the seizure and destruction of all cats that may be found in any of the streets, avenues, parks, lanes, or alleys of this city', insisting that it be done by humane methods and the actual catching of cats (so difficult in the big city) should not be in the hands of children. It was pointed out that what New York lacked was an institution to do such a thing.

A letter to the *New York Times* in August 1880, headlined 'A Plea for Homeless Cats', said:

There is one in London [Battersea]; also one in Philadelphia . . . This is not supposed to be a home where [cats] spend the remainder of their days in luxury, but a place, a building in which they are kept a certain length of time; when, if not claimed by the owners, they are sold, or if not sold, destroyed in the most merciful manner, not by drowning, but by carbonic acid gas . . . Why do not some of the wealthy women of New York who lavish so much fondness on their pet cats and dogs, prove their appreciation by assisting the less fortunate of the species. Let them establish a shelter or place of refuge for stray animals, similar to those in London and Philadelphia.

So there it was, another way for wealthy women to attain their feline destiny – to found a dedicated cats' home ('shelter' would become the defining description) on the practical lines of the increasingly famous dog asylum in Battersea or the Morris Refuge in Philadelphia.

This was cat passion within the bounds of reason. And there was, should a claimant or kindly adopter miraculously appear, the chance of life, the chance of redemption. There would always have to be some killing-to-be-kind. The question was how much.

In Boston, Mass., it was a man who founded a 'home' for street cats and dogs with as little killing as possible. Cat-loving

Captain Nathan Appleton, after a trip to London, where he reportedly visited Battersea, sought to create something like it at home in six acres that he owned of the Brookline district. His Jeffersonian view was clear: cats 'had a right to their lives and pursuit of happiness'. The good captain found a willing backer in Miss Ellen M. Gifford of New Haven, Ct., who endowed his utopian scheme with an enormous sum of money – and more from her estate on her death.

Thus came to be 'The Ellen M. Gifford Sheltering Home for Animals' with its founder subscriber's mission statement emblazoned above the door: *If only the waifs, the strays, the sick, the abused, would be sure to get entrance to the Home, and anybody could feel at liberty to bring in a starved or ill-treated animal and have it cared for without pay, my object would be obtained*. A visitor soon thereafter found accommodation for a hundred felines thus disposed:

> All around the sides of the cat-house are shelves or bunks, which are kept supplied with clean hay, for their beds. Here one may see cats of every colour and assorted sizes, content-edly curled up in their nests, while their companions sit blinking in the sun, or run out in the yards. Cooked meat, crackers and milk, and dishes of fresh water are kept where they can get at them. The cats all look plump and well fed . . .

London readers of *Our Cats* would be informed of the Home's comforts 'when all inmates have roast beef on Sunday. Incurably diseased cats are of course put painlessly out of suffering while convalescents are sent on holiday trips to various parts of the country.'

This was something very unusual in the history of cat rescue. It was a true cat haven – at least for those lucky enough to get in and who were not incurably diseased. Miss Gifford surely recognised that fact, in her 'if only' qualification to her mission statement. She could not save the feline world entire. Nobody could. A hundred cats at a time would have to do.

Five ladies of New York seemed to be on a similar mission when they declared in 1890 that they would devote the rest of their lives to improving those of the city's cats. They had formed something called the 'Society to Befriend Domestic Animals', with the aim 'to provide shelter and food for the homeless and maltreated animals; to secure painless death for animals rendered decrepit by accident or incurable ailment; to secure through educative agencies the repression of all forms of cruelty to animals'.

They were Mrs Grace Georgia Devide, Mrs Sarah Jane Edwards, Mrs Emma Charlton, Mrs Mary Hans and Mrs Mary Wilson.

Mrs Devide, a flame-haired southern belle from Virginia and the animated leader of the movement, lived with her husband in a four-storey brownstone at 230 West 21st Street. She would later tell a reporter from the *New York World* that she had begun feeding stray cats in her neighbourhood around 1875. She was a 'Buddhist', so it was reported, and believed that 'these cats are only the form in which live spirits that some time will be human'.

'We've got the finest place in the world for the poor cats,' she told a reporter. 'Oh, we're going to have a regular little heaven for the cats up there . . . We shall have two meals a day, breakfast and dinner. For breakfast the cats will have milk, oatmeal, and stale bread . . . Sometimes I shall give them toast. They like toast . . .

'My husband refuses to follow me. He is a professor of music and thinks this is craziness on my part.' She pledged to give her life 'to the friendless outcasts of the city, against whom every human hand is turned'.

Under the ladies' guiding principles meanwhile, 'sickly homeless cats of inferior breed would be slaughtered while cats of fine blood and physique would be nurtured', according to the report.

For their cats' asylum a farmstead was sought on the edge of the city so as not to upset the neighbours. An apparently ideal site with rambling barns was found to rent in Washington Heights – later described as a 'frame shanty' on West 185th Street – in the hills of northern Manhattan Island. Much of the funding ostensibly came from Miss Caroline G. Ewen, the hugely wealthy daughter of Civil War Brigadier-General John Ewen (later elected Comptroller of New York City), and one of three cat-loving sisters. The cat spa opened in October 1890 and within six months there were 125 cats at the house with a matron called Miss Conklin.

The ladies encouraged people both to bring foundlings and adopt rehabilitated inmates in good re-homing style. But there was trouble from the start. Mrs Sarah Jane Edwards, General Manager, dropped out of sight for some reason. Miss Conklin sued for unpaid wages and quit. There was a rumpus over kittens born in the asylum. 'It became very heated,' said a mocking newspaper report. 'One woman said there was no use maintaining a home and prolonging the lives of cats if the Society was going to murder the dear, sweet, innocent little kittens.'

Miss Ewen took against a 'spirited tom cat', rescued from a gambling den and called John L. Sullivan after the boxer. 'His claws and teeth are too sharp,' she was reported as saying. 'Miss Ewen will sell him for $10 . . . She also denies the story that the cats are sold to butchers for sausage meat. She thinks Miss Conklin started this story.'

The Society to Befriend Domestic Animals stumbled from crisis to crisis but then it embarked upon something truly novel – squads going out to 'feed strays at night'. The *New York Herald* reported in May 1893:

Several women compose the band, and three times a week they issue forth at the unearthly hour of two in the morning and prowl around until four looking for stray cats. They claim to feed two thousand cats a week in this manner, and they carry the food in tin pails and baskets. Meat the first night, catnip the second and fish on Friday nights.

That summer, for whatever reason, there was an apparent change of heart. The Washington Heights Asylum was abandoned and its cat population dispersed. Although the nocturnal patrols continued, they were now for a very different purpose.

7

A Charming Abode for Felines

MISS WALLY

Female, age (approx.) 5, DOMESTIC SHORT-HAIR black and white, can live with a family.

Hello, my name is Miss Wally. I came into care because my previous owner could no longer afford to keep me. I am a nice affectionate little girl, a little shy at first. I would require to be the only pet in the household and to live in a quiet and calm environment. I would like a secure garden where I can safely sunbathe. Please come and see me?

As in America, so in Britain: the animal-welfare landscape was getting pretty crowded. Along with the venerable RSPCA, eager enthusiasts were keen to proclaim a better idea of how things should be done or find niche causes to pursue. Royal patronage had meanwhile silenced some of the derision that had greeted the first pioneers. Some were by now even claiming *divine* patronage!

The still-strident anti-vivisectionists had been joined by the National Canine Defence League, the Plumage League, the Humanitarian League, the Society for the Protection of Birds, the Vegetarian Society, the Order of the Golden Age and many more, some with religious or quasi-mystic international links and prescriptions for a non-animal-exploiting life that modern post-humanists would recognise.

The Animal Defence and Anti-Vivisection Society was co-founded in 1903 by Lizzy Lind-af-Hageby, a Swedish aristocrat and feminist, and Nina Douglas-Hamilton, the Duchess of Hamilton and Brandon, with a Mayfair HQ to match the splendour of the RSPCA's in Jermyn Street. It was based for many years at Animal Defence House, 15 St James's Place, London. Beyond that was the 237-acre Hamilton ducal estate at Ferne House near Shaftesbury, Dorset (acquired in 1914), where hunting of any sort was absolutely forbidden. The estate would one day prove of great significance in the affairs of distressed cats.

The Society came to widespread attention during the so-called 'Brown Dog Affair' which began when Louise or Lizzy Lind-af-Hageby infiltrated the vivisection for teaching purposes of a brown terrier dog at University College London. The subsequent description of the experiment in her book, *The Shambles of Science* (1903), led to a protracted scandal that transfixed the nation, a much-reported libel case (she lost) and riots by pro-vivisection medical students.

Some activists were campaigners first, some were founders of practical animal shelters – or both; all were animated by intense passions. 'Homes for Lost and Starving Cats' sprang up in genteel suburbs, spa and seaside towns, some little more than a terraced house with chicken-wire huts in a garden, to last a few years before expiring or being taken over by a bigger, more domineering posse of empire-building animal enthusiasts.

The personality and motivation – often religious, but not necessarily Christian – of such groups' founders was important, and power struggles, schisms and policy disagreements were commonplace. Some functioned as virtual cults entwined with spiritualism and esoteric religion such as the Order of the Golden Dawn. Some were true outriders of the 'animal rights' movement that would impact so deeply and with such mixed results on cats a century later.

Like Henry S. Salt, for example, the vegetarian social reformer whose *Animals' Rights: Considered in Relation to Social Progress*, published in 1894, made proposals that would still be passionately argued about today. 'The institution of "Homes" for lost and starving dogs and cats is a welcome sign of the humane feeling that is asserting itself in some quarters,' he wrote, 'but it is also no less a proof of the general indifferentism which can allow the most familiar domestic animals to become homeless.' 'Indifferentism' still has a lot to answer for. Henry Salt would not be alone down the years in blaming feckless humans for the plight of stray cats while also recognising the eccentricity of some who sought to help them.*

Strong-willed, 'let's get something done' societies like Our Dumb Friends' League, founded in 1897, grew very quickly. To begin with, the League's concern was more about the abuse of horses pulling carts in the street rather than the mistreatment of cats and dogs – but pets quickly became a major interest. Within a year it had twenty-two branches. In 1906 an animal hospital was opened in London to provide veterinary care for pets of the poor. Soon the League, like everyone else, would go into the stray cat business.

Those charities that managed to stay independent would be fiercely jealous of each other, competing for patronage, donations and, above all, legacies in the wills of wealthy

---

* In his 1930 memoirs Salt recalled an old clergyman who had been divinely inspired to rewrite the New Testament on vegetarian principles. He was the Rev. Gideon Jasper Ouseley, 'a mystic', whose *The Gospel of the Holy Twelve* appeared (anonymously) in 1901. In the text, Jesus encounters a stray cat who 'was hungry and cried unto him, and he took her up, and put her inside His garment, and she lay in His bosom . . . And when He came into the village He set food and drink before the cat, and she ate and drank, and shewed thanks unto Him.' The stray is adopted by a widow named 'Lorenza' – which is a nice name for a cat. The Messiah's supposed feline encounter would inspire many internet cat memes.

women. Lawyers did well. Cynical journalists prowled around
looking for scandal, social-climbing middle-class women to
mock, rascally General Secretaries absconding with the funds,
loopy wills and crooked solicitors. In a fight over one animal
welfare legacy, it would be stated that the wealthy testatrix (a
Mrs Mary Durant of Kensington) would 'rather leave her
money to a dog than a lawyer'.

Over again, it would be asked by high-minded commentators, what were these ridiculous catbotherers up to when
human misery was so universal? Why care for starving cats
when there were starving children in plain sight? Accounts in
the humane literature of the period regularly compared
animal waifs and strays with their human equivalent. One
kindly lady, a correspondent of the *Animal World*, took
biscuits with her on do-gooding sorties to give to both hungry
dogs and to outcast children as she encountered them on the
streets of east London.

The story of those who would do something for street
animals and for street children would unfold in parallel
throughout the second half of the nineteenth century. Several
prominent personalities in Britain and America would be
involved in both. Under their urging, Parliament legislated.
Donations were invited and freely given. By the end of the
century, a proliferation of shelters, homes and institutions for
infants and young people would be the result. But the idea of
placing a disadvantaged child in a better class of home was
next to unthinkable.

Child adoption into a family was a secretive procedure
with no legal status – and it would not have any such status
in England until 1926; being a 'ward' was different. In polite
society it was stigmatised – inviting Lady Bracknell-esque
comments about being found at railway parcel offices. But
some church societies went actively looking for destitute
children that they might place, not in institutions but in good

Christian 'foster' homes, vetted for suitability, where the lucky few admitted might be expected to be raised to become tradesmen or domestic servants.

There were further informal mechanisms to get children out of the Poor Law system and into family care – without crossing class boundaries. 'Baby farming' (infants for sale to childless middle-class women) excited the gravest scandal. For one such to adopt a street child, even in secret, would be seen as something impossibly daring, even criminal. A lower-class animal coming into the house was just as unimaginable. Shoo it away!

There had always been malfeasance galore in charities established to address human suffering. The so-called 'Society for Organising Charitable Relief and Repressing Mendicity' (usually shortened to 'The Charity Organisation Society') was founded in London in 1869 to try and regulate some of it. In the mood of the times, the Society promoted self-reliance 'with a somewhat undue amount of harshness' to deal with the distressing symptoms, such as child beggars in the streets, but did not tackle directly the social or political causes.

Something must surely be done. But differentiation must be made between the 'deserving' and the 'undeserving' poor. Scroungers and loafers were unworthy of hand-outs.

There were many at the time who doubtless saw swarming street animals as scroungers and those who sought to help them as fools or fraudsters. A sentimental appeal to Help Poor Pussy could open many purse-strings. Muck-raking journalists who a decade before had derided animal advocates as 'mad', now sought to prove that the new vogue for pets-in-distress was a front for old-fashioned fraud.

So what might reassure the sceptics? Ladies with 'intemperate' cat-collecting habits might still be arraigned in the police courts – but it was simultaneously accepted that there was nothing wrong with inviting public subscriptions so that

some vast urban mansion or suburban Eden might be filled
with cats (whatever the neighbours might think), as long as
the treatment of the animals that went through its doors was
perceived to have some practical purpose.

And what might that be? Death was always going to be a
part of it. Battersea had shown the way with its wondrous
killing machine. For example, when Miss Swifte's Home for
Starving and Forsaken Cats had raised enough money and
was taking shape in 1885 in specially created premises at
Grand Canal Quay, Ringsend, Dublin, it was noted:

> It is usual to have a lethal chamber for the destruction of
> animals attached to such homes, and it is intended to get one
> – but its use will be confined solely to dogs . . .
>
> In no case will cats be killed. Miss Swifte intends it to be a
> home in the real sense of the word for cats, and not a slaugh-
> terhouse, and has been promised by an English lady friend a
> legacy for the Home, providing this intention is adhered to.

In fact, the utopian manifesto would have to be abandoned,
but at least Miss Swifte had tried.

'The Home for Forsaken Cats', Ponsard Road, College
Park, Kensal Green, Harrow Road, north Kensington, was
established in 1886 by a committee of well-wishers[*] for 'the
benefit of the lost and starving dogs and cats of London so

---

[*] Known as 'The West London Society for the Prevention of Cruelty to
Animals' (not part of the RSPCA) of which the universal humanitarian, Mr
Ernest Bell, was Chairman and which was headquartered at Mrs Sarah Grove-
Grady's palatial Bayswater house, 20 Norfolk Crescent, W. She donated £1,000
to help start the venture, paid the supervisor's salary and advertising costs. The
Home itself is listed in *Kelly's London Suburban Directory, 1901*, as 'The Home
for Lost Cats (William Bass, Superintendent)', but in general it was by then
being referred to as 'The Mayhew Home' which became its official name
around 1906.

that they should have sanctuary from the cold inhumanity they are being dealt outside'. Cat-loving Miss Anne Mayhew was its first 'Lady Superintendent', presiding over, as it was described, 'a compact and charming abode for felines, whether strays, abandoned, sick, or boarders . . .' Her origins remain as mysterious as those of Mary Tealby, her departure recorded in a stark death notice:

> Mayhew. On the 7th Inst., [August 1897] at the Cats' Home, College Park, Anne King Mayhew, founder of the institution, aged 75.

Nevertheless her name is enshrined as a cat heroine in the title of the 'Mayhew Home for Cats and Dogs' tucked away behind the railway tracks of Willesden Junction, still ministering to north-west London's felines from the same site after 130 years.

The Home was not as quick as some of its rivals to consign its rescuees to a merciful death. In fact, the opposite was true. Its aim was to 'provide shelter, food and care and good homes where possible, for lost and starving cats and dogs'. No mention of killing. In July 1892 Miss Mayhew announced: 'Forsaken cats are taken in, not to be destroyed, but to be well cared for and good homes are found for them . . . [last year] we found upwards of 200 good, kind homes. I have often had their photos sent to me even from Scotland and Wales.' A little later she would make a newspaper appeal for:

> THE POOR CATS, on whose behalf I venture to ask for a trifling assistance, not one farthing for ourselves, but for these forsaken ones. Surely the Almighty never intended the creatures he made should perish from sheer starvation. We seek for and find them in all parts of this great Metropolis, no

longer the sleek well-fed cats but living skeletons. We wish
our Home, College Park, Harrow Road, to be visited (any
foot-sore dog welcomed). Caretakers always there. –
Faithfully Yours, Anne Mayhew, 29, Northumberland-place,
Bayswater.

A little later she would tell a visiting reporter at the height of
the cat-abandonment season in the capital about a cat locked
up in a fashionable house:

> The policeman on the beat heard its cry day after day, till he
> could stand it no longer, and came to tell us about it. Of
> course, we cannot force our way into empty houses, but the
> Society for the Prevention of Cruelty to Animals help us
> where they can. One of their officers came and insisted upon
> the doors being opened. You should have seen the poor
> creature! I had it in my arms till nearly three o'clock at night.
> We found that, in its hunger, it had actually eaten pieces of
> coal. It was a beautiful creature, as you will see . . .

She further confided that the 'freehold ground and building
were paid for by my friend Mr R. Barlow Kennett. He
intended to endow the Home, but died very suddenly [in
March 1890 aged 87]. Since then I have had to depend solely
upon subscriptions. Therefore, you see, we have to be very
careful.'

It might be presumed that most of Kensal Green's proto-
rescue cats (and indeed dogs) were not children of the gutter
but the genteel creatures whose forsaking by their owners
caused such outrage. In a much anthropomorphised but
nevertheless telling piece of writing, a visitor to the Mayhew
Home in summer 1902 described finding a mother cat with
a 'quartet of kittens' in the 'boarders' section' that had
evidently 'been forgotten by its owners'. The poor creature

had been there for four years. The cat spoke to the reporter who had sought her out:

> Yes, it's a disgrace to my family that my offspring should be born in such a place. Everyone is very kind but it reminds me of Dickens's tales of the debtors' prison. I don't know how to go back and face my friends, such eminently respectable suburban folk. I hope they forget all about me and let me end my days here in peace and oblivion . . .

The Home for Starving and Forsaken Cats, Gordon Cottage, Argyll Place, King Street, Hammersmith was opened in 1895 by Mrs Alice Gordon, the wife of Major-General William Gordon, with lashings of aristocratic patronage. A keen anti-vivisectionist, she was also the Hon. Sec. of the newly founded 'Society for the Protection of Cats', which announced its purpose as to 'deal with the question of stray cats in a sensible and humane way' and 'educate the public in their duties to all domestic animals'. Miss Alice Swifte of Dublin was on the founding 'committee of ladies'.

Mrs Gordon got to the point straight away. The Home's chief object, she said, was 'to find an immediate refuge for the many miserable and starving cats haunting the streets of London . . . Every endeavour is made to find good homes for the best cats, and a chloroform lethal chamber ends, by a painless death, the miseries of those for whom no home can be found.' A second home for cats at 5 Wendell Road, was opened for the boarders, 'without contact with the diseased strays', so that was all right.

Mrs Alice Gordon's robust approach was tempered by a belief, as she would tell a newspaper reporter, that 'the human qualities of intelligence, affection, and so forth which a cat has acquired are perpetuated . . . until they reach the higher plane, and in the course of ages reappear in human beings'. It was the destiny of catkind to one day supplant the human race – so it was clearly a good thing to be charitable towards them on the way.

But finding homes, even for the 'best' cats, remained fraught with difficulties all round. Battersea had all but given up trying after the McConnell cruelty scandal (the horrid man who had deliberately acquired cats from the Home to be tormented by his dogs), although 'every care is [being] expended on these unfortunate forsaken animals', so it was said in 1899. 'The Queen's cat and dog doctor', Mr Alfred Sewell, a fashionable Belgravia vet, had been in 'constant attendance upon them'.

'Twice during the past year [to May 1899], the cats were afflicted with influenza, on each occasion that cats' house had to be cleared out and disinfected,' the annual meeting would be told. But in spite of Mr Colam's lifelong enthusiasm for cats, he must be practical. 'If more cats are brought in than there are room for, then the weakest and most useless must be destroyed,' he declared. And so it was.

Of 306 homeless cats received in 1905, so it would be reported, 'homes were found for several but the majority, many of whom were injured or diseased, were painlessly destroyed in the lethal chamber'. Of course they were.

But for those cats lucky enough to avoid any would-be 'rescuers', things were beginning to look up.

8

Posh Cats

BUSYKITZ CURLY HARRY

Is a 6-year-old silver/grey SELKIRK REX male looking for a
loving caring home. His owner has sadly been diagnosed
with heart failure and as such is finding it extremely hard to
care for this lovely boy. He is a domineering cat and would
do better with no other cats in the home. He goes outside
but never goes far away. He can also be a bit rough when
playing and does not like his belly being touched.

By the turn of the century the two feline nations, posh cats
and under-cats, had their allotted places in the order of things.
The 'Cat Fancy', with its stud books, aristocratic patrons and
Crystal Palace shows was (almost) as much a part of the social
order as the Kennel Club.

This general feline triumph was marked by the publication
beginning in 1899 of *Our Cats* magazine (its editorial office
based first in London then Manchester), which would be a
noticeboard for cats at stud, show-cats, pedigree kittens for
sale, cattery anecdotes and much besides. There was a children's page conducted by 'Auntie Nell', its contents more
suitable for tender young Edwardian boys and girls than the
reports on breeding, neutering and euthanasia. The journal
also lobbied for the cause of cats as intelligent, sentient animals
worthy of the highest respect, with tales of their miraculous

faculties, affection, loyalty and intelligence – including an engaging story about a cat that answered the telephone.

It also regularly carried full-page appeals from the shelters, including Mrs Gordon's and Miss Swifte's in Dublin, and every so often it would venture dangerously on to the wild side with reports from the feline underworld. At least it reminded its readers that such a thing existed. Sometimes they found out by themselves.

There was this report, for example, from the second day of the 1903 Crystal Palace Cat Show, when a 'fine sleek black and white cat was seen making his way casually among the cat pens'. A cry went up, 'an angry chorus'. Then, according to the *Our Cats* correspondent, a 'cat hunt ensued with a number of fashionably clad ladies lending their aid until the intruder was captured by a lady with a parrot headdress and stuffed into an empty cat pen'. Was it a show-cat that had got lost? An official pointed out that there was no class for black and white cats. It was a stray, an inhabitant of the Sydenham underworld who had somehow penetrated the cosy circle of pampered show-cats. 'The Chairman promptly ordered the culprit to be banished.'

At a 1904 meeting of the Church Society for the Promotion of Kindness to Animals called to discuss taxing cats, the cat-loving novelist Mrs Bertha de Courcy Laffan revealed that she had 'rescued a stray from death and disease . . . which now rejoices in the name "Lucinda"'. Indeed, Lucinda was transported around the house by the butler on a tea tray and 'having grown well and fat, sits to the table, wears a napkin round her neck, takes her meals with only two paws on the table, and generally [according to Mrs Laffan] behaves as a high-born aristocrat', so it was reported.

And from Manchester came the story of another spectacularly class-crossing feline published in *Our Cats* – a 'Persian tom living the life of a wild cat'. It was captured at last with the aid of a lasso by Professor Alfred Ward ('feline and canine specialist – appliances available for handling vicious cats'), proprietor of the celebrated 'Royal Kennels and Cattery', Stanley Grove, Longsight. The professor, it was reported, 'intends to take it back to his premises and tame it'. He had succeeded in penning it safely but, as he said: 'I find I have set myself a task. This cat is perfectly wild, he flies at the wire and spits at anyone going near. I managed to pass food into him which he eats in the night.'

The abandoned cats of summertime Kensington still lived in a strange limbo, half in and half out of respectable society. There was an especially moving report in *Our Cats* from fashionable Philbeach Gardens, where 'hosts of starving cats sat on windowsills waiting for their families to return'. In the Readers' Letters column, Mrs G. Foulke-Watson, confined by illness to her sickroom, reported watching a 'poor grey cat in the street below following a cats'-meat man, frantic for food, only to be spurned by his foot'. She appealed for kindly people to leave out water for cats in the heat of high summer. There were tales of cruel 'moggy-hunts' by heartless children and, very occasionally, uplifting stories of cat rescue. Like Mrs J. W. Hardy, who was alerted by her husband returning home – 'did she know there was a little cat, apparently dying in the garden'.

It was a six- or seven-week-old kitten, 'soaked and shivering', survivor of an evident attempt at drowning, which was 'revived with hot milk and a few drops of whiskey'. It defied her own 'haughty Persians', she wrote, and was doing splendidly. This was the third waif that Mrs Hardy had rescued this year, she confessed: the 'one before this, a dear little handsome tabby, had gone to a good home'. The latest rescue was available to anyone who would pay the journey expense – 'but it must be a pet and not be murdered again'.

And there were reports of stray cats that rescued themselves by their very usefulness – like the cats of Edwardian

London who inhabited the underground system.* A letter-writer to *Our Cats* reported a 'large tabby on the Metropolitan Railway at Praed Street station', who walked along the track to be admitted by the unseen inhabitant of the signal box. 'Why, it's the rat-killer,' said a porter. 'There are two of them, but one never shows up during the day.' Down the line at Paddington there were thirty or forty cats that all lived underground and only came out at night. Their descendants would still be there, a century later. All the London railway stations had their quota of cats. Plus there were counting-house cats, brewery cats, factory cats, theatre cats, museum cats, Post Office cats and civil service cats living on an official allowance in return for keeping H.M. Government's offices rodent free.

Our Cats magazine honoured them all. And every so often, the patrician members of the National Cat Club, although they would never (most of them) have dreamed of taking a netherworld cat into their homes and hearts, did something to acknowledge the existence of the feline parallel universe.

At the very highest tide of the Victorian age, the two cat nations found a point of contact. It was, of all things, via the cats'-meat trade, the means by which domestic urban cats were kept fed in the first place. Without the cats'-meat man with his skewers of horseflesh and offal, and the wholesale knackeries who supplied them the meat, the cities of Britain would have been feline deserts. It was the same in America.

In January 1901 donations were invited through *Our Cats* so that a grand dinner of thanks for the lowly street-traders

---

* An enduring phenomenon. In November 2013 it would be reported that 'commuters watched stunned' as a ginger cat boarded a train at Seven Sisters station, managed to find a seat and travelled ten stops on the Victoria Line to Vauxhall, where he 'was coaxed into a cat-carrier by a volunteer at Battersea Cats and Dogs Home. Everyone around him was just staring as if they'd never seen a cat before.' Named 'Oyster', he was put up for re-homing.

might be held, hosted by the Cat Club. Why should they deserve it? It was to be 'a slight recognition of the Cats'-Meat Men's invariable kindness to the strays and starving cats of London . . . They feed them, throwing them scraps from a scanty store'.

This was all very incorrect, of course. Everyone could agree surely that the lethal chamber was the solution to the stray cat problem, which street-feeding only made worse. But in this extraordinary way (it was billed as the 'first annual' but was never repeated), wealthy cat-lovers were able to make a nod in the direction of those 'hard-working, soft-hearted men' who might show the teeming outcasts a glimmer of kindness. 'Each man will be given a plug of tobacco and a warm comforter to wrap him up on a cold Xmas morning as he goes on his rounds feeding the cats.' It was a fabulous – a transcendental – moment in cat-human relations.

The novelist Anthony Hope, author of *The Prisoner of Zenda*, was a subscriber to the thank-you fund; so was Mrs Bernard Shaw, along with many anonymous donors. One sent money in memory of 'Dear Little Bimbo'.

A celebrity cast of actors and music-hall artistes was engaged to entertain the gathering, including Mr Alec Hurley, the well-known 'coster singer', and Mademoiselle Natalia Janotha, the famous pianist, accompanied by her equally famed (black) cat 'White Heather', without whom she would not appear on stage.* The feast would be held in the splendid 'baronial room' of the City of New York Restaurant, Hand Yard, Bedford Row, Holborn.

---

* No relation to Queen Victoria's Persian, also called White Heather. Polish-born Chopin-exponent Natalia Janotha had been court pianist in Berlin. Her endearingly eccentric, always cat-accompanied piano act was famous until, on a tide of anti-Germanism, she was expelled from Britain in 1916.

A letter of support (but no money) and 'well wishes for the entertainment' came from the cat-loving Princess of Wales, who greatly regretted that she was unable to attend in person. Her cat-hating husband would surely have disapproved.

Two hundred and fifty cats'-meat men sat down to a dinner hosted by Louis Wain, 'who warmly thanked them for their efforts to look after poor pussy'. On the menu was mock turtle soup, roast beef, boiled leg of mutton and trimmings, plum pudding, cheese and celery. They 'tucked in with gusto'. It all sounded very jolly:

> They were a hilarious assemblage, and greeted the appearance of the soup, the roast beef, and the boiled legs of mutton with prolonged cries of 'Mee-att!' in the familiar notes of the street. At the end of the repast, Mr Wain said that all knew the old tom who ran after the cart and sneaked his ha'porth, and her who said 'Meauw' till she got her bit. They were all right, but he appealed for pity for those poor cats who by chance, circumstances, or cruelty were thrown out into the world.

The Duchess of Bedford, President of the National Cat Club ('whose presence had not been announced beforehand'), arrived just in time to hand round the Brussels sprouts to enthusiastic applause. Her Grace told them:

> I do not know if it necessarily follows that because you are sellers of cats' meat you are all fond of cats, but I think there might be some connection because I have never heard of a case of ill-treatment of cats on behalf of a cats'-meat man and I have often heard of their going out of their ways to be kind to starving pussies.
>
> With some of you, a livelihood may be as hard to get as with poor pussy herself, but this is one way to help . . . to

stop wilful cruelty wherever you meet it and inform the police of lost and starving cats so that the homes in London may send for it.

Then she confessed that:

As the owner of what was once a stray cat* and afterwards fed, I believe, by a cats'-meat man, I have great pleasure in wishing you all prosperity in the New Year.

It was reported the next month by *Our Cats* – along with an account of the death of Queen Victoria – that, 'as a result of the Duchess's speech, cats'-meat men who were not previously kind to the poor cats, now treated them very well indeed.' And no wonder they were so moved. Mary, Duchess of Bedford, Patron of the Society for the Protection of Cats, proto-Suffragette, member of the Zoological Society, bird-watcher and aviatrix (she would vanish without trace in her de Havilland Moth aircraft aged seventy-one in 1937), had established her modernist, radical credentials. She was one of the very few grand ladies of the day to admit to having taken a rescue cat into her home and into her heart.

The cat-rescue world had its saints and sinners. There were mad cat collectors, a very bad thing. There were the deluded rich with their cat utopias – bound to fail. There were the anti-vivisectionist ultras who thought the lethal chamber a better fate all round for street cats. Nobody doubted their compassion for a moment. And there were those like Anne Mayhew who would seek to succour as many as possible

* Identified by Louis Wain as 'a long-haired half-bred cat', later to be buried at the ducal seat, Woburn Abbey, 'where there stands over a very small grave, a plain white stone, on which is carved the simple legend "*Tommy*" – to whose memory her exertions in the cause of the sick and outcast felines are dedicated'. Good woman.

– something the Charity Organising Society thought donors should be warned against.

There were the practical rescuers like Mrs Alice Gordon or Miss Alice Swifte in Dublin with chloroform box close to hand, ready to make difficult judgements and let the 'best' cats find 'good homes'. That was surely beyond reproach. And there were those generally who sought to raise the status of cats, like the stray-adopting Duchess of Bedford. Also, there were those who sought to encourage children* especially to treat cats with compassion and respect. The cruelty of street-boys remained Hogarthian.

It was against this background that a new kind of cat 'rescuer' was emerging. Motivated, organised, businesslike – and in some cases, utterly terrifying.

---

* Like the 'Band of Mercy' movement founded in Britain in 1875 by the veteran philanthropist Catherine Smithies, aimed directly at young people and absorbed by the RSPCA a little later. The movement also took off in the United States. The pledge of both branches was the same: 'I will try to be kind to all living creatures, and try to protect them from cruel usage.' The nursery rhyme 'I Love Little Pussy' about being kind to a pet cat dates from this period.

9

The Midnight Band of Mercy

MISTY

Is a beautiful young unusual silver SOMALI female who was
found in late November 2014 wandering in the Reading area
and handed in to a local vet. She has been with us since
December while she has been assessed and vaccinated. She
has the most delightful typical Somali temperament and
adores people but is not keen on other cats, so ideally she
needs a home alone with lots of attention.

It began, more or less, in New York City. In early summer
1893, dead cats started turning up mysteriously in Henry Street
in the middle of the 'boarding-house district' of Brooklyn; ladies
who ran such establishments liked cats, apparently. The street
was known as 'Cat Lane' for its multiplicity of 'noisy tramp cats'.

When more and more bodies appeared, strewn over waste
ground, it was reported: 'The impression is spreading that
there is a sort of "Jack the Ripper" abroad in the First Ward
in quest of howling cats.'

At the end of June, a woman was arrested for throwing a
dead cat in front of a butcher's shop. The butcher had objected.
The woman claimed she had 'a perfect right to throw the cat
there, it was up to the city to pick up such carcasses. Why,
there was a time we used to put the dead cats in the best parts
of Fifth Avenue because we knew they would be taken away

from there quickly', she was reported as saying. She was Mrs Grace Georgia Devide, the self-proclaimed Buddhist, late of the Society to Befriend Domestic Animals. Now she was an adept of a new society with a somewhat different purpose. They called themselves 'The Midnight Band of Mercy'.*

Their mysterious doings would be the talk of the city through the hot summer of 1893, reported at length in the newspapers. 'An anti-cat crusade is going on over there [Brooklyn]', the *New York Times* reported. 'The Midnight Band of Mercy plan of campaign is – first catch your cat, then chloroform him or her . . .'

There was uproar. Cat-loving Miss E. McGarrah of Stockton Street, Brooklyn, declared it was 'just wrong, cruel, and an outrage on the cats'.

'Why are you so bitter against the new society formed to chloroform stray cats?' she was asked.

'Because they murder the poor things indiscriminately,' she replied. 'Some of my Angoras are worth $50 apiece, and they are just as likely to be chloroformed as any other cats. You can't limit a cat in his midnight prowling. It is impossible to guarantee that he or she will stay in your own back yard. They will get upon neighbours' roofs and there is no stopping them, anyhow.'

Mrs Devide was unchastened. In a later interview she was more illuminating on the details of the Band's technique. They would 'dress in old clothes and toss out catnip to draw cats'. Then they would stuff them into a portable death chamber.†

---

* The first Band of Mercy for juveniles on the British model had been organised in the US in 1882 and the oath-bound humane education ideal spread rapidly. The Midnight Band was, however, something much darker.

† It would later be described as: 'A lined and covered basket, containing a sponge covered with chloroform. Into this the cats (when not too weak to resist) are enticed by various patent devices, and quickly become insensible.

'The basket would shake and the cats begin to protest. In the kindest tones, the felines would be reassured: "Hush, kitty," their rescuers would murmur. "You are going to Jesus, kitty." "Meow!" "Kitty, hush, Kitty; your soul is going to the Lord." "Meow! Meow! Meow!" "Kitty has gone to God. Amen", and all was over.'

One of the Band's members was convinced that the cats were unborn children, and the more she chloroformed, the more she was saving. The *New York Herald* picked up the story when piles of dead cats became a regular feature in Greenwich Village. Rumour had it that a 'veiled lady with a basket' was responsible.

A few weeks later, Policeman Joseph Connelly was patrolling West 135th Street around nine in the evening when he saw a woman calling to a cat, and then a flash of a white rag. Inside her bag he found five chloroformed cats. It was Sarah Jane Edwards, late of the Society to Befriend Domestic Animals. She proudly acknowledged her membership of the Midnight Band and maintained that, under their rules, any cat on the streets after 8 p.m. would be deemed homeless and be put into the basket.

With Mrs Edwards under arrest, Mrs Devide gave a revealing interview. Cats abandoned when a family moved out were 'the most to be pitied', she said. 'Accustomed to food and shelter and to being petted, their suffering is indescribable when deprived of them. They hang round their former home to be driven away and beaten by the janitor or new occupants. They lack the cunning of the genuine street cats . . . Personally I do not love cats, I pity them and do all I can to relieve their suffering.'

Repeated efforts have been made to secure a room where cats might be collected and handed over to the incorporated society to be put to death; but janitors and landlords invariably object.'

Sarah Edwards was arraigned at the Harlem Police Courthouse on five counts of animal cruelty while a lawyer for the ASPCA prosecuted. She was defended by the famous law firm of Howe & Hummel – and a compelling courtroom drama resulted.

Described as a 'middle-aged woman, tall and shapely, with a pleasant face', once on the stand, she held nothing back. She was a member of the Band of Mercy, she said, and also a member of the organisation known as the 'King's Daughters', a recently founded Christian charity. In action they wore a five-pointed gold badge emblazoned with KINDNESS JUSTICE MERCY TO ALL.

The Band numbered about twenty women. 'No men are admitted to the Band of Mercy,' she said, 'because men are cruel to cats, and the animals have a natural antipathy to them.' In three years she had killed more than three thousand street cats – 'that had all been ignored by the Society for the Prevention of Cruelty to Animals'. 'The work is too dirty for them,' she said. 'Consequently they leave it to us and simply because we are women and for the sake of suffering animals choose to depart a little from conventional methods, we are ridiculed and criticised . . .'

Restrained from killing a live cat in the courtroom to show just how merciful an act it really was, instead Mrs Edwards showed off the oilskin-lined basket, from which she produced a dead cat. 'Holding it up, she instructed the court . . . "See what a calm peaceful look is on its little face . . . There was no pain there",' so it was reported.

The grisly performance won her no friends. Justice Charles Welde charged her with 'cruel extermination of cats', fined her $10, and ordered the Midnight Band of Mercy to cease and desist. After the verdict, 'the defendant was immediately surrounded by a host of women friends who tendered their sympathy'. Sarah Edwards declared defiantly that she and her supporters would continue chloroforming cats beyond the court's jurisdiction at summer resorts along the New Jersey coast. She would advocate 'a public pound for cats where kind women and girls would be appointed as cat catchers'.*

The daredevil reporter, Elizabeth Jane Cochrane, the famous female pioneer of investigative journalism, who had found massive fame with her 'round the world in 72 days' stunt three years earlier, kept on the strange cat story, relaying it in print at the very end of 1893 in Joseph Pulitzer's sensationalist *New York World* under her pen name Nellie Bly. It had been tough to put together. The Band's activities in Manhattan had been shut down by the court. The ladies were scattered, wary, living in lodging houses like fugitives. Their financial backer remained mysterious. It clearly all went back to the demise of the Cats Home in Washington Heights and the Society to Befriend Domestic Animals. How had it come to this?

She tracked down Miss Conklin, the matron of the original 185th Street shelter, now Mrs van Orden living in Harlem with four cats. The former matron revealed sensationally that the 'Cats Home was only a shield'. The killing of 'boarding' cats had begun right at the very start. A prominent singer

---

* Ironically perhaps, the ASPCA took over the business of clearing New York strays in 1894 soon after the death of Henry Bergh. 'Any cat found within the corporate limits of NYC without a collar about its neck bearing the name and residence of the owner stamped thereon will be seized . . . which will dispose of the cats in an effectual, though painless, manner,' it was declared.

Brooklyn cats were so incorporated a year later with a shelter in a former tram-shed with a busy 'death chamber using illuminating gas'. Modern so-called 'no-kill' exponents in the US point to this moment as when the 'mighty ASPCA, once a stalwart defender of animals, became a stalwart defender of killing them, beholden not to animals or furthering their best interest, but to a ruthless fundraising machine enriching itself and its leadership at the expense of its founding mission'. The RSPCA similarly went into the mass stray-killing business in London in 1912–13 (see p. 141).

who had been taken ill paid $2 a month for her two cats 'Mousie' and 'Spotty' to be cared for. They had been killed – at once – said Mrs van Orden, while the ladies in charge went on collecting money for their board.

The reporter got the names of several members of the lethal organisation but few had permanent addresses. One of them turned out to be 'Belmont Purdy, a wine merchant, who is the only male member of the Band.' The hunt went on.

Then, after days of searching, the intrepid reporter found Grace Devide 'up the dark stairs of a tall tenement'. Mrs Devide at first suspected her visitor had been sent by the 'Henry Bergh Society' (the SPCA), which 'was up to all sort of tricks to find out what the cat-catchers were doing'. 'She lives like a pauper and dresses like a beggar,' wrote the pseudonymous Nellie Bly. 'She hates religion and hates what seems to her [to be] pretended Christianity.'

Although the Band had been shut down, there was still a stable on West 22nd Street where cat-collecting boxes were kept. The two women went there together. 'As we're no longer allowed to kill them, we keep them here until the SPCA come and take them away,' Mrs Devide said.

'How many cats do you suppose you killed?' asked Nellie Bly. Fifty a night was nothing, she was told. They got the chloroform from an East Side druggist at $2.20 for a 4lb bottle. A thousand cats were born in New York every day, Mrs Devide said; just as well, since some of the members of the Band of Mercy had a 'mania for killing them'. Indeed, sometimes they would bluff their way into old ladies' homes to relieve them of their cats. 'I suppose I am mad,' she told her questioner. 'I have nothing in common with anything except animals, and them I love . . .'

Mrs Devide had been born in Virginia and 'had lived a long time in London', where she clearly moved in animal–advocate circles. She produced letters from 'Baroness Burdett Coutts and other prominent people' including Henry Bergh. 'She is clever and well read,' concluded Miss Bly, but as to the self-confessed madness, the journalist could only agree.

Nellie Bly's clever questioning turned to the mysterious backer of the Band. Was it the same benefactor who had 'joined hands with Mrs Devide and Mrs Edwards' to start the original Cats Home – the famously evangelical Miss Caroline Ewen?

Caroline Ewen was one of three immensely wealthy sisters worth a reputed $20 million living in a mansion on 48th Street and Park Avenue. Although Miss Ewen was 'a devoted friend of cats', Nellie Bly wondered how, with her stated abhorrence of the Church, could Mrs Devide get on with her? The answer was, they had a common pursuit. At night Miss Ewen would also 'dress in old garments' and set out with an oilcloth-lined basket and a bottle of chloroform, so Mrs Devide could reveal. 'Born and bred in luxury she would go fearlessly into the poorest parts of New York to catch cats.'

The undercover journalist went to see Miss Ewen herself, posing as someone wanting to open a home for dogs and cats; the search for her 'lost Fox Terrier', she claimed, had opened her eyes to the fate of street animals in the city.

Miss Ewen was forthright. The Cats Home on West 185th Street had been an idealistic dream. 'We had no intention of killing cats, but after it was broken up, Mrs Edwards suggested chloroforming the homeless cats and I have found it the only remedy,' she said.

'Some of the members of the Band of Mercy have had a life that makes it impossible for good women to associate with them,' suggested the reporter. 'That is true,' said Miss Ewen without commenting further. She told Nellie Bly about the poor animals she had encountered on her nightly prowls and the cruelty inflicted upon them by youthful tormentors. 'What could be more merciful than chloroforming a suffering cat the moment we find it?'

Hearing these accounts of the torments of street cats, Miss Bly confessed she was beginning to understand the enthusiasm for terminating them. This was not to be the end of Miss Ewen's interventions in the affairs of cats.

British newspapers, picking the story up from the transatlantic wires, relayed it in print with an indication that such loopiness could only happen in America – 'the paradise on earth of crack-brained societies'. In fact, there were more than a few cat ladies in London and other cities who thought the Midnight Band's methods were entirely admirable. They did not know it yet, but one day, a big chunk of Miss Ewen's money would be heading their way.

A better time was coming for New York's cats. It happened in a roundabout fashion. In 1902 'Le Dog's Home at Gennevilliers', as it was called, a refuge for the outcast canines of Paris, was founded by the American newspaper magnate Gordon Bennett. Its stated policy was to care for its inmates while inviting the attention of would-be adopters to the dogs' existence – maybe even to take them home. It was not just to be a street-cleaning machine.

Soon after its opening, the Paris refuge was visited by wealthy, animal-loving Mrs Flora D'Auby Jenkins Kibbe of New York City. Moved by what she saw beside the Seine, a year later she opened the 'Bide-a-Wee Home' to operate on similar benevolent lines in a small building on Lexington Avenue, a smart residential area of her home town.

The neighbours objected to the barking (they always did), so Mrs Kibbe moved the shelter to Harrington, New Jersey. It would end up on 38th Street, near the East River, a place where people regularly brought unwanted cats and dogs to drown them in sacks. But the Bide-a-Wee, like Le Dog's Home of Paris, would strive to keep its canine inmates alive while seeking new homes for them. And one day, it would do the same for New York's cats.

10

The Queen of Cats

Tibbs, having been adopted once, had to be returned to the Centre as he was not able to integrate with the other cats in the household. Tibbs appeared very depressed at having to leave a loving home and spent much of his time hiding beneath his fleece. Then a new adopter came who: 'Found him to be a beautiful and gentle cat who was happy to be fussed and would take treats very gently . . . [until] we were delighted to bring Tibbs home with us.

'For the first few days he hid behind the sofa but would venture out when you called him and after two weeks he was given the freedom of the garden . . . Four months on, and as you can see he is a very happy boy who loves nothing better than to run around the garden, laze stretched out on the dining-room table, and sleep on our bed.'

In turn-of-the-century London, the West End Cat Scandal had not gone away. In spite of all the anguish and campaigning, unfortunate felines were still being turfed out or locked up in grand houses for the summer by uncaring toffs; even if the latter had supposedly put money aside for their feed, rascally servants were prone to steal it.

It can hardly be said that nobody was aware of what was happening. The newspapers were as full as ever of indignant letters and appeals. A midsummer letter-writer to *The Spectator* invited readers to go to Stanhope Gardens in fashionable South Kensington, call out 'Puss!' and see the multitudinous forsaken cats that 'came in crowds, big and little, diseased, famished, and most terribly thirsty'.

In 1902 the *Daily Mail* published an abandoned cat's diary – *Left Behind* – with Louis Wain illustrations in which the authorial cat is looking forward to six weeks in Switzerland with his grand family, only to be left behind in the capital with just a saucer of milk. 'Fluff', the lower-class cat next door, is similarly abandoned as his family depart for a boarding house in Margate. The two cats forage together with some success, but when Fluff's family return and provide a nice juicy chunk of meat, they 'shoo me away'.

After three weeks our diarist drags himself into the street 'hoping to be run over and put out of my misery but I heard a young lady say, "What a magnificent Persian, but how thin he is" . . . She brought me here to Ferdinand Street, Camden Town (see below p. 107) . . . there are lots of us here; some of them have had a worse experience than I . . . Feel very sleepy . . .'

There it ends. It was all very amusing but actually heart-breaking. The *Daily Mail* meanwhile would stay loyal to the cause of cats in peril right up to the present day.

Other than the various homes and shelters like Battersea with their attendant lethal chambers, there were hardly any commercial boarding catteries. As cat columnist and author Miss Frances Simpson noted in her 1902 *Cats and All About Them*: 'I wonder that more cat-lovers wishing to add to their incomes do not start boarding-houses for cats. I think there is a great opening for such an enterprise.' She knew of only two ladies 'who receive pussies at so much per week': Miss Harper, of Briarlea, Haywards Heath, and Mrs Carew Cox, of New

Milton, Hants, whose cat-packed home was known some-what forbiddingly as 'The Kremlin'.

Year by year, the adverts for boarding catteries in *Our Cats* would grow. Like pedigree cat-breeding, it would become a profitable and eminently respectable occupation for middle-class women. As could be a philanthropic cats' home – albeit a far riskier proposition. There might be a bit of revenue from the sale of cats, both alive and as carcasses for rendering. And as Frances Simpson usefully suggested to the wider Cat Fancy: 'Healthy foster mothers [for pedigree kittens] can be obtained from the excellent homes for stray cats in and about London. The few shillings go to help the humane work of these excellent institutions.'

Almost all charitable cat shelters both 'boarded' and destroyed, while a very few, like the Mayhew Lost Cats' Home, generously funded by Sarah Grove-Grady, did what they could to keep some disreputable street cats alive even if they were never going to leave Kensal Green. 'It really is a home and not a cemetery or a mart where they may be bought for the tender mercies of the vivisectors,' enthused the ODFL, who provided a small subsidy.

The pioneer boarding catteries were commercial opera-tions. British cats without forward-thinking holiday-making owners faced a less benign vacation. In July 1902 the promi-nent parliamentarian, Barrington Simeon MP, asked newspa-per readers to consider the 'unfortunate cats [who] are left behind to starve, by masters and mistresses of houses who in some cases do not know of the existence of cats which are kept in their own houses, and still oftener in their stables.

'Why not have them painlessly killed before the family moves?' he asked persuasively, and recommended the 'Royal London Institution and Home for Lost and Starving Cats, Ferdinand Street, Camden Town, N.W., which is under the patronage of her Majesty the Queen' to perform such a service. The MP had thereby introduced readers to the most Gothic perhaps of all turn-of-the-century cat ladies – Mrs Zoe Constance Morgan.

Her origins are as mysterious as those of the Countess de la Torre, but over the years her feline infatuation would attract even more press and official attention, several chroniclers telling her story in instalments as her cat-rescue empire rose and fell. The Assistant Commissioner of the Metropolitan Police Criminal Department, for example, opened a file on her in 1903 for reasons which had little to do with animal welfare. It was the potential for a 'Royal' scandal – and use of that word in the title of her much-publicised 'The Royal London Institution and Home for Lost and Starving Cats' – which excited official investigation.

Chief Inspector Charles Arrow, otherwise more concerned with blackmailers and society jewel thieves, set out to probe the matter, interviewing in turn the leading British cat advocates of the age. It was a ticklish affair, involving numerous prominent people; indeed, Queen Alexandra, wife of the recently crowned King Edward VII, was at the centre of it. Was she a clandestine cat lady, perhaps? Like a high secret of state, the inspector's 1903 report would be closed to public scrutiny for a whole century. The 'Suspicions of Mr Whisker' makes extraordinary reading.

Mrs Zoe Constance Morgan, the name by which she would be best known, had begun her cat-rescue career happily enough as an associate of the Mayhew Home, now under 'an entirely new management and ruled by a committee of ladies', as she declared it to be in a letter to the *Morning Post* in July 1895 (with no mention of its original founders). However, there were clearly rumbles of concern over her robust attitude as to which rescuees at Ponsard Road should live and which should die. 'Trouble resulted, which reached a climax when the committee met and found that by Mrs

Morgan's orders, no less than twenty of the inmates of the Home had been put to death,' said the report of the subsequent police investigation. In her Mayhew incarnation she was calling herself 'Zoe de L. M.' and her address to be the 'Ladies' County Club'. Then she was 'Miss William'.

In January 1896 the lady in question, by now calling herself 'Mrs Z. C. Williams', according to the police report 'started a cats' home of her own at 80 Park Hill Road, Hampstead'. A reporter from the *Westminster Budget* had sought her out that summer and found:

> Mrs Williams, who, by the way, speaks with a French accent, explained that she had been led to open the Home on account of her sympathy with poor 'puss'. And, quite in the orthodox way of older 'cruelty' societies, she related the 'experiences' of her officer – in this case a stripling in livery, who goes forth on his missions of rescue mounted on a tricycle, which is fitted with a receptacle for cats.

The visitor further noted: 'Two rooms in the basement of Mrs Williams' house have been set aside for the purposes of the Home. Just before our arrival some cats had been despatched to Battersea, where they are painlessly put out of the way at sixpence per head.' Cats too ill to get that far were 'administered Prussic acid by the Home's vet'. A separate cage acted as the hospital, another held cats for sale, and 'in a room all by themselves were the private and boarder cats'. The article was illustrated by a photograph of plaintive-looking cats with the caption *Destined for Battersea*. A little thereafter, a primitive chloroform chamber had been installed – a chest of wood and zinc with six individually windowed 'compartments for cats'. A blurry image of Mrs Morgan featured in the 1899 report, 'placing a cat in the invalid's last resting place'.

Right at the start, in a typical animal-charity breakaway move, she tried to 'beguile' some of the Mayhew's patrons to come with her; indeed, she urged that the Kensal Green cat asylum should be closed and 'its business transferred'. The coup clearly failed. Mrs Grove-Grady was outraged. But within two years Mrs Williams was announcing a gilded roster of dukes, duchesses and marchionesses as her supporters.* There had been a favourable mention in the *Animal World*, and noted cat-lover the Duchess of Bedford was declared to be a patroness. How much of all this was true would later become a matter of intense dispute. Mrs Williams' ambition would prove boundless. Could she somehow persuade the famously cat-loving Princess Alexandra, consort of the heir apparent, 'capricious, feather-headed and reckless in pursuit of charity' in the judgement of one royal chronicler, to bestow her gracious patronage? There was no harm in trying.

It had all got much more emotionally charged with the establishment of the rival 'Society for the Protection of Cats' soon after her defection from the Mayhew Home, Inspector Arrow surmised, with 'Mrs W. Gordon, the wife of Major-General Gordon, as its moving spirit'. The Society with premises in Hammersmith had promptly joined forces with the Kensal Green old guard to form a 'Party of Cat Workers' in opposition to Mrs Williams, Mrs Morgan – whatever she called herself – and all her works. There were 'statements questioning her probity'. Battersea, however, beacon of lethal efficiency in the matter of stray cats and dogs, had proved co-operative, at least to begin with.

---

* The first principle of animal welfare was to get as many grand personages (overwhelmingly aristocratic ladies) as patrons and/or committee members. By the turn of the century, fashionable actresses were becoming important catches, to be joined in the years to come by music-hall, cinema and radio celebrities.

But in spite of the lady herself having quite recently been one of the Home's most proficient suppliers of strays for destruction, delivering consignments of cats to its south London gates for gassing three times a week in a greengrocer's cart, Mr John Colam found time at the Dogs Home's annual meeting in April 1898 to say petulantly: 'It is reported that somewhere in north London there is a cats' home [Mrs Morgan's] where cats taken off the streets are taken by the hundreds and seldom kept for more than two hours after their arrival (cries of "shame!")'.

'There need be no misgiving at sending cats to Battersea,' he said, 'pets, favourites and strays – where they will be well received and well cared for ("cheers")'.

But within a matter of weeks, Mr Colam was appeased. After a brisk exchange of correspondence, the title 'Home' would be removed, so Mrs Morgan promised (and failed to do) in order to make it clear that 'no one should send their pets which they may desire to be succoured until family homes can be found for them'. That was not the Institution's function at all and people should know it. Twenty to thirty cats might be accommodated in the basement of No. 80 while 'surplus animals brought to her will be mercifully destroyed.' The cat authoress Mrs Ellis Walton (*How to Keep a Cat in Health*) went to Park Hill Road to see for herself and observed 'one of the poor pussies put in the lethal box, and, looking through the glass, watched it sink into sleep and felt what a boon were the rest and peace after its sufferings', as she told *Animal World* readers.

Commenting approvingly on Mrs Morgan's openness, Mr Colam announced: 'There can be no difference of opinion as to whether it is benevolent or not to put cats, whom nobody wants and for whom homes cannot be found, to a merciful death.' He furthermore consented, as announced in *The Times*, to formally become a patron of the north London operation himself. After all, they were already in business together.

So what was Zoe Morgan really up to? Who exactly was she? At her modest enough rented premises at Park Hill Road, Haverstock Hill, as she herself would write: 'The work was first undertaken by myself as a result of seeing so many cats left to starve by heartless owners, cruelly treated and worried by dogs and human fiends. The cats were collected by me with the aid of a servant and taken three times a week to the Battersea Dogs Home to be destroyed in the lethal chamber.'

The charge 'under contract' was 6d per cat, she could reveal. Chloroform was expensive.

'Public attention was soon drawn to the work and cats were received unsolicited in large numbers and in many strange ways, being left in sacks and baskets on the doorstep, tied to the front gate or dropped over into the garden,' she wrote. Her uniformed staff were routinely abused and 'pelted' by street boys as they went about their work of collecting cats.

After four years at Park Hill Road, 'during which time the number of cats received increased from 2,450 in 1896 to 8,381 in 1899, the landlord insisted on the removal of the Institution', she wrote. An emergency plea for funds was printed – much commented on by the press of the time:

A large number of cats, of every shape and colour. A party of them, evidently of strong suicidal tendencies, is endeavouring to gain admittance to a house, across whose front runs a large board, on which is written *To Let*. In the distance is a modest, broken-down tenement, with the word *Full* thereon. The whole country beyond is swarming with serried battalions of cats. Not a living human being is to be seen. They have evidently all emigrated.

Thus it was that 'terribly dilapidated' premises in Camden Town were found, 'which had to be entirely rebuilt at the cost of £1,100'. Mrs Morgan's cat-collecting ambitions expanded to cover the whole of London. The next-door premises were acquired, and the next, in Ferdinand Street, Camden Town, London, N.W.

It was the animal-loving, Danish-born Alexandra, Princess of Wales, who would take Zoe Morgan to the height of feline hubris, and by association, eventually prove to be the instrument of her public humiliation. The lady's royal overtures were at last rewarded when a letter arrived from the Princess's Private Secretary on 16 December 1900 (Queen Victoria had five weeks to live) with stirring news. For its 'kind and useful work', Her Royal Highness had been 'graciously pleased to grant her patronage' to Mrs Morgan's Institution for Lost and Starving Cats. Clever Zoe had pulled it off.

When *Our Cats* announced the news on 16 February 1901, her triumph seemed complete. The self-proclaimed 'Royal Institution' opened soon thereafter. A subsequent letter from Buckingham Palace expressing Her Majesty's 'continued sympathy' referred to the Camden Town cattery by that name. Royal crests blossomed everywhere. The cats of Ferdinand Street met their end By Royal Appointment. Her enemies seethed.

In January 1903 the Royal Institution's Annual Report was printed with Queen Alexandra on the cover, a boastful, picture-packed, crown-bedecked prospectus rather than a dull summary of accounts. Those with urgent cat business might 'telephone day or night on King's Cross 54'. 'The Yellow Tram from Euston passes the door by the Maresfield Tavern,' it said, although Mrs Morgan and her staff seemed more in the business of going out to find cats to 'rescue' rather than waiting for them to come to her by tram or otherwise.

A motor van was acquired (one of the first in London) to go round and collect strays, and would 'call at any house if due notice is given to the Hon. Manageress'. The van kept breaking down. The horse-drawn cart made a comeback, emblazoned with the Home's portentous title, and the words *Free to the Poor* and *Under the Patronage of Her Majesty the Queen* beneath a prominent crown. Male members of staff were uniformed as pages in dark blue with polished brass buttons, the female staff like hospital matrons with gold-lettered hat ribbons, all very smart. This was costing a lot of money. Meanwhile, nos. 36–38 Ferdinand Street were stripped out and rebuilt with all sorts of up-to-date amenities to achieve Mrs Morgan's ends, whatever they might be.

As her own manifesto explained: '*The primary* aim of the Home is to receive and shelter cats, often abandoned by heartless people, until they can be humanely destroyed . . . no experiments allowed on animals . . . strong anti-vivisectionist. Help earnestly required helping clearing the debts. No connection with any other institution.' It was going a bit far perhaps to put a portrait of Her Majesty on the cover. There were mutterings at court. It was sternly pointed out that 'no one in society could make use of the royal title without the permission of HM the King' (no lover of cats). The Home Office took notice. Scandal-sensing journalists began to circle.

A 'Pussy Cat League' of child fundraisers had been instituted, with collecting cards marked at a farthing a time for the relief of stray cats – or at least Mrs Morgan's finances. League members wore a badge in return for a pledge to be kind to all dumb animals – especially cats. Every penny helped. Raising money to pay the debts on the purchase and fitting out of Ferdinand Street seemed to have become the Hon. Manageress's overwhelming priority. Meanwhile, she and Mr William Morgan moved into a splendid new home at

Albert Road, Gloucester Gate, Regent's Park, where she lived in a 'fairly luxurious style'. There were fundraising galas and concerts at fashionable venues.

Mrs Morgan was getting frightfully grand. In the close-knit cat circles of turn-of-the-century London, there was deep disquiet.

But for some the main concern was not Mrs Morgan's showing-off, but her methodology – the lethal absolutism which had caused the original Mayhew schism. This was not a cat sanctuary. Indeed, it was not even a charity and, in spite of all those patronesses, Mrs Morgan ran things as she wanted to. There was scant invitation to the public to come and get a Camden Town cat, although according to the regular plea for funds in *Our Cats*, 'Lady visitors may purchase Cats and Kittens for 1/6d (except Persians)'.

The premises were now centred around an ingenious state-of-the-art lethal chamber. Her Annual Report lovingly described it as a wonder of the age:

> Built at a cost of £365 with an additional floor to the cattery and small lift for the conveyance of cats to the chamber – designed and built by Mr Richardson, son of Dr Sir Benjamin Ward Richardson who constructed the Lethal Chamber at the Dogs Home Battersea, paid for in 1901, which has been the means to a great saving in chloroform and time, in every way superior to chloroforming in separate boxes.
>
> The Chamber is large enough to take 50 cats at once, each cat being in a separate wire cage in various sizes to accommodate large and small cats and kittens.

Miss Frances Simpson gave Mrs Morgan a glowing write-up in her 1903 *The Book of the Cat*, but was frank about her purpose. 'The Camden Town Institution to which H.M. the Queen had graciously given her patronage . . . receives 300 cats per week on average,' she said. 'Not a day passes without several wretched cats having to be destroyed on admission while 80 per cent of cats are destroyed within twenty-four hours . . .

'No charge is made to the poor and only 1s 6d for a painless death in the lethal chamber is asked from those who can afford this most merciful mode of destroying life.

'All lovers of cats owe a debt of gratitude to these truly noble ladies who have begun and carry on such a merciful work in our midst,' she wrote.

But there were many who thought the very opposite about Zoe Morgan. The great London Cat War exploded just as British troops were returning from South Africa from their war against troublesome Boer farmers. Hostilities in the metropolis had been opened by cat-loving the Hon. Mrs Featherstonehaugh, having defected earlier from Mrs Morgan's party, being the most keen to accuse her of 'arrogance' and 'mismanagement', according to Inspector Arrow's report.

In spring 1903 she had approached the editor of the magazine, *Truth*, a kind of *Private Eye* of its day, which specialised in exposing bogus investment 'ramps' and charity frauds. The proprietor, the wealthy Liberal MP and political mischiefmaker Henry Labouchère, could not get enough of what his journal would gleefully dub 'The Cat Home Scandal'. *Truth* duly published a long list of accusations of financial mismanagement and personal extravagance. But its description, published in summer 1903, of what the Royal Institution was exactly for seemed the most damning:

> It is not a home for cats at all, but a slaughterhouse where the animals are received and destroyed in a lethal chamber at a rate of over fifteen thousand an annum, according to the proprietress's last published statement.

This institution is not in any sense a public charity but the private undertaking of a lady who originally undertook it in the name of Miss Williams and has since assumed the name Mrs Morgan alleging she is a married woman dependent on her husband. There is no committee, nor any single independent person associated with this woman in the management of the concern.

Mrs Morgan was mortified. She stormed round to the magazine's office to protest – and had printed a counterblast pamphlet called Truth *and the Cats* in which she berated her enemies – who now included John Colam of Battersea and the RSPCA, who had resigned in summer 1903 as Vice-President of the Institution and Home at the first whiff of public scandal, putting a humiliating public notice of 'Repudiation' in *The Times*.

Mrs Morgan declared:

Ours is a work of love and mercy and because . . . it has withstood the bitter onslaught of its enemies, whose interference and advice have neither been sought nor accepted, it is hated, derided and vilified.

But she found it hard to refute one of the *Truth* reporter's assertions, one that would be familiar to cat 'rescuers' for decades to come. It read:

There may occasionally be one or two valuable stray animals kept on the chance of finding homes, but I was told by either Mrs Morgan or her accountant that this practice has been almost given up as it is found that people do not care to adopt grown cats, preferring to rear kittens . . .

Inspector Arrow's investigation discovered that in the twelve months from November 1900, the bodies of 15,602 dead cats and kittens had been sent from Ferdinand Street to the Battersea Dogs Home for disposal by cremation – at a cost of 3d for a cat, 2d for a kitten. When this proved too costly, Messrs. Hempleman & Co's Guano Works of West Ham were contracted to turn the bodies into fertiliser, removing the corpses for a flat fee of 15 shillings a week. A much better arrangement.

'No account of numbers was kept but the bodies were placed in drums containing twenty to thirty, and from this record Messrs. Hempleman are able to say that they process sixty to seventy cats a day and are doing so up to the present time,' said the inspector. He was not investigating cat-killing, rather Mrs Morgan's financial propriety.

'There is strong evidence that Mrs Morgan does do the work she claims and that so far the funds she collects are not misplaced,' he concluded. The inspector discreetly interviewed Mrs Morgan's accusers, including the Hon. Mrs Featherstonehaugh, Mrs Alice Gordon of the Society for the Protection of Cats, Mrs Douglas of the Mayhew Home, and someone called Miss Kate Cording of 31 Trinity Street, Islington,* described as a 'voluntary worker at Mrs Morgan's Home'.

According to Inspector Arrow, they variously described Mrs Morgan as: 'A painted, faded demi-mondaine of Paris, a cruel slaughterer of cats, a cat stealer, a swindler' – but 'not one could point to any false statement which could be made the grounds for a criminal charge'.

But who was Mrs Morgan?[†] Where had this adventuress-in-cats come from? She was evidently the daughter of Lt-Col

* Later renamed Batchelor Street.
† A diligent on-line genealogist has noted: 'The lady's name is actually Josephine Constance Marie Ruttledge, nee Longueville Clarke; the family name became "De Longueville" in 1870; she was married to Samuel Masters Davies in 1871, divorced in 1876; then to John Knox Ruttledge in 1878.'

de Longueville, ex-Indian Army, resident of Earls Court, so the inspector discovered. She had been born in Calcutta and was a member of the New County Club,* Hanover Square, 'a select ladies club', the inspector could note. More information on her early life and marital status would come out later (see below p. 122) in a fight over the will of an elderly 'aunt' who somehow managed to pass away while actually on the premises of the London Institution and Home for Lost and Starving Cats.

Sometime not long previously she appeared to have formally married Mr William Morgan, the son of a road foreman in the employ of the Hampstead Vestry. 'That he was his wife's social inferior meant he was little in evidence amongst the ladies and others interested in cats,' the inspector noted.

Charles Arrow had visited Ferdinand Street 'privately' and found the work being carried on by staff was just as Mrs Morgan had represented it. Which was not surprising. Zoe Morgan had made no pretence in her Annual Report and her own counterblast to the accusations in her pamphlet 'Truth *and the Cats*' about her purpose and means of achieving it.

She confessed quite openly that 'in the catteries are kept some fifteen to twenty boarders and an equal number of pets of the Institution for the amusement of the visitors who like to see happy cats. Some are life-boarders left with the promise of future legacies, others are pensioned'.

These front-of-house Potemkin pets had a spacious room of their own connected to a 'cat's playground' in a large cage on the zinc roof above the offices; photographs of them looking happy enough adorned the Institution's reports and

* Founded in 1894 as the 'Ladies' Tea and Shopping Club' – 'to provide for ladies of social position the comforts and convenience that men have found in their clubs for years past'.

were widely reproduced thereafter, as if this was some cat Nirvana.

But they were for show only. 'Cats are not kept for the purpose of finding homes for fear of the vivisectors,' so Mrs Morgan stated firmly, 'although my enemies accuse me of colluding with vivisection.' There could be no darker allegation.

Behind this equitable front there was the real business of Ferdinand Street: 77,272 strays had been received since her work began. 'It would have required Noah's Ark to house them all – and to what purpose?' she asked. 'I am accused of running a slaughterhouse. Yes, if you like – but a merciful one where poor animals are sent into their last long sleep with a friendly caress.'

The time from arrival in the Home to reaching the chloroform chambers was only a matter of hours. Battersea Dogs Home destroyed 18,000 dogs in 1900, she stated, to which her own figure of 17,000 cats per annum was comparable. 'There must be 100,000 homeless cats in the capital,' she argued, with a proposal that the London County Council make a contribution to start new branches across the metropolis while making Ferdinand Street the 'Mother House', where London's outcasts should be brought for 'necessary destruction'.

'I am not playing at a Cats' Home,' she said bluntly. 'I have endeavoured to get to the root of the matter by clearing the streets in a practical and humane manner.' She castigated Battersea for only taking 'cats left at their gates', meanwhile sending to her to deal with any request 'to bring in cats' the Home might receive – and likewise the rolling-in-money RSPCA who 'when they get an application to remove a wretched, ill-used animal, send to our poor little Home to do the work'.

Mrs Zoe Morgan's metropolis-wide cat extermination empire was not to be. After the *Truth* furore, the royal connection had to be broken in order to avoid a scandal. And in spite of past expressions of warm wishes from Queen Alexandra, the ghastly arriviste Mrs Morgan was ordered to act without delay.* When she proved slow to do so, humiliating press notices went out in November 1903.

> The Queen has withdrawn her name as patroness of the Royal London Institution and Home for Lost and Starving Cats, which thus ceases to be a 'Royal' institution.

Poor cats, with no Queen to be their protectress. But they clearly had other things to worry about.

It was a cruel blow. Her enemies were jubilant. But Mrs Morgan soldiered on, her death-to-all-but-a-few-favoured-felines policy unchanged. An unpaid bills crisis in 1904 saw her in Bloomsbury County Court where Mr Justice Bacon expressed astonishment that anyone should give her Institution credit. 'A number of ladies of title had withdrawn their patronage and persuaded the Queen to do the same due to mendacious press coverage,' said Mrs Morgan. 'Over the last eight years 86,210 cats have been rescued, the large majority of them killed painlessly.' She faced down her creditors, aided by the affair of the 'Black Cat of Holborn' – an unfortunate feline locked for three weeks in a shut-up confectionery shop

---

* Queen Alexandra remained sound on cats, unlike her husband. It would be noted in a sporting journal: 'Six cats are the favourites of the Queen. One, "Sandy" – so named because born in Sandringham – a valuable Persian, being the particular favourite, and travelling as constantly with his mistress for the past several months as ever the King's celebrated Irish terrier "Jack" did. The feline protégés of Queen Alexandra [including "Ossy" and "Monarch"], find no favour in the sight of Edward VII, for he cordially detests all of them. The Queen's favourite will not come to His Majesty's side of the table at any price, and generally makes himself scarce when His Majesty is about.'

Thus began Britain's royal family's long (and enduring) estrangement from cats.

in central London whose distress caused a considerable stir in the press. 'Well-wishers brought it sardines and salmon, and other delicacies were pushed constantly through the fanlight,' so it was reported, until it was at last set free and taken to the boarders' room at Ferdinand Street.

Two years later, an elderly lady called Mrs Maria Rebecca Bey, of Jersey, died aged eighty-four while actually in residence there, having been removed from her Channel Island home with the aid of her servant to the 'splendid house' in Camden Town three weeks before, along with various items of her furniture. She left an estate worth £18,000, of which through a late-made codicil he himself had drafted, a solicitor claimed to be the major beneficiary. The dubious will was contested in court by a certain 'Mrs Zoe Constance Ruttledge', the Home Manageress, who claimed that Mrs Bey was 'her aunt' and 'had adopted her as her daughter'. Her fortune had been promised to the cats' home. But according to her own servant's testimony, Mrs Bey had been 'entirely indifferent' to cats.

Among other things, the Probate Court was informed that Mrs Ruttledge had been 'separated from her husband by verbal agreement in 1882'. And further that her own father, Colonel Longueville, had 'lost all his money on the Stock Exchange' and that her 'uncle had been killed in the Indian Mutiny'.

'Mrs Ruttledge' was Mrs Morgan, of course. In the case of Maria Rebecca Bey, she also appeared to be collecting wealthy ladies as well as cats and installing them at Ferdinand Street until they died. In the end she got half the money.

By such means the London Institution stayed afloat. Enough aristocratic patrons stayed loyal and by 1913 her subscription list was bringing in £5,000 a year – but this was 'still not enough to cover current expenses'.

Then something astonishing happened. News reached London's cat circles that a Miss Caroline G. Ewen of 23 West

86th Street, New York, had left an enormous sum to animal welfare charities – not just in America but all over the world. Miss Ewen, some veteran newspaper reporters on both sides of the Atlantic might remember, had funded the ladies of the Society to Befriend Domestic Animals. Whatever had happened to them?

Miss Ewen had died in the Hahnemann Homeopathic Hospital, Rochester, NY, on 12 April 1913. There were, however, certain difficulties. Her nephew was contesting the will on the grounds of his aunt's alleged 'testamentary inca- pacity'. And there was the matter of where the money was going: to cats. 'Tramp' cats at that.

The status of American stray cats had not improved since the demise of the Midnight Band of Mercy. In 1910 the US Department of Agriculture reported that outbreaks of rabies, diphtheria, tuberculosis and smallpox had been traced to 'alleycats' consorting with free-roaming pets. 'As much danger lurks in a cat as in a rat,' the Department had warned. And that is where the Ewen fortune was heading.*

Two of the charities named in Miss Ewen's will, the 'Cats' House of London' and the 'Animal Rescue League of Madeira' did not even exist, as far as her nephew, John Ewen – himself a lawyer – could ascertain. He asked for a commis- sion to be appointed to track down the London Cats' House and its mysterious director, named by his aunt's will as 'Kate

---

* Feline bestseller *Pussy Meow* by Sarah Louise Patterson, published in America and Britain in 1903, was the 'autobiography' of a stray who gets adopted by a kindly rescuer. It contained a powerful sequence in which orders are given for the destruction of all homeless cats during an outbreak of smallpox – a move dismissed as 'nonsense' by the family doctor. The rat was the 'real transmitter of germs which gave even the persecuted alley cat the reason for her existence'. Although there are zoonotic infections and parasites that can be transmitted from cats to humans, the killer disease–stray cat assumption would be very hard to overturn.

Renning'. If the Madeira Home was real, he said, each cat on the island was worth $1,000.

The Ewen mansion and other valuable property in New York had yet to be put into the estate. In her will, Miss Ewen had excluded her two sisters Maria and Eliza from any benefit from her share because, it was reported, 'they were not sufficiently enthusiastic about cats'. That seemed more than a little harsh, especially since when Maria Ewen died in 1920, her 'favourite cat would be buried in the casket with her'. Maria had been cold-shouldered, apparently because at the age of sixty she had married a certain Otto von Koenitz, believing him to be 'a baron' with a castle in Thuringia. He turned out to be an ex-convict. The marriage had been annulled in 1911. She should have stuck with the cats.

There was uproar. Reporters on both sides of the Atlantic wanted to know all about the stray cats of London, so apparently enriched. Surrogate Robert Fowler, the court official in charge of probate and estates of New York County, co-opted Mr Richard Westacott, US Vice-Consul General in London, to investigate. He put a diplomatic toe into turbulent London cat waters. The first thing was to find the mysterious Miss Kate Renning . . .

The $40,000 rescue cat hunt was afoot!

11

Waifs of a Great City

FOUND

A smoky grey Persian female cat with amber eyes seen to have
jumped off a furniture van in the Manchester area, has been
taken to the Cats Protection League clinic, Withington,
Manchester.

The Cat, August 1963

What was a London cat to do? At the high tide of fin-de-
siècle feline obsession, there were plenty of mad cat ladies
who had it all mapped for you. Call in chez the Countess de
la Torre in Earls Court and you could end up mummified in
the cellar. Mrs Zoe Morgan was running a self-confessed
slaughterhouse. There was always the Battersea Lost Dogs
Home, a slightly better-ordered affair, but with a trip to the
lethal chamber more or less guaranteed.

The Home itself had earlier reported at its annual meeting
that one anonymous lady alone in 1903 had brought 132 cats
to its gates to be destroyed. 'Does she belong to that class of
person who has a mania for stealing cats?' so Mr Matthias
Colam, the Home's Secretary, had been asked. 'My answer
was "No",' he told the meeting. 'She is a person of means
and uses her means to carry out a work of humanity . . . She
practically said: "When I see cats starving I stretch out a hand
to rescue them" (applause).'

The Barlow Kennett cat bequest of twenty years before was recalled by Mr Colam to general satisfaction. 'It is our boast that everything necessary for the welfare of cats is carried out on the most approved lines,' he said as the meeting erupted in the obligatory cheers. London's stray cats were, in fact, being gassed every day beneath the grisly railway arch and their bodies promptly cremated; everyone gathered in frock-coated self-congratulation for the annual meeting of the Home at the RSPCA headquarters at 105 Jermyn Street was aware of this.

Streetwise cats knew to steer clear of Battersea – and indeed, Camden Town. However, other parts of London were also proving highly dangerous. There were reports of men on bicycles with baskets napping cats off the street for sale to furriers and impoverished families selling their domestic pets for a bit of cash rather than heading for the pawnshop. The going rate was half a crown.

The American Vice-Consul, Richard Westacott, had hired a detective agency to find the mysterious Kate Renning and her 'Cats' House of London', the potential beneficiary of the Ewen fortune. It was more difficult than it seemed, for they discovered the presence of forty 'cat hospitals' in London alone. There were indeed plenty of semi-amateur cat rescuers who had joined the pioneers. Mrs Gordon's shelter in Hammersmith and the Mayhew Home in Kensal Green were constantly full, and in spite of all the problems, Battersea continued its feline work. In 1908–9 as part of wider reconstruction it had erected an eccentric, Arts and Crafts-style 'cats' house' (a little later to be named 'Whittington Lodge') designed by the innovative architect Clough Williams-Ellis: to be used 'for the reception of stray and abandoned cats', as the *Animal World* reported. It was hardly commodious. In discussions with the London County Council over the provision of a fire escape, the architect described it as 'a detached pavilion a few yards square intended for the accommodation of a dozen or so stray cats'. Its actual feline use would be short-lived.

The RSPCA itself was tentatively going into the animal welfare business, supplying lethal boxes where requested by regional branches. The Cheltenham branch began chloro-forming cats in 1902, while the Society generally began to concern itself, just a little, with supplying veterinary care for the animals of the poor. It was in London, however, that the forsaken cat continued to make its very public insistence that something more urgent must be done. There were some Society members now openly demanding prosecutions for cruelty in cases of cat desertion – even of the most illustrious Belgravia householders.

The Society must do something. As well as its long-established personal connections with Battersea and its robust solution for strays, from 1905 onwards the cats of the Mayhew Home – where street animals did not go quite so promptly to their deaths – began to get a small subvention from its central funds. The semi-detached relationship with Battersea contin-ued, while Mrs Morgan remained beyond the pale. In April 1909 an RSPCA 'Cat Sub-Committee' was set up to consider the question of 'diseased, starving and stray cats in London and other large towns'. The move would have major conse-quences for cats – not all of them necessarily good.

Our Dumb Friends' League had also gone into the cat-shelter business. The League had progressed rapidly from a be-nicer-to-horses campaign to become a national animal welfare operation, its rise largely due to the publicity talents of its Secretary and Organiser, Mr Arthur J. Coke, a former tea-trader. He had consistently come up with attention-grabbing ideas, such as paying the dog licences of British soldiers serving in the Boer War. Fashionable actresses were proving better fundraisers than duchesses, he discovered, and

he deployed them at galas, shelter-openings and ODFL benefits with a showman's flair.

The first cats' shelter opened in 1905 when an amateurish
street-cat-collecting operation run by a certain 'Mrs Childs'
at 9 Crookham Road, Fulham, was taken over when she
'found the demands impossible'. It was soon to be 'placed on
a business footing' as the Annual Report described it.

By the end of the decade the League had 'Receiving
Shelters for Stray Cats' – 'in every Metropolitan borough and
suburban district surrounding the County of London, [each
one] in the charge of responsible caretakers and include lethal
chambers', it could report. 'The committee now have six of
these shelters at work – in Spitalfields, Tottenham, Chelsea,
Fulham, Ealing and Richmond – at each of which an average
15,000 cats are dealt with yearly.' The Richmond shelter was
opened by the cat-loving Ranee of Sarawak – otherwise
Margaret, Lady Brooke – in March 1910 with a fanfare of
publicity. The formidable feline grande dame, Miss Frances
Simpson, was on the shelters committee. The League was
very frank about what this capital-wide network was for:

> These shelters should not be confused with Homes for Cats.
> Their special object is to rid the streets of these unfortunate
> animals and not to keep them for a long period without the
> prospect of homes.

The destruction rate was 100 per cent. To underline the
moral rightness of the endeavour, the League's Annual
Reports were full of harrowing stories about the brutality of
street life and the merciful necessity of the work.

Inevitably both *Truth* magazine and the Charity Organising
Society began investigating Mr Coke – but not for his methodology. His fundraising was a little too successful. Was he
perhaps a swindler? He was rumoured to have 'married a lady

in Bournemouth who was supposed to be rich but who turned out to be deeply in debt'. Now he was 'living extravagantly in Belgravia. It is all very scandalous and horrid', so it was reported by a COS snoop, a certain Miss Ethel Bellewes, in 1912. 'People who are engaged in promoting societies for the improvement in the conditions of cats and dogs make reflections on each other's integrity,' noted the investigator. He was right about that.

'You will remember the case of the notorious Mrs Morgan. It is very natural that a powerful sentiment such as the love of animals should afford a field for adventurers in charity.' How true.

But what about the money raised? Was it being spent legitimately? Like the RSPCA, the ODFL made modest contributions to the Mayhew Home, so it turned out. A COS inspector went to see the place for himself. 'The Home is perfectly genuine,' he reported. 'It has had no connection with Mrs Morgan for some years.' All well and good. Then he said this:

> There is one point about the Mayhew Home which is objectionable. No cats are disposed of unless they are very much diseased, and they are kept until homes can be found for them. Subsequently the place is full of strays, some of which are most disreputable.

So there it was, the spirit of the age. 'Disreputable' cats being allowed to live. That would not do.

Among the new, twentieth-century wave of cat rescuers, so the US Vice-Consul's investigators found, was something called the 'Feline Defence League'. Its doings had been reported in the pages of *Our Cats* magazine and in journals of the occult of the kind to be found in esoteric bookshops near the British Museum. Nevertheless it had seemingly utterly respectable credentials since its founding in 1902, with its declared aim 'to deal with the stray cat problem in a practical way'.

'Some people believe in feeding stray cats, and leaving them homeless in the streets, rather than taking them to a shelter. By so doing, they are feeding them up to breed, and bring other unwanted cats into the world, thus increasing the evil,' said the League's founder and moving spirit, a certain Miss Kate Cording.

The League had grown, to make a public splash at a grand meeting in London in 1908 with Mrs Eleanor Penn Gaskell as President. She was a votes-for-women advocate, prominent RSPCA member and soon to be leading light of its Stray Cats Sub-Committee. There were some who thought it all very amusing. *Punch* magazine would include the Feline Defence League ('President, Baroness Puszkin'), its name otherwise unembellished, in its roster of to-be-mocked humanitarian bodies – including the Infants' Anti-Sausage Society, the All-Veg: Universal Brotherhood and the Occult Breathing League.

Among the feline defenders' stated aims were that cats should be 'taxed in the same manner as dogs, and thus be removed from the category of vermin and make them property'. 'Cats suffer from super-sensitiveness,' Mrs Penn Gaskell said stirringly. Furthermore, 'cats were far too shy, and because they loved deeply, they suffered deeply'.

Miss Kate Cording might also be considered shy. She had long preferred to work in the background. Indeed, this middle-aged lady born in Somerset in 1861, now of Islington, north London, who lived and worked not far from where Mrs Tealby had founded her prototype street animals home, had for some time now been very active in the matter of stray cats.

She was one of the ladies interviewed by Inspector Arrow at the height of the Truth *and the Cats* affair five years before, described then as a 'voluntary worker' for Mrs Morgan in the early days of her Hampstead cattery. Like almost everyone else, Miss Cording had meantime fallen out with Mrs Morgan but had pursued her strange cat-related destiny, more dedicatedly, it would turn out, than any of her rivals. There was no grand shop-front, no brass-buttoned pages, and no motor van. For years she had operated from a modest 'working man's cottage' with nothing more than a tricycle and a similarly minded accomplice.

Although publicity averse, in 1902 she had told some of her history in the *Herald of the Golden Age*, journal of the international mystical-vegetarian 'Order' of the same name, founded six years before and of which fruitarian Kate Cording was an adept:

> I am a mission worker and have lived for years in the slums of London. In former days, when I lived the life of a woman of the world in England and abroad, I was quite unaware of the terrible cruelty practised towards dogs and cats in this great city . . .

Then she began to notice. Suffering and cruelty were everywhere − you just had to bother to look. She explained her methods, how she took cats that she found in streets, squares and churchyards or had brought to her, by tramcar, to the excellent Institution in Camden Town run by the benevolent Mrs Morgan; there had yet to be the great estrangement. In November 1902 she described it as:

> A little Paradise with an elegant pink-tinted drawing room to wait in. Courteous young ladies and neat pages in livery tend the new arrivals and everywhere there is brightness, neatness and order. Comfortable quarters are ready for the 'rescued' that they may spend a few brief hours surrounded by plenty before their little boats set sail on the waters of Oblivion.

'What a wonderful apparatus is the lethal chamber!' she proclaimed, while imploring like-minded associates in the Order of the Golden Age, fellow abstainers from meat, feather and fur, to 'get up early in the morning and go out and look for lost cats. Get down from cabs and omnibuses and pick up a poor creature when you see it, crouching forlorn and hopeless. Do not think it is beneath you to save a mere cat.' She told more of her own story in *Our Cats* magazine a year later:

> I was formerly a Church of England mission worker and obliged to live among slums and I became a daily witness to sorrow and want, not only among the poor among whom I ministered but of the suffering among the unwanted and despised domestic cats which swarm in such numbers about the streets and squares and churchyards of London . . . no one helped me much in those days and I was forced to carry on the work of rescuing cats as best as I could. For three years I worked single-handed and lived in lodgings . . . working Shepherdess Walk, Hoxton, Pentonville Road and from my present address in Islington . . .
>
> I went almost daily to Camden Town with my strays, I paid all my own tram fares. I was obliged to wear shabby clothes and go without many a thing some women would have deemed a necessity . . .

In autumn 1901 Kate Cording had taken, as she wrote, 'a small house in Trinity Street, to be joined by a fellow worker who threw her whole heart and soul into the activities of our little home . . . the bare rooms took on a West End appearance rather than a workman's cottage, and we were not ashamed to live here nor invite friends to see us.'

She had published a pamphlet called *Suffering Animals in London*, written articles on her work for the *Herald of the Golden Age* and *The Vegetarian*, while 'kind friends came forward with money, and more and more cats were brought to our door'. The slaughterers Messrs. Harrison & Barber with their knacker's yard behind King's Cross station provided horseflesh for cat food and rendered the carcasses of deceased cats. Soon there would be a mountain of them.

'We live opposite a Board School* and many are the insults we have to put up with from the rough boys who attend there . . .' she wrote. Street urchins called out cruel jibes wherever she passed on her tricycle. She had started a club for boys and girls 'to teach kindness for animals' and was in need of funds for a piano to 'accompany the merry songs about animals' – also for a donkey cart to help in the cat collections.

She talked at length about her motives, of striving for 'mercy and justice for the oppressed', of rescuing thousands of cats from starvation and torture. 'Some of the rescued are sleeping around me as I write, happy, pampered animals full of affection and gratitude to those who saved them. They no longer fear kicks and blows for they now know nothing but love and tenderness . . .'

There were twenty pets running freely around the house: 'All the ones we have "rescued" and can afford to keep, sleep on our beds,' she said. Just lately Mrs Alice Gordon had invited her to affiliate her work in Islington to the Society for the Protection of Cats, she could reveal – presumably after the Mrs Morgan rumpus – and, through the pages of *Our Cats*, Miss Cording invited 'humane women now spending aimless, idle lives to join them in their work – and come and live in the crowded districts of London'. There were not many takers.

She explained her technique of scouring the streets herself, several times over, observing and noting, 'picking up the very

* In 1901, Richard Street School, later Penton Primary.

thin and diseased cats, feeding others and coming again and again before picking up those in good condition'. She would hand out copies of her leaflet *Suffering Cats of London* (more would follow – *London's Lost Legions* and *Waifs of a Great City*) which advertised her services.

Throughout the districts around, there were 'colonies of like-minded, humane people who collect strays and then send to us to collect them', she wrote. 'One devoted husband and wife, belonging to the working classes, feed and receive a large number of strays and have little cages built around their garden to keep them until we bring them up here on the tricycle or by tram.' The conductors of omnibuses and trams, on which the transport of pets was forbidden, did not seem to mind.

And indeed there were male cat-lovers who came to the aid of the Feline League. A mystery benefactor, believed by Kate Cording to be a man, regularly sent her parcels of cash through the post. And a certain Sergeant Major Puttock, a former drill instructor at a German military academy, would become a valiant worker in the cause. He evidently acted as her bodyguard and on 'three occasions had been summoned for assaulting hooligans whom he found ill-treating cats'. He had been dubbed ' "The Cat-man", and I made it my business to catch and feed four strays every day after I had finished my work', he would later tell a gathering of cat-lovers.

On the recent fall-out with Mrs Morgan, Kate Cording was discreet. There had been certain 'difficulties', she said, writing in December 1903. There was 'the expense'. 'So we decided to destroy our cats ourselves,' she said brightly. 'We cannot afford to use the lethal box for any but a very limited number of cats. I, therefore, invented a galvanised wire drowning cage, which is plunged instantaneously into luke-warm water and never comes to the top, but is destroyed in about one minute.' An RSPCA inspector had stood by her, watch in hand, and 'found no fault' with the method, she said. Before long the Society itself would be funding a copious supply of chloroform.

'We never sell cats and rarely give them away – because when we have done so, we have found so often that people have lost them,' she wrote. 'I cannot trust the people with them – I love them too well to give them to strangers.'*

'I call upon a humane public to provide enough funds to keep this house of mercy from going underwater.' No irony was intended. She continued:

> But the work is terrible and more than we can cope with, for we are doing all London and its near and distant suburbs . . . We have no cart, and years of appealing to the public has not brought one.
>
> The people who ask us to fetch cats . . . sweat us to death, taking all we do for them as a matter of course, sometimes bullying and insulting us if we have not done their bidding promptly enough; we are only silent for the cats' sakes. At the present time, we are doing over 530 journeys a month.
>
> We want ladies to come into the slums and actually rescue the starving cats which are suffering and dying there. We beg them to come . . . The ladies of a hundred years hence will do this . . .

The *Daily Mirror*, which had been launched three weeks earlier by Alfred Harmsworth as a newspaper for 'gentlewomen', with a staff of female journalists, picked up the story

---

* In contrast to this outright 'no re-homing' policy, it had been announced to associates of the Order of the Golden Age the year before: 'Any friends who wish to obtain a cat and give it a good home may obtain a suitable one by forwarding to her a description of the animal they require. It is expected, however, that the cost of packing and transport will be paid, and that some small contribution will be given towards the general expenses of the cats' refuge.'

from *Our Cats* and ran its own version approvingly with an illustration of 'Miss Kate Cording, the cat missionary'.

Kate Cording clearly had no doubts about her work, and was sure in the Divine Providence that guided her. There was no shyness at all about the actual business of killing. She published a series of strange confessional articles in the *Herald of the Golden Age*. Like this one: 'It is ten minutes to two this cold November morning – that is to say, the middle of the night – and I have just perpetrated a "deed of darkness" in the back kitchen. I have drowned a poor little suffering kitten, one of the inmates of the cats' refuge . . .'

It had been brought to her door by a woman who told her it had been the pet 'toy' of her one-year-old child. Now she wanted a replacement for the infant's continuing amusement. Miss Cording 'burned with a secret fire of indignation'. Had the little, dying cat been the victim of 'tiny, torturing baby fingers'? She was sure it had been. How could this dreadful woman possibly ask for another one?

'I am scarcely exaggerating when I say that the children around me in the slums of Islington are the cruel offspring of cruel parents,' she wrote. 'Foolish, unreasoning mothers, who would not dream of spending sixpence on a toy for the baby, think a live kitten a fitting plaything . . .'

In spring 1907 she published a further pamphlet, *Waifs of a Great City, More About the Beggar Cats of London*, in which she complained that she could not 'rescue the cats of Slumland' from their impoverished owners as she might wish – 'because there is far too much prominence given to the rights of property and far too little to the rights of animals'.

The story of how she went 'fishing for cats' with 'a net, a big basket and a lantern' ran in the *Daily Mail* soon after publication. 'Secrecy is usually essential as the work is not looked on favourably in lowlier streets,' she was quoted as saying. The quaint account of the 'Fellowship Cottage Lost

Cats' Shelter' and its moving spirit, 'Kate Cording', was picked up by US newspapers and would make ripples in cat-loving circles across the Atlantic. The *Brooklyn Daily Eagle*, for example, would report on the Feline League's doings thus in summer 1908: 'Miss Cording is always ready to go out armed with her basket and blanket in the cause of stray cats, and the lethal chamber at her cats' shelter in Islington is always at work, day and night.' A good thing, surely?

The RSPCA's Stray Cats Sub-Committee was keeping busy meanwhile. As well as helping to keep Fellowship Cottage (in fact a three-storey terraced house) afloat with a trickle of money, it had been looking at broader feline issues. A draft 'Stray Cats Bill' had been prepared by the Society's Law Committee to engage political interest in the question, but by calling for all cats to be somehow compelled to wear collars or be removed from the streets of London like dogs by the police, its passage looked problematic. The Board of Agriculture, the government agency nominally in charge of cat issues, was most unenthusiastic. RSPCA Council member, George Greenwood MP, feared it would be thought of as 'rank socialism' or be laughed at when its title was read out by the Clerk of the House of Commons. It never got that far.

It was resolved by the strays committee therefore to 'support various cats' shelters all over the country' – but not those conducted as 'mere homes for cats – rather those places where cats are collected and destroyed painlessly and in the most scientific manner'. But as the Society could not 'distinguish any particular class of animal in its work against cruelty, the proposal should be progressed through a public appeal for a special fund'.

Kate Cording's strange mission went on. When the 1911 Protection of Animals Act with its proviso against inflicting 'unnecessary' suffering was passed, it did not interfere with her work, nor did the stricture against the poisoning of an animal without unreasonable cause. The cats' fallen condition was reason enough: it was more cruel to let them live.

The number of cats 'rescued' each year was now into five figures. In April 1911 the prominent journalist, Mr W. R. Titterton, of the radical newspaper the *Daily News*, sought Miss Cording out at her 'Shelter for Lost Cats, 31 Trinity Street, Islington'. By now, the drowning cage had been replaced by something more efficient. He wrote:

> Ring the bell of Fellowship Cottage and the door will open on a world of cats – black cats, white cats, tabbies, tortoise-shells – on the floor, on hat-stands, chairs, tables, mantel-pieces, slumbering, as a rule, curled up and content, for their troubles are over now, and no brutal foot will lurch out and kick them . . .
>
> The first impression is of a labyrinth lined with cats – then one realises that the labyrinth is a small workman's dwelling-house and that there cannot be room for very many cats therein. Yet the latest report says that 12,000 cats were dealt with in the course of last year.
>
> 'Where are the rest?' Miss Cording leads me into the garden, opens a door that lets out a deadly, sweet smell – the smell of chloroform – and points to a huge pile of the freshly slain – a jumble of many coloured furs, and then to a number of boxes – one metal, the rest wooden, with a pane of glass in the lid. The legend: *Mors Janua Vitae – Death, the Gateway to* [everlasting] *Life* is stuck above the door of the rough wooden shed.

'How are they caught?' the reporter asked. 'In these,' said Miss Cording, 'pointing to sundry nets on sticks. A little twitch of the arm, and tabby was in the mesh. One soon got expert . . .'

Miss Cording took lots of abuse and threats as she ventured into 'the vilest and most squalid quarters of London'. 'My hat was torn from my head and my body banged about by roughs in Red Lion Square,' she wrote, 'all because I was carrying a cat home in a basket.' There were always sneers that the money she somehow raised might not all be going on cats. But beyond that, nobody defined what she did at Fellowship Cottage as in any way cruel or even unusual.

Her health failing and desperately short of money, she appeared in person before the RSPCA's Stray Cats Sub-Committee with a further plea for funds. An animal-hide dealer, Mr Thomas Columbus Smith, proprietor of the Orchard Street Tannery, Kidderminster, had made an offer 'for the purchase of carcasses of animals destroyed by her', it was noted by the Committee. A twenty-year forward contract was on the table. This looked hopeful. There was a new vogue for catskin among women both rich and poor. It was the 'civet of the Walworth Road' (a working-class district in south London) said a newspaper of the day. Reporting a little afterwards, a prominent fur trade journal noted:

> Of late, cats' skins have increased in demand as it is the mode for ladies' garments to be liberally adorned with tails. Cat tails, soft and hairy, are very suitable.

'Natural black skins' were the most valuable, while 'mottled varieties' were best for dyeing purposes, with a booming continental market for therapeutic cat-fur waistcoats and scarves. Mr Smith's speciality, however, was super-shiny 'japanned' leather. Although it was not spelled out as such, the hides of Islington cats might seem to be destined for the Worcester glove trade. The Society's Stray Cats

Sub-Committee would discreetly consider the best way
forward.

The proposed Stray Cats Bill meanwhile had received scant
political support. It was hardly a surprise. To move with the
spirit of the times, the Society itself would have to get into
the cat-destruction business. Several regional branches had
already installed lethal chambers – and there was always
Battersea. When in 1910 a cat trapped on a Southwark ware-
house roof, 'having survived for three months on only such
food as people could throw up to it', was caught by an
RSPCA inspector in a barrel and 'taken to the Dogs Home
at Battersea, its sufferings ended in the lethal chamber', so it
was reported.

An obvious move was to take over Fellowship Cottage,
lock, stock and chloroform chamber now, with the prospect
of a fur-trade contract, but when the RSPCA's Chief
Secretary, Captain Edward G. Fairholme, and Council
member, George Greenwood MP, went to look for themselves, they found it 'unsuitable and insanitary'. They would
have to find somewhere more commodious. Council
member Sir Frederick Banbury argued that it was all going
to be too costly and that, while north London cats should
continue to be collected, they should be delivered direct to
the newly modernised and extended lethal chamber at
Battersea which disposed of 1242 stray cats in the year to
1914.

But after more discussion it was decided to effectively start
again, as something to be provisionally called 'The Feline
Defence and Rescue League, affiliated to the RSPCA', by
acquiring new premises and fitting them out at direct cost to
the Society. It would be expensive. Miss Cording would 'start
a second depot' south of the river, according to the plan. The
cat-skin proposal was judged to be sound as long as 'the bodies
were disposed of by Mr Columbus Smith in such a way as to

render impossible any reflection on the good names of the League or the Society'. That might be difficult.*

While a new site was being sought, street cats meanwhile would be taken to Battersea for destruction in a specially acquired cart, so it was proposed. At her insistence, Miss Cording should still be permitted to herself 'lethalise cats received at her establishment of such nervous temperament as to make conveyance to Battersea impracticable'. Fellowship Cottage might sputter on to kill a few cats yet.

It was not to be. 'Having given all her money and health to combat the sufferings inflicted on the feline race', Kate Cording was now desperately ill. There was a last bid on her part to stay independent, but the Society would advance no more funding, and a bumper legacy left by a homeless-cat-friendly Norwood spinster would come just too late. Finally, she surrendered. She provided in her will that what might be left of the Feline League would pass to the RSPCA on her death, which by now seemed imminent.

In late 1912 the Society duly took over and began to plan for the lethal cottage industry to move to 'a commodious site'. A rambling terraced house was acquired for the purpose, situated next door to the Angel tube station of the City and South London Railway. The cost of fitting it out would be £500 – including 'electric cages for destroying cats'. If the American innovation did not work, chloroform lethal chambers supplied by Mr Columbus Smith himself would be

---

* Specialist animal products merchant Mr Smith was at the time involved in a tangled and well-publicised court case over the export of '40,000 dogs' teeth' for use as 'currency' in the South Pacific. The RSPCA bizarrely chose this time to issue a warning against cat thieves in London: 'Collectors attached to the Animal Rescue League . . . are satisfied that there is a regular market in good cat's fur [they should know]. The thefts are usually perpetrated during the night – although daylight robbery is also not unknown . . . A furrier's advice to women who own feline pets is "Keep your eyes on the cat, or you may later find it round your neck".'

acquired 'on the best terms possible'. Gassing did not mark the skins.

On 7 April 1913, Kate Cording died, aged fifty-two. Newspapers announced that 'London's cats have lost their best friend'. She left her estate, valued at £87, to the Society. It was reported: '[She] directed that her body be buried in silence and without religious ceremony and desired her friends not to be distressed by the thought that she was an atheist, stating: "I believe in a God and a future state; all men and animals, but, as my religion has nothing to do with the Bible, I do not desire any Christian service read over my dead body".' She further directed that 'all her pet animals should be destroyed as soon as possible after her death'.

It was announced in a eulogy to the late Miss Cording in the *Animal World* that the 'Animal Rescue League' had been formed to continue her work. Miss Eliza Clegg would be Manageress. 'New and larger premises have been found at 357 City Road, Islington', where, 'by the most modern and pain-less methods known to science, the stray cats of the metropolis will be assured a merciful release from an existence of misery.'

Other pioneers were also passing away. Alice May Swifte died in 1913 soon after Kate Cording, leaving her estate to the Dublin Home for Starving and Forsaken Cats – 'and for the special chloroform chamber where they may be painlessly put to death'. A portrait of her own benefactor, Richard Barlow Kennett, was bequeathed to the Dublin Society for the Prevention of Cruelty to Animals.

And there were new arrivals – like the ardent Christian anti-vivisectionist, the Reverend Lionel Lewis, a clergyman who had begun an operation in Whitechapel as the 'East End Cats' Rescue Fund'.* Among the fellow animal workers in

---

* This was not nearly on the scale of the other cat-botherers in the capital. It was noted that 'two poor women receive a pension from the fund for which they feed and keep the cats until a home is found for them.'

his circle was a certain Mrs Maria Dickin to whom he would one day offer a spare basement, where he kept the obligatory lethal chamber, for her own charity. The Rev. Lewis would later become Vicar of Glastonbury in Somerset and a founding scholar of Grail-lore.

Kate Cording had died a pauper, unaware of the transatlantic hunt for the beneficiary of Caroline Ewen. Her 'London Cats' House' was now a semi-detached part of the RSPCA, an organisation skilled in all matters to do with wills and bequests, and whose lawyers had already surmised that Kate Redding was Kate Cording of Fellowship Cottage. The bequest was surely theirs, so Captain Edward Fairholme proposed to the US Vice-Consul.

But there was a last-minute challenger. Zoe Morgan bustled in, claiming that the 'London Cats' House' was obviously her renowned 'Institution', Royal or not, in Camden Town.

New York newsmen loved it. This was a bigger mad-cat-lady story even than the Midnight League of Mercy. London correspondents of US papers were ordered to turn over the cat ladies of the metropolis. A little inquiry discovered Mrs Morgan's Institution's single-minded purpose, unchanged from the battles with *Truth* ten years before. 'Twenty-four hours is the usual time for keeping cats that do belong to the best stray variety,' commented the *Brooklyn Daily Eagle* in December 1913, whose special correspondent filed a rousing story from Ferdinand Road. 'While some pedigree cats might find respite, the democratic cat, the product of the London slums, is invariably despatched to another world shortly after his captor places him within the gates of the institution.'

There were indeed some boarding cats, the correspondent found, 'invariably the pets of aristocratic women who do the Riviera or perhaps a little Swiss mountaineering in the season'. At least those cats were no longer just being abandoned.

Of her staff of twenty-five, only the van driver and account-ant were men. The otherwise all-female staff were employed each night in the 'rescue' work, climbing trees and entering empty buildings with the skill of telegraph linesmen, calling out for cats to come to them, relentless in their determination, roaming the empty (of humans) streets to return to Camden Town at dawn with their haul of strays. In spite of the fact that they 'were all cat-lovers', the reporter observed that the major-ity of the rescued found their way pretty sharpish to the lethal chamber. Subscriptions, legacies and collections just about paid for it all. The lively article featured a photograph of five smartly uniformed, young lady street-collectors with what looked like cardboard cut-out cats – although a recent sympa-thetic profile in *Woman at Home* magazine had been illustrated with a portrait of Peter, the 'collecting cat' with money box. Peter looked grateful to still be alive.*

What would she do with the money? Madam Morgan was asked. Acquire a luxury automobile to help with the work

---

* Whose activities had already excited the attention of *Truth* magazine, which still urged readers to be wary of Mrs Morgan's cats' home, along with all tin-rattling collectors ('flag days' had only just been invented), who now solicited money on the streets of London in apparent defiance of the Vagrancy Act. One of the most prominent, with a pitch outside the Swan and Edgar department store in Piccadilly, was a certain Miss Tyler, who according to her placard collected for the London Institution for Lost and Starving Cats, Ferdinand Street, Camden Town. PLEASE HELP THE PUSSIES! it declared. The authorities were goaded into action.

Inspector Jacobs of the Metropolitan Police swooped. 'By her side was a stuffed cat on the footway with a collecting box supported on its front legs,' he reported in May 1914. When cautioned, Miss Tyler said: 'If you move me on, my living is gone. There are so few places where one can get money given to us' (about four pounds a week, of which she retained a fifth). 'The woman eventually went away and Mrs Morgan complained of Police ordering away her collector,' said the report. The fate of the stuffed cat was not recorded.

– do you know it cost $400 a year just for chloroform alone? Her outstanding desire remained that her Home be granted a government charter.

'During the last year or two a number of enterprising men and women have tried to run Homes competing with the London Institution,' noted the reporter, 'but they are in anything but a flourishing condition.' That might have been Zoe Morgan's opinion but the cash was not hers yet. Meanwhile, political troubles in the Balkans looked irksome – but no more than that. The nation's cats could look forward to a happy 1914.

12

Differences of Opinion

LADY BRACKNELL AND FRIENDS

Found dumped outside a shop in Walberton, Fontwell area,
in the pouring rain – two adult cats and three large kittens all
crammed in together in a small carrier designed only for a
single cat. These five lovely cats were lucky to have survived.
Now all have been re-homed successfully. Hurray!

The death of Kate Cording in 1913 marked the end of an era.
Mrs Zoe Morgan kept up the work in Camden Town but
the time of the go-it-alone cat collector with a basket on a
bike and a chloroform chamber in the garden shed was drawing to a close. The legacy of Fellowship Cottage, already
removed to the City Road, had been discreetly taken over by
the RSPCA. The 'Animal Rescue League' was proclaimed to
be 'an entirely new scheme of work', set at one remove from
the Society itself. That was a shrewd decision.

To fulfil its work all the better, enquiries had already been
made in America about the exciting new device patented by
Mr Huntington Smith, husband of Mrs Anna Harris Smith,
founder in 1899 of the Animal Rescue League of Boston.
The 'Automatic Electric Cage'* would soon be crossing the

---

* There was a different version for dogs and cats. It would be written: 'One
very noteworthy feature of death by the automatic electric cage is the fact that

Atlantic and would make the mass destruction of street animals by gas used by rival Battersea look primitive.

The Animal Rescue League would operate on the principles of its late foundress, Kate Cording; indeed, her partner, Eliza Clegg, would be the Supervisor. The fabulous Ewen legacy was still in limbo, challenged in New York by Miss Ewen's nephew and in London by the vexatious Mrs Morgan – so a great deal more charitable money was still required to fund the Islington operation. Appeals were duly made.

The RSPCA's venture into cat 'rescue' reflected exactly what the other, ever more professionalised, animal charities were up to. Our Dumb Friends' League was still expanding its network of cat shelters in the capital and other British cities. The Gordon Cats' Home, the Mayhew Home, Battersea and others continued their work in London. There were start-ups in Edinburgh, Bristol, Hastings, Birmingham, Manchester, Cardiff, Liverpool, Sheffield, Brighton and elsewhere – almost universally the result of a 'committee of ladies' doing what all right-thinking people believed was best for cats, and all of them *without exception* conducted on round-up-strays-and-mercifully-chloroform-them lines. To perpetuate this 'good work', even beyond a cat-lover's death, there was always a bequest to be made, which often came in the shape of property.* In breezy Brighton, a home for the care of lost and starving cats was opened around 1895 by Miss E.

---

there is absolutely nothing repulsive about it. The bodies come from the cages, relaxed and warm, and so perfectly peaceful in appearance that, if it were not for the widely opened eyes, they would seem asleep.'

* Another near-universal feature of such wills were instructions that on her death, the testatrix's own cats should be destroyed, the implication being that no one could love or care for them as much as the deceased. This would be a feature too of elderly street-feeders who, when they saw their time with 'their' cats drawing to an end, demanded or brought about the destruction of the colony.

Harper in a modest seaside terrace, 63 Coventry Street, but had shut down by the turn of the century.

And in Manchester a cat shelter opened in a small house in St Thomas Place, Cheetham Hill, in 1904 which saw the arrival of 'a vast army of cats'. 'Not all enter the lethal box,' so it was reported. 'Sometimes, if a cat is healthy and comely she will be reserved for a better fate and a good home will be found for her.' The principles of 're-homing' were not to change for a very long time yet.

The Battersea Home for Lost and Starving Dogs stopped receiving cats as boarders in May 1914 because of outbreaks of 'contagious diseases'. Instead, the cats now went to a rural out-station at Hackbridge in Surrey, although London strays were still being brought in by the hundreds by cat-lady street collectors for destruction after five days of confinement under the fatal railway arch. To hasten things along, a 'specially constructed tricycle' had meanwhile been acquired for the 'systematic collection of cats', as it was described. Staff scoured the streets looking for 'poor creatures . . . to rescue from misery and starvation, in several cases cruelly deserted by their late owners,' so it was reported. 'No stray cats are kept with the boarders.'

Cat hoarders continued to be unearthed amid scenes of heartbreaking squalor and prosecuted in the police courts under the taunts of a witch-hunting public, while those cats who had survived were hauled off for destruction. Summer cat abandonment by all classes remained universal and the cruelty of street children ever more inventive. There were still ladies of the night, swooping with nets and baskets and dispensing chloroform. Those who fed cats were still reviled for their foolishness in drawing out the fallen tribe's so-distressing existence.

The stray cat problem had found its solution. The dominion of the lethal chamber was absolute.

But those who might be kind to cats could yet be rewarded. Our Dumb Friends' League raised a fund to reward the crew of a trawler from Bideford, Devon, who had rescued 'a large black cat' found somehow swimming in the sea three miles from land. The League later opened a fund 'for the benefit of the widow and children of Thomas Custance, a barman of Islington', who 'gave his life in saving the life of a cat' when he fell from a tree.

The outbreak of war in August 1914 did not impact much on the affairs of comfortably homed British cats, unlike the great catastrophe that would overwhelm the nation's pets twenty-five years later.* For street animals it was business as usual. The ODFL Secretary, Arthur J. Coke, could appeal thus in 1914 'on behalf of the stray cats of this Metropolis':

> [S]ince the commencement of the war there has been increasing demand upon [our] shelters for disposing of the not-wanted cats. [Further] the charitable public are inclined to allow the war funds to absorb all their interest.
>
> To those who are inclined to sneer at any work for cats, I would point out that we read of our soldiers at the front sharing their food with [them], endeavouring in various ways to alleviate the sufferings of cats and other animals in the devastated areas, and I can tell of many soldiers who have brought their cats to our shelters before joining the colours rather than that they should be left to starve . . .

On 9 November 1914 the Superintendent of the Tottenham ODFL Cats Shelter found a scrap of paper on its doorstep with a note in pencil 'scribbled by a youthful hand' with the words: *Dear Christians. I am a Tabby Cat stray, ill and gentle. Do kindly take me in and so fulfil your work . . .*

* See the authors' *Bonzo's War* (2013)

But no cat. The riddle was answered the next morning when a tabby cat, 'ill and distressed', was found in the front garden by the caretaker. 'Needless to say, the cat was placed in the lethal chamber for a most merciful death,' said the report. Needless to say.

On the matter of 'Soldiers' Pets and Other Animals' abandoned in the first flush of war, the RSPCA's advice, widely published in regional newspapers, was to 'take stray dogs to the police and cats to the chemist to have them humanely destroyed'. Being homeless, for whatever reason, was a death sentence. The welfare charities made sure of that.

Mrs Zoe Morgan made her own extraordinary feline newspaper appeal in January 1915 after weeks of riots in which East Enders with Central European names were attacked by patriotic mobs: 'The Germans in great numbers have left their homes, and their cats and dogs behind to starve,' she wrote. 'It is dreadful to have to ask for help for animals when our . . . dear soldiers require so much, but animals have rights, and animal-lovers will feel for me when I plead for help for our poor little four-footed friends whose greatest and last boon we can at least grant them – a peaceful end . . .'

War or no war, the great Ewen legacy cat-rescue rumpus was still unresolved. Vice-Consul Westacott called the parties together for a showdown at the London Consulate-General at Broad Street in the City in January 1915.

A prominent New York lawyer, Mr Charles Steward Davison, had been sent across the Atlantic by the Surrogates' Court to hear the depositions. Captain Fairholme and Mrs Morgan made their rival cases. The RSPCA Secretary, according to a US press report:

Told how his Society had taken over the Cording Cats' Home and said that his organization, backed by the King and Queen of England, received as much as $280,000 a year in donations. Then he related that Miss Cording had died a pauper on April 7 [1913] last, in an anti-vivisection hospital at Battersea. The Society had paid for her funeral. Everything she owned had been devoted to cats.

Cross-examined, Mr Fairholme said ... 'he did not remember the letter from Miss Marshall, secretary-companion of Miss Ewen, notifying him of the $30,000 bequest'.

It was Mrs Morgan's turn to advance her own claim. She had started her Institution as the 'Cats' Home', she said. Kate Cording had simply been a volunteer who had brought her twenty street cats a week in the early days of her famous Institution. 'Miss Cording chloroformed and then drowned the cats,' she said. She knew no Miss Kate Renning.

But it was a new witness who riveted attention: Miss Eliza[beth] Clegg. She claimed that she had joined Miss Cording in her forays into the nocturnal streets of the capital, each with a basket attached to their tricycles. When her statement was relayed to New York, there was astonishment. This made the Midnight Band of Mercy look like amateurs:

> So many animals were captured that it was necessary to hire a house. This was the inception of the refuge home which had changed its name many times. It had been a 'Cats' House' and a 'Cats' Home', had operated as the 'Feline Defence League' and as the 'Animal Rescue League of London'.

'When Miss Clegg was asked how many cats had been collected and put out of their misery, she replied that from 1898 to the date of Miss Cording's death, the two of them had caught 479,000. All efforts to get her to reduce the figure failed ...' it was reported.

'She had her notebook with her. In it she had kept a complete record of the work. She asserted that between

January 1913 and the date of Miss Cording's death [in April] they had taken over 11,000 animals off the streets.'

The new-made Animal Rescue League got the money. The lucky cats of Madeira got some too. 'A handsome legacy was bequeathed to the League by a New York lady, a portion of which has been received,' it was announced in the RSPCA's Report for 1915, 'but the total subscriptions received . . . were less than one half actual expenses . . . it is to be hoped that increased subscriptions will be forthcoming to carry on this absolutely essential work.' It would go on like this for decades.*

There were somewhat more uplifting stories. The *Animal World* in December 1914 reported the arrival of Belgian refugee pets aboard a fleet of fishing boats, 'thirty-eight dogs plus some cats and rabbits'. The RSPCA moved in to feed 'the derelict band of animals' and negotiate their quarantine, but their fate thereafter is unrecorded. It was further rumoured in cat circles that the nation's martial icon, Field Marshal Lord Kitchener, the Minister of War, had 'a special weakness for cats', and was a secret benefactor of a cats' home.

The real crisis for pets, and not just strays, came in 1916 with the start of compulsory military service – conscription. Mr Coke of the ODFL appealed once more, this time for 'those cats whose owners had been humane enough to bring them to the shelters before joining the colours; [while] others, in the upheaval of home, forgot the cat and these poor creatures, turned adrift, have suffered agonies before they were received by the shelters and disposed of in the lethal chambers . . .

---

* The stone tablet that once stood outside 397 City Road embossed with the words ANIMAL RESCUE LEAGUE FOUNDED BY MISS KATE CORDING is now in the archive room of the RSPCA at Horsham in Sussex. Senior staff in 2015 seemed baffled as to what it was or once signified.

'Cat shelters are not places where cats are petted and pampered at the public expense,' he could reassure the public, 'and the work is far from congenial.' But if such shelters did not exist, 'these cats, dying in out-of-the-way corners, would spread disease in our midst', said Mr Coke.

In the grim coarsening of wartime sensibilities, especially when compulsory rationing of food was introduced in winter 1917–18, domestic pets were turned on in press and Parliament as little more than enemies within. They were portrayed as 'useless mouths to feed'. Anti-dog sentiment was rampant. Showing compassion for animals, other than war-horses serving nobly at the front – which would become an absolute obsession for the charities – seemed cowardly.

When it became known that animals were being expended in poison gas experiments, protest was muted. The vegetarian, anti-vivisection, universal-humanitarian enthusiasts of the years past looked like pacifist cranks. Eliminating pestilence-spreading stray cats was presented, as by Mr Coke of Our Dumb Friends' League, as being hygienically patriotic. Feeding them was traitorous.

The number of cats removed from the streets soared. The RSPCA's Animal Rescue League in June 1916 recorded 75,000 London cats killed in the three years since it had opened. There was evidently some dissent on the totality of killing but there would be no reprieve. In a special feature in the *Animal World* on the League's wartime work it was announced starkly:

> The League neither sells nor gives away any living animal but receives them only for the purpose of painless destruction, although stray cats, whose owners can be traced, can be returned on request. There may be differences of opinion on the rule under which all cats received in the Home are put to death, but everyone who is fond of animals must feel the

greatest concern as to the methods adopted in killing these unfortunate creatures.

There followed a laudatory description of the 'new electrical killer based on an instrument made and used in the United States' (Mr Smith's device from Boston) which administered 2,000 volts – the 'exact strength of current used in an execution chair in the US where murderers are executed by this method', so RSPCA subscribers were informed – thereby inducing instantaneous death. The author of the report noted significantly that the majority of the cats thus being disposed of were 'apparently in good health and doubtless in many cases previously well cared for'.

They evidently were not strays, but cats given up by their owners for whatever reason, fed into the street-cat killing machine. They were casualties of war.

Appeals for funds to continue the work henceforth appeared under the startling headline '20,000 Unwanted Cats' – with the explanation: 'This is not an advertisement for the sale of cats; it is a reminder that the Animal Rescue League, founded by the late Miss Kate Cording, takes from the streets of London twenty thousand cats every year.' It was presented as something to take pride in.

There were other wartime dangers for cats. When a munitions factory blew up in Silvertown, east London, in January 1917, it was reported: 'The Animal Rescue League has recovered 65 cats from the great explosion – which had to be destroyed by the lethal chamber on the spot.'

Miss Clegg and her band of female helpers were on the case for days as a 'legion of homeless cats wandered about the ruins and clinging to homes long deserted by their tenants' in scenes that would be repeated in the Blitz of 1940–1. 'A van from the cats' and dogs' home came down and brought away a number of them,' it was reported. 'The scene was particularly weird at night with all the shattered factories and homes, the swept-up piles of broken glass . . . the absence of people, and amid all the desolation, the incessant cries of the starving cats . . .'

And when Zeppelin airships and Gotha bombers made sporadic raids on British cities it got even worse. 'Cats should be brought inside the house during air-raids' was one supposed piece of advice offered by the enduringly comical Feline Defence League. 'When left on the roof they are liable to be mistaken for aerial torpedoes' according to the leaden humourists of *Punch* – and as the *Weekly Dispatch* reported on 21 October 1917:

> *London's Starving Cats: Hundreds Abandoned by Thoughtless Air-Raid Refugees*
>
> Among the greatest sufferers from air raids have been London's cats. Since the last series of raids, cats' homes have become uncomfortably over-crowded. Many families in their flight from the danger zone have had little thought for anyone but themselves, and hundreds of pets have in consequence been left to fend for themselves – a difficult matter in cities in these times of food shortage . . . These animals, being a danger to the community, are destroyed at once to prevent contagion.

That would have come as no surprise. Nor had the war improved the lot of the humble working animals of the urban poor, the costers' ponies and donkeys in backyard stables. And where there were such, there were also cats. It was this visible suffering that compelled a new arrival on the animal do-gooding scene. Mrs Maria Dickin and her 'People's Dispensary for Sick Animals of the Poor' was founded in 1917 to provide education and some rudimentary veterinary care.

Mrs Dickin had no background in medicine or animal welfare. As a young woman, she had run an elocution studio in Wimpole Street, west London, before marrying her cousin, a prosperous accountant, and moving to leafy Hampstead. Not that unusually for a woman of her age and class, she embarked on social work in the East End, where she was appalled by the poverty she witnessed. The poor, just as they had plenty of children, had multitudinous animals. No one could deny them the right to either. Simply tut-tutting at their neglectfulness, indolence, squalor and immorality did no good. Again, not that unusually, it was the plight of their animals that fired a rage in her that something must be done.

'The suffering and misery of these poor, uncared-for creatures in our overcrowded areas was a revelation to me. I had no idea it existed; and it made me indescribably miserable,' Mrs Dickin would write. Kate Cording had had a similar epiphany two decades before, concerning stray cats in the streets of Hoxton, but Maria Dickin's resolve to act would take her in a very different direction. These were animals that had owners – even if they were the otherwise undeserving poor.

Doubters said that the lower classes would not bring their animals to be tended, either because they did not care or because they were too busy trying to take care of themselves. If they could not pay vets' bills, they should not have animals in the first place.

That was the whole point. Costers needed their donkeys to pull the little carts. Cats were universally kept to eliminate vermin. They lived near the docks – wasn't it obvious? Dogs kept guard of families and humble possessions. The animals were blameless. If their owners could be induced to take better care, and be offered direct help and advice in doing so, there might indeed be redemption.

It was a missionary journey into darkness. An unnamed helper of Mrs Dickin left an account, largely written in impenetrable music-hall faux cockney, of a street market in Brown Street, Whitechapel, a scene of universal squalor. 'If this is their life, what of the animals'?' the middle-class visitor asked. But there was hope. In the middle of all the 'grimy, despairing sordidness' was a cats'-meat barrow.

The genteel visitor was 'aghast' at the sight of the little skewers of horsemeat. But it made her 'heart ache' to realise the barrow's purpose. It was there so that these 'cheerful and dilapidated women', with 'their shilling to be laid out so carefully on necessities', could spend some of it to feed their pets. 'There is to be a "penn'orth for Bob and a ha'porth for Nell and some o' the best fer my Flossie – and Gawd bless the People's Dispensary while yer at it".'

That these impoverished people should care so much for their cats brought tears to her eyes.

This was not the busybody, prosecuting approach of the RSPCA with their assumption that animals required protection from wilfully cruel lower-class owners. Instead, the neglect and suffering of unfortunate pets and working animals might be the result of ignorance and social disadvantage. What these people needed was access to medicine, and for (some of) their animals to be provided with the means to a merciful death. As the Dispensary's own thirtieth anniversary history recorded: 'Owners of animals in poor areas had hardly heard of the lethal box and the very few veterinary surgeons available did not interest themselves . . . [for the veterinary profession] the treatment of small animals is but a sideline and is lucrative only when the animal is of the pampered sort.'

Appeals by Mrs Dickin to existing charities for funds met with no response. There was a war on. So be it: she would pay for it herself. The idea that middle-class ladies should care anything at all about the animals of the poor remained deeply eccentric, with the practical means of doing anything about it – other than killing the animals as some kind of sanitary obligation – only a dream. But one day it would come and Mrs Dickin and her much mocked Dispensary would be part of that.

Thus the PDSA was founded in November 1917, its first little clinic set up in a Whitechapel cellar lent for the purpose by the Rev. Lionel Lewis who, inevitably, as Mrs Dickin would herself recall, 'being a great animal-lover, was doing a good work destroying stray cats'.

She and her co-worker, a certain Mr Hartshorn, an animal practitioner but *not* a vet, set up with 'a first-aid box and a lethal box which had cost ten shillings' – with a sign at the entrance at the head of the stairs that read: *Bring your sick animals! Do not let them suffer! All animals treated. All treatment free.*

After a few hours' wait, a 'forthright woman' appeared with something wrapped in 'a soiled white apron' – the PDSA's first ever patient. It was a cat: 'a fine specimen but without a doubt sick'. It was suffering from mange, according to Mrs Dickin, who did not further record its fate, which is easy to imagine. It was doubtless kindest to put it to sleep. Two dogs soon followed and a donkey – the start of a 'positive avalanche' of cases. The cellar was soon abandoned for a shop on the Commercial Road.

The war was won, but cats did not necessarily join in the universal rejoicing. The RSPCA ('telegraphic address "Cruelty", London') offered this advice in its *Almanac* for 1918:

When drowning kittens, place them in a bag with a big stone so they drown at once. Use plenty of water. If it is necessary to kill a cat, never do it yourself. A lethal chamber is best . . .

The upsets and abandonments of war left, at its end, a multiplicity of urban strays clinging on as best they might. In the capital an observer noted:

> You will not see cats congregated in joyful and vociferous crowds in London, though you may hear their melancholy voices at night; but you will scarcely traverse any thoroughfare without seeing at least one pussy sunning herself on some fence or window-ledge, secure from ill-mannered dogs. Suburban streets swarm with cats; and even in the busy thoroughfares of the City and West-end they go about their own concerns, aloof and dignified.

As London returned to peacetime diversions, cats of whatever social status remained at risk of casual summertime abandonment and a sudden fall into the feline underworld. The new wave of 'Bright Young Things', so it was reported, staged cat hunts with greyhounds in Mayfair streets. There was no parliamentary enthusiasm for a cat tax; indeed, the welfare charities were against the idea because, they insisted, it would cause mass abandonment by impoverished owners.

And anyway, how could it be enforced? Would the police go from door to door looking for unlicensed cats? Cats were still on the margin, and although they had been given some extra legal protection by the 1911 Cruelty to Animals act, there was still the widespread impression that they were officially classified as vermin.

A strange temporary feline refuge had sprung up in 1924 at the British Empire Exhibition held at Wembley, with its grazing daily crowds providing sustenance for a colony of strays: the correct collective noun for cats is a 'clowder' – but it will be 'colony' henceforth. When it was over, 'all the cats that have been living at the Exhibition for six months were collected and placed in a van to be taken to one of Our

Dumb Friends' League homes'. Their fate was predictable. The League meanwhile reported a dearth of funds for stray cat rescue. 'The public seems generally to look on shelters as an extravagance, a place where cats are kept in luxury and pampered', said a post-war report. This was emphatically not so. The shelters were there solely 'to destroy unwanted and diseased cats'. Those 'WHO DO NOT LOVE CATS' were invited to send funds to speed the work.

Over in New York meanwhile, the Ewen legacy was at last finally settled, with a one-tenth share of the sale of 162 building plots in the Kingsbridge and Riverdale neighbourhoods of the Bronx, which realised a huge sum, going to the 'Cat's House of London' as the *New York Times* reported in October 1921. The land, which had been in the family for seventy-eight years, adjoined a park (Ewen Park), which had been given to the city in 1916 by their other sister, Eliza M. Ewen. Now the cash was heading the way of London's homeless cats. However, this windfall was not necessarily to their benefit.

The legacy-enriched Animal Rescue League became busier than ever. In summer 1925, it was reported:

During the past twelve and a half years, 437,429 cats have been painlessly put to death at the headquarters of the Animal Rescue League, Islington, and the rate is now about 1500 a week. The executioner-in-chief, as she humorously describes herself, is an elderly woman, Miss [Eliza] Clegg who, as Manageress, superintends the destruction of the animals as they are brought to her from all parts of London by six lieutenants.

All are women over fifty years of age . . . The animals are killed by electrocution, death being instant. The cats are laid in the drawer of an apparatus resembling a table with the fatal switch on top . . . The dead bodies are removed daily to a

crematorium managed by the Royal Society for the Prevention
of Cruelty to Animals.

The work was not without dangers to the operators. A certain
Herbert Augustus Norris, an 'RSPCA slaughterer', as he was
described, died of septicaemia contracted when he was
scratched by a City Road cat he was about to electrocute, a
coroner's court would be told. The jury returned a verdict of
Accidental Death. A humane commentator observed around
the same time:

> It is no pleasure to those who conduct these rescue places to
> destroy life . . . The fumes of the chloroform and gas produce
> headaches, but the heartaches are harder to bear. Here is one
> of the workers coming into the room. She looks at the cats in
> the cages around the walls and speaks to the caretaker. 'I have
> a home for that kitten. We will keep her, the rest must go.'

Outside of London it was arguably worse. A Mrs Clive of
Yeovil, Somerset, told an RSPCA branch meeting in March
1926: 'It is not generally realised how very difficult it is to kill
an animal in a town. I could tell you a desperate story of how
I spent three hours trying to get a stray cat killed, and failed.
It really is difficult for the poor. Veterinaries charge from 2s
6d to kill a cat painlessly . . . There remains only drowning or
turning it out into the streets to starve.'

Mrs Clive had written hundreds of letters on the subject
and found that 'RSPCA Inspectors were supplied with boxes
to chloroform cats but the method was expensive'. Swindon
Council, she discovered, maintained a municipal water tank
for people to drown their cats.

'When the present RSPCA Inspector took up his job three
years ago, he found it was the great amusement of the idle to
watch puppies and kittens swim round and round till they

drowned,' so Mrs Clive could report, to the meeting's evident horror. The inspector had persuaded the council to do it with coal gas, 'not perfect but very cheap'.

'Last year in Swindon they killed 303 dogs and 730 cats – in round numbers 1000 animals – for about 5s 6d, less the value of bone manure which is made of the bodies . . .'

This represented progress. No one seriously challenged the killing. Not yet. Rescue Leagues were what every city needed. In Penarth, South Wales, Mrs Alice Hacquort appealed in April 1927 that animal-lovers across the nation should do what she and a group of five friends had done – turn their homes into shelters where 'waifs and strays could be tenderly put out of this cruel world'. In five years they had already got through 10,000 of Cardiff's unwanted cats.

In Folkestone, Kent, Lady Ada Douglas established a scheme two years later for 'the protection of cats', as it was described, providing baskets to volunteers for the inevitable merciful purpose. 'The tragedies of cat life are very great, but only want our attention that they may be lessened. It is doubtless known that there is a lethal chamber at the Corporation yard and another at the ODFL Dog and Cat Shelter at Cheriton,' Lady Ada pronounced usefully.

In spite of lawyers routinely challenging cat-friendly wills on the grounds that they were a sign of the testatrix being of unsound mind, legacies flowed ever more generously towards the charities. Over the years to come, several monster bequests would prove of historic proportions. Like that of Mrs Sarah M. Grove-Grady, who died in 1924 leaving £100,000 – the equivalent of around £5.4 million today – to societies and institutions devoted to the care of animals. The People's Dispensary for Sick Animals of the Poor received half of it – a huge boost to the fledgling charity. It was challenged in court by both disgruntled relatives and the Veterinary Medical Association, who saw it as financing the onward march of quackery.

Ten thousand pounds was also bequeathed to the RSPCA by Mrs Grove-Grady, but Captain Fairholme, its Secretary, had to say 'that owing to the [anti blood-sports] conditions attached to the bequest, the legacy has to be refused'. A tenth of that amount from her estate meanwhile went to the Mayhew Cats' Home of Kensal Green whose furry pensioners she had long supported. Hooray! Cats surely rejoiced at the news. It was not enough, however, to prevent the Home being taken over a year later as a branch of the RSPCA.

The will of Mrs Zoe Constance Marie de Longueville Ruttledge, who died in 1929 aged seventy-six – otherwise Mrs Z. C. Morgan of the Home for Starving Cats, 'widow of Capt. John Knox Ruttledge, late 2nd Dragoon Guards', as she was described, was much more modest than Sarah Grove-Grady's but more full of baroque twists.

She left an estate valued at £3,271 – worth £183,000 today. Mr Harold Percy Carter, whose relationship to her is unclear, was bequeathed 'her Webley & Scott automatic pocket revolver with 100 cartridges perfectly new . . .' She 'desired that all her miniatures and family portraits and family seals should be destroyed as I am the last of the family'. The trustees further were to see 'that all animals and cats on the premises on the day of my death be chloroformed at once'.

The still-functioning Institution itself in Camden Town was left to the Our Dumb Friends' League, which took it over willingly. 'In thirty-five years it has reached over half a million outcast and derelict cats,' the League announced cheerfully. As for the revolver, it might be surmised that at some time in her long career, Mrs Longueville-Williams-Morgan-Ruttledge, whatever she called herself, had felt the acute need for self-protection. Possibly from fear of vengeful cats.

13

As Bad as a Funeral

LUCY

Lucy is a four (nearly five)-year-old neutered usual ABYSSIN-
IAN, very sadly in need of a new home as she is not getting on
with her owners' other cats despite many efforts. She has a
very sweet nature and loves laps and cuddles. She must be an
indoor-only girl, preferably with no other cats, and is not
used to children.

(May 2015 update) Lucy has now been rehomed and is
settling well.

There was a big new cause of upset in the lives of urban cats,
including those who had homes, if not necessarily gracious
ones. Slum clearance schemes embarked upon by municipal
authorities with none but the best intentions in the 'homes-
fit-for-heroes' era after the First World War, literally put a
wrecking ball into working-class communities across Britain.
In the bright, brick-built municipal flats that rose in their
place, it was universally a case of no pets.* Mass abandonment
of felines was the result.

For example, a newspaper reporter found a lady in Leeds,
Yorkshire, buying 'seven or eight pounds' of horseflesh:

---

* As would be the case in the post-Second World War high-rise estate building
era.

I asked why she wanted so much and found that she was
going to the Quarry Hill clearance area to give the abandoned cats something to eat. It seems that there are many of
these helpers who combine to feed and catch the homeless
cats left on slum clearance areas . . . some of whom have
become so savage through starvation that traps have had to be
used to catch them.

Although some old-time cat rescuers thought their hour had
come again, this huge new cat crisis could only be met by the
well-funded, well-organised animal welfare charities – with
the lethal box not far away. It was announced:

Two thousand cats and dogs are being collected and destroyed
every week in London. They are pets of slum dwellers who,
under the LCC clearance schemes, have moved to new tenement homes. In these flats and block dwellings the keeping of
any animal – even a dog or cat – is barred. The result is that
large areas are growing in London where the cat population
is nil.

Mr Keith Robinson, the newly appointed Secretary of Our
Dumb Friends' League, thought that: 'Children who are
naturally fond of animals are being deprived of the pleasantest
of all pets, the cat. They will see them in story books and
wonder what kind of animal a cat is.' It was not quite like
that, although he had witnessed many tearful scenes as children were parted from their pets.

The League worked with brisk efficiency. 'As soon as we
hear of streets coming down, we canvass the district with
pre-paid postcards, and people let us know what animals they
want us to collect,' said Mr Robinson. 'Our vans go round a
few days later. All the creatures are painlessly destroyed.' It
would be further reported: 'In north and east London, as

many as 250 cats have been collected in a single day. Often the rescuers have to climb over hoardings or into houses already boarded-up for the house-breakers to capture the terrified cats, which still haunt their former homes.'

This really was mass destruction. In Birmingham two RSPCA officials were themselves prosecuted in 1933 for cruelty – in a case brought by a horrified individual who saw them doing it – for attempting to kill slum-cleansed dogs with carbon monoxide from a car exhaust, because it was 'cheaper'. The Society's Chairman, Conservative MP Sir Robert Gower, insisted that the method was extensively used in America and was perfectly humane.

But some cats clearly evaded the merciful destructors. The League would report in autumn 1937 that: 'Many house-holders allowed their cats to wander away, and colonies of strays were to be found in some parts of London living practically wild.' The feline *Mayflower* had landed on Plymouth Rock. Millions more feral colonists would be not long behind – blown by the winds of war.

The cats'-meat men of London, their venerable street trade suddenly endangered, were described as being 'up in arms against the ban on cats and dogs in LCC flats'. 'It is stated that their trade has dropped 50 per cent,' said a news report. 'A Horseflesh Carriers' Protection Society has been formed, after a meeting at an East End public house, at which the Chairman, Mr G. Casey, stated that a petition was being organised and the question would be made political . . .'

The real political animal welfare ding-dong of the age was the rumbling feud between the National Veterinary Medical Association and Mrs Maria Dickin and her rapidly growing People's Dispensary. By now replete with the necessary patrician patrons and hugely boosted by the Grove-Grady legacy, the charity opened a model infirmary at Ilford on the eastern fringe of London, to treat not just horses but companion animals. Small animal clinics were popping up everywhere, within which those doing the treatment were *not* members of the Royal College of Veterinary Surgeons (RCVS). With some basic first-aid training, they were called 'technical officers'.

At first, the veterinary profession ignored them. They were written off as 'quacks'. But when it became apparent that these new clinics were treating the humblest cats and dogs (but not yet 'strays') as 'patients' deserving of concern, then the profession began to take notice. A whole new territory of companion-animal care was opening up, and just as well, because the working horse, the primary concern of the veterinary profession for generations, was in rapid decline. But this pesky bunch of amateurs looked set to get all the cat and dog business – even in leafy suburbs as their clinic network expanded and their mobile caravan dispensaries rolled into town.

There were anti-PDSA press campaigns, libel suits and legal challenges. There were stories of wealthy women sending their cats to free clinics under the guise of the poorly pet belonging to their servants. But although the outcome might well be prompt humane dispatch at the hands of the Dispensary's 'lethalist', even the humblest working-class cat, as long as it had an owner, could now be the concern of something that looked a bit like veterinary medicine. That idea alone would be far more status-raising than any cat tax.

The RSPCA also had to reinvent itself. It was now a cruelty-prosecuting organisation combined with a stray-cat-killing machine. Its attempts to provide active care for pets were progressing achingly slowly. After more than a century of existence, it was laden with prestige and money but rife with internal dissent. Blood sports and performing-animal issues kept emotions running high. Rumbling dissent within the stately Society was just about kept at bay by the Council, although there was a revolt and mass defection over hunting in 1928, while it, like all animal welfare groups, remained as open to splits and single-issue obsessives as ever.

A 'small group in London' was behind the dissent, according to a pamphlet called *The RSPCA: What It Is and What It Does*, published at the time to counter what it called the 'sensational press reporting'. It was true there had been displays of 'temper and impatience' concerning the method of election to the Council and the status of branch committees, it said, but the Society was doing its job by 'offering free skilled treatment for animals of the poor along with lethalisation centres for dealing with stray cats and dogs which handle hundreds of thousands of animals yearly'.

Everyone could support that. In fact, the more strays lethalled, the better.

And further, no one should forget that the Society's ongoing work on behalf of animals was dependent on subscriptions paid by members rather than what it called 'occasional legacies'. So stay loyal and pay up, otherwise those stray cats might not get what they deserved. It was all very grim but completely in tune with the sentiment of the time.*

It was also certainly true that, even before the PDSA's appearance, the RSPCA had begun to offer some active help to pet owners, including 'the poor'. Its first clinic offering some sort of veterinary services to companion animals had actually opened in 1909. In 1932 the War Memorial

---

* Our Dumb Friends' League went through a similar simultaneous crisis with a revolt over the totality of lethalling at its North London Dogs' Home in Willesden, which from 1914 had a similar contract to Battersea with the Metropolitan Police for clearing stray animals from the northern districts. 'If the present policy of certain influential patrons of ODFL is pursued, it will result in the Home becoming a mere slaughterhouse. Their eagerness to place affairs on a sound business footing means that, under the new regime, no dog is safe,' it was said. Cats were similarly disposed of.

Dispensary was opened in Kilburn, north London, to provide care for animals 'the owners of which could not afford the necessary veterinary fees'.

Two years later a convalescent hospital, described as a 'heaven for sick pets', was opened in leafy Putney, south-west London, thanks to a donation from a Miss Grace Giles. 'The sick or injured animal of a poor person is as entitled to skilled treatment as much as that of a well-to-do person' (unlike the PDSA with their pretend, non-qualified 'technical officers'), said its prospectus. The Putney Hospital had a capacious caged cattery in the garden for convalescing cats. This, however, was most assuredly not a cat refuge. No one except a few cranks would suggest such a thing was remotely practical. This would be the line for decades to come.

On the matter of street cats generally, the charity was bluntly honest about its role. The 'vast army of misery' such creatures represented was being vanquished by painless killing. Turning adolescent kittens adrift was the cause. 'The Society, in this humane work of destruction, performs a duty not only to the animals but to the public at large. Many homeless cats are carriers of disease,' it said starkly in a pamphlet about the role of the Society, now over a century old, towards cats. The public were invited to see for themselves at the Animal Rescue League or at the Mayhew Home, taken over by the RSPCA as the 'North Middlesex Branch' in 1925, which 'provide for the painless destruction of diseased, homeless and injured cats'.

But it was not all killing. Within a few years there would be sixty-four RSPCA clinics, working in co-operation with the veterinary profession to help pets with owners to stay healthy or to bind their wounds. Even the Animal Rescue League had added a clinic to offer treatment to 'animals of the poor' in a bid to counter the 'unfounded criticism made on more than one occasion that it was solely concerned with destruction of animals', according to the *Animal World*.

There were clearly some misguided idealists in the Society who might have discreetly raised an objection to the semi-detached operation in City Road and its single-mindedness of lethal purpose. Indeed, after doubts were raised over the actual 'painlessness' of killing cats and dogs with electricity (it did not work so well with dogs because of their 'horny paws'), the American machines were sent to India to counter a rabies scare.*

Rival Battersea first expressed an interest in the method in 1917 and would at last install patent high-voltage 'Electrothanators' in 1934 after fifty years of gassing. With what would be described as 'certain modifications', their use would be continued into the 1980s.

The lethal absolutism of the big charities was too much for some altogether. There were people for whom going it alone was the only way. A Rotherham vicar, the Reverend S. Claude Tickell, invited fellow cat-lovers to join him in a reborn 'National Feline Defence League' in 1925. He seems to have had little response. The Allnott sisters, Misses Ethel and Mildred, opened their 'Animal Help Society' shelter for 'lost, stray and unwanted dogs and cats' in Goldhawk Road, west London in 1924 – to be eventually taken over by the RSPCA.

And there was Mrs F. M. Ballingall of Barnes, south-west London, who in July 1929 in a flourish of publicity launched something called the 'Friends of Cats Society' with a mission to boost the status of cats via a compulsory licence and an identity badge. Under the plan, 'lost cats will be detained for at least a week, and not slaughtered the next day, as is the

* Where, according to *Animal People* magazine, they stayed in use until 1997. 'One ended up in Pakistan and may still be in use.' The Ewen legacy lived on.

present practice. Only veterinary surgeons or specially
licensed persons may kill a cat.'

Both the RSPCA and Our Dumb Friends' League (although
the latter would change its mind) reacted with alarm to the
suggestion. 'Most of the cats which now have a home in poor
households would be cast adrift', said the League, which
'destroys 50,000 stray cats yearly in London alone, and if a
licence duty and legal responsibility were forced upon owners
this number would be doubled or trebled'. The Friends of
Cats Society faded away, its cat-licence plan like so many
others before and after, doomed to oblivion.

But there was a major human legislative intervention in the
affairs of cats in 1928 when, for fear of rabies, cats entering
Britain were made subject to quarantine; dogs had been such
since 1897. It caused quite a stir among pedigree breeders,
naturally, while those enthusiasts who now had to turn to
humbler domestic types to get their feline fix were shocked
at the general level of ignorance about cats among their
working-class owners. The commitment of the newly
founded Cats Protection League (see p. 178) to education
was one result. Another outcome of the scare was noted:
'Visitors to the Continent for their holidays sometimes take
their cats abroad with them; others occasionally pick up a
stray kitten while travelling and bring it back to this country
on their return. All such cats will in future have to undergo
six months' quarantine immediately on landing as a safeguard
against the risk of their being the means of introducing rabies
from abroad.'

The reality for Britain's street cats, however, was as it had
always been. No jolly foreign trips for them. The journalist
Evelyn Sharp visited Ferdinand Street in 1929 soon after Zoe
Morgan's death. After thirty years, the good old Institution
and Home, recently taken over by Our Dumb Friends'
League, was as busy as ever.

'Those who may think that we have no more right to put animals down than we have to put human beings to death, have still to find a better solution of a problem that exists in every city,' so she began her perceptive report on the 'Unwanted Cat'.

'All day long the telephone bell rings,' she wrote, with cat owners begging for sick, injured or otherwise superfluous pets to be collected. 'Every day the motor-van arrives back from its round at five o'clock with its pathetic load of little cages . . . The lethal chamber, which holds a hundred cages, is then loaded up and closed . . . the chloroform lamp is lit . . .

'When they were strays reduced to skin and bone by star-vation, one felt glad [about their fate]. But it seemed a differ-ent matter when a handsome, well-fed cat was brought in.' She recorded a common cause of abandonment:

'It's as bad as a funeral sometimes,' explained the nurse. 'When someone comes dressed in deep mourning we know what it means – the owner has died and no one wants the poor cat.'

'The unwanted cat is not wholly, or even primarily, a slum problem,' reported Evelyn Sharp. 'The greatest number of cats is brought in during the holiday month of August – sometimes ninety a day – and they come from the better residential quarters, where people go away and leave their cats to starve.'

It was ever thus.

PART TWO

GOOD HOMES
WANTED

1930–1970

14

'A Chance of Life and Happiness'

PEANUT

Female, age 2, DOMESTIC SHORT-HAIR, black.
Hi, my name is Peanut. I came to the adoption centre with
my 5 kittens. At first I was very protective over my kittens
but now I have been separated from them I am beginning to
relax and settle in but will require an owner who has lots of
time and patience as I will need to build my trust and confidence in them . . .

After so much weary destruction, so some cat-lovers were
beginning to ask, after so much 'indifferentism' towards these
beautiful creatures who were supposed to share our lives, was
there really no alternative? What had the mysterious correspondent 'Sans Souci' asked fifty years before in response to
Battersea's installation of the lethal chamber for cats: 'Is this
all we have to offer . . . to hurry them into death as compensation for the miseries of their own lives?' Humans could not
stop being on their case – but nothing had changed. Except
perhaps that the technology of killing had become more
efficient.

An unsigned article appeared in the *Animals' Friend*, journal of the Humane Society, in April 1927 with a call to arms.
In the matter of cats, it was 'passing strange', said the anonymous manifesto, 'that no adequate society had ever taken

root to befriend these household gods who often fall from high estate and their brothers, the strays'.

'Should cats be taxed?' asked the author. 'Can they be taxed? Does chloroform provide the most humane death, or is electricity better? Are the shelters properly run? And many other points are often argued, but never settled . . . Why has no section of the public come to grips with the appalling state of misery and muddle which besets the problem . . .?'

Thus it was that on 16 May 1927 a group of animal advocates met at Caxton Hall in London, when it was resolved 'That a society be formed to be devoted exclusively to promoting the interests of cats and that its name is The Cats Protection League.' Two of its moving spirits were the veteran animal protection campaigner, Ernest Bell, co-founder in 1924 of the League for the Prohibition of Cruel Sports, and his long-time secretary, Miss Jessey Wade, both veterans of vegetarianism, spiritualism, and general animal do-goodery since the 1890s.

Miss Wade, it turned out, was the author of the original anonymous article. Also on the council were the formidable cat advocate, Mrs C. B. Avery of Baron's Court, west London, and Mr William Brown MRCVS, a vet with strong anti-vivisection credentials. They may have been part of the old guard – but the banner they unfurled was new. To some, it seemed alarmingly radical.

The *Animals' Friend* started a special section about League affairs, full of lively correspondence and campaigning ideas. The new energy was tangible. A five-point pledge card was printed. The doleful activities of the RSPCA's Animal Rescue League ('51,280 stray, diseased, homeless or unwanted cats humanely destroyed in the past year', said its most recent report) were sternly questioned. 'Rescue leagues are not enough,' said Miss Wade. 'Something must be done to stem the ever-increasing evil of the need for killing.' But what?

To begin with there was lots of old-style sentimentalism. A plea was made to revive 'Every Cat's Day', when a shilling should be sent to a deserving cats' shelter; first launched in 1907 and progressively forgotten thereafter. There was a glutinous commentary: 'I like to think that the guardian angel of every little lost cat – a nice soft purry angel, with beautiful white fur instead of feathers – leads them, sooner or later, to the right door . . .' Things would soon get much more practical. They would have to.

On the afternoon of 21 June 1928, Captain Fergus MacCunn of the RSPCA, a League member almost from the start, gave a dramatic talk on the wireless on the 'Care of Cats'. It was described as 'the first time cats had been accorded any place on a BBC programme which has mentioned our League'. After fifty years of concern, cat abandonment was still the theme. As the *Radio Times* billed it:

> The Assistant Secretary of the RSPCA will say a timely word to cat owners – particularly timely now that the holidays are here and so many people are apt, in sheer thoughtlessness, to leave their cats to that semi-starvation that is euphemistically termed 'foraging for themselves'.

It was a big hit. 'Many letters were received from listeners asking if we could take stray cats and whether homes could be found for kittens . . .' Just add some celebrities, and a successful broadcasting formula would be assured.

In 1931 the first edition of the League's journal, the *Cats' Mews-Sheet*, edited by Jessy Wade, was published with a bold mission statement on the front page:

> The Cats Protection League came, very quietly, into being some three years ago, and has been during that time, feeling its way towards the creation of a strong and united

determination among cat-lovers . . . to raise the status of cats generally, and in particular to see to it that the present conditions which make the demand for 'merciful death' so essential, shall cease to be.

Another mind-changing, campaigning article in *The Cat* (as the *Mews-Sheet* would be renamed) outlined what an ideal cat shelter should be. It said:

Fully to live up to its name, a cats' shelter should be more than a mere slaughterhouse, for though the majority of its clients need no other mercy than a peaceful death, many of them deserve a chance of life and happiness.

Achieving anything like that would be the CPL's work for generations to come. In 1931, however, the judgement on which cats deserved a chance was harsh. Old cats and sick cats had to go. What *was* an old cat? 'There is too much risk attached to finding homes for cats *over a year old*' (authors' emphasis), wrote Mrs Avery. 'They refuse to adapt themselves and try and return to their old homes, becoming strays as a result.'

Naturally enough, many of the League's early members were old-style street-feeders. Concern for netherworld cats could also be more regulated. A fund was set up in 1931 to give the 'derelict' cats of the capital some sort of Christmas cheer, while special intervention was sought for 'an army of hungry half-wild animals' in Walworth, south London – a very catty spot on all accounts where impoverished locals apparently thought it was 'unlucky to destroy cats'. It was time for a mass round-up and destruction, of course. Meanwhile a survey was made of the cats of the City, apparently living in ancient churchyards and fed from cafés. These would turn out to be 'office mousers' and although pretty hungry, were not really wild at all.

All this was good compassionate cat stuff but the first and most urgent task was to tackle the 'Excess Feline Population . . . otherwise shelters for destruction must go on multiplying and misery must increase', editorialised the *Cat's Mews-Sheet*. 'What causes too many cats?' asked League President Mrs Violet Clive: 'It would hardly be an overstatement to say sentimentality and indifference. The sentimentalist says: "Dear little kittens, it is a shame to drown them," or "Think of their poor mother".

'Of course it is best to leave the mother one kitten if the owner is willing to take the trouble to find it a good home; if not, temporary distress for the mother is less cruel than a whole life of misery for the kitten,' she wrote.

'If the owner wishes for one kitten, a tom should be chosen. It is easier to find homes for one or two kittens than four or five. So, unless it is absolutely necessary for the mother's sake, please do not keep more than two kittens from each litter and be sure they are males.

'The indifferent, of course, think nothing, do nothing, and care nothing,' said Mrs Avery. It was that old problem – 'indifferentism'. Cats deserved the highest degree of attention.

Cats' shelters should keep much better records, and not merely accept anything offered as a candidate for destruction. Too many cats simply disappeared, thanks to a mysterious 'woman with a basket, who snatches up any cat she meets for it never to be seen again', so the League's journal lectured sternly. 'It is a monstrous thing that a happy cat merely having a stroll in his own neighbourhood should be whisked off to a shelter to lose his life.' And who would disagree with that? Miserabilist cat snatchers were everywhere.

And so that genuinely lost cats should have a real chance of being reunited with their owners, there should be much more attention paid to publicity, a noticeboard system to announce the lost and found.

The ideal shelter would 'take pains also to advertise itself so that cat owners would no longer be ignorant of its existence as they are now'. Perfectly healthy cats were being destroyed in their thousands. There was no link yet, other than the most tenuous, between the rescue of netherworld cats and those seeking new homes for them. And anyway, nobody wanted older cats, did they? A 'grown-up cat' would simply rebel and try to find its old home. The editor and correspondents, those that were published, of the *Cats' Mews-Sheet* were deeply sceptical that cats could be re-homed at all. But by degree, education and the spreading of good practice would alleviate the stray cat problem at source – however long that might take. The spell of the lethal chamber might yet be broken.

The way to do it was by neutering,* so Frances Simpson had advised back in 1903: 'Opinions differ as to the best period for a cat to be made neuter,' she wrote, 'but it is generally considered advisable to have the operation performed between the ages of five and eight months . . . A duly qualified veterinary ought to be employed, and an anaesthetic used.'

She had suggested the formation of a 'neuter society . . . for the general improvement of our neuter cats'. The Animals Anaesthetics Act of 1919 obliged the use of anaesthesia in castrations of cats aged over six months. Up until the late 1930s, the spaying of female cats, which required an invasive operation, was rare. Culturally it could be seen as shocking; some cat-owners considered spaying 'cruel, preferring to drown or chloroform (in a sealed biscuit tin), litter after litter

---

* The term can be used for both male and female cats – or more specifically, 'spaying' for females and 'castration' or neutering for males. As Cats Protection explains: 'In a male cat, both testes are removed from small incisions made in the scrotum. In females, the uterus and ovaries are removed via an incision either on the left side or underneath.'

of unwanted kittens while giving little thought for the distress to the mother', as a wise and humane cat historian would write many years later.

League member Miss M. M. Frisbee made it her business to go round 'streets of shabby homes' in pre-war south London dispensing leaflets and advice, telling people not to give away female kittens, nor entrust them to the itinerant cats'-meat man who somehow 'knew how to get rid of them'.'I look forward to the day when every cat in Tooting will be a much-prized [male] neuter,' she wrote.

The CPL would advise: 'If your cat is a female, do not keep all her kittens, only one tom. Take the others to a shelter to be put to sleep.' But it was not easy to tell the gender of newborn kittens. If the supposed male kitten turned out to be female, it too should be taken to a cat shelter to be destroyed, went the advice. At some shelters, the majority of the cats destroyed were older females which had been accidentally kept in this way. And many more cats were destroyed because they were pregnant than because of illness or injury.

In 1935 the League would be bequeathed Prestbury Lodge, a sizeable house in the middle of Slough, Berkshire, the gift of 'Mrs Williams, a very sincere cat-lover'. The new General Secretary, Mr Albert Steward, a local cat enthusiast, took up residence on the first floor, with the rest of the house and garden being used for cat work. There was, inevitably, a lethal chamber in the basement, but unlike almost all the cat 'welfare' efforts of the past, mass destruction was not to be the sole function of the operation. Cat enthusiast clubs in major cities would progressively become League branches.

The new mood began to infect even the stately RSPCA. Its Assistant Secretary, Captain Fergus McCunn, could tell a regional meeting in 1931 that 'an organisation has been built up to find homes for healthy but unwanted pets which would otherwise be destroyed'. The Society's Report for that year announced: '[some dispensaries] now have "Wants Registers" – a record of those requiring and those wishing to find good homes for animals. In one dispensary last year, sixty were found good homes by these means.' The good captain further proposed a 'Cats' Registry Office', one for London at least, to match cats with potential adopters and thus 'save an army of healthy animals each year from the lethal box'.

This was still more a benign vision than any kind of reality. The *Cats' Mews-Sheet* canvassed the opinion of CPL members with 'long experience in cat work' who were doubtful the Registry Office idea could work. Good homes would turn out to be not so good; there might be children or cruel people in the house. Re-homing enthusiast Captain McCunn was now also on the Cats Protection League Committee – *and* on that of the Mayhew Home in Kensal Green, now an RSPCA subsidiary, which would be rebuilt and extended in Art Deco style in 1935 with a caged cattery on the roof. Under its original deed of trust, the Mayhew continued to make its rare stand against lethal absolutism. It did so in a remarkable way. As readers of the *Animal World* were told:

> To anyone who is really fond of cats the idea of having one killed is repulsive. If you visit the [Mayhew] Home you will be shown some cats which are really ownerless and which are kept alive through the generosity of people who love cats. In the ordinary way of things, these ownerless cats would have been humanely put to sleep in the lethal chamber but their lives are prolonged and they are quite happy, due to their benefactors.

In 1931, so the *Animal World* further reported, the Mayhew opened a 'holiday home for cats'. In fact, it was a subsidised boarding establishment, at Eastcote in the north London suburbs. Things were looking much more cheerful all round.

The RSPCA journal was getting dangerously utopian, soon thereafter relaying amazing news from America for its readers, of 'a wonderful society which befriends large numbers of homeless animals but does not kill any animal unless it is absolutely necessary'. This marvel was the 'Bide-a-Wee Home' operating under the banner *No Animal Needlessly Destroyed*. It had been 'founded thirty years ago by Mrs [Flora] Harry Ulysses Kibbie', according to its Secretary, Mr Richard Meaney, on a trip to London which included a fact-finding visit and exchange of views with the good folks at 105 Jermyn Street. The amazingly idealistic outfit on the East River had survived and prospered, as Mr Meaney told his interviewer:

> 'We don't pick up stray animals. All the animals we handle – mostly dogs and cats – are brought to us . . .'
> 'And you keep the lot?'
> 'Well, we have accommodation for 700 animals in New York and at our country place at Long Island. The majority of the animals are dogs. Then, in point of numbers, come cats . . .'
> 'Don't you find homes for any of the animals?'
> 'Oh, yes we do, but we're very careful about the homes.'

There was a free clinic in New York City, said Mr Meaney, and the 'Bide-A-Wee Legion of Kindness to which children can belong – a kind of Children's Club over the air, every Saturday morning, from 8.45 to 9.00, on the Radio Station W-O-R. There are animal stories for the members, lessons on keeping animals, and so on.'

Out of America came dazzling modernity. How things had changed. Just twenty years before, Kate Cording had been in need of a piano for her child helpers to sing merry songs about animals in the parlour at Fellowship Cottage, with the

lethal chamber outside in a shed where so many cats had met
their end.

That was in another age. In spite of economic depression,
swathes of middle-class Britain, London especially, experienced a consumer boom in the 1930s. All those thousands of
semi-detached houses built for aspirant home-makers required
not just wirelesses and domestic appliances: what could be
more symbolic of family life than a cat? A few old-time cats'-
meat men did their best to get out to the new suburbs, but
glimmers of US-style feline novelty were peeping through.
Cat food sold in shops, for example, as Messrs. Spratt's could
announce in 1927:

> Custom has decreed that cats be fed from the leavings on the
> table. But why? The inadvisability of such promiscuous feed-
> ing is as obvious as the fact that the constitution of the cat is
> widely different from our own. Spratt's Cat Food is a perfectly
> balanced nourishing meal specially made for cats . . .

A newspaper could report in summer 1933 that 'there are not
so many stray cats about since people have learned that it is
not kind to let unwanted kittens grow up'. And further: 'cats
used to be wild, furtive creatures' . . . now they could stretch
out in the sun on any street without being chased or abused.
'The cat of today has much more confidence in human
beings, and has responded to more humane treatment by
developing greater intelligence and affection,' said the report.

Another place where cats were not having it so good was
Germany. The Nazis had come to power in 1933, swiftly
enacting strict animal protection laws. But felines were not
among the favourites of the Führer, Adolf Hitler, who apparently favoured dogs and birds.

A 1936 decree on the 'protection of nature' decreed that
cats roaming beyond their homes could be considered

'poachers' and trapped. They had to be treated 'humanely' thereafter but, if no owner appeared, they could be killed. There was a resistance movement. Friedrich Schweingart wrote in his book *Vom Recht der Katze* (On the Rights of the Cat), published in 1937, that cats lived in 'a state of emergency', hated by the majority of the population who were imbued with false perceptions that cats were 'faithless' or 'illbred'. Other cat advocates declared them to be 'hygienic helpers' in the war on mice. But strays and ferals had better watch out. One proposal was that by systematic breeding, cats could be transformed into super rat-killers. To this end, only one or two kittens of a litter should be allowed to live, the others to be 'humanely' killed. Thus so-called 'wild pest cats' (*verwilderte Schädlingskatze*) would be eliminated and a disciplined elite of rodent exterminators take their place. But cats, even in the Third Reich, were not so good at obeying orders.

Could it even be in Britain too that the day of the stray was coming to an end? In the now fifty-year-old contest between the lethal chamber and the fecundity of street cats, the destructors were beginning to draw ahead. Mr Keith Robinson, the Secretary of Our Dumb Friends' League, could announce with some pride in 1937 that the cat population of London was declining rapidly. The prime reasons were 'the increase of facilities for painless destruction, the frequent bans on cats in flats and tenements, and recent epidemics of [feline] influenza'.

Old-style charity cat-swiping continued unabated. In November that year, Marylebone Police Court heard about a nine-year-old pet cat named 'Oo-Oo', 'taken by force by two women officials of ODFL', as it was recorded, accused by Miss Adele Bourne of Blomfeld Road, Maida Vale, of taking her blameless pet. Too late! Poor Oo-Oo had already gone into the lethal box at Ferdinand Street.

'More than 300,000 cats are destroyed every year,' Mr Robinson proclaimed. 'If it were not for the work of organisations like ours, there would be so many stray cats in the streets of London that the authorities would have to do something about it . . .'

Within a matter of months, the 'authorities' would be making plans for all cats – not just strays. In the crisis that was coming, those cats outside human society might just have the better chance of surviving.

15

Blitz Cats

MISTY

Misty is a handsome black and white male aged 4 years old. His life has been tough the last few years; his owners moved away and left him to fend for himself outside on the streets. He was living outside a long time and as a result became distrustful of humans. Who could blame him after how he had been treated! His foster mum has done a wonderful job of bringing him out of his shell . . .

This boy just needs a break . . .

The climb of the cat into the sunlight of middle-class respectability had reached its balmy noontide just as the windows of British suburbia were being measured for blackout curtains.

Unlike the outbreak of war in 1914, the second and far greater crisis for the nation's pets came with plenty of warning. And this time it would be on everyone's doorstep, as it seemed the enemy's horrible bomber aircraft would rain explosives and poison gas on Britain's towns and cities within hours of any conflict beginning. What would cats and dogs do then? It would be a challenge for cat rescuers on an undreamed-of scale.

The Munich Crisis of autumn 1938 when, during 'a throbbing week of tension', war seemed just around the corner but then faded away, had produced two important results for

Britain's cats. It demonstrated that many owners were
prepared to abandon their animals or hand them over for
destruction, and this compelled the authorities to make a plan
to somehow incorporate domestic pets into what were now
being called 'Air Raid Precautions'.

What strays might do in time of war was anyone's guess,
although some cat-lovers would have been intrigued to read
a report in spring 1938 that 'stray cats are to be pressed into
National Service in Germany . . . according to a new order
issued. Henceforth, ownerless cats will not be destroyed, but
collected and put to work at the countless new granaries
which have been erected to house Germany's grain harvest
. . . to keep down the rats and mice'. That might be something worth remembering.

Thus it was that in the months after the Munich scare, a
body called 'NARPAC' – the National ARP Animals
Committee – came into being, supposedly to link the veterinary profession, the welfare charities, police and local authorities in some sort of defensive scheme for pets. What would
happen when cities were evacuated of women and children,
blacked-out or attacked from the air? Would animals go wild
at the first wail of a siren and spread gas or even biological
agent contamination? It might seem 'kinder' altogether if all
pets were mercifully put down, as some officials and senior
police were proposing; after all, the stray-killing machinery
was in place and functioning efficiently as it had been for half
a century past.

It was broadly assumed that evacuation and bombing would
turn every cat on the block into some sort of stray. It had
already been ruled that pets would not be allowed into air
raid shelters or to accompany mothers and children on the
trains heading for the 'safe areas', following an order to evacuate imperilled cities. But cats could be taken or sent to the
country by any other means. In fact, it was officially advised

that they should be. There were going to be plenty of distressed, uprooted felines whatever happened.

Advice crowded in from all sides. In July 1939 the government published a pamphlet called *ARP Handbook No. 12 – Air Raid Precautions for Animals*, available from His Majesty's Stationery Office, price 3d. It offered this advice: 'When an owner has been unable to send his dog or cat to a safe area, he should consider the advisability of having it painlessly destroyed. During an emergency there might be large numbers of animals wounded, gassed or driven frantic with fear, and destruction would then have to be enforced by the responsible authority for the protection of the public.'

The welfare charities were asked to provide details of their pet destruction capacity. It seemed more than adequate. The RSPCA had fifty-two 'cat and dog lethalling centres' in London alone and more in provincial cities. Our Dumb Friends' League was more than ready, so were the PDSA and National Canine Defence League, which offered to also handle cat destruction. Battersea had its bank of high-voltage 'Electrothonators' at the ready.

Lorries and lifting gear would be needed for the collection of carcasses, and 'four-pronged forks for small animals'. It was all very thorough. To dispose of the corpses from London, the firm of Harrison, Barber & Co., slaughterers and fat renderers of Sugar House Lane, Stratford, London E15, was ready to do its bit.

Some enterprising pet owners decided to create their own domestic shelters. Gas was still the biggest fear for humans and animals alike, but most of the advice to pet owners in the event of chemical attack seemed absurd. For instance, 'The contaminated hair on cats should be cut out and carefully destroyed,' recommended *ARP News*.

NARPAC embarked on a mission to recruit a national network of 'Animal Guards', to distribute identity collar badges for dogs and cats and set in motion a scheme for local organisers to register the names and addresses of imperilled pets so that they might, if displaced in the chaos of war, be reunited with their owners. The registration scheme would become an obsession.

As the August crisis deepened and German tanks massed on the Polish border, a draft notice was prepared for the press and the BBC. Headed *Measures to Meet an Immediate Emergency*, it read:

> If at all possible, send or take your household animals into the country in advance of an emergency . . . Put dogs on a lead. Put cats in a basket or box. If you and your family have to leave home at very short notice (you will not be allowed to take animals with you under the official scheme), on no account leave them in the house or turn them into the street. If you cannot place them in the care of neighbours, it really is kindest to have them destroyed.

The existence of NARPAC and what was now called 'Official Advice to Animal Owners' was announced in newspapers and on the BBC News the next morning. And there it was, that seemingly caring line about it being 'kindest to have them destroyed'.

The result was disaster, a tragic over-reaction to the advice so soothingly offered. It had all been done with good intentions, but it was not meant to turn out like this. A despairing Mr C. H. Gaunt, the PDSA Superintendent at the Ilford Sanatorium, told a reporter that they were doing 'the best thing for animals by destroying the pets of evacuated families'. PDSA staff were 'working eighteen hours a day'. They had destroyed 300,000 London animals in less than ten days. The renderers' yards in east London were overflowing with the bodies of dead cats and dogs.

The slaughter of the innocents continued. Other cities caught the frenzy. Those faceless officials who had so casually triggered the catastrophe tried to shut it down in further press briefings. *The Times* commented on 7 September: 'A widespread and persistent rumour that it is now compulsory to get rid of domestic animals is causing many thousands to be taken for destruction. Centres run by animal welfare societies are filled with the bodies of animals. The National ARP Animals Committee emphasise that there is no truth whatever in this rumour.

'Apart from everything else, the huge destruction of cats that is continuing at present may lead to a very serious increase of vermin . . .' Those rats and mice were going to prove very important in the story of wartime cats.

The avuncular vet, Colonel Robert Stordy, Chairman of NARPAC, reported to the Minister of Home Security on 11 August that all estimates had been overtaken by the wave of destruction that took place. 'With the advent of war, it was not only the poor that took advantage of the clinics', wrote Stordy, 'but many of the well-to-do have also had their animals destroyed' (he pencilled *¾ of a million* in the margin). The RSPCA reported: 'From 1 September all the Society's clinics were working day and night. A temporary euthanasia centre was even opened at Headquarters' – 105 Jermyn Street in the heart of the West End; only grand cats there. The destruction was London-wide. Society cats as well as East End tabbies went into the lethal chamber. For once in their hazard-filled existence, strays might be said to have been safely out of the firing line.

Mr Albert Steward, writing in *The Cat*, had this warning of even worse to come. It was not potential enemy action immediately endangering cats but changes in the ordinary routine for such a creature of habit:

It is difficult in the present tragic days to write about the ordinary lives and needs of cats, but it is very necessary to bear
them in mind . . . Many, too, will only think of them in relation to air raids, gas attacks, and so on. But we should not
overlook the domestic difficulties that will cause the bulk of
the suffering of cats in the next few months.

He warned that cats in the charge of indifferent, bad and
'nervy' owners would become strays, either through being
turned out or because they would find life unendurable in
their new homes and wander away. Then there was the problem of 'homesick' cats striving somehow to get away from
the horrid seaside hotel rooms to which they were now
confined – maybe even trying to get back to their big city
homes. Indeed, this did happen in a number of cases. He
addressed the problem of the Wartime Stray directly:

I have no doubt many people would say there is no difference between a stray cat now and one before the war, and to
some extent this statement is true, because the vicissitudes of
a stray cat are the same at all times . . . Under normal conditions a cat becomes a stray either by its own inclination to
wander or through the negligence, cruelty or indifference of
its owner.
    Occasionally circumstances beyond the control of both cat
and owner will result in the loss of the animal, as for example,
being chased by a dog or being picked up by children or
being stolen . . .

'Is it not possible that present-day conditions are likely to
increase the number of strays?' asked Mr Steward. 'When
families or part of families are evacuated from the danger
zones, what becomes of the cats? In some cases they are
destroyed; some are taken by the families to the new home,

others become strays either because they are not at home when the journey is commenced or they become scared and hide away whilst preparations for the removal are being made, and are thus left behind.'

This great whirlwind blowing through the nation's pets was going to uproot some of them like a Kansas twister. Some would come down in pretty extraordinary places. But a major reason was careless owners, said Mr Steward:

> Amongst those who take their cats with them there are quite a number who do not exercise sufficient care when they arrive, and often within a few hours the cat is missing . . . Then there is the evacuee child who tries to replace his or her 'left behind pet' by picking up a kitten or cat and taking it to the new home.

In this time of extreme need, how could any kind of cat rescue be possible? Amazingly, it was. It began in the first days of the pet massacre. There were reports of scuffles in the queues for the charity destruction centres, cats being grabbed out of people's arms. The redoubtable Nina, Duchess of Hamilton, co-founder and President of the Animal Defence Society (the 'Anti-Vivisection' tag was generally dropped in everyday use), was rich and motivated enough to do something dramatic. She rushed from the family seat in Scotland to London with a statement to be broadcast on the BBC. It went out on the morning of 28 August 1939, appealing to those who might offer accommodation 'free of charge for other people's animals in safe areas'. A statement appeared in *The Times'* personal columns the next day:

> Homes in the country urgently required for those dogs and cats which must otherwise be left behind to starve to death or be shot. Remember that these are the pets of poor people who

love them dearly and who will have sufficient worries without those caused by the knowledge that their pets are suffering.

There were plenty more pets locked in houses by fleeing families or simply abandoned in the street. Dr Margaret Young, moving spirit of the Wood Green Animal Shelter in north London, appealed for funds to help the 'scores of animals left behind and slowly starving to death. We know of cases of cats shooting up women's shopping baskets in a vain endeavour to find food.'

The ODFL's London Institution for Lost and Starving Cats (late of Mrs Morgan fame) reported: 'Staff pleaded with owners not to have their animals destroyed but they were adamant. Such people were kindlier perhaps than many others, because staff have continually been called to houses which have been evacuated to rescue some wild, starving cat who has been left behind.'

Abandoned cats would haunt the capital for weeks to come. Our Dumb Friends' League alerted newspaper readers in October to the plight of 'imprisoned cats' still shut up in houses, and appealed 'to owners who have inadvertently left their cats behind, or to people who know of such cases, to write to the League'.

The Duchess of Hamilton's original rescue scheme was to call on rural pet lovers' goodwill to take in urban refugees. This was still the case. 'Letters offering homes in the country came at the rate of 200 a day,' wrote one of her helpers. However: 'Letters begging the Society to take charge of animals came at a much greater rate.' There was a second BBC broadcast, 'an appeal to owners of private cars to help with free transport. This brought much generous personal service and help'.

It was by no means for posh pets only. This was a genuine attempt to save the companion animals of the poor, and many cats and dogs would depart the capital in chauffeur-driven meowing, barking car-loads to be put up in strange new homes. A point was being made. The Duchess herself opened her St John's Wood mansion as a sanctuary – and beyond that lay Ferne, the grand estate in Wiltshire, hastily being converted into a rural refuge for urban pets.

For a cat plucked from danger in 1939 it could not do much better than end up at the Duchess of Hamilton's Wiltshire animal sanctuary. 'Two hundred cats were housed in the private aerodrome,' so it would be reported, 'each one of which was as carefully looked after as the dogs [and] evacuee parrots.' The Duchess described her own charges: 'The evacuated cats were very numerous.' There was a procession of 'grey pussies, black pussies, tabby pussies, white pussies, orange pussies, tortoiseshell pussies, long-haired Persians and shorthaired cats'. 'It became a very real problem as to how to distinguish each one,' she wrote, 'for cats have ways of slipping off collars. Many kind hosts came forward, but the greatest number of cats went to Ferne Sanctuary.' That winter there was an outbreak of feline influenza brought in by an 'evacuee kitten' – but the usual 80 per cent fatality rate was brought down to 10 per cent by 'dedicated nursing'.

The nine months of 'Phoney War' which followed the pet-killing tragedy of late summer 1939 gave Britain's cats a chance to adjust better to blackout and evacuation. With the defeat of the western allies in France in May–June 1940, several French cats reportedly managed to escape with the forces evacuated from Dunkirk. That summer, Britain faced invasion and thousands more cats were abandoned or compulsorily destroyed in vulnerable coastal towns. When whole populations of humans were removed from a seaside area it was ruled that 'a number of cats should be left behind in order to keep down rats and mice'. But the real test came in earnest when bombing of cities and ports began in September

1940. There was a whole new wave of killing and abandonment.

It was time for a forgotten army to come out of the shadows. The cat ladies of Britain were back with their nets and baskets, many of them given a whole new status as 'Animal Guards', the pet-loving militia deployed by NARPAC with a bright brassard on their arms or a NARPAC badge on their bicycles and little carts. It was recognition at last – a cat lady Dad's Army.

Many more rescuers would work under the banner of the animal charity of which they were supporters, the PDSA, the ODFL, the National Canine Defence League and the RSPCA – which, after a policy row, had ended formal co-operation with NARPAC and, for the time being, abandoned their obsession with eliminating strays. With the turmoil of evacuation, with whole city blocks burning and shattered by bombing, such refugee cats were no longer seen as the disreputable beggar cats of old. They were casualties of war.

The old way would have been a quick trip to the lethal chamber in an animal shelter – but surely some were deserving of a chance of survival? And if grubby children and bombed-out families were being placed in strange new homes around the country – why not cats? Class barriers were tumbling.

Albert Steward, writing in *The Cat*, gave a summary of the rival welfare charities' differing policies soon after the bombing began. 'Whilst I can assure readers that assistance has been given to homeless and evacuated animals by NARPAC, it must in all fairness be understood that the scheme was intended to cover Registration and First Aid only.' That is, there was not much actual rescuing going on.

RSPCA staff were, by contrast, 'going out with first-aid kits and searching the ruins for buried animals. Small animals, including cats, of course, have been rescued, boarded temporarily, placed in new homes and fed while their owners were missing. The work goes on.' This was truly a revolution!

In November 1940 the Society appealed directly in the *Animal World* for people willing to take in homeless animals – those who had not been given a painless end in bombed areas. The Society's own report recorded the establishment of a 'wants register' at headquarters for people looking for companion animals: it would turn out to be mostly dogs. In 1940 'new owners were found for ninety-one animals'. War was making taking in a bombed-out pet, if not common-place, at least an act of patriotic pride. This time there was no talk of cats spreading disease.

During September 1940, '10,100 household pets were painlessly destroyed and 5,490 were rescued from bombed premises, fed for a time, boarded in the Society's institutions or provided with new homes', according to the RSPCA's Annual Report.

And of Our Dumb Friends' League and the PDSA, *The Cat* could report, 'cat-lovers all over the country are being asked to form themselves into a voluntary corps to rescue pets found among the debris of bombed houses. People are asked to keep a look-out for stray animals and when they see them to take them in and give them temporary shelter. As soon as possible the ODFL will send for the animals . . .'

As for the Duchess of Hamilton's Animal Defence Society: 'Although this Society's work does not normally include rescue and clinic work, a great deal has been done and is still being done in finding homes for homeless animals and in accepting responsibility for the maintenance of animals at kennels and catteries,' Mr Steward could report. 'The CPL has been in close touch with the ADS for some months, and has given some little assistance with regard to the placing of cats in new homes.' And the Cats Protection League itself was actively looking for:

> New or temporary homes for cats. For many months, tempo-
> rary accommodation has been given to evacuee cats and to
> cats and kittens rendered homeless through 'spots of bother'
> in this neighbourhood [Slough]. At the time of writing all
> available space is taken up. The clearing station scheme is
> making progress, but the appeal for new homes, made
> through these columns [*The Cat*], has met with no success at
> all.

Broadening the appeal had 'necessitated advertising in a daily
paper at considerable cost', wrote Mr Steward – 'but replies
are only now being received. This should mean more new
homes for homeless cats.'

And in places it worked. For example, it was reported:
'The Weston-super-Mare Borough Council recently
appealed to householders for unwanted cats so that they
might be given to evacuees who have been placed in unten-
anted houses in the town. There has been a big response.'

All this was terribly experimental. New homes for homeless cats indeed! But in the great levelling of the Blitz, who
cared now which were posh cats or disreputable strays? Like
bombed-out East End families decanted to suburbia, like nit-
ridden, working-class evacuee children – whose condition
appalled many on whom they had been first billeted – it
might be that even urban stray cats deserved loving new
homes. Like so much else, this war was causing a revolution
in feline affairs.

16

Cats of National Importance

SIDNEY RUFF DIAMOND

Three years ago my partner and I went to the Adoption
Centre looking for a cat that was harder to home than some
of the others. We were introduced to a black cat with the
most stunning big eyes. He was very nervous, hated large
spaces, and had to have a smaller pen than some of the other
cats. We loved him as soon as we saw him.

For about a month we had the door open and he never
came out to the rest of the house until one evening he walked
through and sat watching us. Since then his confidence has
grown and he is really happy. The satisfaction of seeing him
become confident and able to become such a happy cat has
been wonderful . . .

With Britain under fire from the air, rescuing cats meant just
that, saving them not just from some fallen moral state but
physically, from smashed homes and buildings, from trees and
gullies, from wherever they had sought refuge. And many
thousands of ordinary people rose magnificently in the cause.

The organised charity squads did the heavy work. As the
bombing of London's docks intensified, every day the staff of
Our Dumb Friends' League Whitechapel shelter found that
cats showed a universal will to cling to the wreckage. 'Many
piteous tales of cats seen roaming around the ruins of their

homes have reached us,' reported the League. They appealed to the public via local newspapers to 'take them home and wait for us to collect them'. But would-be rescuers just let the cats go again when 'someone failed to turn up in time'.

The League's Customs House and Plaistow District shelter in the London docks told the story of eight cats, trapped in a wood-yard; they had been there for some time before the League was notified. It took two months of patient feeding and building up of confidence before they managed to catch them.

The RSPCA sent a truck into the East End to collect 155 cats. The next day it was sent back to collect another seventy, which had 'reappeared in an endeavour to find their own homes. Cat traps and graspers [a kind of lasso on a pole] had proved their worth in this work.'

In Manchester, NARPAC Animal Guards were reported to be touring the city after heavy raids in winter 1940–1 on foot and by bicycle, organising relief for the 'wild, starving cats' of the city. Scraps of meat and fish from caterers and abattoirs had been collected and mixed with dried cat food stockpiled by the Committee. 'Thirty volunteer women reported the cats' whereabouts and distributed baskets of food to approved animals,' it was reported. 'They carry rope lassos to catch stray dogs, and cat waifs are brought to the lethal chamber.' Miss Rita Cannon, veterinary nurse at the Animal Defence Society's Mayfair HQ, would go out into the streets of the East End in search of pets in distress. She wrote:

> Everywhere the poor folk crowded round me, asking me to take dogs and cats. Many of the cats were so wild that they were difficult to catch, but the children were all helping me and, in the end, I filled the ambulance with animals. I have been up to [blank] Road with buckets of food and drink and went from street to street feeding the cats. As soon as I

appeared they rushed at me twenty and thirty at a time. They all but spoke. I have since paid two more visits to this district, each time bringing away the cats. All I could do for them was to give them merciful release from their suffering.

In Sheffield after the attacks of 12–13 December 1940, People's Dispensary rescue squads had to 'clamber over ruins to collect cats where the owners were dead or injured. Thirty-one animals were dealt with, alas mostly to be destroyed, through owners forgetting to take their pets when they sought shelter,' according to the *PDSA News*.

A cat buried for five days was 'found alive but died from shock very soon after rescue', *PDSA News* reported from the front line. 'Another cat from the same house was rescued, only to come back to the ruins wild with terror and would not let anyone approach it.'

After one raid on east London, an RSPCA inspector reported that 1,400 pets, mostly cats, had been 'found all apparently ownerless'. The ownership of some was traced but 'many of them were of the type that had no specific owners'.* 'In one East End street it took three months to round up 100 cats during early-morning and late-evening visits,' noted the Customs House and Plaistow District shelter of the ODFL.

The organised welfare squads worked by day. The cat ladies worked by night. Right at the beginning, in the first flush of abandoned pets, a Mrs Thornton went out on to the streets of Leytonstone at night, 'looking into churchyards and derelict houses for the victims of callous owners'. She told

---

* Communally tended semi-wild cats in some working-class areas had long survived the attention of the charitable destroyers by virtue of their own fecundity and the defensive militancy of tenement-dwelling cat ladies. The Blitz was their amazing new opportunity.

her story in an ODFL report: 'I noticed a large, old, black gaunt cat. He was starved and neglected. He sat upon a roof where I could never possibly get at him. I began to throw food out to him, and then I found that somehow he came into the factory at night, and I fed him secretly. Of course, he found the food and would wait hours for me to feed him.' Kindly Mrs Thornton was, after some time, able to catch him.

Mrs Lillian Lane of Regent's Park, north London, an Animal Guard from the earliest days, would feature in a newspaper article as the 'Florence Nightingale of Animals', going round north-west London on her bicycle with its NARPAC badges emblazoned on baskets fore and aft, which had 'become a two-wheeled animal ambulance'.

The Cat told a cheerful story in February 1941 about cats who 'refused to leave their bombed-out homes'. They had found 'a friend in London bus driver, Mr Arthur Heelas', who himself had lost his house to the Luftwaffe and knew how it felt. 'Every day he tours the district with food for his furry friends, who emerge from the ruins at the first sound of his footsteps . . .'

Mrs W. Slater of Harborne, Birmingham, was another independent. 'I have rescued hundreds of cats,' she told the *Daily Mirror* in early December 1940. 'Even while a house is burning, a cat will remain there. I throw the lasso cord over its neck and drag the cat out . . . Many of them are so badly injured they have to go into the lethal box immediately and last week three lorry-loads of dead cats were taken away from the city'; the heaviest attacks on the city had been in late November. Mrs Slater and her family had voluntarily become vegetarians, it was reported, 'so that the many cats she has rescued can have meat at her home'.

And Rita Cannon recalled: 'Someone asked me to go and see a poor old woman who lived in a tiny lodging where she kept a number of cats. I found her indescribably bedraggled in a room swarming with cats and kittens, which she had found homeless and befriended. Once convinced of my friendly intentions, she agreed gratefully to my coming back to fetch the cats. Most of these poor people will give their last crust to their cat or dog.'

The *Daily Mirror*, staunch propagandist for wartime cat rescue, made a big story out of a sixty-five-year-old widow, Mrs Caroline Roberts, who 'has fed hundreds of homeless cats in a heavily bombed district of London and every evening makes a fire in her sitting room just to make them feel at home where they doze after she has given them a good dinner of cats' meat, [plus illegally] bread and milk'.

One of the worst conundrums faced by rescuers was the delayed action or unexploded bomb (unforeseen in ARP planning), which meant whole streets might be roped off for days with pets locked in houses or roaming piteously in search of food. There are many accounts of amateur rescuers defying orders not to help them. It was reported:

> In a case heard at a south-west England [Plymouth] police court yesterday it was stated that Hettie Mary Symons defied a constable and risked a time bomb to feed her cat. She was fined £1. It was stated that she asked a War Reserve constable's permission to enter a cordoned area to feed her cat. He refused, but took the food to the cat himself; then he saw Symons in the area. 'I could not let the cat starve,' she told the court.

At least she had some food to give her cat. In fact, it would be food shortages that would disrupt the lives of the nation's cats far more than enemy action. There was no official ration. Housewives must queue for hours for horseflesh dyed green to have something to feed their pets. It was now illegal to give cats milk. Indeed, it was a criminal offence to give pets any food fit for human consumption – a driving reason for yet more abandonment and destruction. Whether they liked it or not, in order to survive, uprooted posh cats and stray cats alike were recruited into the feral colonies now taking over bomb sites and military camps, or surviving from pig-swill bins and cookhouse hand-outs. Some of them would self-perpetuate for years to come.* Displaced cats were very clever at finding new places of safety. Or temporarily so. Our Dumb Friends' League would report in its wartime history:

> The large numbers of stray cats taking refuge in factories was highlighted by the Hammersmith shelter's experience in 1942. 'Periodically Hammersmith is called in to reduce the number,' the report read. 'Kittens have been found under floorboards, cats are heard scampering behind the pipes and along the beams. Still these people will keep male and female animals together and then wonder why there are so many cats.'

But it could also report that 'as enemy attacks lessened . . . a shocking total of 24,070 animals were humanely destroyed in the shelters, over 19,000 of them cats. The majority of these were strays . . .' But thousands more survived in their industrial sanctuaries. The great feral tide was building.

After two years of war, in summer 1941, the Ministry of Food considered launching a clandestine anti-cat propaganda campaign in a bid to reduce numbers – not of strays this time, but of homed cats, whose illegal feeding was consuming

---

* On the Isle of Sheppey, Kent, the descendants of wartime mousers at an RAF airfield adapted to the post-war building of a prison on the site. Tended by auxiliary feeders they would prosper down seven decades. It would be reported: 'They don't interact with the prisoners, but a couple of inmates built them a shelter; although mainly the cats just go and hide in the surroundings.'

oceans of milk, so ministers were told, and whose nocturnal rampages were supposedly menacing Dig for Victory allotments of home-grown carrots and onions. Similar number-reducing moves against dogs were already underway, including 'discouraging charities from finding homes for strays'.

The statutory time for a lost dog to be kept in a police pound was reduced to three days. Plans for the enforced total mass destruction of all 'non-essential' animals were drawn up in secret. That meant compulsory euthanasia of the nation's pets.

The fate of the nation's cats hung in the balance. In late summer 1939 it had been their owners they should have feared most. Now it was the bureaucrats of the Ministry of Food.

But cats had an ally – mice. At this crucial stage in the battle to preserve the very lives of wartime cats, *The Cat* asked:

Is it antipatriotic to deprive the community of so many foodstuffs for one's own pleasure? If the cat were merely a pet, giving no service in return for his keep, the reply would be 'Yes'. But the cat is one of the best food protectors known. He saves the community literally millions of pounds worth of foodstuffs annually. Immense quantities are lost to rats and mice. No cat owner need worry about the rightness of keeping a cat in wartime.

Since the drift of evacuees back to the cities, people were evidently finding 'that mice were over-running their homes, eating their cereals and nesting in cupboards', it was reported. Just as during the slum-clearance era of the decade before, culling cats had left the territory wide open. Teeming, verminous hordes had taken over swathes of Coventry, Swansea and other bomb-blasted cities.

'There is a scarcity of cats,' the *Animal World* had proclaimed in February 1941, 'following the wholesale slaughter of domestic pets last year, and in the East End of London, many ruined buildings are infested with vermin'. Heart-warming pictures appeared in national newspapers of RSPCA staff out on the streets actually feeding plump, healthy-looking cats. The *Daily Mirror* captioned it *Help to the Homeless*. Just two years earlier, the same cats would have been rounded up and dispatched for mass destruction.

The following month Mr Harold Locking, Hon. Sec. of the RSPCA in the blitzed port of Hull, declared: 'The Dogs' Home van will on request collect stray cats in bombed areas . . . it is not in the interests of the city that all stray cats shall be destroyed. If residents in a district will undertake to feed them, much of the vermin that would otherwise find their way into unoccupied areas would be destroyed . . .'

And as the *Veterinary Record* could note in the summer:

> After a severe blitz, the collection of stray dogs and cats is a constant occupation, and while many are returned to their owners, or are provided with homes, there is always a number to be disposed of humanely.
>
> Cats are the most difficult to retrieve, and so long as they are not suffering or starving, the policy [to avert a vermin plague] is to let them remain and, thanks to a kindly public, many of them are regularly fed.

Street cats were an auxiliary army in the fight against the rodent enemy. And so were auxiliary feeders. Cat ladies were in the front line. They should do their patriotic work wherever cats might be found. Kindly people might even offer them the shelter of their own homes. Like the Home Guard platoon exercising in the church hall, cats from all classes were in this fight together.

'Official' cats in warehouses and government food stores had already long been busily engaged in keeping down rats and mice. At the end of 1941 Lord Woolton, the Minister for Food, announced that 'damaged milk powder' would be made available to cats – but only to cats 'on work of national importance'. He was referring only to those feline government employees – but very usefully for cats, the RSPCA, with all its establishment authority, advised immediately after the announcement that the Ministry would take 'a lenient view of reasonable feeding, as most homes have to keep cats to reduce the number of rats and mice'. Work of National Importance began at home.

Faced with an existential threat of mandatory destruction by government decree, cats had rescued themselves by doing what they did naturally. Stray cats and homed cats were now in the fight together. They would see it through to the end with all the solidarity that a wartime coalition of solitary predators could muster.

17

Consumer Cats

HOPEFUL

On Sunday 6 July, we were asked to take a cat who had given birth to two kittens earlier in the day, and who went on to have four more. Poor Hopeful was exhausted but miraculously Mum and kittens all survived. Hopeful has now found a home and went with another cat called Ollie who had been at the centre for a long time and was very nervous. Bon voyage both!

Cats emerged from the rubble of war with their tails held high. Although Britain's dogs might have had a 'better' war (several thousand loaned by the public had served directly with the Army and Air Force and had been given commemorative collars and medals for their distinguished service), cats had boosted morale as ships' cats and military mascots. After the great no-milk-for-cats near-disaster of 1942, they had been recognised both as vital rodent suppressors and family comforters on the Home Front.

But it had been tough all round. Let alone the mass panic killing of 1939 or civil servants plotting to eliminate all pets, homelessness had been the mortal danger. In London, Battersea had destroyed 77,217 'unclaimed stray' dogs brought in by police during the conflict, peaking in 1940–1 and 1944, so it was recorded at the end of the war. The ODFL's north

London Home accounted for 9,236. 'There is no statutory requirement on police as regards cats. No figures are therefore available about these animals,' wrote an official when an account of the wartime record was asked for by (for some reason) the Royal College of Surgeons. But many thousands had gone up in smoke and thousands more had gone underground.

Cats of national importance continued their hard work through the post-war years of austerity and reconstruction, as guardians of food stores and patrollers of government offices. There were numerous Post Office, factory and railway cats with sums formally allotted for their feeding and care. They were part of the British landscape.

There had recently been an important legal victory for cats. An old lady's cat-benefiting will had caused the usual ructions. Miss Dorothy Moss, cat-lover of Wimbledon, had died in July 1947 leaving half her estate in the intended form of a charitable trust to her friend Miss Heather Harvey, spinster, for use 'at her discretion for her work for the welfare of cats and kittens needing care and attention'. Disgruntled relatives ('Hobrough and others') contested its validity. Under the law, a charity had to be of 'public benefit'. Where was the human good in fussing over cats? It was reported:

> The evidence showed that Miss Harvey, for more than thirty-five years, had been sheltering stray cats and kittens and those no longer wanted by their owners [up to fifty at a time]. She found homes for some of the healthy ones, but if the cats and kittens were badly ill or hurt, or if she was unable to place them in homes, she had them put to sleep in chloroform lethal boxes.

Mr Justice Romer, having recalled his own judgment in the great Sarah Grove-Grady legacy case of two decades before, in which that lady's proposed utopian sanctuary where animals 'would be kept free from molestation by man' was deemed not to qualify as a charitable trust, now determined that Miss Moss's bequest was different. As he explained:

> . . . [One] has to see whether the present case passes . . . the test [of] whether the gift produces some benefit to mankind. In my judgement, it passes that test with honour. It seems to me that the care of and consideration for animals which through old age or sickness or otherwise are unable to care for themselves are manifestations of the finer side of human nature, and gifts in furtherance of these objects are calculated to develop that side and are, therefore, calculated to benefit mankind.* That is more especially so, perhaps, where the animals are domestic animals.

Hooray! That presiding truth which all cat-lovers had known from the beginning of cat-time was now enshrined in law. Solicitude for the welfare of cats, especially strays, was morally improving for human beings. Let the legacies flow!†

---

* 'The advancement of animal welfare' is one of the statutory descriptions of charitable purpose under the Charities Act 2006, provided that it is 'for the benefit of the public' in accordance with the Act.

† The Moss legacy case was soon followed by the release in 1951 of the Hollywood film *Rhubarb*, the story of an 'initially unlovable stray' that steals golf balls and is adopted by a millionaire, who leaves the cat a fortune including a baseball team.

Real-life strays continued to do well in legacies. 'Goofy' became a stray when his Sussex owner died in 1982 but 'RSPCA officials decided to capture it' when he was left £13,500 in owner John Smith's will. In 2003 eight-year-old tom cat 'Tinker' was left a north London house and trust fund by his adopter, Mrs Margaret Layne, on condition 'he did not stray again'. In 2011 Italian widow Maria Assunta left her £10 million fortune to 'Tommasino', a 'stray cat she had found and looked after because of her love for animals'.

The status of cats was changing – and not just in charity law. In the immediate post-war years, as sundered wartime households were remade, there was both a baby boom and a boom in pets. For family entertainment, a goldfish circling its humble bowl or a budgie in the parlour would have to do – plus a kitten or a puppy to keep the kiddies amused. They came from pet shops, in turn enjoying a high-street revival, something that invited official examination of the pet trade generally. The pet boom in part led to the UK Pet Animals Act 1951, which required 'any person keeping a pet shop to be licensed by the local council'. The selling of pets from market barrows (as in east London's Club Row) continued but was now subject to licence and inspection, while the door-to-door peddling of pets which had long been a way of disposing of kittens, was banned.

House cats meanwhile still had to subsist on a turgid regime of horse-meat and lowly scraps, but as the century passed the halfway mark, the new age of tinned cat food and kitty-litter was just a paw's stretch away. The nation itself stood on the threshold of TV-advertised consumer affluence and mass foreign holiday travel – things which would bring pet-related issues of their own. Better times were tangibly coming for cats generally.

But would homeless cats get any more consideration? Not yet. The semi-official protection they had enjoyed as rodent-removers was now at an end. And there were just so many of them, busily reproducing away on the urban moonscapes that the war had left behind. Bomb-site cats would get an unaccustomed moment of celebrity with a much-commented-upon photo essay, 'Cats of London' by photographer Thurston Hopkins. Published in February 1951 in *Picture Post* magazine, it featured 'alley-padding mogs . . . with no fixed address'. It was noted perceptively alongside:

Cats never spurn human company deliberately, they stray. This hand-written Lost Cat placard (right) remains full of emotional intensity after over a century. Did the Lewisham Black Cat with white whiskers ever make it home?

Strayed

On Sunday evening 3rd inst a Black Cat with black face, white whiskers white under the throat & Stomach, fore paws tipped with white, one hind leg partially white, the other all white with one black spot on it. WHOEVER will bring her to 5 East Place Avenue Road will be rewarded

Lewisham 6th April 1864

Queen Victoria was famously fond of dogs but her passion for cats became ever more apparent as her reign progressed. The RSPCA caught the mood in an illustrated account from May 1873 (above left) of a royal visit to a Scottish crofter's cottage when the Queen's collie frightened a cat to HM's acute displeasure.

The Society meanwhile campaigned tirelessly in its journal Animal World (above right) against the casual abandonment of cats. This 1881 engraving of a forsaken cat by animal artist R. H. Moore would be much reproduced.

Mrs Zoe Constance Morgan (above left, with her cat-collecting cart) was perhaps the biggest show-off of several fin de siècle cat-lady charitable entrepreneurs. Her self-proclaimed Royal Institution and Home for Lost and Starving Cats in Camden Town inspired huge jealously among her rivals. The destruction rate was total.

As it was at Miss Kate Cording's 'Animal Rescue League' based at Fellowship Cottage, Islington (above left), which in the space of ten years managed to drown or gas almost half a million street-caught cats. The RSPCA took over.

When the 'cat's house of London' was later left a fortune in an American cat lady's will, Zoe Morgan claimed it was hers (previous page, bottom left) but the Society got the cash and installed an electrocution chamber at the Angel, Islington, (seen top right in 1916 and bottom left a century later) killing an astonishing 1,500 cats a week. The founder's plaque (below) survives in the RSPCA archives.

THE SOCIETY

FOR THE

PROTECTION OF CATS.

PATRONS:—

THE DUKE AND DUCHESS OF BEDFORD, EARL PERCY.

STRAY HOME:	BOARDING HOME:

Gordon Cottage, Argyle Place,

King Street, Hammersmith.

THE chief object of this Society is to find a refuge for the many miserable and starving cats haunting the streets of London, for which purpose Homes are being established.

Any humane person may assist in this work by feeding a poor stray until it can be caught, and then sending it to the above Home. Margarine baskets are very suitable for this purpose, and can be purchased for 4d., and Carter Paterson or Pickford will carry cats from any part of London for 6d. Every endeavour is made to find good homes for the best cats, and a chloroform lethal chamber ends by a painless death the miseries of those for whom no homes can be found.

Good cats may be obtained. No cat is permitted to be taken from the Home without the consent of the Hon. Sec.

Pet cats or birds painlessly put away in Lethal Chamber for 1/-.

The Boarding Home is very roomy and comfortable, English Cats 2/6, Persians from 3/- per week.

The Veterinary Surgeon visits the home twice weekly. No charge is made unless a cat is ill, but it must be distinctly understood that the Hon. Sec. shall be permitted to expend 5/- in case of any sudden necessity, while awaiting communication from the owner.

No cats can be admitted whilst suffering from an infectious disease, but arrangements can be made for surgical cases.

Every care is taken of the cats, but the Society cannot hold itself responsible in case of the death of any cat.

Visitors are welcomed between the hours of 2.30 and 5, except Sundays.

The Committee are most anxious to raise £400 in order to purchase premises, just taken. Donations and subscriptions will be most gratefully acknowledged, and further information supplied, by Mrs. Gordon, Hon. Sec., 7, Nevern Road, Earl's Court.

Our Dumb Friends' League opened cats' shelters across the capital from the 1900s. Its Fulham Road operation (top left) looked cosy but the destruction rate was total. Mrs Alice Gordon's pioneer Society for the Protection of Cats, Hammersmith, was taken over by the ODFL (left) in 1910. A Blue Cross hospital still operates on the site a hundred years later.

The pioneer Mayhew Home, Kensal Green, was taken over and rebuilt by the RSPCA (detail inset, bottom right) but kept a few cats alive in line with its founder's principles. Operating independently on the same site, it remains a beacon of cat welfare after over a century.

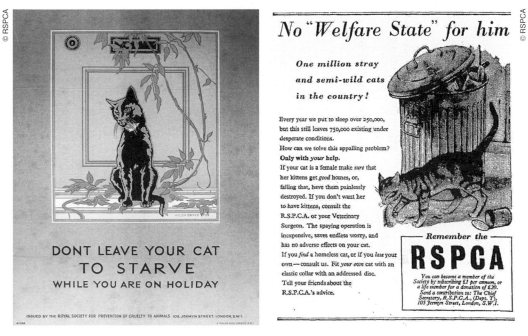

DONT LEAVE YOUR CAT
TO STARVE
WHILE YOU ARE ON HOLIDAY

ISSUED BY THE ROYAL SOCIETY FOR PREVENTION OF CRUELTY TO ANIMALS. 105. JERMYN STREET. LONDON, S.W.1.

No "Welfare State" for him

One million stray
and semi-wild cats
in the country!

Every year we put to sleep over 250,000,
but this still leaves 750,000 existing under
desperate conditions.
How can we solve this appalling problem?
Only with *your* help.
If your cat is a female make *sure* that
her kittens get *good* homes, or,
failing that, have them painlessly
destroyed. If you don't want her
to have kittens, consult the
R.S.P.C.A. or your Veterinary
Surgeon. The spaying operation is
inexpensive, saves endless worry, and
has no adverse effects on your cat.
If you *find* a homeless cat, or if you *lose* your
own — consult us. Fit *your own* cat with an
elastic collar with an addressed disc.
Tell your friends about the
R.S.P.C.A.'s advice.

Remember the
RSPCA
*You can become a member of the
Society by subscribing £1 per annum, or
a life member for a donation of £20.
Send a contribution to: The Chief
Secretary, R.S.P.C.A., (Dept. T),
105 Jermyn Street, London, S.W.1.*

The RSPCA meanwhile kept up campaigns against summer abandonment (top left a poster from the 1920s) and for sterilisation (top right press ad from the 1950s) while opening veterinary clinics that offered more than just destruction (below left, the waiting room at the Animal Rescue League, Islington, c. 1950).

Meanwhile, the Cats Protection League, founded in 1927, set out a new moral imperative with feline champion Mrs Nerea de Clifford (below right) advancing the impossible-seeming idea of 'rehoming' as well as neutering. Taking off from the 1960s, it was a moral revolution in the affairs of cats.

Wartime bombing of British cities forced millions of cats into the streets. The cat ladies' happy time was back again (top left, Mrs Caroline Roberts feeds East End cats, November 1940) and continued post-war, feeding their myriad descendants in the ruins (centre, near St Pauls' Churchyard, for example, c. 1960), while striving to keep the exterminators off the scent. The Blue Cross charity called them 'grotesque sentimentalists'.

Celia Hammond (left) meanwhile made cat rescue look more glamorous. In 1969, she was filmed tending London cats with fellow model Sue Gunn.

A cultural shift in attitudes saw the stray cat being ever more celebrated in films like 'Rhubarb', 1951. Even the cat lady would be culturally rehabilitated, like Mrs Scratchen Post in the 2014 Lego Movie (below).

© Lego/Norton

By the new century rescue cats were top cats (from top to bottom) – at home in Downing Street ('Larry' prepares for royal wedding), as pets for pop stars (Florence Welch and Battersea rescue 'Missus'), and were the subjects of bestselling books and films ('Street Cat Bob'). Charities airbrushed their past record of mass-killing to fit the new mood. These 2016 Liverpool ferals meanwhile looked grateful for some old fashioned street feeding.

Most of them have sad histories, there's a bomb somewhere back in the family records. War made their parents homeless . . . [now] they hunt in the daytime in the country growths that have blown to the heart of London . . .

They were glamorous outriders of the hipster strays that would be so fashionable in the decade to come. As to numbers, during a well-publicised cat-stealing trial in 1953, the prominent barrister, Mr Michael Sherrard, acting for the defence,* had made headlines with his apparently well researched claim that there were '500,000 stray cats in London'. Although animal welfare societies could not precisely quantify the cat population of Great Britain, it was reported:

The total has been variously estimated to lie between 5 million and 7 million. If, as has been further suggested, from 8 to 10 per cent of cats are probably strays, there may be 500,000 or more stray cats in the United Kingdom, and 200,000 of them may live in Greater London.

Other estimates for the capital varied from '250,000 to 500,000'. The authoritative-seeming figures given in the court case could be worked out from the destruction rates of strays as reported by the charities. The People's Dispensary for Sick Animals was 'putting 20,000 cats painlessly to sleep every year at its dispensaries', it was said. In 1951, Our Dumb Friends' League had destroyed 86,000. 'The RSPCA destroys something over 100,000 cats a year in England and Wales,' so it was reported blandly. 'Between them, these three organisations alone remove 200,000 unwanted cats every year.'

---

* After the defendant's conviction for stealing eleven cats for sale to 'research centres', Mr Sherrard was said to have been 'threatened by cat-lovers'.

So there it was – after a wartime amnesty the welfare charities had returned to the old street-cleaning routine of trap and destroy with the same moral excuse. 'It was altogether kinder that way.' There was no debate. The PDSA, for example, were summoned in 1949 to deal with a cat crisis at the Tower of London. They did so willingly. A Dispensary official said:

> Not only are the Quartermaster's stores in danger of being invaded by cats, but the yeoman in charge of the Tower's ravens [had informed him] that the cats are also attacking his birds. The sleek, well-fed, respectable cats who live sedate lives in the homes of the officials at the Tower hardly dare to poke their noses outside the back door for fear of being set upon.

The wild cats were 'defying all efforts to catch them by hand. If this does not succeed, we put traps down baited with fish and other titbits.' The outcome was predictable. According to the PDSA man:

> Once caught, the kindest thing is to kill the cats painlessly as they are never happy in captivity and cannot be domesticated. One cat-lover persuaded us to let her have two wild kittens we had caught in hope of domesticating them but it was no good. After the kittens had nearly scratched her to pieces, they were put to sleep.

It was further reported: 'The official said that the cats were descendants of domestic cats who were Blitzed out of their homes during the war. They are very cunning and become quite clever at looking after themselves.' They would have to be.

Such cats had once been largely a rural phenomenon, living in barns and grain stores with minimal human contact. Now they were everywhere – doing best naturally enough where there was most food – and there was more food in cities even amid continuing rationing and austerity. Cat ladies would make sure it was so. The battle between the charitable exterminators and the nocturnal cat-comforters had been resumed. As it was reported in *The Times* in 1952:

> Londoners may not know [that] cats have made a home in more than one bombed area and depend on the charity of the kind-hearted. The history of these cats began when a number, terrified by the destruction of their homes, took refuge in the ruined basements . . . There they remained, living precariously . . . In time the wild grasses and willow herb softened the outlines of their bricky wilderness and even converted it into a miniature jungle that, in summer at least, cannot be unpleasing to the cat-like mind.
>
> Their lives, however, would have remained nasty, brutish and short if it had not been for the kindness of one Londoner. She, a working woman, first saw the cats in the bombed areas which lie on the slopes of Ludgate Hill between the railway viaduct and Water Lane. She . . . realised that they must be starving. From that day – it is now six years ago – she has brought scraps of fish and other food to supplement their diet.

There was another bomb-site colony of cats, 'off Eagle Street in Holborn [which were] also under her care. The Holborn cats were slightly better off, for they live in a residential area where they had already attracted the attention of householders nearby. The woman noticed, however, that while scraps of food were thrown from time to time, no one thought of giving them anything to drink . . . When the cats breed, as they do frequently, she takes it on herself to look after the kittens. Where possible she finds homes for these – she has four in her own house – otherwise she has them painlessly destroyed.'

The anonymous Holborn feeder was clearly not alone. The wartime cat ladies had never demobilised. They would be described by one feline chronicler as the 'underground movement of the cat world':

> It is not easy to find out who they are. A chance Christian name may sometimes come your way; if you know one feeder they may disclose that another feeder comes after or before them on account of the dishes left there.

They stayed mysterious and anonymous, not because they feared ridicule or for their position in society, but were fearful of all officialdom, the council officials and their contractors who would trap and eliminate the objects of their devotion. Blue Cross (the renamed ODFL), never shy about its robust approach, would describe those 'ignorant people feeding cats on bomb sites' as 'grotesque sentimentalists' – appealing meanwhile in its winter 1958 journal for funds to continue the merciful work of rescuing 5,000 London strays per year from their misery. 'Hundreds of kittens could be saved', the charity conceded, but 'the rest are so wild they could cause serious injury to anyone trying to handle them'.

The war had impacted on cats' relationships with humans in other significant ways. Evacuated and bombed-out cats parted from their original owners had found plenty of wartime well-wishers to take them in. A principle had been established. It might seem that cats in trouble of whatever age could find new loving homes.

As well as its educational and neutering-campaigning (especially females), the Cats Protection League was now striving to establish dedicated 'shelters' to provide what they described as 'a temporary refuge' for cats in need. But the financial outlay was daunting. In 1950 it had received a legacy specifically for that purpose. A sprawling property in Haslemere, Surrey, was taken on as the site for a 'boarding home'. This was pretty new. Nor had the League's wartime campaign to find new homes for homeless cats been forgotten. Indeed, it seemed to be an idea which people might subscribe to, all over again.

For example, reporting the post-war boom in bomb-site cats it was stated in *The Times* that the RSPCA 'found homes last year [1952] for nearly 8,000 cats . . .' while it was 'easier to find a home for a dog than for a cat', so the charity had found. On the novel idea of finding new homes for cats, one Scottish newspaper commented:

> [Cats] are attached, either by choice or through adversity, to one human habitation. It is eloquent of the place cats have gained in the domestic arrangements of man that if one of these animals does not have a home, the conclusion is that it ought to have. The animals, for the most part, share that opinion . . .

Those lowlier cats that had catapulted across class barriers were also prospering as adoptees in their smart new homes. The Duchess of Hamilton's sanctuary in Wiltshire, Ferne, was as full of cats as it had ever been. It was reported that 'Maggie' and 'Rosie' – a black and white Manx and a tabby – had been evicted from their home in Salisbury and would have been destroyed. They had adopted Mr Colsey, the ducal butler at Ferne House, and 'refuse food given by anyone else; they also refuse to live anywhere but in the rose garden'.

The 1950s generally were proving good for cats. The number of owned felines climbed to more than five million, to overtake dogs as domestic pets some time towards the end of the decade. Dogs, subject to the purchase of a licence, actually fell in number, according to a report:

Animal welfare societies attribute the fall-off to the great spread of council housing estates and flats where dogs are frequently banned, coupled with the growing number of married women who go to work and, sensibly enough, decide to forgo the added responsibility of a dog about the house.

They would rather have a nice cat instead. And now with the arrival of commercial TV in 1956, cats were to be increasingly 'commoditised' both for what they were and what they ate. They were a burgeoning new consumer group (a bit like teenagers) to which, via their female human owners,* an ever more sumptuous range of tinned feline food would be offered, not just in pet shops but in chain grocery stores and the shiny new supermarkets. The cats'-meat man was ancient history.

To attend to their further needs, the British Small Animal Veterinary Association was formed in 1957 by a forward-looking group of practitioners who, as it would be said, 'saw the small animal (dog first, then cat) as a suitable recipient for a new type of scientifically driven veterinary medicine, where cost was not always a limiting factor in deciding upon treatment, as it was with [farm] livestock'.† The Feline Advisory

---

* Mrs Nerea de Clifford, pillar of the Cats Protection League, noted in her mould-breaking three-year study of 200 TV-watching cats – published in 1963 as *What British Cats Think About Television* – that: 'Most cats show an interest of some kind, though it is often of hostility', and further, 'generally cats are not interested in TV once the novelty has worn off. But when they do react, it is usually to sudden, quick movements, possibly likening them to the flight of birds or the creep of a mouse.'

† Vets had traditionally been a country-based profession, concerned with livestock and horses. As horse use declined rapidly in towns, they had turned to companion animals as their newly lucrative practice. Treating cats was always sensitive. *Our Cats* had noticed a tendency for the servants to smirk when a vet arrived at a grand Edwardian house to treat a cat. A hundred years later it would be written: 'In veterinary circles in the 1970s, male vets with interests in feline medicine could be thought of as "wearing suede shoes", a euphemism for homosexuality.'

Bureau ('FAB – We Know About Cats') was founded the same year, to raise the life-science profile of cats and the application of good practice by commercial breeders and boarding catteries. Advice on setting up and running cat-rescue shelters would follow.

Cats were 'members of the family', sharing the bounty of the new age of affluence. The Animal Medical Center in New York was even referring to cats and dogs as 'companion animals', so the bemused *Pet Trade Journal* told its startled British readers in June 1960. Whatever next?

The great 1950s pet-food explosion showed just where modernist hep-cats were going. Only yesterday's cats tolerated leftovers to eat or put up with indoor earth toilets. Cat litter was another wondrous innovation. The mighty Petfoods Ltd. of Melton Mowbray was 'spending ten times as much on TV advertising as any of its competitors', so the *Pet Trade Journal* reported in 1959, 'and uses as one of its chief ingredients, more than half the whale meat imported into the UK'. So that is what it was.

'Many hardened scrap-users still refuse to tamper with their pets' familiar diet and manufacturers have devised [as well as TV advertising] elaborate sales promotion schemes to break down their resistance,' so the magazine reported.

And the brands kept coming – 'Pussikin', 'Perky' ('keeps cats healthy, sleek and satisfied'), 'Whiskas' and 'New Whiskas' ('builds cats to be proud of'), 'Spratt's Fish for Cats' ('just what your cat needs'), 'Queenie' ('keeps your cat in first-class form'), 'Minx' ('inside satisfaction, outside protection'), 'Kit-E-Kat' ('the complete cat food'), 'Mish', 'Wise Cat' ('well balanced and delicious'), 'Happy Cat', 'Sprinkle' ('just add water'), 'Wow', 'Zest' and 'Tucker Box' ('contains no rabbit'). In 1958 Spratt's launched 'Top Cat', an event that would have a cultural significance for cats that extended way beyond the feeding bowl.

Then there was 'Felix' ('crisp and crunchy'), advertised by 'Felix' himself, 'the beautiful thoroughbred, Colour Point [Siamese] whose every move is aristocratic', as he was described. Out of all of these, in 1960 the Consumer Association could recommend Kit-E-Kat (the cheapest) as the best value, even if, like the rest of the products, it was more than 40 per cent water. It cost ten old pence a day to feed a cat – along with kitchen scraps, milk and bread.

There were few obese cats. Neutering was something for better-off owners and vaccination was a novelty.

Affluence was not all good for cats. The *Animal World* reported a story of a cat being presented to an RSPCA Inspector with a demand for it to be put down by a couple because it did not complement the new decor of their home. As well as not matching the new curtains, excuses for dumping cats ranged from 'we're going to Spain on holiday' to 'they keep having kittens' or 'they're ruining my lawn'. At least they were given up to some sort of care. Many more were just left by some roadside.

Shiny new urban motorways were barging through Britain's cities. Birmingham CPL reported mass cat abandonment by 'many families' – whole streets full of strays – and cats being pulled from rebuilding rubble just like in the war. The high-rise blocks that were supplanting humble terraces were universally council-enforced cat-free zones.

Greed and callousness went with affluence. *The Cat* had a story of the death of an old lady, after which the relatives descended, stripped the house of furniture and turned her cats out on to the street. Across the Atlantic, the US Humane Society would later blame 'working women' and family breakdown for the new heartlessness: 'the cat and the dog . . . are now subject to the same whims of affection and rejection that characterize human relationships'. Throwaway pets were new versions of the forsaken animals that the Edwardian cat ladies had considered it a higher duty to put out of their misery.

Mass package holidays meant a new wave of midsummer abandonment by the cat-owning working class – and one holidaymaker in Tunisia complained that it had all been spoiled by the sight of so many starving cats.

But there would be unlooked-for benefits for cats. The end of coal fires would mean no more hot ashes and therefore fewer metal dustbins in the streets. New-fangled plastic food refuse bags would one day be a boon for not-so-choosy cats prepared to have a go with their claws. It was like that wondrous wartime episode when there was a pig-swill bin at the end of every street. Just like then, the pickings would be good for another feline character whose time was coming round again.

Out there in the darkness, the third feline estate were also benefiting from the rising tide of affluence, sustained by their adoring nocturnal minders and the bricky warmth of the city. In fact, bomb-site cats were teeming, several generations removed from their Blitzed-out domesticated forebears.

At the start of the 1960s, fifteen years after the last V2 rocket had fallen on London, there were cats in royal parks and in fashionable squares. There were cats in mental hospitals and street markets. There were cats at the Tower and in the vast bomb-blasted wilderness around St Paul's Cathedral. There were cats in Knightsbridge and in Kennington. There was a colony in Green Park round Pall Mall – not far from the decades-old feline-free zone that was Buckingham Palace. Were they to be tolerated or eradicated? Some people seemed to like them; plenty of lunchtime sandwiches were going their way.

'The grandest colony I have ever seen was in Harley Street,' wrote a later visitor to the exclusive enclave of private medical consulting rooms where, in the garden of an elegant house, numerous cats were being fed on best mince from Harrods Food Hall three times a day by the butler of a society lady.

Another colony inhabited the 'warm, rabbit-warren basements' of the British Museum in Bloomsbury; perhaps it was the Egyptian connection – although it was reported that they 'did not get into the galleries'. They had been there for as long as anyone could remember, and their presence had been tolerated until some staff members started complaining of the prevalence of fleas. At last, Mr D. L. Paisey, the Museum's Assistant Secretary, would complain to the Ministry of Works when it came to a crunch in October 1963: 'There are some hundreds of cats on the Museum premises, all of which are quite wild.'

'The ridding of the Museum of stray cats is not a service that can be undertaken by this Ministry,' came the reply. The Ministry of Agriculture in turn feebly suggested some kind of physical catproofing. The Animal Rescue League did a bit of desultory trapping, but more cats just moved in. A 'Sunday shoot with beaters' was suggested, but it was pointed out that this would be illegal. One faction of the staff and lots of public sympathisers kept feeding the Museum felines, in spite of stern DO NOT FEED THE CATS! warnings.

Although it was strictly Cats Protection League policy not to concern itself, news from the wild side kept turning up in their magazine, *The Cat*. As London was rebuilt, the bombsite cats must move on. The League's house journal ran a hugely evocative piece about the cats around St Paul's Cathedral, once 'the Mecca of cats' but now a giant building site. A certain C. B. Cousins wrote about a little, now departed, black Siamesey cat she used to feed: where was she now? In January 1963 she said this:

Most of the cats are gone to where no one knows. Some were taken to homes, the rest vanished in that inscrutable way cats have. All except poor old Fluffyduffy who is old now but who was once a beautiful young black Persian tom cat. He now sits very bewildered in the Car Park trying to stay warm . . . a remote and dejected figure – all his cat friends departed.

There were stories about a thirty-strong colony at the Tate Gallery, Millbank, tended by a Mr Milton who found homes for the kittens at London County Council-run old people's homes. There was another at the LCC headquarters, County Hall, on the south bank of the Thames, where a certain Mr Midge, a messenger, was feeding them daily at 6 p.m. The League had sent a parcel of food. The family of fourteen strays 'was controlled by a female called "Bonzo Number One"', so it was reported.

There was outrage too in the same September 1962 issue at the report of 'the shooting by a pest control firm of about fifty cats at Barking Power Station'. 'This horror must not be repeated', said *The Cat*, which demanded 'a top-level probe'.

Quite right too. For years to come, the wild cats of British cities that managed to dodge the eradicators would breed and multiply. It could not go on for ever.

18

Cool Cats

NO NAME

I'm looking to rehome my 7-year-old BENGAL cat. He was abandoned outside my house about 18 months ago, and we tried to find the owner, but no one came forward so we took him in. He's a lovely-natured cat, but requires a sensitive diet.

Outside of these ailments, he is a lovely cat, affectionate, likes to know when someone is going to be around, and cuddles in with me at night. I think he has come along a lot since we first found him, and he has become more settled, which is why I am trying to find a way to continue his regained confidence.

By the middle of the nineteenth century, the cat, companion of witches, creature of the night, had begun to be culturally de-demonised. A hundred years later, the skulking stray was about to go through the same transformation. Some cat-lovers were beginning to think that the fallen domesticated cat also had the right to life, liberty (on terms to be negotiated) and the pursuit of feline happiness, whatever that might be. A change of mind was in the wind. Feline TV capers would give it a nudge.

Human cultural politics had already led the way. Advertisers, film-makers, TV soaps and writers of the beatnik 1950s into the Swinging Sixties were falling over themselves to promote all things working-class. Just like the extraordinary (and one-off) moment when the Duchess of Bedford sat down with the cats'-meat men of London sixty years before, no uptown event was complete without the presence of a gritty working-class pop singer or actor. The cats'-meat men had sadly vanished.

Just so, the stray cat, child of the streets, was all of a sudden wildly fashionable. In the paw-steps of the 1951 movie *Rhubarb*, the Hanna-Barbera cartoon *Top Cat* ruled TV screens in 1961–2 – first in the US then in Britain – with its fabulously cool feline fables played out among the dustbin-dwelling alley cats of New York City, pursued not by the Midnight Band of Mercy, but by Officer Dibble. What Disney's Bambi had done for deer, TC did for stray cats.

In the middle of its first thirty-show run, the legendary title sequence for the film *Walk on the Wild Side* coincidentally appeared in cinemas, featuring a lithe black tom cat on the nocturnal prowl. It became iconic. In the 1961 Hollywood movie, *Breakfast at Tiffany's*, Audrey Hepburn's gamine credentials were immeasurably boosted by her ragamuffin cat, 'Cat' – played on screen by the talented animal actor and *Rhubarb*-star, 'Orangey', along with several stand-ins. The writer Paul Gallico's book *Silent Miaow* of 1964, ostensibly written by a stray cat, was a 'manual' for opportunist felines on how to take over otherwise cat-indifferent homes. They were pretty good at it. Stray cats were top cats.

TC and the gang's back-street, dustbin-dwelling status had a further significance. A distinction was beginning to be made in American cat-rescue circles between so-called 'alley cats' and 'strays'. Efforts were being made generally to get everyone, not necessarily just cat ladies, to take more responsibility for the free-roaming cats they fed and tolerated in their backyards and porches. A 'stray' cat was defined as a 'once-homed waif' who could and should be adopted, according to humane literature of the era.

But an 'alley cat' taken off the streets and placed in a shelter was considered to be much less likely to find a home because it knew no home but the street. It was a recognition of the existence of the third feline estate – out there in the shadows, the cats that had taken over London bomb sites, the Liverpool docks and the crevices of American cities – the semi-wild cats, the feral cats. Their time was coming.

BBC Television had a terrific run with *Top Cat* but had to change the title to *Boss Cat* because of its sensitivities on commercial advertising: the cat food of the same name was being pushed on the other channel. Cat food advertisements also introduced several live-action celebrity strays. In 1966 'Arthur', the paw-spooning Kattomeat cat, would begin his garlanded TV career. Arthur, a neutered tom also known briefly as 'Samantha' – it's complicated – already had a back-story more exotic than most. It seems generally acknowledged that he was a 'stray facing destruction' aged about four when he came into his original owner's possession. He would have plenty more adventures, including court appearances, kidnap and a diplomatic incident.

France would be briefly transfixed by 'la chatte Félicette', a black and white 'stray from the streets of Paris' (others claim she was obtained from a dealer, but let's discount that) who, on 18 October 1963, made a 100-mile ascent atop a Véronique rocket above the Sahara Desert and then returned to earth safely via parachute capsule. After three months of observation at the space medicine lab in Paris, Félicette was 'put to sleep'. A second cat died in an abortive launch. No wonder France's space strays were made so little fuss over, although the Comoros Islands issued a commemorative stamp in 1992.

And in America there was Morris, 'discovered' by an animal talent scout in 1968 on the brink of being destroyed at the Hinsdale Humane Society shelter in Chicago. The following year he made his TV debut for '9 Lives' cat food, while being described as 'the world's most finicky cat'.* It was rapidly becoming the case that charity stray cat elimination squads could no longer solicit donations for their work with such moral certainty. After all, they were lining up TC and his pals Chooch and Benny, and now Morris and Arthur for euthanasia.

The BBC's flagship children's programme, *Blue Peter*, introduced a cat in May 1964. They missed a trick. 'Jason', curled up on presenter Valerie Singleton's lap, was a very regal Seal Point Siamese. He joined full-time after appearing in one show with his mother, brother and sister when a three-week-old kitten. Mumsie *Blue Peter* was not quite ready for the stray invasion – but it would come.

Cat consumer goodies meanwhile were all over television. Could unwanted cats in search of homes themselves be 'commoditised'? In 1960 the very first pets for adoption had appeared on the BBC TV *Wednesday Magazine* hosted by the affable David Jacobs. It was on in the afternoon following *The Flowerpot Men*. Pet author Josephine Hunter fragrantly unveiled a series of cats and dogs in search of good homes, with a uniformed RSPCA Inspector hovering uncomfortably in the background. It was an instant hit.

Not to be outdone, grubby commerce had a go. In summer 1968 something called the Animal News Service announced a 'home-finding' plan centred on pet shops across the nation with newspaper adverts running nationwide under a photograph of an appealing kitten and a heading saying: *Please, Does Anyone Want Me?* It went on:

---

* Like Arthur, the Kattomeat cat, Morris underwent several *Dr Who*-style regenerations. In 2015, Morris IV was on Facebook.

> Thousands of healthy kittens are destroyed each year because good homes cannot be found for them. If you have kittens you cannot place and want a good home guaranteed – take them along to any of the pet stores listed below.

The Cats Protection League reacted with deep alarm. League Secretary Mr Steward announced: 'From years of experience I have found that there is often much more in finding good homes for kittens than appears on the surface . . . The way to deal with the problem of unwanted kittens is to stop it at source – by spaying and neutering.'

The Animal News Service turned out to be a front for the mighty Petfoods Ltd., makers of Whiskas and Kit-E-Kat. It was a sales promotion scheme: everyone loved kittens, even unwanted ones. But it was a little breakthrough in the wider cause – TV and a pet food company putting a whisker or two into the Good Homes Wanted business. That could not be a bad thing, surely? Maybe older cats might be next. The point had been made. 'Re-homing' could be a practical reality – and a little innovative marketing could speed it along.

There was a whisper on the wind that animals generally might not just be there to be eaten, petted and cast aside when no longer convenient. The Irish novelist Brigid Brophy published a famous essay in the *Sunday Times* in October 1965 with the attention-grabbing title, *The Rights of Animals*, which dramatically stripped pet welfare of its fusty vegetarian Edwardian garb and plonked it on the tables of trendy north London. When promoted afterwards by the Animal Defence Society, the imagery featured the author clutching an enormous tabby.

This cultural shift in feline affairs found the charities suddenly being much more discreet about the destruction of strays. The Animal Rescue League was barely mentioned in the RSPCA's reports* and its affairs had disappeared from the pages of the *Animal World*. Conscious that old-style mass destruction was ever less palatable, a big change of direction had already begun, led this time by the other-wise ultra-cautious RSPCA. It had effectively started when the Old Etonian Chairman of the Bath Cats and Dogs Home, insurance broker Mr John Hobhouse (later to be National Chairman), was elected to the RSPCA Council. At his small animal shelter at Claverton Down he was an exponent of as little putting down of animals as possible.

The former RAF officer worked hard to establish a new sub-committee within the RSPCA to focus on 'Homeless Animals', with himself as Chairman. That itself was pretty radical. When it came to announce the programme in January 1958, the plight of stray dogs and cats would be dramatically described as being 'the biggest issue in animal welfare'. It was a statement that would come back to haunt him.

'Because the number of cats, homeless, unwanted and strays is so vast, the RSPCA is concentrating first on this aspect of the problem,' it was announced. British dogs did not live semi-wild and, for all sorts of reasons, the number of stray dogs was falling. Not so cats. The Society had been doing a bit of scientific research – an early outrider of the many, much more extensive stray and feral-cat studies to come. In a remarkable turn-round of policy, the Homeless Cat Sub-committee reported:

---

* In 1964 the RSPCA did, however, pocket a large sum from a hugely contested will left to animal charities by former Wimbledon tennis finalist, Mrs Phyllis Satterthwaite, part of which was in the Animal Rescue League's name. Like the contested Ewen will case of 1913–21, the testatrix had written garbled details on a brown paper bag of animal charities she had vaguely heard of. The League was among them.

Unlike the dog, the cat can adapt herself to a semi-wild state and once that state is achieved, has the pleasure of complete freedom and, although often hungry, this cat is reasonably happy.

It was more a moral judgement than a scientific fact, but a century of sentimentalised certainty about merciful killing had been overturned at a stroke. The very radical declaration continued:

For this reason the RSPCA is not in favour of collecting these healthy semi-wild cats for humane destruction unless they are ill or injured . . . a great many of them do the valuable job of keeping down vermin.

So leave them alone. But 're-homing', as it would one day come to be called, was also impractical:

The RSPCA does not believe in catching and placing semi-wild cats in new homes as the genuine stray does not settle down to a domestic life where freedom is curtailed, and many of them die of cat flu or enteritis . . .

For the 'unwanted cat, whose numbers form the great majority of strays', there was, however, better news. '[These] unhappy and lonely creatures whom we catch up whenever possible, particularly young males, are often placed in new homes by the Society. Last year [1957] 12,206 were so placed,' said the report. Getting overall population numbers down would need a neutering campaign, and public education to reduce abandonment and make people aware of the dangers of cats stowing away on vans and general nocturnal wanderings. Emotive press ads appeared, revealing both the astonishing overall numbers and just how many the Society was killing:

No Welfare State for him:
One million stray and semi-wild cats in the country! Every
year we put to sleep over 250,000, but this still leaves 750,000
existing under desperate conditions. How can we solve this
appalling problem? Only with your help. If your cat is a
female, make sure that her kittens get good homes, or, failing
that, have them painlessly destroyed. If you don't want her to
have kittens, consult the RSPCA or your Veterinary Surgeon.
The spaying operation is inexpensive, saves endless worry,
and has no adverse effects on your cat . . .

The Secretary of the Research Defence Society – the British
lobby group for animal experimentation – made an unfortunate response: 'The RSPCA has recently conducted a survey
of stray cats in this country, thereby drawing attention to a
state of affairs of which none of us can feel proud,' said Dr
William Lane-Petter in a letter to *The Times*. 'They quote
figures of 250,000 cats and 100,000 dogs destroyed each year
. . . mostly by the RSPCA itself . . . [but the Society] stead-
fastly refuses to supply any of these animals to laboratories
carrying out medical research.'

Would it not save tax-payers' money all round, so he
argued, if the muddle-headed charity could be induced to do
so? What was the difference between being lethalled in an
RSPCA clinic and being experimented upon under anaesthesia? Although Dr Lane-Petter, who was also Director of
the Medical Research Council Laboratory Animals Bureau,
did not point it out, across the US, municipalities were legally
obliged to raise revenue by turning impounded stray dogs
over to institutions for 'research purposes' in a process known
as 'pound seizure'.

His intervention was a clumsily insensitive throwback to
the days of the Brown Dog riots, but it glaringly showed up
just how many cats were still being 'painlessly' killed in the

name of animal welfare. It also boosted the morale of the amateur street-cat-killers, still out there with their lethal boxes, determined to save poor pussy from vivisection, fear of which was still the biggest obstacle to the acceptance of home-finding for adult cats.

The very radical-seeming homeless animal initiative was complemented in 1960 by the success of the Society's long campaign to bring the abandonment of pets within existing cruelty laws. Under the new 'Abandonment of Animals Act', owners leaving an imprisoned pet with a few bowls of cat food, or 'casting away animals' – a phenomenon of mass car ownership, with cat dumping combined with a 'joy-ride' – would now face prosecution and three months in prison. The forsaken cats of Victorian Belgravia might get their ghostly day in court. But according to the peerless cat historian, Sarah Hartwell: 'Owners would try to make out that the cat was not theirs but a stray. Ownership was generally impossible to prove when new-born kittens were abandoned; this being a common abuse which could bring conviction for cruelty even before the 1960 . . . Act.'

More was to come a year later when the RSPCA embarked on a programme, as it announced, of turning local branches into actual shelters. 'In every large town we aim to have a shelter which can take over the police responsibility for [lost] dogs and provide a temporary home and merciful end for cats.' Liverpool's strays (fed by dockers, apparently) were especially in need of attention. But as well as old-style mass putting to sleep, there might be a chance of redemption in the shape of a new good home, backed by a sound money-raising reason, according to Mr Hobhouse: 'A great number of legacies received by the Society are the direct outcome of the love of a cat or dog adopted from one of our homes,' he declared in the *Animal World*.

Meanwhile the Society pursued its usual business of show-casing its prosecutions for cruelty – every issue of its journal having *Warning: Horror Pictures Inside* and a centre spread of cruelly abused cats and dogs provoking disgust and despair at the human condition and, it was to be hoped, a legacy heading for Jermyn Street. It would go on like this for decades.

For the welfare charities, big or small, home finding was still largely a question of 'make it up as you go along'. BBC TV's *Wednesday Magazine*'s Adopt-a-Pet was a tiny experiment. Branches did what they could by word of mouth and by who-wants-a-cat intelligence gathering. For individuals it was a small ad in the paper or newsagent's window: *Good Homes Wanted* or *Kittens Free to Good Home*. But at least the RSPCA was pursuing the revolutionary idea of looking for new homes for adult cats that were unwanted or stray for whatever reason.

This was a challenge to which the Cats Protection League must respond. But how? 'Are we getting any nearer to formulating an active policy on Homeless Cats and Kittens?' So Albert Steward asked at the outset of 1960 in *The Cat*. 'The answer is "yes" but the young lady around whom we were hoping to build our trial phase is in hospital as a result of cat scratches.' He promised to struggle on. The pace was hardly quick. Seven years later he was able to pronounce on the question of 'Unwanted Cats' at the onset of the summer kitten season:

> For years it has been recognised by Animal Welfare Societies that for at least three months every year there will have to be a daily slaughter of the kittens, cats, puppies and dogs . . . The imagination boggles at the immensity of the problem that would face any organisation that attempted to meet the demand that homes should be found for all and sundry.

That was not the view of an increasing number of CPL members. There were too many cats, that was clear. What to do? Address the supply side or boost demand? A logician would point out that the supply of cats was geometric, involving many offspring, generation after generation. Adoptions were arithmetic – home-givers being able to deal with only one or maybe two animals at a time. The problem for the supply-siders was that dealing with cats for adoption and boosting demand was so much more fun.

19

Strays, Strays and More Strays!

What to do? The Cats Protection League, in its delightfully
unregimented way, fussed and fretted about whether to
concentrate money and volunteers' time on neutering, which
was the Executive Committee's view, or rather on the more
immediately gratifying business of sheltering, rehabilitation
and home-finding for cats in trouble.

League members already did that willingly, of course, but
it was not official policy. Mr Steward confessed to having
spent many years receiving heartbreaking requests for help
from people forced to part with their pets while having to
explain that the League was unable to help find homes for
cats.

That home-finding was 'fraught with difficulties' had long
been the view at League HQ. The Executive was deeply
suspicious; Mr Steward indicated that it could be a front for
cat collecting, a dreadful thing, with the old bogeyman of the

vivisector lurking in the bushes. He promised to investigate – but he could not advocate 'willy-nilly passing on fully grown cats that are perhaps temperamental or nervous'. How wise! Maintaining the 'attitude of a home for every cat was just not practical', he wrote.

Cat activists generally were getting fed up with stern lectures from central committees about how neutering was the only thing that mattered – that, plus a perceived readiness by their favoured charity to kill healthy animals. Some of these activists, confronted with the rough end of cat welfare, wanted even more rescue, and the pleasure of turning a rufty-tufty stray back into a purring object of mutual adoration. Even – *whisper it softly* – the cats that lived out there on the wild side of things. If it could be done.

Whatever the feelings of its members, the League, like the other charities, would not let cat birth control slip for a moment as their top priority. Sentimentality was as big an enemy as ignorance, all right-thinking people could agree. The newly established Feline Advisory Bureau used its newsletter to attack irresponsible loath-to sterilise pet owners for allowing 'a flood of unwanted waifs to swarm their way into the world faster than they can ever be absorbed'. The language was emotive:

> To give away an unspayed female is the primary cause of the tragedy we are trying to combat. The very kitten YOU gave away could be the cause of that gaunt, emaciated mother foraging in bins, her eyes haunted in the losing struggle for survival of herself and her puny, frightened kittens.

Faced with a growing split, the Cats Protection League Council agreed to let donations and legacies (but not subscriptions) be earmarked by well-wishers for one cause or the other – neutering or the rescue of cats in trouble by finding homes.

It was clear which was going to be more popular. After all the doubts and delay, a 'home-finding and rehabilitation service' was at last formally established in 1965 – 'inviting inquiries from anyone who wants a kitten or is prepared to adopt a cat' – with fifteen regional representatives, two of whom were men. There was some basic home-checking of would-be adopters, and a signed pledge would be required promising to meet the future welfare needs of the cat in question and, if a kitten, which they overwhelmingly were, to have the animal neutered when it was old enough. It was primitive but it was a start. Adult cats proved as difficult to shift as ever, but there would be no looking back. Cats Protection was now Cat Rescue in all but name.

Members loved it, crowding in with stories of rescue for publication in *The Cat*. Like the little cat found wandering the streets of Birmingham with a broken shoulder. 'Her owners were finally traced but were uninterested in her welfare. We were on the point of having to decide her fate when along came a delightful couple who took her home.' Accounts from the neutering table were not nearly so heart-warming but Mr Steward, who was now editing *The Cat* himself, liked to feature them as part of the campaign for Cat Population Limitation.

'I think the Neutering Programme is wonderful,' wrote a correspondent in 1966. A neighbour's friend had told her about her daughter's cat, which had just had kitten number 104. It seemed to be a matter of pride.

> 'What became of them all?' . . . 'Oh, we gave some away and drowned the rest.' I suggested spaying but was told it was cruel! I cannot understand the mentality of such people who help increase the vast army of unwanted cats and strays.

Finding homes for strays was much more rewarding. In summer 1968 Miss M. Wilson of Glossop, Derbyshire, told of how:

> During April we admitted four strays, two of them, 'Tabitha' and 'Minnie' expecting kittens. Homes were found for six kittens and three older cats; at the end of the month we have twenty-three cats in our care . . .
>
> We also help to feed about forty strays and old people's cats at a cost of around four pounds a week. Female cats are spayed and sheltered until homes are found. One lady over eighty years of age has two cats of her own and feeds about ten strays. She has made a shelter for them in her cottage garden . . .

But Miss Wilson was keen to tell members of the wider problems faced, especially:

> [The] general exodus of the industrial north, the annual Wakes holidays, which is a time of headache and heartache for workers in animal shelters, who are regularly sickened by the number of pets brought in for destruction. An appeal in the *Lost and Found* section of the evening paper with the largest circulation in the north of England, for a home for stray cats and kittens brought No Response At All! We leave you to judge the extent of our difficulties.

The Sussex branch reported:

> Strays, strays and more strays! Scarcely a day passes without a call from someone needing our help . . . 'My neighbours have been evicted and left their cat behind. He sits all day outside the empty house crying to be let in. I give him food, but cannot take him in as my two cats fight him. Can you help?'

He is now in our shelter waiting for a home, a lovely black cat, and very gentle.

However emotionally rewarding, finding new homes was indeed fraught with difficulty. Re-homing stalwart Mrs Walledge of Edmonton, north London, let readers of *The Cat* know in autumn 1969:

> Mrs Walledge would like to say that she is tired of people bringing kittens and dumping them on her doorstep. Also CPL members telephone Mrs Walledge and demand that she takes in various cats and kittens into her sanctuary and keeps them; these members will not hear of these cats being put down, and as Mrs Walledge is a voluntary worker there is a limit to what she can do . . .

The Glossop and District branch was caught by the cost-of-living squeeze, reporting:

> The recent purchase tax on pet foods has been a big blow to us . . . old people with several cats of their own and feeding strays are finding things increasingly difficult. We are at a loss to know how we can continue to help them. The absolutely destitute strays must be our main concern.

The business of helping cats must go on, however, like the plight of this street refugee family:

> We recently have taken in a little mother with six kittens found straying in Droylesden. A man rang to say he had found five kittens and would we take them? We agreed on condition he brought in the mother and looked for any more. 'Timmy' duly arrived with six, the last one being found asleep on a wall.

When Mrs Lettice MacNeal, of Ocho Rios, Jamaica, left £60,000 to the League in 1968 it was stalled by the inevitable legal dispute. It all looked terrific – lots of money for cats in trouble – but when the money was eventually released after much legal wrangling, it was the boring old neutering campaign to which the MacNeal legacy was allocated by the League Executive – thus causing 'confusion, disappointment and discontent among members and a mass of correspond-ence – and we still have not been able to straighten it out', according to a despairing Mr Steward.

A sponsorship scheme launched somewhat grudgingly thereafter for cats judged to be 'unhomeable' proved much more popular. 'If our shelters were to be filled with such cats, our work would come to a grinding halt,' pronounced Mr Steward in *The Cat,* 'but £10 per month would allow an unhomeable cat to live a happy and satisfactory life . . . to pay for food and veterinary care for a cat at a shelter where he lives, details of which will be given to the sponsor who in return can arrange to visit "his" cat.'

It was the utopian ideal of the Mayhew Home a century before with its elderly in-pensioners. But what was it doing for the greater feline good? Could a cat sanctuary ever work? It looked like an open door to those dreadful bomb-site cats – the ones that had never been domesticated, the untameables, the unhomeables. What a waste of resources they would be.

But they kept claiming attention. 'It is a desperate situa-tion,' said Mr Steward in August 1967, 'surrounded by a fog of facts and fancy.' He was right about that. Getting some sort of scientific information was vital, so he suggested wisely.

Miss Kit Wilson, a correspondent of the anti-vivisection journal the *Animal Defender,* waded in with a stern attack (reprinted in *The Cat*) on 'misguided people who feed these poor creatures . . . the kittens of which, and there must be hundreds, are for the most part interbred'. She also surmised, just how, she did not explain, that '60 per cent of the cats encountered [by night feeders] had come from homes and were there for the extra food'. Wicked domestic cats! Pretending to be wild to get a bit more to eat! Things were becoming really murky now.

Miss Wilson, who was, in fact, the League's former PR chief, advocated a 'constant campaign of neutering and spaying to stop the breeding not only of the alley cats but also of pedigree stock not specifically used for breeding under the licence of the Grand Committee of the Cat Fancy'.

She was not, however, worried about them falling into the hands of the vivisectors as 'they are too careful not to get scratches'. But East End furriers were after them, as always, she was certain. 'In the case of these derelicts, a humane end is the best thing,' she counselled.*

Such hopeless cases were clearly beyond any attempt to give them a home. But surely some wayward cats were capable of redemption. The anguish and recrimination grew. The

---

* For a century and more the spectre of the cat thief, swiping pets for fur and for vivisection, was a constant motive for cat-activists. In 1950 the PDSA warned of the 'cat spiv', the 'man with a sack' loitering on London street corners, and outbreaks of mystery cat disappearances were long-time staples of local newspapers. The grass roots local action of many years later that would eventually lead to the closure of Hill Grove, a 'cat farm' breeding for medical research, reportedly began when Mrs Cynthia O'Neill's cat, 'Snowy', disappeared one day in 1991 from her Oxfordshire garden, 'and she became determined to act against vivisection'.

'She now thinks that hundreds of cats were stolen each year to be sold to laboratories in Oxfordshire alone,' it was reported at the time. Rather than process stolen or street animals, Hill Grove bred 'specific pathogen-free' cats under government licence – along with accommodating B&B guests at the same property. Nevertheless it was a 'stolen cat' that triggered the long-drawn-out protest that forced the place to close in August 1999, the last UK facility to breed cats specifically for experimentation. Eight hundred cats were removed by the RSPCA for a crash national re-homing effort. Not many years before, they would all have been discreetly destroyed.

ageing Mr Steward tried to keep order, appealing for calm amid a rash of anonymous phone-calls. He addressed members sternly in the January 1969 issue of *The Cat*, when he asked:

> Can anyone doubt that what we propose to do is right in having placed a definite priority on neutering? It is the only way to arrest the flow of kittens, all too many of which are destined to become part of the vast army of the unwanted that degenerate into the homeless felines that . . . depend on the nightly visits of cat-lovers who often travel miles in order to feed their protégés.

On 'home-finding and rehabilitation' he promised to 'honour our obligations within limits'. But the big question he asked readers to consider was: 'Should every unwanted cat or kitten be rehabilitated regardless of the expenditure involved, or should there be a limit to the time they are kept pending a satisfactory home being found?' And of the ever-pressing issue of strays, Mr Steward further asked in 1969:

> Should we be responsible for providing food indefinitely for homeless cats, here, there and everywhere, or should we do so for a limited period pending their 'rescue', in most cases by trapping; and should we keep them indefinitely, trusting that time will restore the balance between semi-wildness and domestication?
>
> Should we accept the responsibility for the care, housing, treatment, etc. of cats that have to be adopted, as so many are, because the original owner cannot or will not provide for them any longer?

The CPL's view was now to stick with neutering and do as much re-homing as would keep members happy. But the 'feral' was out of the bag and some people were just getting on with it – while beginning to tentatively take their passion for the clandestine feeding of outcasts into a more acceptable 'welfare' arena. Both feeders and fed were stepping blushingly into the daylight.

20

How to Market a Three-Legged Cat

Ellie is 8 years old and is in perfect health. Recently we have had two bully cats move into our Close and Ellie isn't coping well at all. Unfortunately, this means we need to re-home her for her own good. Ellie is a standard moggy cat. Affectionate and well behaved.

An adopter who has lots of land and not near a main road would be great.

In America some clever people were beginning to look at the demand side. They were asking themselves could new marketing techniques, mail shots, TV advertising, celebrity endorsements, be used in the cause of getting unwanted pets out of shelters and into loving homes? Could scruffy, unloved, too-many-miles-on-the-clock pets be somehow represented as being just what your family is looking for? This was how some of the re-homing enthusiasts at the Cats Protection League were already beginning to think. The rescue animals on their hands were there for human reasons: loss of job, loss of home, divorce, death, pregnancy, illness. Rescue cats were not damaged goods. The job now was to tell the world. It could be done – and a cat shelter in New York State would show the way for everyone.

The North Shore Animal League, of Port Washington, Long Island, was on the verge of dissolution. Run out of a garage with a few animal pens, since 1944 it had functioned more or less as a sanctuary with a deeply eccentric policy of striving not to kill its street-rescuees, 'not even older and ailing ones'. Local resident Mrs Elisabeth 'Babette' Lewyt heard about its plight and brought her semi-retired, inventor-businessman husband, sixty-six-year-old Alex Lewyt, to a board meeting. French-born Mrs Lewyt was already a committed walk-in stray adopter. 'My wife adored animals, and I adored my wife,' so Mr Lewyt would recall. What did the North Shore League need? They needed money. He donated $100 on the spot. But Mr Lewyt saw what they really needed – which was marketing.

It was summer 1969 – the small start of a big revolution in the affairs of rescue pets. Mr Lewyt had made a fortune by turning his wartime ordnance business over to making vacuum cleaners, which his genius for selling had put into millions of North American homes. Before long, a roster of innovative sales techniques would be employed in putting, not vacuum cleaners, but Long Island's pre-loved cats and dogs into those same homes.

It all looked quite simple. The Lewyts recruited their dog-loving neighbour, the singer and television star, Perry Como, to serve as mail-shot endorser. Lewyt produced a letter featuring a photograph of a puppy and a kitten. The letter asked its 28,000 recipients: 'Would you give a dollar – just $1 – TO SAVE THEIR LIVES?' The mailing brought in $11,000 in donations. The next step was to market the animal themselves.

'We have the same concept as bringing any product to the public,' Mr Lewyt would later tell the *Wall Street Journal* when interviewed in 1975 under the headline: 'With Right Tactics, It's Easy to Market a Three-Legged Cat'.

'The key moment,' he said, 'is when we bring the prospect and the product face to face. But we have to have point-of-purchase material since, after all, the product can't speak for itself . . .

'And if a product doesn't move, we have a [sales] promotion,' he went on. 'Most animal shelters are run by well-intentioned people who don't know anything about fundraising or running the place like a business. The only reason they don't go broke is that a little old lady dies every year and leaves them something.' There were always just about enough little old ladies.

Never before had a humane organisation paid to advertise their animals for adoption in direct competition with pet stores and breeders. Other humane societies objected that Long Shore was treating animals like 'commodities' – while, as it would be pointed out, 'those same societies were killing more than a quarter of a million dogs and cats in New York City alone per year'.

By 1972 North Shore had pushed adoptions up to 3,000 annually, leading the world, and was actually running low on adoptable animals. Mrs Lewyt would reportedly drive her station wagon round municipal pounds and pay $10 each for as many dogs as they were willing to release from death row. A professional trainer was hired to rehabilitate disturbed dogs rescued from pounds. Babette Lewyt would one day famously say:

> These are not strays, there's no such thing as a stray. All these animals had homes at one time or another – some were good, some were bad. But they all deserve another chance.

With its celebrity endorsement and marketing as slick as any in corporate America, North Shore was a model for other shelters – with a message that re-homing could be fun, re-homing could even be glamorous. If pre-loved pets were commodities, they were desirable ones – even three-legged cats. Those three-legged cats were something else . . .

21

Cats Have Rights Too

ANGEL

Female, age (approx.) 9, DOMESTIC SHORT-HAIR, white.
Hello, my name is Angel. I'm a mysterious lady who would like a more certain future. I was found and adopted about seven years ago by a kind gentleman, but my life with him and where I originally came from is a mystery . . .

So no one knows anything about me at all! I would love a home with just adults, or a family with older children who will be calm around me . . . I like a bit of time to myself sometimes, but if you have food and fuss to offer then my heart will likely be yours . . . X

Cats did not know it yet but, just as the question of what to do about strays was being intensely debated between the sentimental and practical wings of cat rescuers, the very idea of animal 'welfare' was about to be turned upside down. Old-time cat ladies of either persuasion had talked about 'The Cause' as they fed (or chloroformed) street cats on their nocturnal mercy missions as if in pursuit of some higher moral purpose. Now a new cause had arrived. It was called 'Animal Rights'.

The concept had been there since the late nineteenth century, had simmered away through the years until the 1960s, when it would explode in a wave of uncompromising activism. It might be localised in inspiration but would be played out over a much broader agenda in the future. 'Welfare' meant doing something about helping animals – admitting a stray cat in from the cold. 'Rights' meant doing something about changing the minds of people, by waving placards, writing books, sending hate mail, making death threats. Whether they liked it or not, pets were to become part of human politics.

Old-style animal advocates could be equally attracted to both, but now they had to declare which side they were really on – welfare or rights. The new wave would be underpinned from its start by an eruption of academic and philosophical discourse which has echoed down the decades since – especially the 'Oxford group' of animal-rights-vegetarian-vegan philosophers behind the publication of the collection of essays, entitled *Animals, Men and Morals*, published in 1971. The publication four years later of *Animal Liberation* by the Australian moral philosopher Peter Singer, and the passions it inspired, reinforced the student sit-in-style debate that was rapidly supplanting the gentler discourse of a cats' home bring-and-buy. Helping poor pussy was not 'posthuman' enough.

In a critique of the 'old established groups', as he called them in his book, Mr Singer would argue that 'people came to think of "animal welfare" as something for kindly ladies who are dotty about cats, and not as a cause founded on basic principles of justice and morality'. What Mr Singer perhaps overlooked was that being dotty about cats and concern for morality were not mutually exclusive. Showing compassion for street animals was something people could do something about. Whales and tigers not so much.

American philosopher Tom Regan pushed the debate forward with a telling attack on the routine 'putting to sleep' of healthy companion animals by shelters in his canonical 1983 book, *The Case for Animal Rights*.

In these rarefied discussions, having pets around at all began to be questioned. It was 'the exploitation of animals in the name of transitory love'. Henry Salt's dictum of 1894 was rediscovered: 'Pets . . . are usually the recipients of abundance of sentimental affection but of little real kindness – so much easier it is to give temporary caresses than substantial justice.' Although very few people as yet sought to prohibit outright the keeping of companion animals, the time was not too far off when a mainstream mass-membership US animal rights group (PETA) would proclaim: 'We believe that it would have been in the animals' best interests if the institution of "pet keeping" – that is, breeding animals to be kept and regarded as "pets" – had never existed.' But pet keeping *did* exist – and what was a cat-lover without a cat?

In the new mood of questioning everything, the result would be years of turmoil, especially at the RSPCA, as the ageing 'cats and dogs brigade' on its Council were pushed aside by an ever more vocal 'Reform Group' and the fox-hunting proclivities of Britain's royal family were held up for scorn. It was all agonisingly awful. Cat rescuers, with their singularity of feline focus, were much better placed to ride out the storm, although out of sight they too were developing a Provisional Wing of feral enthusiasts.

Within the RSPCA, immediate policy could be driven by motivated members via the election of the council – the body the reformers were intent on capturing. In the long term, however, it was the perception of the charity's presiding welfare ethos that persuaded elderly sympathisers to vote with their wills. The little old ladies who kept it all going, as Mr Lewyt had observed of his Long Island undertaking. Forget its views on seal-clubbing or battery hens for a moment – was the Society sound on cats?

By the beginning of the 1970s mass destruction was no longer such a come-on for charity fundraising. The ever-rising status of cats, domestic or otherwise, had seen to that. But the killing went on. The charities knew whose fault that was. The RSPCA could state in 1969: '[We are] often criticised for reports in the press over the large number of animals destroyed in the large industrial towns . . . it is irresponsible owners, not the Society, who should bear the blame.'

But behind the scenes the Society knew it had a problem. On the rising tide of 'stray and wild' cats, an internal report by the Homeless Animals Committee had a little earlier proposed the setting up of a truck-borne cat-liquidating mobile commando – with an ex-SAS officer in charge! – to be called in by regional branches for special actions. The idea was dropped because 'it was very easy to earn a bad name by the collection of stray cats and their destruction'.

So things really might be changing – at least in terms of public perception. The Homeless Animals Committee could further note, but not publicly: 'The argument to destroy a fit cat to "prevent its suffering" is a complete paradox.' And that had been the justification for a hundred years!

It was an outrider of the killing-healthy-animals-is-wrong imperative that would transfix animal welfare for years to come. In any case, it was noted, demands to trap and remove problem cats came overwhelmingly from 'a small section of the public' who had 'never given the RSPCA a penny'. Meanwhile, as internal correspondence noted, the Society was scooping up and 'daily destroying many homed cats', something which was not just bringing a public image of clumsy cruelty but also raising the prospect of prosecution under the revised Theft Act of 1968 . . . which made it an offence for the first time to steal any cat, not only those with a pedigree of high financial value.

The RSPCA was 'fast gaining the reputation of being the *animal murdering society*' (authors' emphasis), a confidential

October 1971 Homeless Animals Committee report said, extremely bluntly. The work would be better done by public health authorities and pest contractors, it was suggested. That way, the charity's hands would stay clean. Reputation was all in protecting those legacies.*

Just as the animal rights storm blew up on both sides of the Atlantic, across America humane societies and individuals were energetically opening a new wave of animal shelters. The millionaire adventurer and Lake Tahoe menagerie-owner, George Whittell Jr., died in 1969 leaving a typically legally contentious will – dispensing $40 million to those animal-welfare organisations who might persuade the lawyers that they could meet its term of 'relieving pain and suffering amid animal, bird and fish life'. Scores of cat and dog shelters applied, plus various moose-sanctuary pranksters. It took years to sort out, but a rash of cat-friendly Whittell memorial-named shelters, clinics and humane education centres would be the result.

It should be noted, however, that as cats were rousing themselves to supplant dogs as America's top pets, these new-wave shelters 'failed to predict and plan for the increased numbers of both owned and unowned cats'. Their cages and runs were configured for canines. That would have to change.

In Britain, to set up a go-it-alone cat shelter, all you needed was council planning permission to make pens outside if you were minded to, and some veterinary input. Charitable status was only necessary if you were going to try

---

* Animal rights proponent Richard Ryder would later note: 'The Society's very bad publicity throughout the 1960s and early 1970s had compounded the council's natural fear of the media. By the time that Reform Group members arrived on the council in 1972 they found . . . the council was attempting to keep all its deliberations secret. Almost every council document was labelled *Strictly Confidential* and meetings were held in an aura of conspiratorial self-importance.' Dog and cat destruction rates were especially sensitive.

and raise significant funds. The Cats Protection League recognised the urge of many cat enthusiasts to be independent, but advised a degree of co-operation (they called it 'group practice') to better cope with how the increasing complexities of modern life impacted on cats and those who cared about cats. They stressed the need for some basic book-keeping and admin skills, plus the need to be alert to the danger of the cat collector. Of their own 13,000 members it would be said in the early 1980s: 'Central guidelines are given to groups by Headquarters, but individual feelings are respected if some groups feel they do not want a single cat destroyed.'

The inward flow of cats was still unceasing. But having been seen as somehow disreputable or unworkable since the start, finding homes for homeless mature cats was now the main concern, at least for the Cats Protection League. As Mrs Nerea de Clifford, its staunchest advocate for so long, wrote in *The Cat* in summer 1976:

> Of all the ideas we have launched, that which has been salvation to the greatest number of cats has been home-finding for adult cats. Year by year, numbers have mounted and many cats have had happy lives and lived to contented old ages instead of being destroyed when their first homes had to give them up. We have worked out rules for the new homes: no children under school age, no dogs, no busy road nearby, and the promise of care or return to us, with no passing on – all laid out in our acceptance forms. Home-finding has been a great work and one which we can look upon with pleasure.

The Animal Rights tide was bringing changes for pets in every home. In the Anglo–US felinosphere, the domestic cat was already considered a family member, a 'companion animal' no longer to be lightly thrown away for convenience. Those who abandoned cats in a shut-up house or by the side of the road were not just stupid and cruel but now, in Britain anyway, they were also criminals.

But those who thoughtfully had them 'put to sleep' (PTS in the shorthand of the day) before a trip to the Costas were not. The kitten season and holidays combined to make midsummer the time of peak destruction. The time-worn tragedy of the killing of healthy animals, 'unwanted' for whatever reason, would be an increasingly raw issue in animal welfare. Not before long it would become *the* issue.

The RSPCA went into deeper crisis. The council had been infiltrated by fox-hunters, it was alleged. Pets were being put down in 'circumstances compared to Nazi death-camps'. Euthanasia by electrocution was very publicly discredited at the same time.* There was a further drama in 1972 when it was revealed that the Society, along with the PDSA and Battersea Dogs Home, had been selling the carcasses of euthanized animals to a company in east London – the Smithfield Animal Products Trading Company – to be rendered for tallow and fertiliser and the hides for leather. What's more, they had been doing so for many years. 'We make no money out of it,' said the PDSA. In fact, 'The company charge us a collection fee.' It was cheaper than cremation. The trade continued.

---

* In 1974 the manufacturers, Electrothanators Ltd, were forced to admit that their apparatus did not conform to the set standards and had never done so. Although the main control could ostensibly be set first at the 'stun' position and then at 'lethal', there was no allowance for a current to be passed directly through the brain to produce unconsciousness in cat or dog before the lethal 1,000-volt shock was delivered. Labelling of the control knobs was a front. 'To use intravenous injection as an alternative method of humane destruction was impossible,' an RSPCA spokesman was reported as saying. It was 'too expensive'. In spite of vocal campaigns, both Battersea and the RSPCA would continue using 'the box' to destroy cats and dogs for another decade.

The RSPCA's one-time homeless-animal champion, John Hobhouse, was driven out as Chairman. Describing outcast cats as the biggest issue in animal welfare had not been helpful. The 'cats and dogs rural conservatives', as Richard Ryder would characterise them, were now at open war with the 'internationally-minded campaigners'. To counter allegations of financial mismanagement, a stable-cleaning independent public inquiry was set up in 1974, directed by Charles Sparrow, an eminent QC. According to the reformers, the Society's actual expenditure on homeless animals, which had been reinstated as an animal rights-leaning policy worth pursuing, was a mere £17,000, they alleged.

'In fact, the sum spent was over six times that amount, £108,643,' insisted the Society's own counsel. 'In addition, branches of the Society spent £237,921 on homeless animals.' At least unwanted cats were still an issue. As part of the bitter internal propaganda war, it was reported in 1974 on the stray cat front:

> Cat-lovers, who take in and care for London's strays, complained last night that they were not getting support from the RSPCA. Seven of them told the inquiry that they wanted to bring to light the plight of thousands of stray cats in central London. Mrs Charlotte Gibbs, a member of the Society, who runs a home for strays in a converted garage at her home in Mostyn Road, Merton, said: 'We are desperately in need of help.'

She told the inquiry that she had been helping stray cats for twenty years and went to the East End two nights a week. She used a shooting-brake as a cat ambulance, but she wanted the RSPCA to run its own mobile unit. Mrs Gibbs said that hundreds of women cared for London's strays – but RSPCA officials did not want to know about voluntary workers. 'They tell us to leave the cats alone and they will go away.'

Mrs Angela Cope, Chairman of the Society's central London branch, said in response: 'If a stray is brought into one of our eighteen clinics in the Greater London area, we will find it a home, but if it is wild, it is far kinder to destroy it.' The Society did not round up strays, she explained, but did finance animal hospitals that took them in.

The embattled Society did manage to pull off a rescue cat PR coup, however, when a stray kitten from their Hounslow branch was installed as the 'Office Manager's cat' at No. 10 Downing Street in July 1973 during Edward Heath's tenure as Prime Minister, with a Cabinet Office-funded living allowance. It was Office Manager Mr Peter Taylor's mother who arranged the adoption, dutifully filling in the right forms, 'because the RSPCA need to know the thing's gone to a good home', as he explained.

The rescue cat was given the name 'Wilberforce' from a nearby statue of the nineteenth-century politician and humanitarian. 'He was a very scared cat when he first came here,' Mr Taylor would later recall, 'and he's still a bit shy if someone makes a quick move.' Wilberforce would prowl on through the Wilson–Callaghan years into the Thatcher era – the longest ever feline survivor in the political jungle.

A year later, the renewed threat of rabies arriving from continental Europe, and the possibility of it being spread by cats, provided a distraction for the embattled RSPCA council as it published its Annual Report for 1975. 'The tremendous increase in the urban fox population' was a direct concern. Foxes could carry rabies, and while they were 'afraid of dogs, would mingle quite happily with cats' apparently. It was a licence to carry on lethalling.

'New homes were found for more than 73,000 dogs and cats', said the 1975 report. 'But 163,000 animals had to be humanely destroyed.' So the killing went on and, just like a century before when the Home Secretary, Henry Matthews, had been urged to arrest cats on the street, the threat of rabid cats gave it a public health moral authority.

That same year, the Animal Rescue League shut down after sixty-two years of industrialised cat destruction in the City Road. It just did not seem to fit any more. For years to come, however, much as some members might want to, the RSPCA would find it impossible to stop killing unwanted animals – and would keep coming up with good reasons why. It was mostly because foolish owners let their pets have kittens and puppies.*

In London, still the teeming felinopolis, Battersea Dogs Home chugged away with military efficiency (much of its staff were ex-servicemen), offering cheap and cheerful electrical euthanasia for what it called the 'four-footed friends' brought to its doors. It remained quaintly Edwardian in its destructive purpose – described as a 'NECESSARY PUBLIC SERVICE [conducted] as much in the interests of Society as in that of homeless and starving dogs and cats'. The police as ever brought in stray dogs, while ageing cat ladies and local councils continued the timeless feline street clearing. But even after the Electrothanator scandal (see p. 259), Battersea would not give up killing by electricity for a decade yet.

According to annual 'returns of cats and dogs', in the twenty years from 1959, of cats brought to its gates, 6,233 were 'sold' and 7,825 'destroyed', a re-homing rate of 39 per cent – actually quite commendable. 1963 was a bad year: 514 cats destroyed and 197 sold. Ten years later it was a bit better: 379 destroyed and 449 sold. Home-checking was basic. The old-guard regime was changing ever so slightly, with the arrival of kennel-maids in 1974.

---

* 'Euthanasia is forced on the RSPCA by irresponsible ownership' is the standard policy statement repeated unchangingly each year from 2006 onwards.

Thus it was that by the third quarter of the twentieth century, admission to a 'shelter' for a cat on both sides of the Atlantic was still a virtual death sentence. Survive in the wild and the pest destroyers had a contract on you. Find 'sanctuary' with some kind cat lady and she would soon be floundering. The crisis had come and to do something about it, the focus of cat welfarists everywhere was still on the supply side, aiming for fewer unwanted animals, with sterilisation, sterilisation, sterilisation as the only policy. But was it working?

22

'Why We Must Euthanize'

DARCY

Darcy is a lovely neutered male 6-year-old NORWEGIAN FOREST CAT. He is looking for a home on his own with no other cats, dogs or young children. He is microchipped, fully vaccinated and in good health. Darcy is currently an outdoor cat but lives in a very rural area. He has no road sense as he has never needed it, so an indoor home would perhaps be better . . .

If you think you may be a suitable slave for Darcy then please call the number above for more information on this handsome young man.

In America, just at the same time that the RSPCA was engulfed yet again in crisis, a big fuss was also being made about 'unwanted animals'. It was the very issue that the Society itself had so pioneeringly raised fifteen years before, although no real solution had yet been found. Neutering and spaying were being pushed everywhere with missionary zeal.* The ostensible reason was the sheer horror of what was happening as the annual destruction rate of unwanted pets across America hit a gruesome twenty million animals. On

---

* One later theory for just why everyone was getting so excited was that it was part of an undercover campaign to find a new market for the recently developed human oral contraceptive.

Long Island, the Lewyts at least were trying to climb out of the pit with their strange conviction that rescue animals were just as marketable as commercially bred puppies and kittens.

There was no shortage of anguish within what would be called America's 'animal shelter community', where the moral compass was being centrally calibrated by the politically powerful Humane Society of the United States. The Society had been founded in Washington DC in 1954, after a typical animal advocate doctrinal split, aiming to serve as both a lobbying and welfare organisation (although the hands-on side would fade). The new degree of anguish was not matched by any flood of ideas on how to scale back the killing.

How the Humane Society decided policy, how it demonstrated techniques and determined best practice, would be followed by almost all animal welfare workers across America. The formidable Miss Phyllis Wright, former US Army Korean War dog trainer, had been appointed as its first Vice-President for Companion Animals in 1968 and had immediately castigated pet owners who might be a bit slow to sterilise, by saying: 'People who let their dogs and cats have litters to show their children the "miracle of birth" should come and witness the "miracle of death" performed in the back rooms of animal shelters all over the country!'

It was shockingly true. She further suggested that men were reluctant to have pets spayed and neutered because it felt as if they themselves were being emasculated. Her overall position meant defining a clear moral line on what to do with the unwanted healthy dogs and cats being dispatched in their millions by all those independent shelters across America.*

---

* Miss Wright would also coincidentally be a driving force behind the shift in the US to the use of sodium pentobarbital injection for small animal euthanasia, in opposition to the use of gas and the horrible 'decompression' chambers that would be the standard killing methods used in the US until the early 1980s.

Phyllis Wright was a revered beacon of humane practical sense in her day, but did not live long enough (she died in 1992) to see herself held up thirty years later by some as a moral monster, the so-called 'matriarch of catch and kill', placing her in a direct line from the lethal absolutists of the cat underworld of turn-of-the-century New York and London.

Her historic 'crime' was to have made a statement called 'Why We Must Euthanize', in the form of an article printed in the Society's journal for summer 1978. It reportedly would be pinned on the wall of animal shelters everywhere across America as some sort of solidarity-inducing manifesto among euthanasia-technicians, and would disappear just as universally when it went out of fashion in the ideological battles of the future. It was fantastically politically incorrect. Miss Wright declared:

> We all know people who never want an animal euthanized, who insist it's best to keep the animal alive . . . regardless of how badly the animal lives . . .
>
> That is the worst thing we can do. Our objective is to prevent and release animals from suffering. We know that death, humanely administered, is not an evil, but a blessing to animals that are of no comfort to themselves or to the world . . .
>
> I know it is difficult to put animals to sleep. I've put 70,000 dogs and cats to sleep – and I'm aware of the trauma. But I tell you one thing: I don't worry about one of those animals that were put to sleep. And I worry a great deal [more] about dogs and cats that have to spend their lives shut in small cages . . . without affection or companionship.

Human companionship was the key to pet well-being, she said. She told the story of a Texas woman whose will left money for a 'perpetuated home for stray and lost dogs'. Twenty-five dogs were placed in a cage, fed each day while otherwise being abandoned. They went insane. Her manifesto continued:

> Being dead is not a cruelty to animals. Being half alive is. We have the responsibility to release these animals from suffering . . . We also have the responsibility to work towards a time when all pets will have responsible, caring owners and euthanasia is no longer needed.

An HSUS-sponsored 'National Conference on the Ecology of the Surplus Dog and Cat Problem' had been held in Chicago in 1974 – a step on the road to Phyllis Wright's 'infamous' manifesto. 'It is a problem, the solution of which will require the intensive effort and co-operation of veterinarians, government officials, the pet industry, pet food manufacturers, and all of us in the humane movement,' announced the HSUS. Ferals were barely mentioned but at least strays were being considered, even if the solution proposed was not entirely a favourable outcome. The Society published a special report in January 1975:

> With an estimated 80 to 100 million cats and dogs in this country already, kittens and puppies are being born at the rate of 2000 to 3500 an hour. The Society learned in a recent survey that 15 to 17 million cats and dogs were turned in to the nation's animal shelters in 1973. Of that number, a shocking 13.5 million were put to death! This means that only 13.5 per cent of the dogs and 9 per cent of the cats were adopted or redeemed.

All this was costing $500 million a year – 'for the feeding and care of unwanted animals during the five to ten days they are held for adoption, killing the 80 per cent that are not adopted or redeemed, and disposing of the carcasses. The result is both an unconscionable waste of life and a needless drain on public and private money.'

Why was it like this? The delegates had all sorts of explanations, but looking at the conference's conclusions forty years later, the pioneer 'no-kill' (see p. 341) advocate, Nathan Winograd, would castigate the 1970s welfare generation and Miss Wright in particular for firstly, 'blaming the animals themselves' – their own lack of adoptability required their killing; secondly, 'blaming the public' – for inadequately confining their animals and for general irresponsibility; and thirdly, for demanding stricter animal control laws. As Winograd would write:

> In response, laws were passed across the United States that confined dogs and cats to their homes, required dogs, and to a lesser extent cats, to be licensed with local authorities, limited the number of animals a family could care for, prohibited feeding stray animals, and provided authority for animal control officers to seize and destroy animals they themselves deemed a 'nuisance' . . . Where these laws were passed, kill rates tended to increase as a result.

It was a harsh judgement but it was broadly true. Both in the US and Britain, destruction rates stayed unconscionably high and rates of adoption (the word 're-homing' had yet to be invented) just as tragically low. In less strident terms than Phyllis Wright, Mrs de Clifford told Cats Protection League members around the same time that it was inevitable that 'some must die' and suggested a special fund for the putting to sleep of 'wild strays'. Sanctuary enthusiasts were outraged.

Something must be done. If there were too many healthy cats and not enough homes, it was, according to the mainstream charities, something that only education (of humans) and sterilisation (of cats) could turn round.

That would take years. But for the old-time cat ladies and younger animal rights activists alike there was something that could be done. Save one cat at a time and the whole cat world might be saved entire. Do it with the cats that could never be homed. Nobody cared about them. Do it with the bomb-site lot. Do it on the wild side.

It was beginning to happen already, more or less out of sight. For years there had been fights, and not just theoretical, over what to do about the Third Estate of the cat realm. They were fought between those who pursued trapping and destruction and those who sallied forth with bowls of food, went gooey over the kittens and dreamed of sunlit sanctuary for all catkind. The stand-offs and suspicion reinforced a code of secrecy because a lone feeder knew that where she might go prospecting for cats, a less kindly bunch might be following in her footsteps.

It was time for the rituals in the dark to come out in the light.

PART THREE

A WALK ON
THE WILD SIDE

23

The Third Estate

HARRY

Hello, my name is Harry. I'm a very handsome chap but I've been through the wars a bit. I was living as a stray, having to fend for myself, never knowing where my meals were coming from and always having to watch my back. Then I came here, where it is safe and warm, and I get lovely regular meals. But the humans found out I have something called FIV, which means my immune system isn't as strong as it should be, and I will need to lead an indoor life from now on. I'm a friendly chap, and would love a home where I can have lots of love and cuddles.

It might be called the third wave of cat advocacy. First there was the domestic cat, worthy of respect and care. By the third quarter of the twentieth century that battle had been more or less won. Cats were installed in the heart of loving homes, adored by millions for their grace and charm – although gruff, anti-cat sentiment was still seen as amusing. How droll to find a use for a dead cat or to declare 'I Hate Cats', a publishing phenomenon of the 1980s. There was no 'I Hate Dogs' canine equivalent. Nobody would dare.

Then there was the stray, the fallen cat, mewing at a strange door when forsaken by heartless owners for stupid materialist reasons, or, having got lost on an over-adventurous foray, ending up in a feral street gang like some feline Oliver Twist.*

This was the cat that the charities loved to scoop up into their shelters – tell heart-wrenching stories about human cruelty and plead for funds for them. After years of persecution, the stray cat was clambering its way back into the light. It was time too for those kindly people who would adopt a semi-wild cat which sought to adopt *them* by 'ghosting around' the defended home territories of domestic cats, to be more open about their secret friends.

In 1973 *The Cat* reported from Bournemouth a sensation at the Wessex Cat Show where 'Mandy Lou', 'rescued from death by the CPL fifteen years before', had won an entirely new class; she was 'Best Rescued Cat'. (Mandy Lou afterwards 'glowed and purred, talking to everyone'.)

But out there, always, had been the wild side. It was still barely spoken of, something for female guerrilla bands to stealthily attend to in the darkness, only their little bowls of left-out food giving away their presence. As it had been since the beginning, there were those who fed them and those who had a different end in view. The two groups just about tolerated each other.

In summer 1973, for example, the Cats Protection League's north London branch could report: 'Trapping of semi-wild strays continues. Our grateful thanks are due to our two helpers, Miss Mervyn and Miss Tompkins, who during the year have spent many of their evenings each week clearing sick and hungry cats from building and derelict sites.' 'Clearing' was a loaded word.

---

* Researching a feral colony in Regent's Park in the mid-1970s, animal protectionist Jenny Remfry observed certain cats happily approaching lunching office workers for bits of sandwich and some affection. A stroke and cheek-rub maybe. These central London cats were clearly domestic strays. Several of them enchanted their new Parklife friends so much, they indeed *took them home*.

Meanwhile the same branch, based in the Caledonian Road, Islington, was struggling to cope with 'a borough swarming with abandoned cats', as it was described, kept alive in their fallen, flea-infested state by the inevitable old lady feeders. What were practical cat-lovers to do? 'In 1972 the branch took in 1956 strays but only managed to find homes for 10 per cent,' so it was reported. Mrs Maureen Davies, the Branch Secretary, told the *Islington Gazette*, 'That's where you get stuck, when nobody offers them a home. You get so fond of them once you've pulled them round. But if they can't find homes, then we have to put them to sleep.'

It was as if Miss Cording was still in residence just round the corner at Fellowship Cottage. But on the rising tide of 'animal rights', change was in the wind.

The idea of reaching out to the truly wild ones had been there ever since the 'homeless animal' problem had first begun to claim attention – and it was different from changing minds about once-domestic stray cats being vermin to be rounded up and destroyed. That was still a good fight and by no means yet won. Paradoxically perhaps, it was the old guard of the RSPCA that led the way with its campaign proclaiming that the unwanted cat was the biggest problem in animal welfare.

All of a sudden, a new idea was taking hold. If neutering house cats was the answer to an exploding birth-rate, could not ownerless strays be caught and then, instead of being euthanised, be given similar treatment? Who would do it? Who would pay? It seemed bonkers but it was worth a try.

Cat-lovers, timelessly drawn to hands-on welfare with all its nocturnal dramas, heartbreaks and triumphs, might do more than just put down food for hungry bomb-site cats. Here was a fabulous new adventure – luring cats, trapping them, giving them up to a vet for neutering and – whisper it softly – *returning* them to where they came from. Such a mad-seeming idea would first break the surface of public consciousness, not in some hospital culvert or railway-arch junkyard, but in the back alleyways and canals of Venice.

Cat ladies of the past had kept their ambitions reasonably close to home. Like cats themselves, they had territories, a favoured square or churchyard, which must be defended against rivals and intruders. Kate Cording's 'patch' had stretched to half of London. Zoe Morgan wanted the entire metropolis. Some thought even bigger. Mrs Dickin's People's Dispensary, with a very different agenda, burst out of its Whitechapel cellar to go nationwide and, for a while, its international ambitions to succour animals seemed boundless – until war intervened.

For many years, wealthy English cat-lovers had indulged in feline tourism, not necessarily to seek out exotic breeds or see how the rest of the world treated its house cats, but to encounter, especially, the fabled semi-wild free-roaming cats of southern Europe. The cats of Rome had been on cat ladies' 'must-see' lists since Victorian days. These were not forsaken cats, nor even strays. They were effectively wild animals wrapped up in familiar beguiling form that might, just might, accept a proffered titbit from an outstretched hand.

Greek island cats had plenty of adherents – and always would have – although the cats that inhabited the ruins of Trajan's Forum and other archaeological sites in Rome were the most famous. They had been there for ever. It was noted before the war that wealthy British and American lady tourists would arrive in taxis to call out 'pussy pussy' while entirely ignoring ruins of archaeological importance more than two thousand years old. Concern for the cats' welfare had been raised when the otherwise animal-loving Benito Mussolini had moved in 1930 to clear them up as part of the general makeover of newly re-imperialised Fascist Rome.

The feral colony had crept back, survived the war and clung on as they might, like the post-war London bomb-site cats. Kindly Roman cat ladies came each day to feed them on pasta as they had always done. Florentine cats of the Boboli Gardens* were another famous calling point on any feline Grand Tour but it was the cats of Venice which excited the greatest emotions.

For many visitors, discovering Mediterranean cats was pleasant enough, but tempered by anguish at their apparently undernourished† and diseased condition.

However compelling the desire to 'rescue' such unfortunates, doing so was clearly impossible. But some thought that something must be done and devoted their own lives to doing it. Mrs Eleanor Close, for example, wife of the British Council representative in Athens, founded the Greek Animal Welfare Fund in 1961 to help all animals but especially street cats and dogs. In 1965 she was given the RSPCA Victoria Medal, the one that the Queen Empress had insisted almost a century before should contain the likeness of a forsaken cat.

In 1965 Mrs Helena Sanders, Chairman of the CPL West Cornwall Branch, began to make a noise about the cats of Venice. After an exploratory trip in March, she could report

---

* Although one English lady visitor complained at 'every alley in Florence being peopled by scrawny, diseased, undoctored toms assaulting every female cat they could find'.

† Biologist Roger Tabor would later point out in his splendid column for *The Cat* that appearances could be misleading. Southern European cats were more evident in daylight hours (northern ferals ruled the night), which made it appear to the newly arrived visitor that they were indeed swarming everywhere looking for hand-outs in fish-markets and at tourist sites, where in season food might be guaranteed. Their slim build denoted descent from Ancient Egyptian desert cats, so as to manage their body temperature better than chunkier-built, northern European cats. There were stories of cat-napping by campervan-borne tourists. 'Do not try to bring them home. Give the local cat shelter a donation,' was his advice.

in *The Cat*: 'Not all of them are starving; some are well-fed family pets.' She had observed 'one sleek tortoiseshell and white riding in a gondola ferry, quite unconcerned by the wake of the water buses'.

But she was shocked to observe that 'Venetian cats breed unchecked' . . . and her hostess, Signora Rafaella Pucci, a dedicated cat-rescuer, had showed her the darker side of the Lagoon's cats, telling her: 'for every stray I send to the vet [for destruction] there are ten more.' The authorities dealt with it by putting strays in a sack and throwing them into the canal.

Soon after her return to Cornwall, Mrs Sanders's manifesto 'The Cats of Venice: An Appeal', appeared in *The Cat*, proposing that an 'English person set up home in the city [and] undertake a massive programme of rounding up strays and putting them to sleep'. But this was to be accompanied 'by a massive plan of neutering, otherwise an endless stream of strays would continue to arrive'. It would be performed by vets and paid for by well-wishers. The neutered cats would be returned to their canal-side life but in drastically reduced numbers. Thus would a much smaller but manageable population thrive in the city of the Doges, still tended by the Venetian ladies in black with their parcels of fish scraps and pasta – the 'cat mothers'.

The formidable Miss Mabel Raymonde-Hawkins, founder in 1952 of the Raystede Animal Sanctuary in Sussex, read the appeal in *The Cat* and offered her help. The ladies invited and got charitable funding, including some from the League itself, and they would venture to the Adriatic in October to make more inquiries and more of a fuss. There were reports of their intentions towards the cats of Venice in the Italian press. This could be big, attention-grabbing stuff. Would it help or hinder the cause of Britain's strays?

At the outset of 1966 ('we went in January because the hotels are closed and the cats are at their hungriest'), Mrs

Sanders returned again to the Adriatic, intending this time to actually do something – with an apparent mission to apply a Kate Cording-style solution to the unacceptable condition of the city's estimated 28,000 stray cats. A Fleet Street tabloid had picked up on the story on the eve of their departure, declaring that they were 'going to tour the city in a gondola with a big cage on it' while giving Venice's old women a payment of 100 lire to give up cats. It would all turn out to be a bit of a misunderstanding.

There was uproar. The *Gazzettino de Venezia* called them 'Suffragettes of Feline Euthanasia on Safari'. *The Times* reported:

> It began two days ago when the two cat-loving Englishwomen announced their departure from England, having obtained sufficient funds from animal lovers to launch what is evidently an unappreciated campaign. The situation of Venice's cats, Mrs Sanders is said to have written, has become deplorable. The number of cats is thought to exceed that of mice; there are not enough mice to keep the cats busy. Hence Venice is menaced by stray cats, which belong to no one and live like savages . . .

The missionaries were offering small sums to those who might assist them ('old women', as Mrs Sanders described them in *The Cat*) to 'collect all the sick and homeless cats whose fate, after a medical examination, will then be decided'. They had brought a large number of specially made cardboard cat boxes with them from England, with *Raystede Pussy Pack* boldly emblazoned on them. The locals were baffled.

After the Italian press had reported that they 'intended killing all the stray cats they could find in Venice and sterilising the rest', the ladies had to be given a police guard. Surrounded by shouting pressmen, a chastened Miss Raymonde-Hawkins explained that she and Mrs Sanders had been asked by Venetian friends to help get something done.

'During their last stay in October, they had made some suggestions. In the meantime there had been an improvement,' she explained. They suspected the local authorities of having done some cosmetic rounding up of strays to salvage the tourist trade.

Signor Giulio Silvan, Director of the Ente Nazionale per la Protezione degli Animale, 'a man with his white hair dyed blue', according to Mrs Sanders, was furious. The Guardia Zooifili had been mobilised to protect Venice's cats, he declared. Crowds surrounded the ladies in the Piazza San Marco, shouting, 'Inglise Go Home!' The women had little choice but to prepare to do just that.

The *Corriere della Sera* announced: *Dangerous Times Over for the Cats of Venice*. The English invaders were in retreat, there would be no massacre, and Venetians would be free to continue to spoil and cosset their cats. Excited reports appeared in the British press and on TV news bulletins featuring bemused reporters in gondolas, and interviews with locals and cats – lots of cats. Tom Jones' recent hit 'What's New Pussycat' provided the soundtrack. It was *Carry On Cat Lady*.

The mission was parodied in song on the TV satire show *BBC–3*. 'The women are due to leave Venice on Saturday,' came the urgent news. 'If they do not leave the canals littered with dead strays, the first extremist alarms about their objects will have proved exaggerated. The horror is understandable in a country which looks upon the care of animals in a quite different way from the Anglo-Saxon world. Though Italians can be cruel to animals, they have a respect – excessive in some minds – for life itself, so that the majority is against such measures as sterilisation and what is euphemistically referred to as "putting to sleep". They got to Marco Polo airport with a mob of paparazzi still in pursuit.'

On her return to Cornwall, Mrs Sanders was unbowed. 'So far, only a very few badly injured or very ill cats have been given euthanasia. There has been no spaying or neutering,' she said. But it could be judged a success. 'World opinion has been focused on the plight of the cats of Venice and made the Venetians realise, as nothing else could, their responsibility,' she told *The Cat*. To counter the Italian view that sterilisation led to degeneration she intended getting her own castrated cats into the Venetian newspapers. Meanwhile she could fully account for her and Miss Raymonde-Hawkins's expenses, including air fares, hotel bills, payments to local cat ladies and the hire of a translator, to concerned League members. Their opinion was divided. Should not charitable money be spent on cats closer to home?

'I have seen the cats of Venice, an emaciated miserable crowd, never a purr from them,' was the view of one disgruntled CPL member. Asked for his comments, the Director of the Universities Federation for Animal Welfare, Major Walter Scott, said:

> A stray cat which is getting enough food and is enjoying his hunting is probably quite happy. It is a common misapprehension to imagine they are not. Cats which go over the wall may be simply connecting with the ways of their ancestors.

It was not a contribution to the stray cat welfare discussion that would be welcomed by all. 'They should worry about their English cats, not ours,' had been the head of the Venice Animals Society's response to the mission – and indeed, there were some cat-lovers doing just that at home. The condition of the unowned cat was entering a decisive new phase.

24

The Untouchables

HUGO

Male, age (approx.) 5, DOMESTIC SHORT-HAIR, black, can live with mature family. You'll have noticed Hugo's ear . . . (caused by a old injury). And if you've entered his pen, he has possibly hissed a hello . . . By this stage he probably isn't seeming an attractive proposition. But Hugo is a big friendly giant. Ignore the initial impression and give him a little reassurance and time, and you'll find he loves a fuss. Say hello, don't rush him and see what you find.

Mrs Sanders and her friends had been all over the papers and on TV. Not so Mrs Sheila Young, a ward sister at Mount Vernon Hospital, Northwood, Middlesex. Like many hospitals, it was home to a long-established 'feral' cat colony whose numbers and consequent fleas were raising public health issues. It was recorded: 'For all those years [since 1965 when she began trapping and neutering cats], the hospital managers tried to oppose her on the grounds that she was encouraging rather than exterminating the cat population.'

She had just got on with it in semi-secrecy. A decade later the management would concede that a managed feral colony was better than outright destruction, when new cats or descendants of survivors moved in to claim the brutally emptied space. It was 'the vacuum effect'. 'Sheila thus gained recognition for her work with the cats at Mount Vernon and was soon visiting other hospitals to help them set up their own control groups,' it would be written. Sister Young then established a group of three neutered male ferals at the Middlesex Hospital for 'nine stable years' but a new administration insisted on their removal. Two females moved in and within eighteen months sixty cats were in residence. 'Staff who feed this type of colony all too often have to do it surreptitiously and are made to feel like criminals,' wrote Sister Young. After months of stand-off and official grumbling, she and her feline watch-keepers were invited back and a small manageable colony was re-established.

But all that was a long way in the future. In 1966 those who would publicly admit to supporting the trap and neuter concept (or in the Venice case, trap, kill, neuter and return some) were on the extreme spectrum of eccentric cat lady. *The Cat* in December 1968 reported a rumpus in Coventry when cat feeders tried to protect a colony in Chain Gardens, Spon End against the council pest destroyers. The same in Mount Bingham, St Helier, Jersey where a certain Mrs Lecoq led a bid to save 'a colony of unwanted cats' she had been feeding for five years. 'Some were trapped and destroyed by the Jersey Animal Shelter, some were rehabilitated,' it was reported.

By happy accident, the much-mocked cat feeders got a celebrity champion in the shape of twenty-something fashion model Celia Hammond who, it would be said, 'converted to herbal cosmetics and synthetic furs after she sat next to an old lady with a handbag-full of slaughterhouse pictures on a bus at Marble Arch'. Again on a London bus (models of the time were not yet quite so Super), she spotted a cat at the window of a boarded-up house in Kilburn, 'broke in with a crowbar' and found the wraithlike creature with three dead kittens. 'I took her home, and that was my first rescue,' she would later tell an interviewer.

Her cat advocacy was immediate and practical, with an understanding that the three cat worlds did indeed come together, interact freely, and that unneutered domestic cats and strays were the source of a continuous stream of free-roaming cats and feral kittens. The outcasts would have to be dealt with first – but not by killing.

A Pathé newsreel was shot in colour of Miss Hammond and her friend, fellow long-blonde-haired model, Sue Gunn, at work in battered-looking, late sixties London rounding up cats and kittens in a sunny daytime car park (lots of Hillman Minxes) with RSPCA-supplied kipper-baited traps and wicker baskets.

'There are thousands of semi-wild cats on derelict building sites in London. This is a problem for the RSPCA as the cats spread diseases,' said the narrator sternly.

'The girls sometimes keep the cats themselves – Celia has fifteen in her London flat and will soon move to a house in the country with more space.' How nice for everyone! No mention was made of neutering and returning.

Miss Hammond carried on trapping, neutering and finding homes where she could for wild-side cats until in 1971 the willowy former model, who had given up her career to work fulltime with ferals, started, as a temporary measure, to put them back where they had come from.

It seemed to work. Neutering was apparently stabilising colony numbers. Colonies were independent and did not interact with other colonies even over comparatively short ranges, it could be observed. The returned cats on their reappearance were reported to be more docile – even affectionate – which made it all the more rewarding for the little bands of feeders who came to tend them.

It would be written: 'The main lessons she learned were the importance of researching the site before starting to trap, in order to get to know the cats and the feeders [who must be persuaded of the rightness of what was being done] and the importance of monitoring the site after the cats were put back, preferably by the feeders, so that sick cats could be given treatment and new cats moving in be monitored.'

With her cat-rescue credentials firmly established, Miss C. F. Hammond was elected to the RSPCA Council in 1974 on the Reform Group ticket. But she would become a familiar face of animal advocacy thereafter not so much for her well-known anti-fur trade stance (she had been a noisy fur-coat refusenik in the fashion industry) as for her very unusual brand of cat advocacy. She and other reformers would move to set up further various specific-issue working parties on the Society's ambitiously broad new agenda.

One result would be the setting up of a 'feral cats working party' with funding from the RSPCA. It was chaired by an eminent veterinarian, Mr Oliphant Jackson. Also aboard were Miss Hammond, CPL veteran Mrs Nerea de Clifford and the animal rights philosopher, Richard Ryder, who would be the RSPCA Council's Chairman for two years in the late 1970s and still be very active on the Council forty years later. The working party would meet sporadically as the years passed, keeping its head down as civil war raged in the Society. The official RSPCA line on ferals remained trapping and destruction. It was also the official policy of the Cats Protection League and the other major welfare charities. What's more, it was pointed out by the many sceptics that releasing ferals at unmonitored sites constituted abandonment – and thus was illegal under English Law. But who was going to do the monitoring?

Whatever the critics might say, the idea of Trap, Neuter and Return was now well out of the bag. The Danish Society for the Protection of Cats had established the technique of clipping one centimetre from the left ear of a free-living cat under anaesthesia during neutering to mark it as 'vetted'; this procedure was taken up. Some trapped cats, as it turned out, had already been neutered, indicating that they were one-time pets. Experiments with an oral contraceptive, pioneered in Denmark and taken up by Dr Jenny Remfry, were meanwhile proving extremely problematic.

A London vet experienced in dealing with trapped ferals ('the untouchables' as he called them) told readers of *Veterinary Practice* magazine of his amazement 'at how many trapped and homed cats, especially the young ones, became so surprisingly tame after six months [of human company]'.

But the adult feral tom (all the ones he had dealt with were in 'superb physical condition') was effectively a ferocious wild animal, he said, 'astonishingly strong and fast'. One had clawed its way to freedom through a mattress. What to do with them? He could not condone killing them. 'I can only admire their stamina, power, grace and intelligence,' he wrote. Such splendid feline gladiators deserved some form of sanctuary which certain CPL members were evidently trying to provide.

Much about these extraordinary animals remained unknown. Would neutered cats really become friendlier? Would 'entire' toms attack neutered cats or wander away seeking punch-ups and other excitements of life on the wild side? Could feral cats ever be homed? Would neutered cats be territorial? And there were moral questions.

Was feline feral life in cities with its disease and pain, deformed inbred kittens and general squalor, a man-made freak show which should be suppressed by the most immediate means available? What were auxiliary feeders but mad cat collectors who had just taken their cruel passion out of doors? These debates would continue for decades to come.

The TNR advocates still needed proof, more scientific research and hard facts to demonstrate that this was not just a potentially expensive excuse by a new wave of bothersome

cat ladies to save poor pussy one more time. The neuterers
had, in fact, found a niche habitat where the established charities would not go, and they swarmed in to exploit it.

In spite of the CPL's doctrinal opposition, a request for
information on location of colonies was published in *The Cat*
– along with a list of dos and don'ts for feeders: no chicken
bones, take pregnant females first, and beware of cat thieves.
And don't start feeding cats unless you are prepared to
continue! Nerea de Clifford did not know what to do. 'Little
Wildie Kittens,' she wrote, 'it is hopeless to put them into
pens or sanctuaries.' It was much better 'to take the pregnant
cats as soon as they are noticed, even if they might have to be
put to sleep. Could anyone suggest a better way?'

With the RSPCA paralysed and the CPL dithering, an ad
hoc 'National Cat Rescue Co-ordinating Committee' set up
its stall with the veteran welfare activist Miss Ruth Plant as its
driving force, Born in the Edwardian era with impeccably
eccentric do-gooding credentials, she had been 'cat indoctri-
nated' by her mother; between them, they had sheltered a
large collection of wartime feline refugees at their agreeable
home in the Chilterns. Miss Plant's post-war interests would
embrace all sorts of causes including a 'National Rescue
Service for Dogs', with municipal dog-catchers replaced by a
uniformed Dog Warden Service. '[Our] policy is to chase the
owner as well as the dog,' she would say – and it would
happen.

Two members of the Universities Federation for Animal
Welfare,* Dr Jenny Remfry and her assistant Peter Neville,
who had been researching ferals since the early 1970s,
provided the necessary scientific resource. The Committee's
first public meeting was held at Caxton Hall in September

---

* Set up in 1926 as the University of London Animal Welfare Society to find
a humane way forward on the treatment of animals by scientific researchers.

1975 with Celia Hammond as Chairman. Richard Ryder and Mrs de Clifford of the CPL were also on the platform. It was the same place where, seven decades earlier, Kate Cording had raised the banner of the Feline Rescue League and where in 1927 the Cats Protection League had been launched.

These seemed like good omens. But was the new committee to be wrapped in old-fashioned do-gooding sentiment? In fact, it was very practical, announcing that rodent control on the kind of sites that ferals prowled was a boon to human society and a cost-saver for local authorities. Just as significant was their pronouncement that the connection between outcast cats and humans still existed. If they could be caught and rehabilitated young enough, juvenile ferals might indeed 'make good domestic pets'.

What was needed more than anything was an understanding of the science of it all. Supporters recruited from cat-lady ranks were asked to keep records of the animals they encountered: the data they kept track of had to be about true ferals, not strays that had wandered in nor the kittens in the supporter's own house that had already been handled by humans and thus been semi-tamed. Early results were remarkable: 76 per cent of kittens became completely tame on homing while neutered adults became notably less shy with time. It was also a general finding that cats became fatter and sleeker after neutering and the males fought less – altogether a good thing.

In 1977 the National Cat Rescue Co-ordinating Committee turned into the snappier-sounding 'Cat Action Trust'. Clunkingly sexist press attention focused on its photogenic figurehead. It was reported:

Celia Hammond, that wispy model of the mid-sixties, who shocked the fashion world fifteen years ago with an unfashionable refusal to pose in furs, drew blood yet again for the animal kingdom yesterday ... [T]he delectable Miss

Hammond launched the new organisation called the Cat Action Trust and announced that even cats living in feral colonies have rights. The aims of the Trust will be to ensure the security of these cats (good news) partly by controlling their numbers through sterilisation (less good news), and to find them more foster homes and sanctuary accommodation.

Miss Hammond told me: 'For many years feral cats have been treated as vermin, and we have to elevate their status. They are in the state they are because of man's ignorance and lack of caring. They have rights and must no longer be persecuted.'

Miss Hammond would be the Trust's patron. The young biologist Roger Tabor of the North-East London Polytechnic, and Jenny Remfry of UFAW provided the veterinary and animal behaviour advice. Mrs de Clifford had to resign, as the CPL's policy at the time was euthanasia for ferals.*

It began modestly enough with volunteers taking calls and making connections, urging those with feral cat issues to adopt Trap Neuter and Return as the best solution. Some politically modernist councils gave them experimental contracts. A colony of hep-cats prowling the gritty alley and fire escape behind a jazz club in Oxford Street, central London, co-existed with a number of tramps. It was reported:

* It was not for want of compassion. Mrs de Clifford had written a perceptive article in *The Cat* in 1973 about 'cats running on sites'. These were 'the strays' . . . the 'ones we are trying to help' – which she considered to fall into three categories: 'the shy ones who could be reclaimed at any time', 'the nervous ones who might take years to become friendly cats again' and 'the wild cats taught by their mothers from birth that humans can never be trusted. Those cats could have cheerful lives in the country.' But beyond that, wrote Mrs de Clifford, were 'the tragic ones who have let go, so sunk in terror . . . there is no real cat-mind left . . . I hate to advocate destruction for any cat, but for these I think there is no happy future . . .'

'CAT stepped in and now four of the neutered favourites have become valued mascots and energetic mousers. What about the tramps? "My sympathies don't extend as far as that," the cat person said.'

The British Museum solution, in the end, was to turn those pesky staff feeders into a committee with a cat warden in charge. A move to make certain feeding sites 'official' reduced random feeding by the visiting public. A large weatherproof cattery was erected where neutered cats could sleep comfortably enough. The Tate Gallery colony got less benign treatment – they were trapped and destroyed.

One of the first trappers was Mr Rex Sheppard, the British Museum cat man. Jenny Remfry remembered him in his warder's uniform decked out with homemade badges and an armband saying CAT CONTROL. 'He was sent by Ruth Plant to trap all the cats at the BBC TV Centre in west London . . . which he did very successfully – some of the broadcasters offering homes to the kittens.' Sister Sheila Young of Mount Vernon Hospital feral cat fame joined the committee. Hospitals would be important clients for the pioneers, especially the big old mental asylums around London, gothic cathedrals in wooded grounds, all absolutely full of cats. Jenny Remfry recalled how patients drew special comfort from them – including one elderly woman who had been there for decades apparently unable to speak or make any human connection. But she would talk to her cat, the chosen one from the colony. That the NHS should employ pest-control firms to shoot them seemed appalling.

In her book, unpublished at the time but incorporated by Jenny Remfry into her biography of the tireless cat-campaigner, the then sixty-five-year-old Ruth Plant described being taught cat-trapping by Celia Hammond. The former model would 'wait quietly for a cat to walk into the trap to take the bait' and then pull a string to close it. They went to work after pub closing time in a yard near Claridge's Hotel in Mayfair and were given encouraging words by an approving policeman, although another tried to arrest them for a breach of the peace.

'Passers-by would notice [Celia] and think she was a beautiful vagrant wanting help and would rush over and offer her aid, thus disturbing the cat she was patiently trying to catch . . . But Celia would go on until all the cats had been trapped and stowed in the boot of her car.' Covent Garden remained full of cats, and while famous actors and publishers also indulged their secret cat-feeding passion, some old-style cat ladies – and cat collectors – were still in residence. Accompanying a theatrical friend, Miss Plant was surprised at their sense of proprietorship.

A cat with an injured eye was the object of a dispute. When her friend attempted to feed it, an ardent supporter of the cat arrived, 'a thin pale lady dressed in long black clothes':

> She was the daughter of one of the original market traders of Covent Garden, now dispersed since the fruit market had gone. She declared it was her cat and she could offer it a home and that it had been her responsibility to feed it. She had a good vocabulary of some exceedingly colourful words and spouted these out in a torrent. The atmosphere became so electrically charged that we withdrew apparently defeated [a policeman is summoned and the cat fed by middle-class hands].

The biggest menace to the Covent Garden animals, however, were those ladies who could not bear the idea of anyone else tending their cats after they themselves had become unable to do so. As Ruth Plant recorded:

The strangest people of all are those who, moved by apparent motives of compassion, turn killer towards those they set out originally to help.

First in this category are the so-called rescuers who have become so caught up in the system of killing that they have become rather like the ladies who took their knitting to the guillotine to watch the heads fall. Mostly it gets round the grapevine: 'she is a killer – don't let her get hold of any cats'.

Mostly these ladies have their own lethal boxes and there is no investigation of their methods, which they do under the evasive cliché of 'putting them down'.

The second type is the long-term feeder of a colony, very emotional people, for whom when the problem becomes just too big, they subconsciously feel this is the only way to throw it off – by terminating the cats. For instance, after one feeder had been forced to give up feeding a colony for financial reasons, she had demanded that all the cats were killed, although there were other feeders to carry on. I was the recipient of mysterious anonymous phone calls in which an eerie voice cried out: 'Mary's cats are sick. They must die.'

Miss Plant, a veteran spiritualist, thought that such people should consider the prospect of being haunted by the spirits of the cats they had so cruelly killed – 'remaining in an after-life existence in a state of terror close to the place of their destruction'. She had plenty of personal experience herself of visitations by ghostly cats – but in her case, all purringly benign. Cat killers better watch out!

On a much more inspiring note, a woman in Woolwich, Miss Emily Dyer, was still feeding cats in a south-east London churchyard at the age of a hundred. Miss Plant discovered this Edwardian survivor from the days of Kate Cording and Zoe Morgan – who between them might have had plenty of ghost cats to worry about. And there was Mary Wyatt, who had been feeding the cats of Fitzroy Square ('a plump flock') from her little trolley since the early 1950s.

Miss Plant and Miss Hammond worked in the semi-ruinous former electricity sub-station at St John's Wood, after difficult negotiations with both the site owners and the gaggle of anonymous feeders, who regarded every outsider with suspicion. Fulham Broadway underground station was next for treatment with a big colony fed by passengers and ever growing in spite of the attention of pest control contractors. The response to notices saying *Do Not Feed the Cats* had been that more food was put down by both public and devoted auxiliary feeders. One of them, a Mrs Dennis, cleaned offices by night and spent most of her wages on food for 'her' cats. 'The work went on night after night – batches of cats being driven by Miss Hammond to her vet in Sussex for neutering.' As Ruth Plant would write:

> The cats in the station colony have now grown into a beauti-
> ful healthy happy group of cared-for cats without the
> emotional strain of having kittens to carry and defend.
> Controlling the numbers of a feral cat colony is a race against
> time with kittens produced faster than the adults can be
> trapped and neutered. A solution to this problem would be a
> safe birth control pill which would permanently sterilise the
> cat with one dose. I have never ceased in my quest to find
> one . . .

Ruth Plant, with her concern for cat activists as strong as that for cats themselves, emphasised the role of auxiliary feeders in the new urban ecosystem. They must be organised for every site, she insisted, 'because feeders will eventually grow old, ill or move away.' She would like to see a 'Guild of Feeders', so it was reported, 'which could send a locum whenever or wherever the system broke down'.

Herding cats was notoriously difficult. Herding cat ladies might prove equally so. And not all of those actually in favour were fit enough to spend a sleepless night clambering about some derelict post-industrial landscape in the dark.

The new mood was internationally infectious. In 1979 French cat advocate M. Michel Cambazard began to argue for the protection of free-living cats at the Montmartre Cemetery in Paris, where the cats were routinely trapped and killed by municipal contractors. A year later, the deputy mayor of Paris in charge of environmental matters, Mme Jacqueline Nebout, issued a 'Declaration of Rights of the Free-living Cat' and M. Cambazard founded the École du Chat which soon thereafter trapped, neutered and returned its first French feline.

In England the RSPCA, with the reformers still ascendant on its council, was proving a willing fellow-traveller of all this pro-stray, even pro-feral sentiment. As the arguments over the Society's royal patrons' fox-hunting, about factory farming and the rest of it got ever more raucous, it was feared by some of the surviving traditionalists that all this trendy radicalism would threaten the Society's key source of funds – legacies. But it might be said that the by-now expiring Edwardian generation had always been sound on cats – certainly not excluding strays. The Society's concern for all cats was surely a plus, as was a declared attempt after so very long to move away from euthanasia of any healthy animal – stray, semi-wild or otherwise. All of a sudden, ending the killing was a burning issue. It was what both traditionalist members and reformist zealots wanted, surely?

In April 1978 the RSPCA had set up an 'Unwanted Animals Working Party' chaired by the self-avowed reformer

John Bryant who was coincidentally Manager of the Ferne Animal Sanctuary.*

Six months later it recommended in principle that a 'commitment be made to cease the destruction of healthy animals' before the end of the decade. That was fantastically ambitious. But it looked as if the ghosts of Fellowship Cottage might be laid to rest at last. Surely this was something the warring wings of the Society could unite behind?

They could not. According to one partisan pro-Reform Group history of the Society, published when the issue was still very heated, the bar on healthy animal destruction was bitterly resisted by the branches, 'where people boasted about the number of animals they put down, affirming that they were not going to stop'. Re-homing was, apparently, 'too much trouble', and ferals were beyond the pale. Ruth Plant recorded an encounter with 'the military organiser of a big welfare society' (presumably the RSPCA). '"I have no use for wildies", he said. "All those will have to be put down". He indicated an area outside his window.'

After more bruising infighting, Mr Bryant resigned and the 'no destruction of healthy animals' imperative was overturned by the new (some might say 'realist') council, which was elected in 1981 under the chairmanship of Conservative MP Miss Janet Fookes. With a cash crisis looming, amid general sackings and resignations, it was soon announced that the Mayhew Home would close, as 'part of a big package of cuts to save the Society from disaster'. An RSPCA spokeswoman disputed the Mayhew manager's claim that the home handled

* Nina, Duchess of Hamilton died in 1951 with a clause in her will that Ferne should remain as an animal sanctuary in perpetuity, but the restrictions were reportedly so stringent that the house was unsaleable and was demolished in 1965. The animal sanctuary moved to Chard in Somerset and a new house was built on the site in neo-Georgian style for the 4th Viscount Rothermere, proprietor of the *Daily Mail* newspaper, long a champion of cats.

13,000 animals a year. She described it simply as a 'stopping-off refuge'. In fact, the unique institution would be promptly rescued by a breakaway faction and resume its proud independence.

Another decade of RSPCA turmoil would follow as the animal rights exponents were themselves purged from the council, whilst claiming simultaneously that the 'battle of ideas had been won'. Much had changed, but business as usual was resumed. The killing would go on.

Even good old Battersea caught some of the new mood. Always at the grimier end of the urban dog business, a new Director General, Colonel Anthony Hare, expressed anger in the Home's Annual Report at the treatment of companion animals in the 'throwaway society' of the 1980s and the stream of 'sick and frightened animals' arriving every day.

There were practical changes. After half a century, euthanasia by electrocution was at last abandoned in favour of lethal injection. A proper veterinary hospital was established. Checks on potential adopters became much more rigorous. It would be said: 'For the first time, dogs and cats could be given a complete medical examination before they were allowed to leave.' Cats for re-homing were alive and well, and living in hope at Battersea. Things could only get better. And they would.

25

Feral Frenzy

TESSIE

Female, age (approx.) 7 DOMESTIC LONG-HAIR, black and white, cannot live with other cats.
When Tessie went to her previous home several years ago it was a quiet home. However, with the addition of a baby, Tessie found it hard to cope with the changes. She was not getting on well with the other cats in the home either so now finds herself looking for a new home. A lovely cat who just wants a quieter lifestyle.

As the RSPCA writhed in turmoil, in the United States the animal welfare establishment would get its own equivalent culture shock with the beginning in 1980 of 'People for the Ethical Treatment of Animals' ('PETA'). It was co-founded and energetically led by the Surrey-born Ingrid Newkirk, who would famously date her conversion to animal rights to a moment when she took her neighbour's abandoned cats to a squalid, broken-down 'shelter' in Maryland where they were promptly all destroyed. Over the next three decades, PETA would grow to become, reportedly, the largest animal rights group in the world.

Whether the ever more powerful PETA would function as a rights campaign or as old-style 'welfarists' (the term was used in a derogatory sense) would be a matter of deepening controversy and have some unlooked-for consequences for cats everywhere.

The stately Washington-based Humane Society of the United States, which had itself come into being as the result of a doctrinal schism, inevitably, it might seem, began its own slow, uncomfortable move in the animal rights direction around the same time. Its own running of shelters would progressively end. In the search for doctrinal purity, at least the RSPCA did not consider doing that. It might have been more convenient all round if it had.

Academic research into cat behaviour generally was becoming respectable. But not much had really been done thus far on the feline wild side. Life scientists were suddenly taking the utmost interest in the feral colonies which the new-wave cat activists were finding so beguiling.

How did cats, so famously aloof and only happy in their own company, operate in groups? Were they really 'colonies' or agglomerations of convenience? Did they work differently in the country and the city? In 1975, the biologist Roger Tabor began work on his famous study of 'the wild life of the domestic cat', observing free-roaming cats in west central London at a time when the ravages of war were by no means entirely healed.

His attention turned to Fitzroy Square with its early nineteenth-century terraced houses now largely occupied by offices. For many years it had been home to a colony of free-living black-and-white cats said by some to have inspired T. S. Eliot's nocturnal Jellicle Cats, as the poet wandered over to Fitzrovia from his publisher's office in nearby Russell Square and observed their tuxedoed routine on the eve of the Second World War.

If that was so, then the cats were there before the wartime upsets which served to turn London into a feral cat megalopolis. Whatever the truth about their origin, Roger Tabor's work would make the Fitzrovia felines, for a time, as famous as any Roman amphitheatre cat.

Why did the inner city remain such a feline magnet? It was warmer than the outer suburbs, he explained, and devoid of the delineated gardens of the outer suburbs which territorial, one-family domestic cats found so convivial and worthy of defence. The railings, areas and basements of the terraced-housing pattern south of Regent's Park were particularly amenable to free-living cats.

West London also tended to support more feral cats because an older, wealthier population meant more auxiliary feeders. Sandwich-sharing office workers provided extra lunchtime sustenance. And over the years the inhabitants of Fitzrovia had not seemed concerned enough to urge St Pancras (later Camden) Borough Council to bring in the exterminators. In fact, they were keen to keep them out.

Another feral 'colony', in rural Devon, studied by Dr David Macdonald and P. J. Apps of Oxford University in the winter of 1977–8, was found to include one adult tom (called 'Tom'), and three adult females: 'Domino', 'Pickle' and 'Smudge'. They lived around a barn, but also wandered over the surrounding farms and their outbuildings. On-cat micro radio transmitters tracked their progress.

The cats seemed to like each other. In the course of two six-hour sessions under observation, each animal approached every other member of the colony amicably. Throughout all the months of observation, only seventy-two aggressive interactions were noted, and exactly half of them were directed against a stray male, 'Shadow', who was chased off whenever he put in an appearance.

Of thirteen 'internecine struggles', none were serious, and twenty-two were directed by Tom towards Domino, who pestered him with her attentions. Thus, out of 1200 observed social interactions, there were only fourteen instances of spontaneous aggression among the four. This was a small cohesive cat tribe with developed manners and mutual support systems. Even solitary predators could be social.*

The Devon farm cats received the nutritional equivalent of two mice per day in the form of powdered milk prepared by human hands. For the rest, they hunted. They ate what cats are supposed to eat – rodents and insectivores, such as house mice and wood mice, shrews, voles, the odd mole and young rabbit. They also caught small birds – blackbirds, hedge sparrows and marsh tits. What's more, they proved more adventurous and less choosy in their diet than cat folklore might have predicted, killing and eating brown rat, weasel and slow-worm plus a great many insects – mainly grasshoppers.

Was this uncontrolled population explosion by a 'superabundant' and successful predator about to massively disrupt Britain's wildlife – already under pressure from environmental change? It was not just ferals, of course, but the ever-increasing number of domestic cats having a go at whatever might be in the garden. Many bird-lovers thought the cat catastrophe was already upon them – a view that would grow over future decades as the cat population continued to increase.

Being pro- or anti-cat, like being pro- or anti-fox, took on a political dimension. People had to choose sides. It was easier perhaps to get away with outright cat-hating, as long as they were pesky 'non-native' ferals consuming songbirds and field

---

* Concerning rescue cats, behaviourist and historian Sarah Hartwell would note: 'Cats in captive colonies at animal shelters often form close friendships which last for many years.' She recounted the case of 'Eagle', who 'shared an enclosure with eleven other "unhomeable" cats. The other cats frequently rubbed against Eagle and chose to sit close to him. When Eagle died, the relationship between the other cats broke down and the colony fragmented into several small groups. The super-sociable Eagle had been the glue that held them together.'

mice rather than canned whale-meat, which was, inciden-
tally, banned as a pet food from the early 1970s.

There would be storms ahead. But at least there was no
rush on behalf of scientists to discontinue their research into
that now very fashionable and fascinating animal – the cat.

More studies by Roger Tabor and Dr Jenny Remfry of
UFAW looked at both semi-wild urban cats and the 'vast
army', as they were described, of old ladies who acted as 'auxiliary feeders'. The cat-lovers would turn out to be much harder
to study. Observing the social life of feral town cats meanwhile
showed it to be just as complex as their rural equivalents. They
did indeed tend to live in 'colonies', which in towns commonly
contained an optimum number of twenty to thirty animals.
Any smaller and there might be a surplus of food or whatever
attracted the cats in the first place, so that more would be
drawn in, making the colony 'unstable' and 'likely to frag-
ment', as observations were beginning to show.

At the time there was much debate on whether these gath-
erings really were colonies – or were they what some researchers, in the case of farm cats, called 'unstructured aggregations
around the milk churn', or, in the case of city cats, around
the cat lady who came to feed them.

Dr Macdonald concluded that his Devon cats had 'complex
social structures' – while Roger Tabor observed that free-
living town cats dwelling in mother/sibling families within a
colony would be joined by unrelated cats, including strays,
living in as solitary a state as they might, but forming up
together in the evening at a specific time and then moving off
as a group to find their feeder. It was completely fascinating.

The role of the auxiliary feeders was vital – although
nobody suggested rounding *them* up – but this was only part
of the survival mechanism. In a paper delivered to the Feline
Advisory Bureau's annual conference in 1979, Dr Remfry
wrote: 'Our familiar fireside cat is still not totally

domesticated in that it is not really dependent on man . . .
cats abandoned on derelict building sites in central London
will do remarkably well on rodents, birds, frogs, contents of
dustbins [as well as] the food left for them by sympathetic
cat-lovers.'

In 1975 Dr Jane Dards began a study of feral cats in the
Portsmouth naval dockyard. There were about a hundred
females in the colony producing four hundred kittens a
year. All the infants contracted cat flu to some extent and
the mortality rate was high. The coat colour genetics of the
colony cats, she found, were very different to those outside
the dockyard, which had been enclosed by a high wall since
the early nineteenth century. The naval cats had survived
in their cut-off genetic island down the generations ever
since. She wrote: 'As I studied this enclosed high-density
population, I realised that the cats were living in social
groups, and that much of their behaviour paralleled that of
the lion, which was previously considered to be the only
social cat.'

The studies were published in learned journals then exam-
ined at a UFAW-sponsored symposium held at Royal
Holloway College, University of London, in September
1980. It was a real turning-point. The gathering estimated
the number of free-living cats in Britain at an astonishing one
and a half million. The RSPCA's Feral Cat Working Party
gave a very useful interim report on why there were so many.
The reasons were:

> Unwanted kittens being foisted on families who neither want
> nor intend caring for them.
>
> Queens having litters in outhouses or on wasteland and
> which then grow up wild.
>
> Cats being encouraged into factories or hospital grounds as
> rodent suppressors.

Abandonment of an entire female rather than humane destruction.

Cultural resistance to sterilising cats or destroying unwanted litters, kittens from which are either abandoned or sold.

In addition, cats sometimes wandered off from human company sensing neglect or indifference, or they were driven out by other 'bullying' cats.

Sister Sheila Young gave useful advice on the mechanics of capturing cats: use a big cage to do the trapping but a smaller one to transport the animal – specifically the UFAW-approved 'crush-back version' which could restrain the animal and still allow the vet to anaesthetise and neuter it.

'Before trapping, one must find a vet willing to handle feral cats which will be very angry by the time they reach the surgery,' she said in her detailed submission. 'Some cats will have to die – the very old, unhealthy or injured cats which would normally have crept away to die in a corner.' Once they were returned, the cats must be fed and monitored by carers. As for homing, it was very possible, said Sister Young, who remarkably advocated bringing prospective adopters to the colony's site to feed and fuss over them, thus allowing the cat to 'choose her rather than the other way round'. 'Feral cats can become domestic cats, as I have proved with great satisfaction several times over, but great patience and under-standing are needed,' she said. Everyone could agree on that.

Miss Hammond told the conference that in the eighteen years she had been involved in cat rescue, attitudes had changed from regarding strays as 'vermin fit only for extermination' to recognition both of their 'innate right to life' and their useful role. It was not just rodent-suppression. A big part of why ferals were good for us was by providing 'a reason to live for many lonely old people who feed them and suffer deep emotional crisis when their cats are swept away'.

Professional cat trapper Michael Jackson described the use of a baited trap with its swing door operated by a line at a range of 200 yards. A blanket should be thrown over the once-trapped cats to 'quiet them down', he explained. Nets and graspers were used in corridors or crevices. Mr Jackson's company were commercial cat trappers responding to clients' requests; up to now those requests had been for destruction on public health grounds (around a hundred cats per week). Now they were in the cat rescue business. 'We still use the chloroform box,' he told the conference, 'as do the RSPCA . . . if used correctly, it is better than injections. The cat doesn't get banged about so much.'

Roger Tabor's contribution to the conference would be expanded in a popular paperback book. The publication in 1983 of *The Wild Life of the Domestic Cat* did much to bring Britain's strays culturally in out of the cold. As well as providing a fascinating account of how feral colonies had begun and managed to stay in existence (places to hide, plastic sacks versus metal dustbins, auxiliary feeders, acquired disease resistance), he advanced novel-seeming reasons why managing them without destruction was viable and practical. And doing so was not necessarily 'animal rights' based. According to him:

> The feral cat is not necessarily a health risk to either ourselves or our pet cats; indeed, they try to keep themselves clean and healthy and away from us.

But what about the quality of their life, the perceived suffering and brutishness which had been the moral excuse for so much destruction down the decades? Were they not lost in savage darkness? The opposite seemed true. They were leading lives with a harmonious social structure. At Fitzroy Square, the central London object of special study, the long-established colony of similar coat colour that had made it their family territory displayed 'social interactions of a friendly nature', he wrote. On the arrival of the auxiliary feeder, at regular times, the cats would acknowledge both each other and the feeder herself with the 'tails-up greeting'. The only real aggression was shown to outside cats.

There were dangers. Feeders, for instance, regularly caught ringworm – while cats on hospital sites might need some control. One hospital in south London reported that the 'maintenance staff were terrorised by the feline residents prowling the basements'; their fleas also got into the heating ducts, and 'there have been dramatic stories of fleas migrating as far as the operating theatre', as Dr Jenny Remfry had reported to the symposium. But in other places, it might be best just to leave the cats alone.

Roger Tabor also importantly described the 'vacuum' effect, when survivors of eradication attempts started breeding again or new arrivals were sucked into newly feral-cleansed territory. The science showed that both in a rural setting and isolated urban sites, eradication by whatever legal means could effectively control numbers for a long period. But in big cities, especially London, if the site was good enough to support a healthy colony, eradication left an empty space that 'envious cats around the corner are only too keen to fill'. It had been observed crucially that neutered and returned ferals continued to defend their territory. Leave a guard contingent in place and they would keep out the opportunists (with some crossover of very determined strays). This would be the Trap Neuter and Return advocates' core argument.

And so it would work out as, over the years to come, urban colonies were brought under increasing control, lots of domestic cats were spayed/neutered or became 'indoor cats', and habitat niches were vacated for other predators and scavengers to occupy. Amid the concrete and clay, all sorts of new wild-side opportunists would begin to make their presence felt.

The RSPCA's Feral Cat Working Party, a relic of the now retreating reformist tide, was still working away as best it could. Its investigators managed to survey 704 colonies, with an estimated population of about 12,300 cats. It reported formally, at last, in March 1982 just as the Society reached a new peak of internal infighting (there were suggestions in the press at the time that it would be 'kinder to have it painlessly put to sleep'), observing that:

> Colonies of feral cats, previously largely confined to farms, developed in towns and cities during the Second World War bombing, when whole rows of houses were destroyed and domestic pets were left to fend for themselves. Since then, indiscriminate breeding, a diminished public sense of responsibility towards pet animals, the inclination of many people to feed strays, and restrictions on pets by local authorities [in council flats] have contributed to their increase. There were heavy concentrations in the large metropolitan areas, and 52 colonies were found in one 10-square kilometre of central London.

The survey discovered that in nine out of ten colonies studied, someone either working or living on the territory was actively feeding the cats. The UFAW researchers would also conclude in parallel that the main influence on a colony's survival was the auxiliary feeder.

And as for the Society's own policy on ferals henceforth, the council could formally advise: 'Where their presence is welcomed by the owners of the site, the RSPCA advocates sterilisation of these cats, provided the instructions concerning humane procedures are followed.'

The RSPCA had joined the club. The question remained: who was going to do the sterilising? The crisis-torn Society itself clearly was in no fit state to do so. Where the Cat Action Trust was leading, others were following. As the old-guard cat welfarists stayed aloof, the feral aficionados had found their own vacuum and were rushing to fill it. Like 'SNIP' for example, the 'Society for Neutering Islington's Pussies', which began life in 1983 under the inspiration of cat activist Kate Horne to cover the part of north London where Kate Cording and Eliza Clegg had long ago swished their nets – but with very different outcomes in mind. As she told the story:

> Where I worked in central London there was a tortoiseshell cat which kept having kittens in the street which were captured and dealt with by the RSPCA. I heard about Celia Hammond and she arrived one Sunday afternoon to trap the cat.
>
> The cat came to live with me in Islington afterwards, named Cecilia after her. Celia saw my enthusiasm for the TNR approach and set me up with a trap. Islington Council asked me to talk to them about running an official scheme.

Thus it began, after a 'grilling by the Environment Committee', with the award of a small grant. Indeed the council's enthusiasm would draw grants-for-lesbian-judo 'loony left' accusations from some quarters for allegedly promoting 'cat neutering on the rates'. SNIP would later split, in good animal welfare tradition, into rival factions with Kate Horne leading a TNR drive into the eastern Mediterranean under the banner 'SNIP International'.

In 1980 the remarkable 'Cats in Industry' charity was founded in Sheffield by Mrs Myra Hammond and Miss Pat Finch to meet a feline emergency when the factory cats of the city were effectively abandoned during the national steel strike. The wider plight of free-roaming, blue-collar cats across the nation was dramatically highlighted: 'few received veterinary care and many were outright ferals attracted to canteen scraps', as it would be recorded. De-industrialisation would present the biggest challenge to rust-belt cats since the Second World War. *The Cat* usefully pointed out meanwhile that the veterinary and food costs of farm and industrial cats were tax-deductible.

Mrs Myra Hammond and her supporters 'lobbied factory managers to set up proper feeding stations for the cats and to provide veterinary care and vaccinations. Where that failed, she sought individual employees to adopt and take home the tamer cats.'

Cats in Industry soon had around five hundred subscribers and small shelters – in Middlesbrough, Southampton and South Wales, fundraising, making cat-food collections and appeals on behalf of working cats. A strong campaigner for neutering, Mrs Hammond realised that companies were not going to pay the £16 fee. An alternative was to add oral contraceptives to the cats' food – a move which feline life scientists were experimenting with, and which was proving difficult.

CPL member Sue Gross would tell the story of 'Martha', born in April 1967 at British Steel's works on Teesside, an industrial cat looked after by the 'works cat man', a Mr George Carroll. Martha had her ear burned in a furnace in which she had been sleeping overnight. The next day she had three kittens. Sue met Martha and George in 1979 when he was looking after sixty steelyard cats – which had been put on the payroll. They were made redundant, along with every-one else, in 1981 with no plan as to their fate.

Over the next two years the CPL managed to evacuate, Oskar Schindler style, 122 cats and kittens to local homes.

Martha refused to leave, even when demolition men found her, 'a dirty, scrawny cat sitting on a bogie' inside the vast, abandoned steel mill. Sue Gross caught her, 'calmed her down a bit', and at the age of sixteen Martha had two 'beautiful long-haired kittens'.

Cats in Industry, sadly, would fade away. Health and Safety regulations and de-industrialisation progressively doomed the working factory cat. The last Post Office Headquarters official cat, 'Blackie', died in 1984. And 'Tiddles', the enormous tabby adopted as a stray kitten who had ruled the ladies' lavatories at Paddington station for thirteen years, would check out of her subterranean realm in 1983.*

Where things had gone really feral, mainstream animal charities would move in to do the trapping and destruction, while commercial pest controllers were contracted to deal with both feral colonies and the rats and mice which once had been the excuse for many a corporately homed office cat.† White-collar cats generally were being put out of a job with a few high-profile exceptions, like 'Wilberforce' the Downing Street cat (see p. 261). National Health Service cats were already finding their own special way forward.

---

* Ex-stray, two-stone Tiddles, described by one observer as being 'not unlike an overweight puma', received fan mail from all over the world and was an international feline media phenomenon long before the internet. He reportedly had an official British Rail fridge packed with donated pet food at his bulky disposal.

† Pockets of feline employment held out. In January 2016 it would be announced: 'The last working animals from a British coal mine – four feral cats – have been rehomed by Cats Protection following the closure of the Kellingley Colliery, the UK's last deep coal pit', in Beal, Yorkshire. 'Florence', 'Betty', 'Leia' and 'Solo' had been 'well cared for by the miners who had provided food, water and shelter, and were in great condition', according to Cats Protection's York Adoption Centre who had been called in by 'concerned miners'. The semi-wild rescuees began new above-ground lives as farm cats.

26

The Moral Maze

MURIEL

Female, age (approx.) 12, DOMESTIC SHORT-HAIR, black.
Muriel is a gentle-natured lady who would be great for an older family home where she can have lots of fuss and attention. Muriel would be perfect if you're looking for a companion, as she is so affectionate. The lovely Muriel is very much a homebody – going outside is just far too much effort! A warm spot on the sofa is far more appealing than outdoor adventures. Muriel would really need to live as an only pet as she isn't at all keen on other animals. Could you offer this sweet lady a fresh start?

Cats were suddenly everywhere – especially ferals. 'What is a feral cat?' it was asked in Parliament during a debate on the sanitary state of NHS hospital kitchens and their reported infestations by 'disease-carrying' pests.*

---

* 'My understanding is that it is a cat that has gone wild,' replied London Labour MP Frank Dobson, promoting the removal of 'Crown Immunity' from prosecution for food hygiene transgressions, so that troublesome cats might be eliminated more readily. 'In certain hospitals, considerable numbers of feral cats roam round the premises,' he said, 'but because they do not fall within the definition of vermin, it is difficult to deal with them under the law.' Future Labour leader Jeremy Corbyn (who had a tabby called 'Harold Wilson', his first wife would one day reveal) supported the move.

With a boom in TV wildlife documentaries and populist life-science publishing, cat-lovers generally got a chance to find out more about life on the wild side. And there were big questions all of a sudden. Let alone rights, did cats, domestic or otherwise, have emotions? Could they feel fear, anxiety, joy, sadness, jealousy? Were they capable of love? In their treatment of live prey, could they be judged to be wilfully cruel? Lots of owners when surveyed thought they could. The feline personality was being analysed as never before.

In early 1984 the BBC 1 science show *QED* picked up on the wild life under Londoners' noses with an unprecedented primetime look at the capital's ferals. The programme was presented by writer and broadcaster Roger Tabor. There were problems, however. Known territories at the British Museum, at Covent Garden (survivors from the now transplanted fruit and vegetable market) and the famous Fulham Broadway ferals were scouted out. But all these colonies, it turned out, had already been trapped and neutered by cat welfare groups. Where was the on-screen drama in that?

Conscious that the film should not tell 'a bland, idealised story of the behaviour of a single colony of wild cats', a suitable unaltered population on which to go to work was found at a two-storey derelict factory site in Camden. Reviewers also noted the human side of the nocturnal proceedings:

> Old ladies, on the whole, appear to be long-suffering and kind to the feral ones, taking them supplies and presumably making them less independent and also less likely to depart. Some councils worry about them. Foremost among these [councils] is that one where social concern is well known to be finely honed – Islington. It has a society, SNIP (Society for the Neutering of Islington's Pussies), and a council cat-catcher. Both pursue a kind of cat-napping, doctoring the

animals and returning them to site. The cat-trapper's name is
Joy. She said her work was rather exciting.

The show also depicted a more direct approach featuring Mr
Melvin Driver, a 'professional cat catcher and putter-downer,
with technological traps and lots of chloroform'. He had been
brought in after a manufacturing company put out a contract,
following a complaint from a union. 'He seemed a kindly
man.'

Roger Tabor's book and the TV show which followed
gave the public the most intimate glimpse yet of both feral
cats and feral catchers in action. They also raised the question
that went back to the dreams of the nineteenth-century cat
utopians on both sides of the Atlantic.

Having plucked the animals from their grimy colonies,
instead of neutering and returning them to their original
stomping grounds, should attempts be made at transferring
them to some ideal 'sanctuary'? Would cat adopters or fosterers even be able to take them into ordinary homes?* What of
the burden that a new wave of migrants from the wild side
would put on an already overstretched shelter system?

Some old-school welfarists found the concept of cats as
wild animals impossible to grasp and would still rather euthanise healthy ferals so as 'to save them from their predicament'.
Others thought a second abandonment into the wild, even
when monitored in some way, was compounding the original disaster. It might even be considered illegal. Wracked by
such doubts and unable or unwilling to launch its own

---

* Cat sanctuary enthusiasts might well be city dwellers, fighting a constant
personal battle not to tip over into cat collectors. A correspondent of *The Cat*,
Patricia Mukhoty, of Shepherds Bush CPL, frankly admitted she was a 'cat
addict . . . with sixteen in her house', having to live 'one day at a time' to resist
the temptation of taking in any more. Others she knew had been unable to
resist – with disastrous consequences.

programme, the RSPCA made a small subvention to the Cat Action Trust towards paying veterinary fees. Cat rescuers were about to enter a whole new feline moral maze.

Sometimes the 'return' component was impossible anyway. The colony in question might be on a development site with bulldozers ready to move in, presenting the rescuers with a time-urgent choice of euthanising the wilder cats or keeping a proportion captive in some enclosure until a suitable new site could be found. To complicate things even further, by the early 1980s the utopian, all-must-be-saved advocates had found a new voice, starting, as it had a century before, in America – with the first outliers of what would become the 'no-kill' movement (see p. 341).

The most contentious issue was 'sanctuary' – miniature game reserves for untameable cats, an idea that had always proved contentious in law and in practice. A former riding instructress, Miss Veronica Huthwaite, had founded such a thing on the Kent Downs near Folkestone, amid some controversy. It had begun in the 1950s as a Burmese-breeding stud, then, as the charity's long-serving Secretary explained:

> Veronica began to take in stray and unwanted cats into her boarding cattery. In those days 'stray cat' tended to be a term of abuse, and there was not the concern for abandoned pets that there is now. On many farms there were still colonies of inbred diseased cats who were given nothing but whey [a by-product of cheese-making] and were required to subsist by keeping down the vermin.

Planning permission for a cat 'sanctuary' was sought. The *Kentish Express* reported: 'A haven for the accommodation of homeless cats is being planned at Rhodes Minnis. It will have everything that stray pussies dream of on cold nights . . . shelter, regular meals and a heated clubhouse for a feline get-together.'

Amid some controversy, permission was granted. The charity was registered in 1970 and began the familiar cat-shelter routine of admitting strays and looking for new homes. It was, however, a lot less eager than some to dispose of the difficult cases. Then, ten years later, as it was explained:

> The Feral Sanctuary was founded, at the furthest end of the plot behind the bungalow. Veronica had taken in a colony of about thirty undomesticated cats from one of the London University buildings. They would otherwise have been rounded up and euthanized . . .
>
> The Feral Sanctuary caught the imagination of supporters who liked to visit and observe the colony, many of whom liked to perch in a large laurel bush, safe from the stresses of the outside world. All these cats are sponsored by supporters who understand their situation and visit to get a sight of 'their' cat until he or she skitters away into the long grass, or hides in one of the refuges provided.

Miss Huthwaite died in 1996. After almost five decades the mission of Rhodes Minnis Cat Sanctuary remained as it was from the start – its aim to 're-home as many of the cats that are brought to us as possible . . . those [cats] which cannot be re-homed, because they are too timid, dirty, bad-tempered, on permanent medication or just won't settle in a house, stay with us for the rest of their lives'.

As it was explained: 'If a new home cannot be found within three to four weeks the cat is let out of the pen to join the hundred-plus who inhabit the Big House dormitory building.' After that, individual sponsorship was sought for the 'unhome-ables' – who might live out their lives just as Anne Mayhew's pensioners of Kensal Green had done a century before.

The post-banking-crash crisis would hit the Home badly. Re-homing rates collapsed while admissions exploded. It was explained: 'With a guarantee never to put any healthy cat to sleep, we are besieged with inquiries from people and other organisations and charities who want us to take cats, whilst we are largely dependent on people from our home area of East Kent to provide new homes.'

The open admission cats' home on the Kent Downs really was a sanctuary – the bravest, most resource-intensive end of cat rescue. The good ones were always full. The bad ones quickly went under. Jenny Remfry recalled a so-called sanctuary where all the cats escaped from confinement to 'roam the surrounding fields, coming back each day at feeding time, [which was] all right for a favoured few but hardly an ideal solution'.

That was an important reason why the Cats Protection League, for one, remained so wary of the new vogue for ferals. The cat behaviourist Roger Tabor advanced his own humanely sage view on the 'sanctuary' argument:

> The vast number of totally free-living cats certainly makes [concentrating on abandoned domestics] a more realistic proposition, but the people in the former camp [sanctuary for rescued ferals] have a missionary zeal in their outlook. The suggestion that free-living animals, perhaps into generations of such life, especially in rural settings where the territorial range is so large, might not really appreciate being 'saved' by being put into the narrow confines of a penned cattery is a strong bone of contention . . .

'The argument that animals can be tamed to live with man is not a valid argument for their being happier in that state,' he wrote convincingly. 'The feral domestic cat is certainly a part of our wildlife and has been so for a long time, whether we admit it or not.' There were, however, not just academic researchers, but high-profile 'wildlife' advocates who would strongly disagree.

Reports from the British pioneers and TNR's growing profile in veterinary and scientific journals had made ripples in American cat welfare circles – where the feral population, rural and urban, was estimated at up to an astonishing 60 million. For instance, there had been a discreetly maintained colony at California Disneyland since its 1950s beginnings.*

Private backwoods projects had already been going on for some time when the concept was more publicly codified by the publication in 1982 of *Maverick Cats* by New York architect Ellen Perry Berkeley. Inspired by a stream of feral visitors (the first being 'Honey Puss') to her Vermont retreat backyard, she had begun to explore their mysterious condition. She discovered and studied the pioneering means adopted by cat-loving humans in England and Denmark to find a way of interacting with them.

Municipalities attempting trap-and-destroy programmes had had a universal lack of success. The 'traps were sabotaged by well-meaning people', so it was reported, while a ready supply of food from restaurant trash bins or feral cat feeders simply lured in a replacement crew.† In 1991 in San Mateo County, California, a feral cat pact was established between the local humane society, which already contracted with the county on animal population control, and local freelance auxiliary feeders. It was agreed that 'persons caring for barn

* At Sleeping Beauty Castle apparently. Sixty years later it would be said: 'It is estimated that the current cat population on Disneyland property is about 200. The cats actually live a pretty mundane life, similar to most other feral cats you might have in your neighbourhood. Of course, they do so in the Happiest Place on Earth. They generally stay hidden out of sight during the day and only come out at night to have free run of the park.'
† In a national survey of pet 'care-givers' commissioned by the Humane Society of the United States in 1993, respondents were asked if they fed stray cats and, if so, how many they fed. From those polled it was possible to extrapolate that American auxiliary feeders were regularly tending about 32.7 million cats.

cats or a colony of feral cats' had to register with the County Animal Control Services and undertake to:

> Regularly feed or arrange for the feeding of the cats, including on weekends and holidays. Trap or make a reasonable effort to trap all barn or feral cats over the age of eight weeks in his/her care, and have them spayed or neutered.

Initiatives like this were popping up all over America. A 1989 plan to reduce the big feral colony on the campus of Stanford University, California, by old-style trapping and destruction was challenged by an ad hoc 'Stanford Cat Network'. But when they turned to the local humane society and the HSUS for help, they were reported to be 'shocked to learn that these groups supported the eradication plan'.

The Stanford group instead implemented its own 'Trap–Test–Vaccinate–Alter–Return' (as the policy would generally be called in the US) programme. It was seen to be a success. A year later, 'Alley Cat Allies' was founded in Washington DC by South African-born Louise Holton and Becky Robinson, broadly speaking as America's version of the Cat Action Trust. It was all still wildly controversial. Emotions were mixed.*

The prestigious HSUS, in fact, would remain against the sustenance of feral cat colonies, even monitored ones, for years to come, claiming they represented 'subsidized abandonment'. Miss Phyllis Wright was especially adamant. It was observed in return by one Trap Neuter and Return campaigner: 'The [HSUS] view was that feral cats live short

---

* Jenny Remfry recalled being on a lecture tour in the US in 1995 when the story of the Jellicle Cats of Fitzroy Square came up. When she revealed that not one was left, since neutering had caused the colony to die out, a great sigh of 'No!' went up.

brutal lives in the wild and should be destroyed for their own well-being. However, this view could be taken to its logical conclusion in which case all American wildlife, including deer and raccoons, should be destroyed.' Another so-called 'nativist' view was that feral cats, although quite capable of surviving on their own terms, were a man-introduced invasive species whose predations on other wildlife must be redressed.

In 2006 the HSUS would announce a change of mind: that 'the goal of any feral cat management program should be to maximize quality of life for the cats and to eliminate the existing colony over time through attrition'. Neutering would extinguish the race.* 'Removal of kittens and friendly adults for possible placement in homes' was permissible. A feral free America was still the goal.

And a decade later in summer 2015 the Australian Environment Minister would declare: 'I want to see two million feral cats culled, five new islands and ten new mainland areas as safe havens, free of feral cats, and control measures applied across ten million hectares.' Monster cats weighing up to thirty-three pounds were killing and eating eighty million native animals each day. This was assuredly *not* TNR. It would be further reported:

> The elimination of wild cats will involve the use of detector dogs, fencing, and shooting, as well as the use of a new poison bait called 'Curiosity', which has been developed by the government and a private biotech company over several

---

* At a cost. According to the Washington State Feral Cat Spay/Neuter Project, 'The average cost to alter one cat is just over $50. This includes the costs for the surgeon, veterinary technician, anesthesia, sutures, pain relief, surgical pack, rabies vaccine, and other direct and indirect costs. During a typical clinic, up to fifty cats are altered, including twenty-five spay surgeries.' UK costs averaged £80–100 per cat.

years. A toxic compound in the bait stops the flow of oxygen within the poisoned cat, and is described in the government's plan as 'the new humane feral cat bait'. It will be placed inside pieces of meat that are moulded to resemble sausages.

It was that impossible thing about cats again – that their innate capacity to be domesticated marked them out for special treatment. Feral cats only existed in their ostensibly tragic condition because humans had mislaid them somewhere along the way. Now that carelessness could only be atoned for by killing them.

But the debate over ferals would be as nothing compared with the passions that were about to be unleashed by the so-called 'kill/no-kill' divide (see p. 345).

Such arguments thus far were confined, more or less, to cat welfare enthusiasts. Since the everyone-loves-a-stray revolution of the early 1960s, popular cat culture in Britain apart from 'Arthur' had been pretty tame. But there was a new message to reinforce, of responsible cat ownership – and that meant no cuddly kittens, even on children's television.

In 1986 'Willow' first appeared on TV screens as the *Blue Peter* cat ('a beautiful female Burmese . . . she was horribly noisy, and could also be vicious') – supplanting silver tabby 'Jill', who had been in residence since 1976. The progress of Jill's kittens, born three years after her own first solo appearance, had been a big on-screen attraction. But this time, rather than similarly follow Willow's career as a mother, it was decided that Willow should be the first *Blue Peter* cat to be spayed (sorry, children, but you'd better know about this stuff). This was to underline a solemn message from the RSPCA about the 'vast numbers of unwanted pets destroyed [many at their hands], every year'. Willow retired from the programme in 1991 to be replaced by two even more politically correct cats.

Wilberforce, the RSPCA-nurtured stray turned No. 10 Downing Street, four-administration-spanning Office Cat, had died in 1988. After a catless year, a black-and-white cat was found wandering near the heart of government by a member of the Cabinet Office staff. Where had he come from? It was utterly mysterious. Enter 'Humphrey', the one-year-oldish stray who not only got himself adopted but was taken on to the staff: 'his food was paid for by the departmental budget'. The cost of £100 a year was said to appeal to Mrs Thatcher 'because it was much cheaper than hiring a pest-control contractor (the previous one charged £4,000 a year and was said never to have caught a mouse)'. Mrs Thatcher would soon be heading for the one-way catflap herself, but would be judged righteous among cats as the only Premier to have presided over two rescue cats in succession. Incoming PM John Major would also approve of Humphrey, of whom you will hear more in the next chapter.

All the feral frenzy meanwhile was serving to clutter up what the mainstream charities saw as their real work: the general welfare of cats and the rescue of those cats, where possible, which had fallen from domestic grace. Even though its magazine had long since become a rogues' gallery of lovable rescued strays, the Cats Protection League could not take animals that were effectively 'untameable' into its rehabilitation and 're-homing' (the word was now in widespread use) system. No ferals, please. RSPCA and Blue Cross policy was the same.

On the cusp of the new century, Battersea would go on insisting that urban ferals 'were far happier being left to fend for themselves as they've probably been doing for years'. It could also reveal in a report that of 2,614 cats admitted the previous year (1999), 60–70 per cent were 'most likely not strays at all but pet cats that had roamed from home'. The forsaken, un-micro-chipped tide had been brought in as street-finds in the time-worn cat-lady tradition.

But wild-side cats were not being entirely ignored on the wider stage. In 1991 'Kari' and 'Oke' were taken as kittens from a feral colony by volunteers and placed in the care of the Wood Green Animal Shelter in Hertfordshire. Oke had been found abandoned in a bush and the staff of the Centre set about the task of trying to encourage Kari's mother to adopt Oke. The plan worked and the pair effectively became brother and sister. Six weeks after being rescued, the former feral kittens made their debut on *Blue Peter*. Ferals were now in the forefront of TV feline celebrity.

Everybody loved kittens, of course, and the remarkable capacity of feral kittens to be 'tamed' by human contact was overwhelmingly appealing – although one distinguished cat expert has likened 'handling an angry feral kitten to wrestling with an animated cactus'. What was not stressed so much on the Kari-Oke show was that, out there in the wild, 80 per cent of feral kittens died in their first year. Further, that even of those trapped young enough, a proportion were never going to be tamed.

Cute-looking, one-time-feral kittens were the rescue cat's most appealing ambassadors. Cats really were, it seemed, programmed to love us. Catch 'em young and all would be fine. Or not. In reality, it was going to be a lot more difficult than that.

27

Asylum-Seeking Cats

KITTY

Female age (approx.) 8, DOMESTIC SHORT-HAIR, tortoiseshell.
Hi, I am Kitty. I was very much loved in my last home but
the young human was very ill and in hospital. An allergy to
cats was mentioned. I am an independent girl and like to do
my own thing but I do like attention and being treated like a
princess. Please can I be the only pet in an adult home.

Looking at things from a cat's point of view, there was nothing to stop an intrepid stray with enough residual domesticated charm from rescuing him- or herself by somehow
getting in the right door. Thousands of outsider cats did that
all the time and always had done. Cats had been adopting
people, even Prime Ministers, for generations.

Humphrey, for example, had his paws well under the table
at Downing Street. In March 1992 a detailed memo was
prepared on the stray who had wandered in from the streets
of SW1. 'He tends to eat little and often – no doubt because
he knows he can always get food whenever he wants.' And
his security vetting was good: 'He is a workaholic who spends
nearly all his time at the office, has no criminal record, does
not socialise a great deal or go to many parties and has not
been involved in any sex or drugs scandals that we know of,'
said the memo. In November 1993 Cabinet Office staff were

told that Humphrey was suffering from a minor kidney disorder. 'As well as being treated by a vet he has been placed on a controlled diet and is not to eat anything other than the prescribed food,' it was noted. 'Staff are therefore asked that, for his own good, he is not fed any treats or titbits.'

Humphrey had sought asylum in no ordinary household. Veterinary care and general well-wishing were on tap. But in humbler circumstances when a stray knocked on the door, the subsequent relationship required a special level of love (often unrequited at first) on behalf of the rescuer. They might need all the advice and support that cat welfare experts could offer once the scruffy, difficult, often sick, injured or pregnant new arrival made its presence felt. Then there were the kittens.

The Cat, for example, journal of the Cats Protection League, was proud to tell readers the story of 'Ginge', who appeared one morning in the south London garden of Mrs S. M. Parratt. 'He was very thin and dirty and had obviously been a stray for a long time. He would fight any cat that came near and our own two tabbies were frequently attacked,' she wrote. Weakened by a facial abscess – an infected wound from fighting – he seemed close to death. 'He hadn't the strength to fight me so I wrapped him in a towel and took him to the vet,' Mrs Parratt recalled. But not for destruction. The wound was drained and after a fortnight in the ward he returned to be lodged in the garden shed. 'Ginge let me bathe his wound, he took his tablets and used his litter tray. I would sit in the shed and read to him to keep him company.'

Ginge spent a year on the fringe of the family, nosing into the house and disappearing through the cat flap at the first approach of human footsteps. 'We called Croydon CPL thinking he would have to be re-homed,' wrote Mrs Parratt.

Their advice was to stick by Ginge. 'The lady at CPL said he felt very insecure . . .' That at last he had found somewhere nice to live but was in danger of being thrown out by these two other cats. 'Give it time and he will settle down.'

The advice proved right. 'Ginge lived happily with us more or less in harmony with the other two tabbies.' After two years he died of liver failure. 'About a week after his death a young ginger tom cat appeared at our back door looking skinny and filthy . . . maybe Ginge sent this little cat to fill the gap he has left', Mrs Parratt noted. Maybe he did.

Another correspondent, Mr John Halsall, told the story of finding mysterious saucers in the garden then discovering his wife, Muriel, secretly feeding a stray cat in the shrubbery. 'Some weeks after I had discovered my wife's secret, she called me out and I saw that Tiddles [they had called the stray 'Tiddles'] was in the process of giving birth.' Mr Halsall made a tent for the new family in the porch out of old sheets and a clothes-horse. A call was made to the CPL, who said they would take the kittens if the Halsalls could take the mother, and advised: 'Handle the kittens as much as possible as soon as you think it wise to do so.'

'The four kittens grew very quickly', wrote Mr Halsall, 'and when I opened the door I would be overwhelmed by a tidal wave of kittens eager for play.' Treatment for ringworm followed, twenty-one days of isolation and a cancelled holiday. The kittens indeed found good homes via the CPL, 'while it was out of the question to return Tiddles to her home in the shrubbery'.

And there was 'Orky', who had lived semi-wild in a village churchyard, well enough tended by cat ladies to produce multiple litters of kittens, before taking up home in the garden shed of Mrs M. Isaacs. 'You could not have met a more unappealing or unfriendly cat', she wrote, 'who would only hiss over the garden wall', but little by little, Orky encroached on the house, coming into the kitchen and allowing herself to be stroked when she was feeding. Now Orky had learned to use the cat flap and would sleep quite happily on the spare bed. There was happiness all round.

Cats might need rescuing for all sorts of reasons. 'Tiny' and 'Ginger', for example, were rescued by CPL member Mr Les Spragg after the 'brutal murder of a Bristol woman [Mrs Violet Milsom, aged sixty-two] in her basement flat'. At the request of the police, Ginger featured in the BBC TV *Crimewatch* show's reconstruction of the slaying.*

Or 'Toby' of unknown origin adopted from a shelter, who, when let out of his basket in Mrs Karen Wood's Staffordshire living room, 'turned into a monster'. For months afterwards 'he could only be handled with gardening gloves but after immense effort he now adores to be fussed over and never wanders far from us', she told readers of *The Cat*. Or 'Basher', the beaten-up stray who otherwise lived in an old van in the street. After a lot of hissing at Mrs Rosemary Burston, she was suddenly allowed 'the privilege of stroking his coarse tabby fur'. The next day Basher formally came in from the rain and mutual love soon blossomed.

Stories like these underlined how the nation's feline flagship, the Cats Protection League, now saw its primary mission. Thirty years before, Albert Steward had sternly lectured members on the importance of neutering over the cuddlier but contentious business of finding good homes. Now its members could talk of nothing but adoption. Readers' letters and branch reports in *The Cat* were packed with heart-warming stories of triumph over tragedy, feline endurance and human self-sacrifice. It was cat-rescue heaven.

---

* Both cats were successfully re-homed. After thirty years the murder remained unsolved.

The 1995 *Annual Review* proclaimed outright: 'Rescue, Our Main Aim'. Neutering was somehow 'an investment for the future' – and education was 'the way ahead'. 'The League's primary aim is to rehabilitate and re-home unwanted cats and kittens with the emphasis on re-home,' said the *Review* unreservedly.

Rescuing strays, however, could be fraught with difficulties. Presented with a foundling, shelter volunteers should ask – is it a genuine stray? Could it be a new cat to the neighbourhood brought in mistakenly by a well-wisher, or even an owned cat being deliberately given into a shelter as a stray, as a cynical way of getting rid of it?

Rehabilitation was admittedly difficult. Aggressive, bad-tempered, and excessively timid cats needed lots of work. But the League was confident that these 'unco-operative characters' could be helped and that 'somewhere there was a suitable home for all its rescued cats', according to the *Review*. Even grouchy cats could find forever homes.

The third stage, 're-homing', was by now a carefully managed operation, conducted to agreed protocols with plenty of experience to draw on for volunteers to assess 'both people and places' on exploratory home visits. There were dangers to look out for – a nearby busy road or the balcony of a high-rise flat. Human signals must be discreetly observed. Then there was the obligatory follow-up visit, a week to ten days after the initial placement. Authority to repossess a cat or kitten had been written into CPL rules since the re-homing programme had begun in the 1960s. Technically, the cat always stayed the property of the League with a contractual obligation on behalf of the adopter to have the cat or kitten neutered by a certain date.

The first ever CPL 'Re-homing Conference' was held in 1995 to compare and codify good practice, with Pedigree Petfoods as the sponsor. Representatives came from the

RSPCA, Blue Cross (as Our Dumb Friends' League had been known since 1950), the National Canine Defence League, Battersea, and Wood Green Animal Shelter.

There was a continuing boom in independent shelters, many of which maintained good relations with the big societies. The latter acted as overspill fosterers or sources of technical advice as the new imperatives of vaccination against Feline Infectious Enteritis (FIE) and cat flu plus microchipping (from the mid-1990s) were becoming much more commonplace.

There was still a ramshackle amateurishness about it all, however. The Cats Protection League's sixtieth anniversary history captured it when it said:

> Accommodation varies but standard of care does not. Bigger branches have custom-built catteries with a live-in superintendent while others make do with portable huts and wire runs in members' gardens. Small groups with minimal facilities are, however, undaunted; there is always the secretary's guest room or a snug corner in the treasurer's airing cupboard.

Freelance cat sheltering became trickier after Parliament made one of its intermittent interventions in the affairs of abandoned animals with the passing of the Environmental Protection Act 1990. It required local councils to treat all unaccompanied dogs on public land as strays. Stray cats were not legislated for, but the new Act did affect cat rescue directly.

According to the advice of the Cats Protection League, the Act's wide-ranging provisions meant that: 'If large numbers of cats are kept at a domestic residence the Local Planning Authority . . . may require the owner or occupier to make a planning application for a change of use. If this is not granted, the owner or occupier may be required to reduce the number of cats kept at the property.' The tipping point, it seemed, was twelve.*

In the emotionally charged world of TNR there were also splits and defections, mostly amicable, some not so. Celia Hammond went it alone in 1986, setting up the Celia Hammond Animal Trust, 'CHAT', to 'care for and neuter those cats which have nobody else to befriend them'. Then regional branches of Cat Action broke away in a clash of personalities and a dispute over a revised constitution, leaving the original founders to start a new charity: 'Cat Action 1977' (the year of its original foundation).

It would be recorded of the original Cat Action Trust's work in 1991 that 'many thousands of cats on thousands of sites have been trapped, neutered and returned, many thousands more cats and kittens have been fostered, tamed and homed, and many hundreds more re-sited when unable to return to their previous site. Only a very small proportion have been euthanised because they were beyond help.'

The Trust still faced indifference and hostility from some site owners. Some RSPCA branches refused co-operation in neutering ferals while the Cats Protection League was still not interested, although some individual members were, according to the snapshot of Cat Action in its fifteenth year.

And the League did, indeed, remain sceptical. It might have embraced Trap Neuter and Return as a concept worthy of respect and even funding, but could not burden its existing

---

* Best practice advice from the Cat Group states: 'The same principles apply to how cats are kept in a rescue centre to those for boarding establishments. They should be housed individually (or in groups if that is how they have come into the centre). Cats should have sleeping accommodation with heating and a run where they can exercise. Cats from different origins should not be able to touch or sneeze over one another and the establishment should have a good management system for keeping them clean, warm and well fed.'

operation with animals regarded by all right-thinking people as untameable. According to the League's own 1995 *Review:*

> The likelihood of re-homing feral cats is slim, although some of our more imaginative branches have met with occasional success in this area [the south Dartmoor branch had placed some of them with farmers for rodent control].
>
> Usually there is little chance of re-homing ferals and the League has developed a policy that, provided a colony is being fed and cared for, Headquarters will sponsor the neutering of all adult cats – and then return them to keep away other cats and continue to catch vermin.

In 1995 approximately 10 per cent of all cats helped by the League were feral, according to the *Annual Review.* That same year, 41,000 cats and kittens overall were rescued, rehabilitated and re-homed.[*]

The League's emphasis had still to be on the animals cast out of human society for whatever reason. Their volunteers meanwhile were also having to deal with the human emotional baggage that accompanied each feline refugee. An old lady with severe arthritis, for example, offered her beloved cat for fostering – but would phone all the time asking about its welfare, while questioning the suitability of any potential adopter who showed interest.[†] The

---

[*] Cats Protection would continue to back TNR but not those 'many people who believe that feral cats should be somehow "made back" into domestic pets', as CP's chief vet, Maggie Roberts, told the authors in 2015. 'The truth is that a lot of feral cats are perfectly happy and would much prefer to be left to themselves,' she said. 'We don't want to tame feral cats because it is terrible welfare, not because of lack of resources. There is an issue with feral kittens when it is possible to socialise them, but it is very difficult and resource-heavy. They are better neutered and returned to site.'

[†] In a later move the League would disbar those who gave up pets for re-homing from knowing the details of the eventual adopter or attempting to contact them (or their cat).

Peterhead Branch newsletter told the heartbreaking story of a man who turned up with both a cat and his seven-year-old daughter:

> The little girl played with a kitten I had in my care at the time while we dealt with the paperwork and the cat's health record. The gentleman explained he was loath to give up the cat but he was working away from home [the relationship with the girl's mother had ended]. The daughter started to realise that the cat would not be going home with her and began to cry and begged her daddy to take the cat back.

The branch Chairman explained that he understood the hurt of losing a pet. 'Comforting his daughter, the gentleman told me the cat's love and comfort had been the only thing that had helped her through the heartache of the marital rift.'

What about older cats, often left behind when an elderly owner had died? There was this story from Miss D. Hall of Collyhurst, Manchester, who went to a CPL shelter looking for a kitten to 'make us laugh again' after the death of her and her partner's long-term companion cat. There, sure enough, was a kitten – and another mature cat in need of a home. But there also to greet her was 'Fluffy', an 'old black and tatty long-haired who was desperate for affection. I pulled my partner away, saying that Fluffy was too old and I could not go through the upset of losing another cat again.'

So Fluffy stayed at the shelter. Miss Hall could not get him out of her mind, however, and went back to adopt the over-looked veteran. 'He was very affectionate, adored being made a fuss of and got on very well with the other cats. It was wonderful to see him enjoying his old age. We decided we should always keep a space for an oldie.'

Indeed, good and kind Miss D. Hall returned to Tameside CPL and asked to home their oldest cat. Thus arrived 'Toby'

— 'a bit tatty and no oil painting, but who is nowadays rarely off our laps and enjoying his old age. We know we won't have him around for years to come but he deserves to be loved, asks for so little and gives so much in return.'

In 1996 the CPL published a special booklet by feline advocate Sarah Hartwell, *In Praise of Older Cats*, which very splendidly did that just that. It featured the story of 'Esmeralda', aged eighteen, 'surely a record age' for a re-homed cat, described as a 'cantankerous old dowager who could hardly walk' — but having been given a home by a lady in Buckinghamshire, soon turned into a beautiful and affectionate animal.

The work of gathering in cats, fixing them up and getting adopters through the doors of the League's shelters — soon to be renamed 'Adoption Centres' — went on in the timeworn way. Many deeply happy relationships would be made this way. Like Alfie Teale, whose memoir of his young life in London, *Bringing Down the Krays*, would become a best-seller. One happy day in Archway, north London, he first encountered 'Molly'. He remembered:

> When my wife, Wendy, and I returned to London from living and working in Tenerife, we found a flat in the same block as our son, Mark . . .
>
> Mark had wanted a cat and found Molly, a brindled tabby, from Cats Protection in Archway. Staff there told him that Molly and her sister were both strays and had been found wandering in the street half-starved.
>
> As both Mark and his partner were out at work all day, Wendy and I quickly found Molly making her way up the stairs to our flat each morning instead. I soon bonded with her, so much so that I started to think of her as my cat.
>
> Molly had all sorts of adventures during those early days. On one occasion after she had gone missing for three days, I

heard faint meowing coming from the trees in a Victorian graveyard nearby. It was night-time and very spooky. But I recognised Molly's cry straight away. After calling out the fire brigade they cut through the iron bars of the locked gate and to my joy, rescued her and put her back in my arms.

But Molly's worst adventure happened not long after this when Wendy and I were alarmed to hear terrible screams coming from the staircase one morning. Rushing out, we found Molly had been cornered by a Staffordshire bull terrier who had bitten her badly on her rear leg.

Fighting the dog off, we managed to get Molly into our flat. Poor Molly was in a terrible state with blood everywhere. Sadly, the vet said Molly's leg was too badly damaged for him to save it, but he offered to amputate it in order to save her life.

The next day we got a call from the vet to say that although the operation had been a total success, Molly appeared to be pining for me so badly that they feared she wouldn't pull through. So I went to collect her, and bringing her home, put her in her basket next to my bed. All that night I sat up with her, feeding her little pieces of ham and melon. In the morning she seemed much more energetic, and thankfully in a few weeks was running around the flat on her three legs almost as well as she had before.

That was over sixteen years ago now and apart from my wife, Molly remains my dearest and most affectionate companion. She still sleeps next to my bed, licks my face and hair, and cannot bear to be parted from me. I count myself lucky to have found such a wonderful cat.

But still those pesky strays kept turning up at people's back doors all by themselves. Like the marmalade cat 'Cockle' who appeared at the Vicarage of St Martin in the Fields, Trafalgar Square in central London. 'He was obviously a stray and had been hanging round the church and crypt for some weeks, getting food from some of the down-and-outs who frequented the church.' One piece of pre-internet era advice from the CPL was that if a cat turned up on a cat-lover's doorstep, they should put an elasticised collar on the mysterious feline, bearing the message *I am a stray – does anyone own me?* or advertise locally with *Found* posters and other announcements. Thirty years later it remained standard advice. But lots of people 'adopted' by a stray in this way were quite pleased when the 'owner' failed to materialise. So, more often than not, was the cat.

The PDSA, whose mainstream welfare work since the war years had not been concerned with animal rescue and rehabilitation, could not resist publishing the story of 'Patch', a homeless animal around two years old who had adopted Thomas and Carol Parry of Liverpool. After a few years, an increasing appetite combined with weight loss concerned them. A charitably sponsored veterinary examination diagnosed hyperthyroidism, which would need 'daily medication for the rest of his life, along with regular veterinary checks', something his owners and the veterinary charity were totally committed to providing.

But ferals too kept knocking, asking to be let in. Resistance was wearing down. Approaching the new millennium, Cats Protection, which had dropped the word 'League' in 1998 in a modernist makeover, was now admitting stories of feral adoption – and not just of kittens – into its journal. Members were clearly sympathetic, even if Headquarters remained deeply suspicious.

There was the story of 'Grisn', 'little grey one', a two-year-old feral who was the 'special favourite' of Andrea Taylor in a colony that she fed. Andrea was desperately worried when he appeared, then vanished again, with a mangled leg, evidently having been caught by a trap. He somehow survived and 'on his reappearance I decided to adopt him there and then', she wrote. 'It took me a long time to win his affection but that was all the more special when he let me kiss and cuddle him.'

And what about 'Rufus', the feral High Wycombe cat who lived in the neighbours' back garden until they wanted him removed as a 'nuisance'. He was neutered, lived in the back door lean-to and seemed happy enough. As Mrs Patricia Shakespeare wrote:

> I wanted desperately to give him cuddles but he was fright-ened to let me and I was afraid to try. Each time I reached down, he ran away ... one day he closed his eyes and accepted the stroking. As of last year I can pick him up and carry him around, which he seems to enjoy ... but he will NOT come into the house ...

CP member Sharon Riley, an oriental breeder with a cattery in Essex, was regularly visited by a large feral tom cat she called 'Panda', 'who would not take no for an answer' and who managed to father some kittens.

A Cats Protection-loaned humane trap got the better of Panda, who was taken to the vet 'for neutering and general overhaul and returned to live semi-wild in the garden'. One day he disappeared. Mrs Riley promptly acquired two replacements from her local CP shelter in the form of two six-month-old 'untameable' kittens, 'Chloe' and 'Charles', with a plan to confine them in a large pen for three weeks 'at least to acclimatise them to regular feeding'.

'They were released and disappeared into the undergrowth ... hissing, spitting and defiantly cowering from human contact.' At the time of writing they were living wild in the garden, still hissing at the approach of a food-bearing human. 'But there is no doubt in my mind that Charlie and Chloe are happy,' she wrote. 'To anyone who has a large garden and can apply constant care I would say think about adopting a feral . . .'

And there was the story of 'Oscar', the outside tabby tom who Liz Davies, a Cats Protection member, began to 'feed at the back door with the intention of trapping him'. It did not work. Her own three 'quite elderly' cats withdrew inside and refused to go out. After a bit of long-range stroking she managed 'to get Oscar in a basket and a quick trip to the vet followed'. He recovered in the garage and began a long campaign to get further and further inside the home and into the family's affections . . .

'He remains gentle and calm and despite the growling and hissing of the three original feline residents, his greatest pleasure is to sleep in their favourite haunts.' So Oscar was one that did get in the door.

These were rescue cats, apart from Chloe and Charles, which had never been in the shelter system. They re-homed themselves, like so many other cats, while the welfare group was there to provide technical support and advice.

By the time of the new millennium, the very concept of a 'cat shelter' would be questioned by some, as animal rights idealists pursued ever greater doctrinal purity. Killing healthy animals had already long been a very dispiriting thing, not just for those who did it professionally, but because it worked against the securing of donations and legacies. It was a statistic to be buried in obscure bar charts in Annual Reports. Now it would become total anathema, according to the ever-louder advocates of what would be called the 'no-kill revolution'.

It happened first in America.

PART FOUR

RESCUE CATS
ARE TOP CATS

1990–2020

No-Kill

CHARLES

Charles is a 2–3-year-old black male looking for a new home. He is part of our home-to-home scheme which means he will stay with his current owner until a new home can be found as we don't have the space to bring this little chap into care at the moment.

He is a lithe and beautiful cat. He is lively, wants to play, and is mischievous and can be very giddy. He is very determined and knows his own mind. He is finding it difficult to adjust to living with another cat which is why he is being re-homed . . .

He is less bothered about stroking but does like the top of his head rubbing. He is neutered and chipped and vaccinated.

It began on the US West Coast, led by the animal rights, theory-heavy wing of animal advocacy; but 'no-kill', as it came to be called, would impact directly on the hands-on welfare enthusiasts wherever they were, and on the many thousands of cats in their charge. As always in the cultish nature of animal politics, individual charismatic personalities and interventionist charitable funding would prove very important. Nathan Winograd, the Stanford law graduate who had been involved in the campus cat colony removal rumpus in 1990, was one of these key figures, and would later confess to having been strongly influenced by his mother, 'who was the neighbourhood cat lady'. Richard Avanzino was another: he had been appointed in 1976 as President of the San Francisco Society for the Prevention of Cruelty to Animals.

Mr Avanzino, who was already known for his controversial stances on cat and dog issues, had dramatically announced in 1984 that the Society was 'getting out of the killing business', and could no longer contract to the municipal authority to get rid of the city's unwanted animals. Nathan Winograd became the SFSPCA legal counsel and would later move to Ithaca, New York, where his directorship of the Tompkins County SPCA became an East Coast model for the 'no-kill' movement. Meanwhile he became an object of scorn for his opponents – especially regarding his claim that there was 'no pet over-population crisis' and that it was the unreformed culture of existing shelters that was leading to so many healthy animals being killed.

Rather than accepting the time-worn approach that the best thing shelters could do for homeless animals was to find homes for some and kill the rest, he came up with the startling idea that a shelter could save '100 per cent of healthy and treatable animals, and 100 per cent of feral cats'. In the face of much opposition and ridicule, Mr Winograd set out to try and prove just that.

The rise of no-kill would represent a change in the interrelationships of cats, humans and those various free-roamers caught in the middle, a change as fundamental as the much-copied installation of the lethal chamber at Battersea had been a century before. That had been courtesy of the will of Mary Ann Kennett and this time too, a fabulous charitable funding line would propel a second revolution.

For decades past the most contentious issue among professionals in animal welfare had been: what was the most humane way of killing?* In the matter of a few years, the debate would change to: should an unwanted animal be a candidate for destruction at all? Before no-kill could be achieved, the existing means of addressing pet over-population without mass destruction had to be made much more efficient: high-volume, affordable sterilisation; trap, neuter and return for ferals; and high-volume adoption for shelter animals and adoptable ferals.

In the impassioned arguments that would follow, definitions would become very important, even if some of the more theoretical concepts were way beyond the concern of many cat rescuers (and indeed cats). A 'no-kill shelter' would be defined as one striving to save all healthy or treatable animals. At least 90 per cent and more of the animals entering the shelter were expected to be saved – that figure based on

---

* The 'extinction of life', as Sir Benjamin Ward Richardson had called it, by chloroforming had generally been supplanted in animal shelters in Britain and America by carbon monoxide gassing from motor vehicle exhausts or compression bottles. The RSPCA had ended its use of electricity in 1928 after a big internal controversy. Battersea continued with electricity for another fifty years. US post-war techniques included decompression chambers and lethal injections. By the twenty-first century, 'direct injection of sodium pentobarbital (referred to as Euthanasia by Injection, or EBI) remains the most humane method available', according to the USHS in 2014. The top brand in the US is 'Fatal-Plus', an injection of which leads to 'Instant unconsciousness . . . with simultaneous collapse of the animal', according to the manufacturer, Vortech Pharmaceuticals of Dearborn, Michigan.

According to the Humane Society of the United States Euthanasia Reference Manual, 2014: 'A lethal IV (intravenous) dose of sodium pentobarbital causes a mammal to lose consciousness within seconds, and results in clinical death within just minutes.

'Cats tend to resist even the gentle restraint associated with IV injection, so IP (intraperitoneal abdominal) injection is often preferred over IV for conscious, well-socialized cats.' The Society further noted: 'As we come ever closer to achieving zero euthanasia, the challenges become greater, and the debate over which animals must be euthanized and which can be saved seemingly grows more intense.'

all animals entering the shelter, not just those judged to be 'adoptable'. The save rate or 'live release' rate was what mattered.

It would be pointed out that careful attention should be paid to those self-proclaimed no-killers who might blur the definitions of 'treatable' and 'adoptable' – not admitting black or diabetic cats for example – in order to manipulate statistics of outcomes. As public perception of the principle spread as being generally a good thing, the way things were worded became exquisitely sensitive.

For example, although the century-old Boston Animal Rescue League could not declare itself to be 'no-kill', it proclaimed a benign up-front policy of 'not putting animals to sleep on the basis of length of stay, accommodation space available, or breed'. However, it operated a 'flexible admissions policy', by which 'problem pets' would be offered to 'another shelter partner'. 'For cats that are unable to adapt to indoor life, for example, we work to place them in a barn cat program.'

Thus the distinction would be made between a so-called 'limited-admission shelter' which might take only those animals judged at the outset to have a prospect of finding homes, and 'open door', which took whatever they might be presented with. But because they were not sanctuaries, open-door shelters perforce had to cap their population by euthanising animals that were healthy or had conditions treatable by veterinary intervention. There was never enough room, never enough money, never enough fosterers, never enough adopters.

An important subset of such 'open-door' shelters had always been those run by official environmental control agencies or under contract – such as, in the British context, the Battersea Dogs Home (which added 'Cats' to its name in 2002). Their responsibility was to both keep the streets clear and be a clearing-house for abandoned pets in need of homes. Those not so placed were killed. It had been that way for ever. After the advent of 'no-kill', suddenly nothing was certain.

As arguments raged, the practical arguments of the open-doorers with their apparent readiness to end the lives of viable, adoptable, lovable animals would be likened by some to abortionists. The no-killers meanwhile prided themselves on a compassionate commitment to fight for the individual animal, however difficult finding a 'forever' home might seem. They were the ones full of missionary zeal, the ones making the most noise, the ones in command of new media and attracting the most attention. Soon they might be attracting the most money.

All this might seem dryly theoretical, something for animal rights obsessives to argue over, but it would have an immediate impact on the actual practice of cat rescue in America, Britain and beyond. Those who worked on the open-access side began to find themselves accused of revelling in the business of killing. The old guard were portrayed as cruel – as cruel as anyone who would put a cat in a microwave or abandon kittens in the woods. The no-killers in turn were held up as delusional sentimentalists who franchised out the rough stuff while otherwise condemning pets to years of incarceration. It would be written:

Typically, shelter workers see themselves as compassionate people who put animals out of their misery in a humane way while blaming the public for causing the killing [by failing to neuter]. They deny their killing is cruel, even when they euthanize animals that might be adoptable, let alone young, attractive and healthy. They just see no other option for handling the numbers of animals brought to shelters.

The no-killers had gained a powerful patron in 1994 when the Duffield Family Foundation created 'Maddie's Fund', which offered generous financial support for those seeking to practically pursue the ideal. In 1998 the San Francisco SPCA opened Maddie's® Pet Adoption Center, a facility that reportedly housed 'dogs and cats in condominium-style rooms featuring accoutrements such as television sets, cat trees, toys, and live aquariums. The facility is named for the pet Miniature Schnauzer of PeopleSoft founder Dave Duffield, who concentrates his philanthropy in the animal welfare world via the private foundation Maddie's Fund.' The $300 million endowment fund's director would be Richard Avanzino.

Nathan Winograd's No Kill Advocacy Center would open in Oakland, California in 2004 with several imitators – 'No Kill Nation', 'No Kill Revolution' and 'nØkill Network' – soon following. The internet meant that no animal lover, shelter worker or humane activist could plead ignorance of the no-kill alternative, which was even beginning to look as if it might become the mainstream. Mr Winograd's passion-ately argued 2008 book, *Redemption: The Myth of Pet Overpopulation and the No-Kill Revolution*, went so far as to introduce the concept of 'hospice' care for terminally ill shel-ter animals that would normally be destroyed. It was described as a 'third door between adoption and killing'.

And there would be more new-wave utopians, like the 'Best Friends Animal Sanctuary' which was founded in 1984 near Kanab, Utah, with 1960s-style, cultish, religious-spiritual origins that the vegan adepts of the Order of the Golden Age a century before might have found familiar. By the early 1990s, the mystic elements had been entirely supplanted by no-kill zealotry, taken even further when they replaced their already ambitious mission statement 'No More Homeless Pets' with 'Save Them All'.

One veteran US animal welfare commentator called the change 'desperate, unhinged . . . a task doomed to fail from the outset'.

In 2003 there was a high-profile court case when Kelly Reistrom, thirty-one, a veterinary technician with the Tinton Falls, New Jersey shelter of the Associated Humane Societies, was accused by a co-worker of euthanising six cats that might otherwise have been adopted. She was dubbed 'Killer Kelly' by the ultras in a direct echo of Zoe Morgan's fall-out with the Mayhew Home committee a hundred years before. 'There was justification for the action. The kittens were sick. Ms. Reistrom had gotten permission from her supervisors and she followed all required procedures,' said her lawyer. 'The decision had been heart-wrenching.'

The trial judge would decide that the euthanasia was not needless and that Ms. Reistrom was innocent and had simply been performing her job. 'I hope to go back to working with animals,' she said at the end of the trial. 'That is my love and was always my love.'

The American arguments crossed the Atlantic but without nearly the same stridency. In the first years of the new millennium, a stated reluctance to kill, or something very like it, would become the face of British feline rescue – without grandstanding individuals claiming that theirs was the only way. Maggie Roberts, Director of Veterinary Services at Cats Protection, told the authors in 2015: 'We never put a healthy cat to sleep – so we don't euthanise them due to lack of space.' But she added tellingly: 'People look at the National Cat Centre and say what a beautiful building it is – but it is a prison rather than a hotel for cats.'

Like the best of cat rescuers, she wants their rescuees to move on and out into homes as smartly as possible. 'We firmly believe that there is a loving home out there somewhere for every cat' is Cats Protection stated policy. Those who have any contact with the organisation know straight away that they will do their utmost to achieve it. Anyone can join the stream of visitors to the National Cat Centre – and the commitment of the people working there is tangible. It is tempting to imagine that the cats know it too – but the reality, according to Maggie Roberts, is that 'cats are stressed when they enter a shelter and this stress decreases as they become more familiar with the routine'. But stress levels rise again as cats get bored and frustrated in what is effectively benign captivity.

The counter-accusation by those who advocated or ran open-admission shelters in America was that no-kill led to 'pet warehousing', the unending confinement of cats who, for whatever reason, failed to find a home. One visitor to such a shelter described a spotless set-up with 'air-conditioning, climbing-trees, toys and good food – but when you walk in, they were all over you . . . I had cats attached to my legs and arms, cats on my head. These cats were starved for human contact, that's what breaks my heart about these places . . .' A visitor to the very best-run cat shelter, with cats socialised, played with and cosseted by kind staff and volunteers, could tell you something similar.

In fact, the most significant counter to the no-kill enthusiasts came from animal rights behemoth, PETA. It uncompromisingly called the no-kill apostles 'alleged animal rights activists' – whose 'warehousing solution' made it so that 'cats and dogs suffer a far worse fate than destruction in an open-admission shelter'. Their line was clear:

To be able to offer refuge to every animal in need, open-admission shelters must euthanize unadopted and unadoptable animals. The alternative – turning them away – is cruel and leaves the animals in grave danger . . . Many animals who are refused by turn-away facilities are dumped on the road, in the woods [or] in the yard of the local 'cat lady' (also called a 'hoarder').

PETA's line on cat ladies was equally uncompromising. Cats who fell into their hands would suffer a 'far worse fate than euthanasia administered by caring shelter workers'. The group also took a stern line on 'cats who are let outdoors, where multiple dangers abounded', suggesting that 'like dogs, cats should be allowed outdoors for walks on leads'. 'Cats are not native wildlife . . . Their hunting instincts exist no matter how well fed they are. They terrorize, maim, and kill countless native birds and other small wild animals,' said PETA. British wildlife enthusiasts would vocally agree. The organisation was also tough on ferals, calling TNR 'Trap, Neuter, Re-abandonment'. It would be stated:

Having witnessed first-hand the gruesome things that can happen to feral cats and to the animals they prey on [an important consideration for the organisation] PETA cannot in good conscience oppose euthanasia as a humane alternative to dealing with cat over-population . . .

We believe that although altering [neutering] feral cats prevents the suffering of future generations, it does little to improve the quality of life for the cats who are left outdoors, and that allowing feral cats to continue their daily struggle for survival in a hostile environment is not usually a humane option.

In fact, PETA would also question the rightness of pet keeping at all. 'The international pastime of domesticating animals has created an overpopulation crisis . . .' so the organisation declared. 'As a result, millions of unwanted animals are destroyed every year . . . This selfish desire to

possess animals and receive love from them causes immeas-
urable suffering . . .'

The Victorians were the original sinners evidently, having
invented 'pets' in the first place with their 'fantasy relationship . . . visible in the trope of the animal as child, the pet as
a member of the family', according to an American cultural
historian. We had never moved on. It might be counter-
argued that, in the sensibilities of the nineteenth century (and
no less so afterwards) being kind to cats was a first step to
imbuing respect and compassion for all living creatures.
Especially in children.

The good cats–bad cats debate was dramatically revived in
Britain with the publication of a report by the Mammal
Society, 'dedicated to the study and conservation of British
mammals', which drew attention to the devastating impact of
the nation's cats, both home and astray, on wildlife. The
Society's 2001 report, based on research conducted in
1997–8, would conclude:

> By virtue of their abundance in many ecosystems, domestic
> and feral cats are a major predator of wild animals in Great
> Britain. While their impact as predators and the necessity of
> measures to mitigate this are a controversial topic, there is a
> clear need for analysis of the numbers of animals affected and
> of the factors influencing kill rates.

The survey claimed that Britain's estimated nine million cats
(domestic and feral) were killing an estimated 275 million
animals per year, of which 200 million were mammals, 55
million birds, 10 million reptiles and amphibians and 10
million other creatures including worms and moths. 'There
are twenty-six times more cats than foxes, and six times more
cats than all other wild terrestrial predators combined,' it was
stated. The BBC wildlife presenter, Chris Packham, declared

in response that cats were 'sly, greedy, insidious murderers' which made him want to 'reach for my shotgun'. It did his subsequent TV career no harm.*

Perhaps cats were themselves the worst offenders. That innate ability to be domesticated had already brought all sorts of trouble down on their heads. To the animal rights purists, they were wilfully colluding in an abusive relationship with their 'owners', while turning their claws on hapless garden birds and defenceless voles. All pets were parodies of wild nature, 'biological slaves' collaborating in man's own ruthless predation.

Animal advocacy organisations could argue away about other people's (and other animals') rights and wrongs as much as they liked. It was much harder for the hands-on welfare charities when, although they did not know it, they were about to be overwhelmed by the abandoned furry casualties of global economic turmoil and recession. A big new rescue-animal crisis was looming, and it would need more than philosophical point-scoring to meet it.

---

* In October 2015 he revised his opinion, stating: 'Only a small percentage of domestic cats are rogues. It's about one in ten which regularly takes wildlife,' after a study by the University of Reading found that two-thirds of cats brought home no prey over a six-week period.

29

Love Me, Love My Rescue Cat

ELLA'S STORY

Tabby and white Ella came into our care after a dog attack
left her needing veterinary treatment, that her previous owner
could not afford to provide. An operation to remove her
badly damaged left foreleg went well . . . After several weeks
recuperating Ella was finally ready for re-homing. She
received quite a bit of attention and it wasn't long before
Teresa and Phillip fell for her charms.

Teresa writes: 'Ella settled into her new home with us and
now has us wrapped around her little paws, but returns this
with love and affection in abundance. Her missing leg does
not hold her back at all; she still tears up and down the stairs
when she's in her playful mode. She is a chatty little girl and
very welcoming when we come in the door after work.'

By the first years of the new century, domestic cat numbers
in Britain were at a record high. Cat food, pet insurance,
luxury brands, big-box pet superstores and on-line find-a-
feline marketing had created a multi-billion-pound industry.
Meanwhile the unstinting advocacy of campaigners had made
cat rescue part of the landscape. Cats Protection launched its
'Tough and Tender' campaign in 2000 ('tough' in insisting
on neutering, vaccination and micro-chipping of rescued
cats, 'tender' in its 'strict non-destruct policy').

The first of the 'Rescue Cat of the Year' awards soon followed,* won by abandoned-on-a house-move 'Mitzi', who was now a star turn at a care home for humans. The CP shelters were recast into smartly branded so-called 'Adoption Centres' to better declare the re-homing imperative. Proper scientific research began on what made some 'long-stay' cats more difficult to re-home, and on the stress-related behavioural issues that affected institutionalised cats. When the organisation moved to a purpose-built 'National Cat Centre' in East Sussex which looked like a Silicon Valley research campus, nobody batted an eyelid. Rescue cats deserved the best.

British animal charities had ridden out the political turbulence that had marked the previous three decades, and remained more or less intact. The no-kill debate in America had not crossed the Atlantic with the same degree of rancour. Animal rights militants had moved on to new issues expressed with new levels of passion, while unwanted cats were still up there as a cause worth fighting for. One cause, among many.

Cats Protection would emphasise its 'no killing for human-convenience policy' while the RSPCA, under a new director, former PR executive Gavin Grant, would a little later very ambitiously declare its goal of ending euthanasia of re-homeable animals within five years.

The cultural shift was absolute. In mainstream public perception the number of healthy animals destroyed by welfare charities had become an outright badge of shame. The 'merciful release' mantra had not worked for years anyway. Nor had the threat to public health of disease-

---

* The contenders' back-stories – one 'used as live bait in a dog fight', another 'shot by poachers' – could have come straight from a cats' shelter report of a century before, but with this difference: rather than a merciful end, these battered survivors were all given a new chance of life.

carrying feline swarms. The past record of the way street animals had been dealt with was airbrushed out of history.

The age of the celebrity pet sugar-rush had truly arrived. It was good for fundraising. Would it also be good for cats?

It was altogether a good thing for Battersea, which celebrated its 150th anniversary with its 'Cattersea' initiative and a fabulous £5 million cattery opened by the Duchess of Cornwall. A cat behaviourist was appointed to boost re-homing rates. And with the advent of the new facility it would be reported: 'A noticeable difference was detected . . . because every aspect of the building had been designed with animal welfare in mind. The isolated air systems stop the spread of disease, each cat has its own window to look out from and the large pens have allowed them to be increasingly confident. Consequently, re-homing rates in the new cattery [have] increased by almost 30 per cent.' And they would progressively improve. In 2014, 3,401 cats were received at Battersea, of which 3,007 were re-homed. For the first time in the Home's long story, more cats were re-homed than dogs.

But for politicians and celebrities, adopting a rescue cat was all of a sudden something to be shouted from the rooftops – or rather emblazoned all over the burgeoning new world of social media.

The internet also served to spread rescue cat best practice and put images of cats in search of homes, wherever they might be, a mouse-click away.

For example, one day in Nanjing, China, a high-school student called 'Kevin' read about TNR 'on the RSPCA website' and with co-founder 'Chaser', set up an organisation called 'Mao Pu Da' – 'dedicated to the Trapping, Neutering and Releasing of feral and stray cats who are being fed in parks and the community by caring feeders'.

Cat-loving Mr Dau Dau of the Da Dou Dou Cat Café, at No. 205 Ning Hi Rd, Nanjing, offered his agreeable café to

be their public headquarters, dedicated 'to promoting attention and kindness to cats, especially street cats'.

In the Chinese capital Mr Dong Bin founded 'Beautiful
New World' in 2005 – described as 'a group of people in
Beijing who could no longer live with the appalling condition of stray pets in their neighbourhood'. After a decade,
while it was still the case that in 'China no governmental
organisation cares for stray animals', almost all the capital's
individual care-givers had been converted to the cause and
'were working closely with animal hospitals in Beijing to do
en masse TNR so as to get good prices'.

Across the world, rescue cats were climbing into the sunny
snoozing spot which pampered domestics had occupied
before. Then in 2007–8 came the global banking crash and a
whole new crisis engulfed cat owners and their pets – but
more of that later. The cultural status of the British Domestic
Stray meanwhile was about to get its biggest boost in fifty
years.

Film stars had long since replaced duchesses as animal
welfare ambassadors. And now, new-millennium rescue cats
had no shortage of celebrity adopters. Although they seemed
to overwhelmingly favour dogs, singers, actors and reality TV
stars were queuing up to offer a home to, and set up a social
media account for, a cat in trouble. Politicians too got aboard.
After several post-Humphrey catless years under New
Labour,* it was noted that vermin were reappearing in the
heart of government – or rather scurrying in front of TV
news cameras outside No. 10 Downing Street.

When staff were said to be pressing for a new feline recruit,
and a spokesman for the newly elected Prime Minister, David

---

* Walk-in, Thatcher-era stray Humphrey had 'retired' in November 1997
after encountering a reported frostiness from the Prime Minister's wife, Cherie
Blair.

Cameron, confirmed that there was a 'pro-cat faction within the building', Battersea Dogs and Cats Home helpfully pointed out that they had many rescue cats waiting to be re-homed. They suggested a three-year-old tuxedo cat, 'Crocket'; he could be ideal. Mr Cameron appeared unmoved.

For reasons unknown there was a change of mind nine months after the coalition government had been installed. It was reported that officials had asked Battersea 'to recommend a suitable cat. They didn't mind about its sex, colour or age but asked that the cat should 'be happy meeting new people . . .'

Step forward Larry the rescue cat. It would be reported:

Nothing is known about Larry's past, save that he is aged about four and was rescued early in January [2011] after apparently living rough. He was taken to Battersea Dogs and Cats Home, neutered, and nursed back to fine fettle by its re-homing team.

It was the Home who had put Larry on a shortlist of rescue cats and the PM reportedly asked his young children to choose. Battersea staff had described Larry as 'lively, confident and sociable', with 'a strong predatory drive'. Thus it was that Larry 'arrived [at Downing Street] in the passenger seat of a blue van from Battersea and was carried into his new home in a basket shielded by a blanket. Set free, he hid under a table.' But was No. 10 a 'forever home'? Had Battersea checked out the suitability of the adopters? Apparently not. But Larry, it transpired, was in for the duration – and beyond.*

---

* The Tory-supporting *Sun* newspaper stated bluntly that Larry would be 'shockingly kicked out of No. 10 and left homeless' should Ed Miliband be elected PM in the UK election of May 2015.

Celebrity Cats

CLIVE AND SUZY

Clive, 4, tabby DOMESTIC SHORT-HAIR lives with Suzy in a Wendy house in the garden of a house that has been sold. The previous owner is now in a nursing home. Clive is a big, beautiful, demanding of affection, boy.

Suzy, 2, is Clive's companion. White, tortie, female. She is a little timid but not feral. When we go to feed her and Clive, she runs alongside Clive miaowing, so it would be great if they could be homed together.

An even bigger stray cat sensation than Larry would break a few months later. It began in summer 2010 when a nameless but soon-to-be very famous cat met busker and *Big Issue* (the homeless people's magazine) seller, James Bowen, in the hall-way of his flats in Tottenham, north-east London. The mystery ginger tabby had no collar or identity tag, and an infected leg wound. Bowen, then in a drug rehab programme, reportedly checked with other residents of the sheltered accommodation to see if the apparent stray belonged to any of them. When none claimed ownership, he 'decided to help the cat himself'. The walk-in cat had pulled a classic stray, 'pick-up-a-human' routine. And he had chosen wisely.

James Bowen took the cat to RSPCA's Harmsworth Memorial Animal Hospital in Holloway – to where, in a nice historic twist, the work of the Animal Rescue League had been transferred in 1975. What happened next, as recorded with the help of Battersea Dogs Home chronicler, Garry Jenkins, would turn out as a classic of rescue animal narrative, as engaging as the *All the Year Round* correspondent's visit to Mrs Tealby's establishment, also in Holloway, almost a century and a half earlier.

The waiting room was 'a scene from hell', full of aggressive, tattooed young men with Staffies on strings that almost certainly, thought Bowen, 'had been injured in fights with other dogs, probably for people's amusement'. He wrote:

> The cat sat on my lap or on my shoulder. I could tell he was nervous, and I couldn't blame him. He was getting snarled at by most of the dogs in the waiting room. One or two were being held tightly on their leashes as they strained to get closer to him.

After four and a half hours, the nurse ushered the cat and his adopter in to see the vet. 'I told him how I'd found the cat in the hallway of my building and pointed out the abscess on the back of his leg,' wrote Bowen.

It was and remains RSPCA policy to refuse a 'healthy stray' for rehab and re-homing – but luckily for this street cat, he was clearly in trouble and already had someone who might offer him some kind of a home. It was not the vet's job to make human or feline character judgements – he was there to ease animal suffering and that is just what he did. Bowen would write:

> He could tell the cat was in pain and gave him a small dose of diazepam. He then explained that he was going to issue a prescription for a two-week course of cat-strength amoxicillin.

The cat was free of fleas and a scan showed no microchip. His back-story was unfathomable, but even though a stray, he was happy enough in human company. A feral would never have adopted anyone – even in Tottenham.

He should be micro-chipped, urged the vet, and neutered, giving the ginger cat's adopter 'a form advertising a free neutering scheme for strays'. The RSPCA dispensary charged £22 for the two-week course of antibiotics. 'It was a lot of money for me,' so James Bowen would write, 'a day's wages. But I knew I had no option: I couldn't let my new friend down. I'd been given a sample of scientific formula food at the RSPCA and tried it on him the previous night. He'd liked it so I bought a bag of that. I also got him a supply of cat food. It cost me around nine pounds, which really was the last money I had.'

So the cat and James Bowen were now bonded together, for at least as long as it took to get through the course of anti-biotics. But the degree of bonding was remarkable. The cat began to follow his bemused adopter around. He'd better have a name. How about 'Bob'?

Since Bob seemed so keen to accompany him, Bowen constructed an improvised harness from shoelaces and began to bring him, travelling by the number 73 bus, to his regular pitches in Covent Garden (from where the feral colony had long since departed) and Islington, where he was a regular sight among the fashionable shops and cafés of Upper Street. Bowen had a *Big Issue* pitch outside the entrance to Angel tube station[*] where he was spotted by a London Underground blogger called Annie Mole; she posted an on-line picture of

---

[*] Round the corner from where the RSPCA's Animal Rescue League had dispatched hundreds of thousands of London's street cats. The spectral shade of Kate Cording and Fellowship Cottage would at last be expunged by Bob's triumph 100 years later.

man and cat in July 2010. A local paper, the *Islington Tribune*, picked up the story in September.

While Mr Bowen was performing, Bob would calmly sit in his guitar case exuding feline calm. The effect on the day's takings was dramatic. 'The best to manage' Bob, as it would be written, he was equipped with a more rugged 'blue woven-nylon' body harness and lead, neutered and micro-chipped as the RSPCA vet had advised. The public began uploading videos of Bowen and scarf-wearing Bob to YouTube and tourists would seek them out for selfies. The lovable pair's public profile attracted the attention of Mary Pachnos, the veteran literary agent responsible for the UK rights to journalist John Grogan's *Marley and Me*, the canine bestseller-turned movie.

The Battersea Dogs Home chronicler, Garry Jenkins, was put on the case – with the outcome being a moving narrative of mutual redemption, Bowen first getting the wounded ginger cat back to health and in turn being rescued himself from drug abuse and street living by Bob's loyalty and trust. The result was an international bestseller and a Street Cat Bob franchise which made everyone very happy, including readers of the heart-warming story and rescue cats generally. Who would dare disrespect a stray now? But a new wave was coming, driven by the exploding attention economy of social media. It was all about image. Was a cat cute? Was it funny? Bob was an agreeable-looking ginger tabby; the only props he needed were a woolly scarf and a lead made out of street-approved string.* He would now be challenged, however, by

---

* Less heart-warming was a spate of news reports from Scotland in summer 2013 of 'foreign men' begging in Princes Street, Edinburgh with 'sedated kittens'. A West Lothian Cats Protection branch member pointed out that it was a result of the 'Street Cat Bob bandwagon' and was technically an offence under the Performing Animals Act 1926 (as indeed was harness-wearing Bob, being used as part of a busking act, if not actually begging). The Scottish SPCA

a freakish bunch of attention-grabbing cats who would become internet sensations simply because of the way they looked.

The Tottenham stray found James Bowen and traditional media found them – after the post in a blog of an endearing digital image of the pair outside an Underground station. When a literary agent, ghost-writer and publisher came into the menage, Street Cat Bob moved uptown.

It did not need traditional media to make 'Lil BUB' a global sensation. The feral kitten from Indiana went viral (almost) all by herself. Lil BUB became an internet cat star by simultaneously satirising the look-at-me social media world in which lolcats thrived – and exploiting the very same in a tsunami of lucrative merchandising deals.

And by being cute. And by looking a bit weird. And by being a rescue cat. It was perfect. Like a clever girl from the wild side, she had captivated an army of on-line auxiliary media feeders. She did it like this:

Mike Brivadasky, a thirty-four-year-old 'bearded musician with wise eyes and tattoo sleeve' from Cleveland, already had four rescue cats. A call from a friend at a shelter in Bloomington, Indiana, led him to an encounter with an extraordinary cat. A tiny female tabby, the runt of the litter born to a female feral, she had been found in a rural tool shed in summer 2011.

Her extra-terrestrial strangeness was her charm: her short, stubby legs, polydactyl paws, and a genetic mash-up which had detained her for life in big-eyed kitten wonderment. As a champion for the right to life of misfit cats, for showing that

---

was blamed for doing nothing to help the 'poor wee cats'. The RSPCA had long concerned itself about 'mendicants' animals' – typically 'pipe smoking' and begging dogs. In 1908 its magazine had featured (not that disapprovingly) a blind pedlar in Whitechapel, east London, a 'familiar sight' with his attendant black cat.

being different is no bad thing, and that adopting a rescue pet is the best, Lil BUB could not be beat. She was given lavish veterinary care, micro-chipped, vaccinated and spayed – and provided with what every feral cat had always dreamed of – some clever social media management.

'Lil BUB is a healthy, happy cat living in the care of her "dude" who treats her like a queen,' said her Facebook page reassuringly. 'She is always calm, and surprisingly comfortable and at peace in just about any situation. She loves to travel and gladly sits on her dude's lap in cabs, subways, planes and even his shoulder as he walks around outside.' In February 2014, Lil BUB and the ASPCA announced Lil BUB's Big FUND, a national fund to provide grants to shelters with special-needs pets.

Lil BUB acquired a boyfriend, 'Smooch', an exotic short-hair with an unusual physiognomy, also from Indiana. And she unsurprisingly faced ever more competition, as anthropo-morphised caricature cats crowded in like it was a casting session for a live action remake of *Top Cat*. Other web sensa-tions, such as the gloomy philosopher tuxedo cat, 'Henri, Le Chat Noir', and 'Tardar Sauce' aka 'Grumpy Cat' failed to provide suitable rescue-shelter credentials. Their merchan-dising potential was, however, undiminished.

But then here was 'Hamilton the Hipster Cat', a grey and white rescue whose facial markings adorned him with a handlebar moustache ideal for prowling the achingly hip thoroughfares of Hoxton or Harrisburg, should he have chosen to do so. But Hamilton might find that all a bit too cool for his undeniably wild nature. He had been found with his sister ('Flower') on the streets of San Francisco and taken to the Humane Society of Silicon Valley. It was reported:

Being ferals, both Hamilton and Flower did not trust people or their new environment. Both of them would have to have a lot of special care and attention before they could be put up for adoption.

Hamilton's adopter in July 2012 was local stand-up comedian, Jay Stowe, who in spite of being hissed at a lot, persevered with the aid of a behavioural specialist to get the remarkable animal into a homeable (and presumably merchandisable) state. With an enviable social media constituency in the bag, it would be noted:

> Once you earn the trust of a feral cat and give them the love that they deserve, the bond you will form is unlike any other you can have. Hamilton is now a fully loving, playful, fun-loving kitty.
>
> Hamilton and his family are advocates for adopting versus shopping for your next pet. Rescue pets are the best pets!

All-black Persian rescue cat 'Princess Monster Truck' of New York had fewer Instagram followers but equally attention-grabbing features – described as 'yellow were-cat eyes, a vampiric underbite and a head that looks as if a fur pom-pom exploded from her neck'.

According to her adopter, artist Tracy Timmons, PMT 'came tumbling out of a Brooklyn bush when we were walking home one night from dinner. Her hair was totally matted, she was really thin, and obviously hungry.'

Her subsequent social media exposure was 'to encourage other people to adopt and rescue pets', it would be said, but after Buzzfeed featured PMT, she became a real internet celebrity and 'brands and charities started to get in touch'. They would do that. A portion of Princess Monster Truck's revenue was pledged to animal rescue shelters.

And how about Scandi rescue cat 'Monty', acquired from a Copenhagen shelter in 2013, who 'was born without a nasal ridge, or a nose bone [through a] chromosomal abnormality'. 'We wish for Monty to be an ambassador for cats that may not look perfect in everyone's eyes,' said his owners on Monty's Facebook page. 'We also want to raise attention to the fact that looking different doesn't mean you can't be fantastic.' Admirable motives.

The new wave of 'unusual'-looking cats with oddly human attributes offended some welfare purists as being an on-line freak show – although who could begrudge the glow of feral-rescue-friendly sentiment they inspired? This time the cats were the celebrities, not their adopters.

Tottenham Street Cat Bob was already in a lucrative partnership. But who was the celebrity? Was it Bob or his street-performer friend? James Bowen and his media advisers had no doubt about the answer: it was Bob himself. Other celebrities would not be as self-effacing as they put their rescue cats on social media. A new phenomenon was in the making. Love My Rescue Cat, Love Me More.

Attention-hungry British comic, Russell Brand, was named PETA's 'Sexiest Vegetarian Celebrity' of 2011, and was subsequently pictured with his agreeable black and white rescue cat 'Morrissey'.

In 2014 singer Florence Welch adopted a four-year-old tortoiseshell cat called 'Missus' from Battersea Dogs and Cats Home that had been left with the charity 'after her owner could no longer care for her'. The cat was reportedly chosen because of her 'friendly' nature, which in rescue cat terms was not strictly politically correct.

Actor Robert Downey Jr. adopted two kittens from a rescue centre that had been found under a bush in West Hollywood and named them 'Montgomery' and 'Dartanian'. 'I would kill for these young, sweet little feline souls, these two boys. I would protect them with my life,' he was reported as saying.

The Social Network actor, Jesse Eiscnbcrg, became well known on social media as a 'fosterer of rescue cats in need of homes' – while his 'own best friend and cat is called Mr Trunkles'. In 2012 *Family Guy* creator Seth MacFarlane announced the creation of a no-kill cat shelter in partnership with the Heaven on Earth Animal Society, to be called 'Perry's Place', named for his late mother. The shelter is described as 'a cage-free, no-kill sanctuary in the San Fernando Valley of Los Angeles County that serves as a haven for homeless special needs cats'.

Founded in 2000, Heaven on Earth had taken on the toughest of briefs, 'to implement community-wide spay/neuter programs, sustain an adoption program for rescued strays and provide long-term care for animals with low adoption potential due to medical conditions, disability, temperament or age'.

Rescue cat 'Mr Peeps', belonging to singer and animal advocate Ke$ha, developed an enviable social media pawprint. In 2012 Mr Peeps' owner was appointed Global Ambassador for the Humane Society International.

Country music sensation turned 'cat mom', Taylor Swift, was reported in 2011–12 as having 'adopted' two Scottish Fold cats, 'Meredith' and 'Olivia'. In spite of both being highly attractive representatives of the fashionable 'owl-like' breed, they were described in tweets and press reports as having been 'homeless rescue cats'.

31

Cat Crisis

Rescue cat celebrities might boost the cause of adoption but could do little to help welfare charities still mopping up the casualties of the new recession. The banking crisis of 2007–8 was not only bad news for the world's economy but also a disaster for cats. It worked two ways, with people resolving to give up their pets because of cost or the loss of a job, of a home, or through having to move to rented accommodation where they were not allowed to keep pets.

Then there was the reluctance by potential adopters to take on new responsibility in uncertain times as recession rippled onwards into homes and families. The squeeze meant all charitable donations were down. Less cash and more cats.

Year on year, feline adoption onward figures would fall. The number of cats taken up from Cats Protection, for example, were: 55,185 (2009), 52,583 (2010), 48,000 (2011) and 46,000 (2012), prompting desperate appeals by the cat charity for more people to be aware of how animals were suffering. The summer holiday-plus-kitten season was tougher than ever, with adoption centres reporting 'nobody coming in and looking at the cats'.

Cats Protection appealed specially for its 'unwanted older cats aged twelve years and above' – now waiting an average of ninety-six days before being adopted – more than twice the charity's average adoption rate of forty days.

In 2010 the Blue Cross took in 1,175 kittens dumped in bags or left at roadsides. RSPCA figures showed such a rise in unwanted animals that the charity announced itself to be struggling to cope with the nation's 'ever-growing cat crisis'. More coming in and fewer going out meant a grisly upswing in destruction.

The RSPCA would note that 'although the overall trend in the euthanasia of re-homeable cats and dogs has gone down during the past twenty years, in 2010 we had to put 33 per cent more dogs and 28 per cent more cats to sleep than we did in 2009 . . . The cat population in the UK has reached crisis point,' it announced dramatically. 'The charity is full to capacity and is having to rely heavily on private boarding establishments to house the many unwanted and abandoned cats . . . As 75 per cent of the UK's cats are acquired as kittens, the market for adult rescue cats is already, by comparison, very small.'

A big survey in 2014 unsurprisingly found that younger, poorer cat owners were slow to neuter while old myths and prejudices still pervaded: 'Female cat owners apply anthropomorphic tendencies to their female cats (e.g. "I don't want to take away her right to have babies"),' said the subsequent

report. An important concurrent issue among welfare professionals was *when* to neuter. It was generally stressed that
owned cats be neutered at a pre-pubertal four months, rather
than at the historic norm of six, and rescue kittens be neutered
as early as eight weeks, prior to re-homing. Some vets resisted.

'Initially it is unnerving to look at such a small kitten on
the operating table . . . now it is completely normal to operate on a 500 gram/eight-week-old kitten', said a partisan for
early intervention.

'The castrations are a little more fiddly, but not beyond
anyone. Once you overcome the mental barrier associated
with the smaller animal, the benefits to the individual and
population become clear,' said a vet with Wood Green
Animal Rescue.

Battersea Dogs and Cats Home were aware that many
more pets were being given up by struggling owners for
economic reasons than were coming in as strays – although
these might well have been simply abandoned. A visitor in
2009 found the 'feline wing . . . close to bursting point. The
exhausted staff are struggling to cope with a record 143
inmates . . . waiting patiently for new homes, plus a further
175 standing by for an empty pen.' The press report continued: 'Usually it takes just 27 days to find most cats a new
owner, but the 10 per cent fall in the number of new owners
coming forward means that "Smudge", "Bella", "Dingle"
and their neighbours could be here for well over a year. But
a good number are simply dropped off at the door, together
with cat tray, blanket and favourite toy by owners who just
can't – or won't – cope with them any more.'

'Many landlords will not allow tenants to keep pets', said
the Home, 'and in the context of increasing pressures on
housing and rent, the impact can often be the displacement
of a dog or cat from a home'. The emerging Generation
Rent was not necessarily Generation Pet.

All the charity help-lines were overwhelmed with desperate pleas of: 'Unless you take him, I'm going to have him put down anyway' – or worse. Outright abandonment was back to 1960s levels. 'Every year we have suffered a fall in our cat adoptions. We are down by about a third compared to where we were in 2010,' said a Wood Green volunteer. 'We are also swamped by requests to take in cats for the same reasons. However, as we are already full to bursting, we have little option but to add further cats to a waiting list or point owners in the direction of other charities who may be able to help them.'

Or much more likely, they too would be 'full to bursting'. Cats were shuffled from shelter to shelter, to outworkers and fosterers, with as much care and tenderness as could be given. It was a time of grave crisis for cats.

It was a very unfortunate time therefore for the RSPCA to embark on a brave new initiative. In January 2012, a new Chief Executive was appointed: Gavin Grant, a public affairs professional and centre-left political activist. Soon afterwards, as the second of 'five pledges' (the first was to 'end over-population of companion animals'), the Society announced it was 'Intending to end the euthanasia of any re-homeable animal in our care during the next five years . . .' It was a goal, so long wished for, but which had never even remotely been in sight. The timeframe, inevitably perhaps, would one day be quietly dropped.

The ending of euthanasia could be effected when 'more good homes were available and more people chose RSPCA rescue animals as pets', said the Society. That was no surprise, but what was new was the general expression that it was down to the charity itself, its management, its workers and volunteers, to work towards these admirable ends – specifically by providing better support for adopters and developing a fostering network. A re-homing tie-up with horrid commerce (the Pets at Home stores, see below p. 389) was announced in parallel.

This time, the traditional blaming of irresponsible owners for pet over-population was played down. It was the Society itself that must try harder to end shelter-killing. This was almost a no-kill manifesto.

With moves like this, the RSPCA's enemies detected a renewed shift from welfare to rights under the Grant regime. Lots of stories about the 'RSPCA forcibly taking beloved pets and destroying them against the owners' wishes, then pursuing the owners with charges of cruelty' began to pop up on-line and in an acquiescent press, along with (and this was new) right-to-life animal-lovers being persecuted by the Society. The presence on the Council Reform Group of veteran, 'pet-banning' philosopher Dr Richard Ryder excited special anger among 'country' interests and their newspaper allies. Cats would be caught in the crossfire of the new proxy war.

The Society could not win. It had a torrid time as ex-employees were paraded in the media describing a regime which placed 'prosecution and persecution' of owners ahead of protection of their pets. Families had beloved cats swiped by callous inspectors. There was a row in autumn 2013 because, according to press reports: 'The owners of independent animal refuges claim they have faced disproportionate attention from the charity.' Mr Gareth Edwards, co-founder of something called 'The British Association of No-Kill Sanctuaries', had had his County Durham refuge raided by RSPCA inspectors and a prosecution for cruelty brought against him.

He accused the RSPCA of 'bullying' and said: 'A no-kill policy, such as the one we operate, means a higher standard is being met, and that is very threatening to the RSPCA who cannot and will not guarantee that no healthy animal will ever be put down,' as it was reported.

In another case, RSPCA inspectors, accompanied by two policemen and a vet, raided a cat rescue centre, removing sixty-two cats which were allegedly in an 'unsatisfactory condition'. When presented in the press as heavy-handed harassment, the RSPCA in reply said it supported the work of 'well-run' animal sanctuaries and that the Society itself had promised to end 'the euthanasia of any re-homeable animal, and a number of our own branches operate non-euthanasia policies'. But it was still merely a promise, not a reality. Indeed, the fate of the 'unsatisfactory' cats they had themselves removed was not recorded.

Another Society-baiting story soon turned up, this time concerning an elderly couple who had 'hit out at the RSPCA after it refused to help remove a feral cat that had invaded their home' in Canterbury, Kent. The cat's very presence seemed in some way to be the charity's fault.

'Bruce and Eileen Gough were left cowering for two days after the cat climbed into their house through an open window and ran amok,' it was reported. 'When Mr Gough attempted to remove the animal it attacked him . . .' But when the couple appealed to the RSPCA for help, they were told there was nothing they could do because the feral cat was 'healthy and not in any distress'.

The delinquent feline had begun 'urinating and defecating in the house and then broke a treasured heirloom' (a Victorian ewer which fell off a mantelpiece). Mrs Gough said that 'when they contacted the RSPCA expecting someone to come out and remove the animal, the charity refused and told them to try a local cat protection charity'.

Canterbury Cats Protection provided a cage trap 'in the hope they could tempt the cat down and catch it . . . however, when that failed they turned to neighbour Andrew Fox, a retired fire-fighter and keen motorcyclist. He donned his full leathers and helmet and managed to wrap a blanket around the cat before releasing it outside.'

An RSPCA spokesman said: 'Our donors expect us to use our limited resources on animals who are suffering or in distress or danger . . . So long as a feral cat is healthy, he or she will live happily outside.' We do not know the subsequent fate of that particular cat.

In February 2014 Gavin Grant quit as Chief Executive, for 'health reasons'. His enemies were jubilant. The search for a replacement to take this 'well-established, premium brand', as the animal charity was described, 'forward into a new era of achievement', went unrewarded. A spokesman for an anti-badger-cull group gave a rousing statement in Mr Grant's defence in the *Guardian* newspaper: 'He was doing exactly what the RSPCA was set up for . . . It's not there just as a sanctuary for people who can no longer look after their dogs and cats.'

There were still a few people, however, who would have been happy if that was exactly what it *was* there for.

32

Cat On-line

GLORIA

Female, age (approx.) 6, DOMESTIC SHORT-HAIR, black.
Hello my name is Gloria. I came into Cats Protection care as
a stray from the Langley area. I am a lovely little lady with a
shy but sweet nature, I enjoy fuss and strokes once I have got
to know you. I prefer to live with older children. I would
like a home that is quiet and calm with access to a garden for
me to explore and a family to love me.

The surplus pet problem, it seemed, had long been down to
a simple equation. There were too many pets being born (or
abandoned) and not enough homes. The agonisingly slow
retreat from mass killing had been matched by an emphasis
on a new technology to address the supply side: mass sterilisation.* For many decades and without too much fuss, the

---

* In 2014 RSPCA research would indicate an overall UK neutering rate of 86
per cent, which was 6 per cent short of the target for a static population. The
shortfall meant 30,000 'excess' cats being born per year. Traditionally, both
male and female cats had been neutered at six months old while feral kittens had
been neutered on capture at a much earlier age, sometimes just eight weeks old.
So-called 'early neutering' became a lively issue in cat welfare. According to the
Cat Group: 'There is no evidence to show that neutering earlier than six months
(and as early as seven weeks), has negative developmental or behavioural conse-
quences. The perceived increased risks of surgery/anaesthesia are now consider-
ably reduced by . . . improved techniques and agents.' Neutering at four months
could be recommended.

mainstream cat charities in Britain and America had run programmes to spay and neuter the felines of the not-so-well-off, to spread the principles of responsible cat ownership, provide voucher funding schemes and pool resources.

The London Cat Care and Control Consortium ('C4'), for example, was founded in 2002 to do just that in the capital with seven charities aboard including Cats Protection, the Mayhew, the RSPCA and CAT. It also offered help for ferals and multi-cat ('six or more') households. It was all terribly worthy but a little bit dull. Quite soon, the companion-animal charities, when appealing for donations and legacies, would hardly mention neutering at all. Kittens looking for homes were much more appealing.

Now the new technology of the internet seemed set to revolutionise the demand side. Petfinder.com, for example, founded in the US by Betsy Saul in 1996, which began by posting pets available for adoption from thirteen shelters in New Jersey, would be set for astonishing growth. Ten years later, *Forbes Magazine* would call it 'one of the internet's greatest – and most touching-success stories'. And they were right.

With this fabulous virtual marketplace becoming universally available, it would be simple, surely, to match a rescue cat in need of a forever home with kindly, responsible people looking for a lifetime feline friend. This was much more exciting! In fact, it was going to prove a lot more difficult than it seemed.

In the mid-life crisis of the Cats Protection League back in the 1960s, Albert Steward had bemoaned the lack of interest

---

The forty-year search for a viable oral or injectable feline contraceptive had also been unrewarded. In 2015 the John T. and Jane A. Wiederhold Foundation of Connecticut announced a $130,000 research grant towards an injectable contraceptive for free-roaming feral cats.

by members in promoting neutering. They would much rather make a fuss around cats in trouble. That was where the dramas were, both feline and human. It was where the satisfaction was – and always had been. It was where the love was. More to the point, it was where the donations and legacies were. *The Cat* had run a report from the CPL's Croydon Branch in the mid-1980s discussing the art of homing difficult cats:

> We had a lot of cats in the rescue pens which had been there for a very long time. However, by concentrating on them in our publicity we have recently homed ... 'Pandora', 'Marleigh' and 'Chester'. The owners of these three difficult cats are quite special types and we were very careful to whom they went. A sob story in the local paper is always the answer and we are lucky enough to have Pat Davis who is a master at them.

And it was just the same thirty years later when the web really arrived and cyberspace opened for business as a giant feline photo opportunity. A good sob story was still what was needed.

The internet also gave an 'adopt our cats' platform to the smallest shelter and breed society, allowing them to stand up just a bit to the tide of corporate professionalisation that made the big boys with their out-of-town campus HQs, eager marketing and legacy appeals all look increasingly the same. The individualists battled on in the cause of cats, even when an umbrella organisation like the Cat Group could announce sternly:

> Houses with rooms full of cats kept by well-meaning people are no longer acceptable – cats kept in large groups may be very stressed and liable to become infected with the many

infectious diseases which can affect cats such as cat flu, enteritis, feline leukaemia, feline immunodeficiency virus or ringworm.

Whether it was designed to lure potential adopters to a 'room full of cats' (that is just where we found ours) or a glossy Adoption Centre, the emerging internet rescue-cat subculture showcased lots of felines in need of homes accompanied by lovingly crafted mini-biographies packed with heartbreak, hope and the promise of redemption.

Some purists wailed about the dangers of only displaying the most adoptable cats. But the dramatic back-story approach was designed to do the job as their well-meaning authors saw it, to shift cats in trouble out of shelters and into homes. Their rescue cats had origins, destinies, triumph-over-tragedy narrative arcs. They had personalities. Each one could give and needed special love.

They included oldies, grumpies, three-legged cats, timid cats, one-eyed cats, FIV-infected cats and even feral cats. Some of their mini-sagas have been shamelessly used in this narrative.

While all this newly internet-enabled take-me-home stuff was fun, some in the business urged that attention should still be turned to the supply side, not just neutering, but specifically to shutting down commercial puppy farms and 'kitten factories'. 'How Much Is That Doggie in My Browser' was the attention-grabbing title of a damning 2012 report into US 'puppy farms', claiming that the internet had become a vast, unaccountable marketplace for the long-reviled 'back-yard breeders' to offload their production-line animals.*

---

* In September 2013, the US Department of Agriculture announced that breeders selling puppies and kittens directly to the public through the internet,

The British Parliament debated the matter in September 2014 after a 125,000-name e-petition demanded action to outlaw 'irresponsible puppy and kitten breeders'. The move did not get much further than that, but at least MPs did take time to consider the welfare of cats.*

Some find-a-pet aggregator websites featured cats both for adoption and for commercial sale – with welfare charity pop-ups simultaneously urging: 'Adopt Don't Buy!' Confusion reigned.

Kitten factories and puppy farms also damaged the standing of breed-specific clubs and professional pedigree breeders. The latter too had been infected with rescue cat frenzy over the years – there had been reports of feral Persians turning up in urban colonies – and had sloughed off much of the elitism and snobbery of less egalitarian times.

The Duchess of Bedford, hostess of the cats'-meat men's grand dinner of a century before, would surely have approved the roster of breed- and type-specific sites that bloomed across the internet – with an acknowledgement that even the posh-est of cats can get into certain difficulties. Of the 115 cats,

---

by mail or by phone, would be subject to the same licensing and inspection regulations as those selling to brokers or pet stores. More than 400 kitten farms were targeted. So-called 'hobby' breeders, breeding three females or fewer, were not affected.

* British law-makers of all parties proved anxious to declare their pet-loving credentials during the debate by name-checking their pets and thus getting them into *Hansard*. Tory cats included 'Naughty Cat', 'Mango' – plus 'Monty' and 'Maggie' – who came from 'properly licensed breeders'. Labour cats 'Polly' and 'Lucy', in contrast, were politically correct rescue cats obtained from Cats Protection. 'We went through a fairly rigorous process to get them. We had a visit to our home, and we then had to follow the proper processes to ensure their subsequent welfare,' Meg Munn, MP for Sheffield, Heeley, told the House. Labour's John McDonnell, the soon-to-be Shadow Chancellor, thought that the opportunity for MPs 'to put their pets' names on the historic record [was] a valuable contribution to our civilisation'.

clubs, societies and associations listed under the umbrella of
the Governing Council of the Cat Fancy, nearly all of them
featured welfare or adoption contacts showcasing pedigrees
in peril. All of them – of course – fabulous.

Cats Come Home

QUEENIE

Female, (approx.) 5, DOMESTIC SHORT-HAIR, tortoiseshell, can live with mature family.

Queenie has had a difficult start in life. Her previous owner was unable to cope so she has not had the socialisation that she deserved. Queenie would need a lot of time and patience for her to be able to build and gain confidence. We have found her very food-orientated so encourage her out of her pod and she will love to play and fuss round your legs if you have treats. If you are lucky she will let you fuss her but this we are still working on, as at the moment it scares her. She is a beautiful cat who just needs a loving owner to help her along.

The internet had changed so much, but so much still stayed the same. For all the rescue cat's cultural street-cred, for all the buzz around celebrity adopters, for all the social media rumpus around Lil BUB and the literary success of Street Cat Bob, for all the no-kill-style reflection that it was down to shelters to try harder and not blame the owners or the cats, the take-up rate of rescue cats leaving shelters for loving homes stayed stubbornly low. Whose fault was that?

The statistics from the US and Britain over the years were remarkably similar. The work of the US National Council on

Pet Population Study and Policy showed the percentage of lost cats returned to their original owners by shelters to be vanishingly small. That had always been the case.

On the crucial issue of where pets in homes originally came from, surveys and analyses showed the majority of them were obtained from acquaintances and family members including 'born at home'; 15–20 per cent of dogs were purchased from breeders, and up to 10 per cent were purchased from pet shops. At least 20 per cent of cats were adopted as walk-in strays and – this was the most significant statistic – 20 per cent of cats and dogs were adopted from shelters and rescues.

As Nathan Winograd argued in his 2008 book *Redemption*, there were 165 million cats and dogs in US homes, topped up each year by the acquisition of millions more. And 20 per cent of that happily homed population were obtained from shelters.

On his figures, 4–5 million unwanted pets were killed each year in shelters, of which 90 per cent were 'saveable'. Get the adoption rate up by just 3 per cent and there would be nothing left to kill. It looked like a done deal when the HSUS waded in to say, 'If we can increase by a few percentage points the number of people who get their pets by adoption, we can solve the problem of euthanasia of healthy and treatable dogs and cats.'

The historic trend was remarkable. Four to five million animals per year were being re-homed in the mid-1980s, when shelter killing was running at 18 million dogs and cats. Thirty years later, the re-homing rate was broadly the same, four to five million animals per year, but on 2013 figures, the killing of otherwise viable, adoptable cats and dogs had come down to just over three million: sterilisation had seen to that by pinching off the supply. Making that figure zero seemed tangibly close.

But there were and would always remain structural problems. As the veteran American shelter professional turned animal news blogger, Merritt Clifton, pointed out in 2014:

> Among the most cherished . . . myths afflicting the [US] animal rescue and sheltering community in recent years is the notion that with intensified effort and investment we could adopt our way out of ever having to euthanize an animal . . .
>
> Since Americans annually acquire at least four times more pets than the numbers of dogs and cats killed in shelters, the argument runs, merely persuading more people to adopt a pet instead of buying from breeders and stores should end pet over-population.

This was in essence the no-kill platform, one of its precepts being that effective promotion could push the shelter adoption market share of overall pet acquisition significantly higher. But over the years, so Mr Clifton noted, the cost of marketing as part of the average expense of receiving, sheltering and re-homing an animal in successful US shelters 'had already increased from almost negligible to more than half of their operating costs'. The internet was terrific but it was still just a marketplace. Would people want the wares on show?

But at heart it was about numbers – and that other factor that had been in play for half a century: sterilisation. 'Since every pet has to be born somewhere, and since shelters and rescues are supposedly not in the breeding business, at least half of all pet acquisition will always be other than through shelters and rescues,' Merritt Clifton pointed out. Along with the fact that the total number of animals re-homed from shelters peaked in the 1980s, when most of them still received abundant litters of accidentally born puppies and kittens – the cute pets that people always wanted.

That was it: people still wanted kittens, and however fashionable rescue pets might be, however many celebrities polished their hipster appeal by being associated with a rehab street cat with Munchkin legs and polydactyl paws, there was also the defining factor that a pet was seen as a family member. Decisions about which would be taken by Mom and Pop. Primarily Mom.* And Mom could be pretty unhip sometimes.

But nobody ever said you had to be part of a nuclear family to be a cat-lover. Singles, couples, young adults, same-sex couples, all could be forever-home providers. And they could be just the sort of person in need of a cat to make themselves more attractive to other humans. Any reason to adopt a rescue cat was good.

It was just so when relationships ended and families broke apart – always a big reason for pet abandonment. But when the cat was still wanted, who got to keep it? In the US especially, pet custody battles would become a lively subset of divorce law, when it was by no means a given that the primary caregiver (nearly always female) had the strongest emotional attachment to the contested cat. 'Get two pets' became standard advice – while PETA could counsel: 'Please do not allow your companion animal to be needlessly euthanized during times of crisis. Take the appropriate steps now to ensure that he or she is well taken care of even after your divorce or death.' It was all mapped out.

---

* Cats Protection have long been aware that in traditional UK households, 'on the whole it is usually the woman in a family who makes the decision as to whether to get a cat as a pet, and the one also who is more likely to take the cat to the vet, and to do most of the care-taking.

'We tend to appeal to women in our marketing. Calendars with cats, Valentine appeals, etc., are all primarily female-focused. There are, of course, many singles and same-sex partners who are committed cat-lovers.' In addition, Dr Jenny Remfry, pioneer feral expert, accounts for 90 per cent of feeders being women.

There were successes. Those shelter pets being re-homed did now include many more of the 'difficult' cases that would not have had a chance before, because there were 'so many younger, cuter, healthier kittens and puppies in line for adoption ahead of them', according to Mr Clifton's analysis. And the percentage of rescue animals becoming family pets in American homes overall was significantly up over the years – from 15 to 25 per cent. But the reason for that, he argued, was because only a fraction as many pets were being born into their homes as in the forty years past.

Mass sterilisation had created a kitten vacuum. 'Currently 91 per cent of all pet cats and 83 per cent of all pet dogs have been sterilized', he wrote, 'according to the 2013 American Pet Products Association survey.' Thus the in-home pet birth-rate had plummeted. It was exactly the same in Britain.

A second reason for the missing pets was that, because far fewer people were allowing dogs and cats to roam unsupervised, and thereby get lost to be found and adopted by someone else, acquisition of pets by simply finding them in the street or at the back door had also gone down. There was more room for shelter adoptions as the self-adopting stray got rarer.

It remained the fact, however, that every cat acquired from a pet shop or garden centre, or on-line retailer, or breeder, or neighbour, or born in a litter at home – meant a home-seeking rescue cat waiting in a shelter. Self-adopting strays were, of course, entirely blameless. They did their own marketing.

But for all the politically correct arguments about not 'commoditising' cute, adoptable cats, too many cats were not leaving shelters to go home with anyone. Something new must be tried. There was a way – and it was already big news in America.

Pet supply retailer PetSmart Inc., founded in 1986 in Arizona, had long since spun off 'PetSmart Charities, Inc.', described as a 'a non-profit organization dedicated to ending euthanasia and finding homes for homeless pets'. An innovative move was to invite shelters to showcase their roster of rescue cats and dogs physically in the parent company's stores. Like this:

> PetSmart Charities®Adoption Centers – in more than 1,300 PetSmart®stores – provide a clean, quiet and convenient place to get to know your new furry friend. The centers feature adorable cats and dogs from local animal welfare groups . . .

The rival Petco pet products retailer, founded in San Diego in 1965 (it had never sold commercially bred cats and dogs), had begun to promote cats from local shelters soon after it started. As it grew and spread across forty-nine states, the principle grew with it. It was announced in December 2013:

> Through a unique partnership with Petco and select animal welfare groups, we have created satellite animal shelter locations within local Petco stores, introducing loving adoptable animals to lots and lots of prospective pet parents. These mini-shelters are open whenever Petco is open and provide access to adoptable dogs, cats and other small animals by a very desirable demographic of potential animal adopters.

What was not to like? Petco even made a statement explaining why adopting a shelter animal from an actual shelter might be difficult. They 'could be a very stressful place for a homeless dog or cat', apparently. 'The constant barking and meowing and . . . people looking to adopt can be both scary and intimidating. Many cats and dogs are also bewildered as to how they got there in the first place.' According to Petco:

Many animals may appear timid, may hide in the back of their cages or may even hide under their bedding. As a result, it can be very difficult to get a grasp of their true personality. That shy, timid, frightened pet may actually become a fun-loving clown when you bring him home. Many animals begin to blossom once they are in a loving home environment.

Few would argue with either statement. And by such means many millions of rescue cats and dogs had indeed already found loving American homes. PetSmart Charities Inc. also backed feral neutering groups and funded the 'Rescue Waggin' program', a bussing operation to 'transport adoptable cats and dogs from areas that are overpopulated to partner shelters where adoptable animals are in demand'. Why could not such innovative, successful methods be brought across the Atlantic?

In 1997 PetSmart's UK assets were bought by the eight-year-old British-founded company, 'Pets at Home', itself set on a path of expansion on the US model. Part of that was establishing a charitable foundation which in 2006 became 'Support Adoption for Pets', with a mission to raise and dispense funds to British 'pet rescues' of whatever size. 'Organisations can be national animal welfare charities or independent rescue and re-homing centres. Branches of national animal welfare organisations which receive minimal or no funding from central funds can apply for financial support,' said its grant funding criteria.

Tiny 'sanctuaries' with an income of less than £500 could apply. But just as significantly, the Manchester-based charity also established 're-homing centres' in hundreds of Pets at Home stores, featuring small animals, rabbits, guinea pigs, unwanted for whatever reason.

In 2010 Pets at Home was acquired by a US investment fund for £955 million. It was floated on the London stock market four years later for £1.23 billion. Even in a recession, pet commerce was on a roll, riding out the banking crash when many pet owners lost their homes and 'foreclosure pets' were big news.

There was some muted outrage but no surprise therefore in British animal welfare circles when in 2012 Pets at Home announced a 'partnership' agreement with the RSPCA, to put live animals on sale in their warehouse-style stores where they could be purchased by the public for an 'adoption fee'. The first opened in Stockport in November. The doomed Gavin Grant cut the ribbon. It was for cats and rabbits; dogs at weekends. 'It took just five days to re-home our first four cats – a litter of black cats that had been at Rochdale RSPCA for eight months – their entire lives,' it was reported. Who could argue with that? Dogs Trust and Battersea Dogs and Cats Home soon got on board.

The take-me-home animals were on their websites, why not live in person? Having in-store pets was upbeat, family-friendly, great for 'footfall' and, even better, they were rescue animals. In October 2013 Battersea opened a 'mini version of the rescue charity' within the Pets at Home store in Sydenham, south London, manned by Battersea's own staff and unpaid volunteers. 'Jeffrey', four, and 'Pepsi', six, were the first cats out of the door.

But it seemed to some that decades of campaigning had been overturned. Mr Michael Jessop, past President of the British Small Animal Veterinary Association, called it 'an appalling idea. Animal welfare organisations have fought for years to keep dogs and cats out of pet shops and you no longer see puppies and kittens in shop windows.'

The charities put out bland statements about following strict procedures and reaching out to new customers. But when Cats Protection came aboard, many of its '8,500 unpaid volunteers flooded the charity's private forums with expressions of concern', so it was reported. One said: 'The thought of cats being screamed at by unruly kids with parents who will get them one to appease them, is frightening. It feels wrong and irresponsible.'

There were more concerns. Would older, timid or unfashionable cats be included in the new feline beauty pageant? (In fact, they would be.) Cats Protection were unabashed, saying:

> The centre in Pets at Home will contain spacious pens that have been custom-built to our welfare standards and the cats will be cared for by the charity's staff and volunteers. It has purposely been separated from the rest of the store to avoid large numbers of people passing by the pens, thereby minimising stress to the cats. Potential adopters will go through the same process as they would when adopting from any Cats Protection centre, ensuring people cannot buy a cat on impulse.

Their kindly hosts, Pets at Home, said 'we always put pets' interests first and will make no money from this partnership'. But it could only be good for getting people into the shop. Thus it was that Cats Protection opened its very first UK Homing and Information Centre in the Newbury, Wiltshire, Pets at Home store on 29 April 2014 in a branded, discrete area of the big box. It was announced: 'Cats will be displayed in pens provided by the store, with shoppers able to choose a cat and, after paying a £65 adoption fee, return the next day to pick it up.' For that sum, the cats would have been vet-checked, neutered and micro-chipped, if old enough (five to eight weeks), vaccinated and come with four weeks' free insurance.

The first in-store cat to be re-homed was five-year-old 'GiGi', adopted by Louise Harrison and her ten-year-old daughter, India. GiGi's original owner had had to go into a hospice. Louise had apparently spotted GiGi after she 'popped into the store to buy food for her other cat', 'Tuppence'. Two days later she came back with India, 'hoping any cat they adopted would help her daughter learn how to care and be responsible for a pet'. There, still on the shelf, was GiGi. The adoption fee was paid, the Harrison household passed the criteria, and lovely GiGi was heading for her new family twenty-four hours later.

Within a month, ten more cats had been re-homed out of the store, an achievement described as a 'fantastic start'. Cats Protection's chief vet told the authors in summer 2015: 'It's been brilliant. We have one-eyed cats on site, black cats, the ones usually harder to re-home, and we will have more. It has been incredibly successful in terms of finding families and homes for our cats.'

The old-established charities' alliance with a giant pet shop might offend the purists but it was in tune with the times; the charities had been doing deals for years with pet food and insurance companies while the veterinary profession tried its best to stay semi-detached. American animal rights advocates were calling it the 'Extended Pet Industry' worth a staggering $55.7 billion a year in 2014, only $2.23 billion of which went on live animal purchases.

It was in the pet product merchandisers' interests to keep cat and dog numbers up along with their share price, the animal rights advocates said, and it was that which was driving the supply side of the pet population crisis. They effectively accused the commerce-compliant, charitable re-homers of having made a pact with the devil.

But what was hard to object to in all this was the fact that *rescue* was the brand. Breed did not come into it. 'Oh, we got a rescue.' It made adopters feel good about themselves (the authors certainly did). And why not? It was like being Brad and Angelina. When a big-screen movie of Street Cat Bob's story went into production in London in early 2016, a feline actor called Oscar and seven stand-ins were stepping in the talented paw-steps of *Rhubarb* star Orangey. Were they being exploited? Surely not – and what a boost for all those rescue cats without film contracts looking for a nice home. As lovable cats pleaded soulfully from their branded, merchandised enclosures, as children smiled with delight and wonder, only the most doctrinal animal-rights, all-pets-are-cruel ultra could say it was somehow wrong. It was what everybody wanted.

Cats were going home.

Innovative web use might do much more. In April 2015, for example, Wood Green put 200 cats on the Handy domestic-help app on a fostering basis as rodent controllers. 'Chico' and 'Elsa' led the way. 'Naturally, this is all about the cats,' said the charity, 'and we hope that Londoners will fall in love with some of the attractive mousers that come to stay, potentially turning temporary residences into permanent ones.' Forever homes were waiting. Let's match them with fabulous cats however we can.

It had been a long journey for a humble stray – from being scooped up by Mrs Morgan or turned into fancy leather gloves by the Animal Rescue League, to being eyed by a nice adopter in a big-box superstore in Sydenham. The authors know where we would rather end up. And we are sure that nine out of ten cats would agree. Now please, pay the adoption fee and – *Take Me Home*!

Postscript

CAT LADY TO THE RESCUE, 1904

The scandal of the forsaken cat went on for decades, and for just as long a time, cat-lovers published poems and stories bewailing the animals' plight and the thoughtless cruelty of those who abandoned them. It was part of the century-long campaign to raise the status of cats from throwaways and vermin to an animal worthy of respect and love. The fight goes on.

This story from the pages of the *Animal World* in 1904 had a happier ending than many:

A CAT'S TROUBLES

You talk of poor dumb animals in voices soft and kind,
And then you take a brand new house and leave your cat behind.
We're left behind to starve and thieve and find another place,
There's no name upon our collar to publish your disgrace.

The cat was troubled and perplexed; she could not make out what was going on. All day long, men had been tramping in and out, carrying tables and chairs, pulling down curtains and taking up carpets, etc. Everyone was far too busy to take any notice of her even when at the usual dinnertime she lifted up her voice and signified her hunger by mewing several times.

The people she lived with did not care for cats. Where rats and mice were concerned she was looked upon as a necessary evil but in other ways she was considered a nuisance and banished to the kitchen or out of doors – and the love she willingly would have given was rejected. She would hear them say that cats were selfish, who only cared for what they could get, so it was not surprising that when Puss ran from one to the other, she was pushed to one side and told to get out of the way. Not understanding, she got into a sunny window and after dejectedly washing her paws, curled herself up and tried to sleep – but without success. It was all so strange and uncomfortable. She wanted a little milk, her mouth was parched and she had had none that day. Presently she heard her mistress say: 'What about the cat? Shall we take her?'

'Take her? No,' replied the master. 'What's the good? She would only run away. Besides, she is no longer a kitten and we can easily get another if we want one. Put her outside – she will get her own living and take care of herself all right. When the new people come, perhaps they may be glad to keep her.'

'But if they should not, John? I should not like even a cat to starve.'

'Starve? Not she,' replied John. 'Cats can always find plenty in a town, let alone the mice and birds they catch. If she could speak she would tell you she would rather stay about here than go to a fresh home. She does not care for us as a dog would. Cats only attach themselves to places, and provided they get plenty to eat they are quite happy.'

Pussy tucked her head tighter under her paws. She could not speak to contradict them and though her heart might ache, she was unable to express her feelings or let them know either how she longed for a fond caress or how gladly she would have returned it with all the wealth of love that despised heart of hers contained.

At last she got so hungry she was obliged to go out and see if she could catch something for her supper and when once more she returned, she found the door and windows closed against her. Now indeed her troubles commenced for the new tenants would have nothing to do with her. They cared even less for cats than the last people had done and gave foolish, affected screams when Kitty came near, as if she were some dreadful wild beast about to do them some harm.

Things were not so bad while the warm weather lasted, for some of the neighbours were kind, especially a little old maid; many a saucer of milk did she give the deserted waif, stroking her gently the while. Puss never feared to go to her, though the many hardships she had gone through had made her mistrustful of people in general. She would have liked to have gone indoors and adopted this kind friend as a new mistress but the good lady had many pets of her own to study and felt she could not take another.

Time went on and winter came. One snowy night poor Kitty was wandering about in the freezing air looking hopelessly for some place of shelter; she was cold, hungry and miserable. All that day in turn she had tried for admittance at the doors and windows of her old home with piteous cries that might have melted a heart of stone; but in vain for either she was chased away or else left to mew till her throat ached. At last she dragged her weary body into the shelter of the porch and lay down on the front-door mat.

Before morning, cold and hunger were forgotten as in a new joy that had come to her. Three tiny blind kittens crawled aimlessly around her and she purred her happiness as she washed the wee faces of her darlings. But alas! Troubles were to come back with the returning daylight. The door opened and the maid, with a pail of water, came out to clean the steps, but as soon as she saw the cat and her kittens she gave a shriek, rushed back and banged to the door again with all her force. A voice from upstairs called out sharply: 'Mary! Mary, what are you doing? Whatever is the matter?'

'Oh! if you please, mum, it's that 'orrid cat,' answered Mary hysterically. 'She have been and got kittens outside of our front door on the mat.'

'Dear me! How I do hate cats. How tiresome it is,' said the owner of the voice peevishly. 'Well, Mary, the best thing you can do is to put them in your pail and get rid of them at once.'

'Me, mum, me drown 'em? Lul, no. I couldn't touch them with a pair of tongs.' Each member of the family in turn, one by one they would open the door, peep, and shut it again with a shudder, as though some noxious reptiles were there instead of a harmless cat whose hunger and thirst no one thought of satisfying.

By and by the charwoman was fetched and soon the poor little atoms (whose eyes were never to be opened in this cruel world) had finished their short career while their broken-hearted mother was again driven away. She picked up a few scraps of food and returned to wander all that bitter day round and round the house, her plaintive cries becoming weaker and weaker, until at last as night approached, she crawled once more to the porch where a few short hours ago she had been so happy, and stretching herself out, she curved her paws out and tried to imagine her lost darlings were still with her.

Time went on; the moon rose and looked down at the stiff, cold form of poor Puss, not dead yet, but almost sense-less from cold and want of food. Two figures entered the gate and came up the drive; one was the daughter of the house, the other, the little old maid who had been kind to the friend-less creature no one loved or wanted. As they reached the door, the girl started back, exclaiming, 'O! That horrid cat again!'

'What cat, my dear? Why, bless me, it's that poor thing I have given food to. I wonder what brings it into such a plight. It seems almost dead with cold. We must take it in and try what we can to save its life.'

'Not into our house,' said the girl crossly. 'Let it die! Since we have been here that beast has been a perfect nightmare for us and this morning we found it with three wretched kittens. However, we soon had them put out of the way and if we get rid of the cat too, perhaps we may have some peace.'

The little old maid's face flushed, her eyes blazed and she stamped her feet on the snow, crying sharply, 'Peace? You cruel, heartless girl! Do you expect peace – you who ruthlessly tear all the poor thing's babes from her, and then leave her to starve like this? You, who say that once you get rid of the unfortunate beast, you hope to have peace? Rather until the end of your life you may expect to be haunted by her starving form and sorrowful cries.'

Her indignation was let go no further; stooping down, she gently lifted the cat in her arms and turned on her heels without another word to her callous companion. On reaching her own home she relented not until she had done all in her power to restore the life of her helpless burden. At last her efforts met with success and Pussy, after swallowing a few spoonfuls of warm milk, purred feebly and tried to rub her head in a grateful manner against the kind hand that had saved her life.

Needless to say, in spite of the many other pets, Pussy was not again turned adrift. She had found a home and someone to love her at last, and proved how much the saying 'cats only attach themselves to places', was worth by the faithful devotion she gave to her dearly loved mistress.

Grace Wildash

CAT LADY TO THE RESCUE, 2007

Urban redevelopment and Trap Neuter and Return campaigns had cleared feral cats from much of inner London over the decades, but plenty of determined survivalists remained in the de-industrialised east of the city. When clearance began in summer 2007 of the vast derelict landscape allotted for the Olympics, as yet five years away, just 'a few kittens' had been spotted. But then contractors reported 'many cats roaming all over the site'.

The Celia Hammond Animal Trust was called in to do what they could, working against the clock. Ms Hammond's first assessment was gloomy. She wrote:

> We are so concerned at the scale of the problem. Not only the number of cats that need to be brought to safety – many are wandering, traumatised and disorientated, due to the destruction of their habitat – but the limited time available to us to try to make sure that cats and kittens are not injured or killed in the demolition process.
>
> Some are nervous rather than feral as they were fed by the previous owners of businesses, but many will need to go to farms, stables and smallholdings. All will be neutered, vaccinated and micro-chipped and we will give advice and support to introduce them to their new location.

It took months. There were multiple success stories and re-homings of the tamer ones but a number of cats proved impossible to trap, including 'Victoria' and 'George', who had made their home in a bus . . . until in October 2007 it could be reported:

> Victoria appeared forty-eight hours ago at a different bus station in the same road, where the many cats we recently

rescued [including George] had been regularly fed by Larry, one of the bus drivers. She was all alone, terrified and crying pitifully. She was so ravenously hungry that it only took a matter of minutes to get her to enter the trap.

One cat in particular has proved, so far, impossible to catch, in spite of all my forty years' experience. A large long-haired black cat we call 'Blackjack' has been seen just about everywhere on the site, and seems to constantly move around . . .

If he is still there, I can't help him now . . .

Winter came. No black cat. As spring arrived the Olympic Delivery Authority grew ever more exasperated at the hold-ups. Relations broke down. Meanwhile, the hunt for Blackjack had attracted a global following. 'One lady from New York has been calling every week, asking: "Have you caught him yet?"' so Ms Hammond reported. Fifteen thousand cat-lovers signed a petition. The rescuers were barred from the site. Then a factory worker called to say that a black, long-haired tom had been seen in a next-door alleyway on the western edge of the site.

It was reported: 'Miss Hammond set traps in the alley, which runs next to a canal beside the 2012 hoardings. For three weeks, night after night, she or one of her assistants waited in the dark cabin of her van, clutching the end of a length of twine, ready to spring the cage. There was no sign of Blackjack.'

Then, very early on the morning of 11 July 2008, came the dramatic news: 'Blackjack – safe at last!'

It was just past 4 a.m. and we were waiting to rescue another cat at a factory adjacent to the canal bordering the Olympic Park: when suddenly Blackjack appeared, coming across the canal from the towpath on the other side, making his way to our feed site. We could hardly believe our eyes when he went to the trap and walked around it for what seemed an age.

Eventually, after a nail-biting wait, he couldn't resist the chicken inside it any longer and we caught him. We were ecstatic!

Blackjack – the 187th and last known cat on the 800-acre Olympic site has finally been rescued and is now recovering at our Lewisham Clinic.

Blackjack made the BBC News. 'To be honest, once we had left the site in May I didn't think he was still alive,' said Ms Hammond. 'He has calmed down a lot . . . at first he was so wild, I thought he was feral. Now I think he must once have been someone's pet. He has spent the last year fighting to survive on that building site. We will put him with a family without children. He just needs a nice quiet home.'

And that is what Blackjack, just like Pussy over a century earlier, did find.

SO YOU WANT TO ADOPT A RESCUE CAT?

You have made a good choice. Rescue cats are immensely rewarding and, as the authors know from our own family experience, they are intensely loving, funny and affectionate. But they are not problem-free, and depending on each cat's personal story, may need a bit of time before they settle in with you and start to feel really at home.

Why does any cat find itself in a rescue shelter? This is important to think about as it will not only be an indicator of your future pet's behaviour, but is also key to knowing how best to handle them. Your rescue cat may have been badly treated, had an elderly owner who died, or been abandoned completely and left to survive and become semi-feral.

Sometimes the owner may have wanted to keep the cat but found it impossible due to an allergy, some aspect of the cat's behaviour or hostility from other animals in the household.

But for whatever reason, a rescue cat has suffered the trauma of being separated from his family and home territory, and his confidence will have been affected as a result. The good news is that, with the support of a loving stable home, he still has a strong chance of living a long and happy life with you.

HOW TO FIND THE ONE (OR MAYBE THE TWO)

There are thousands of cats in rescue centres, and they all need good homes. With so many to choose from, there is bound to be the right cat just waiting for you to come and claim him. What are you waiting for? Cats Protection now also operate a Cat Match programme, including a personal app and Android to help you find The One.

But remember, looks are not everything. It isn't about choosing the cutest kitten. Many adult, elderly, or disabled cats would love to find a home, and you will have the added satisfaction of knowing that you are helping an animal which may not otherwise have found love again. And if you are older yourself, you may find a slower, snoozier animal more appealing anyway.

Black cats and white cats also tend to be less popular than other colours, on the absurd grounds that 'they have no personality' – as do nervous and 'timid' cats who are frequently overlooked in favour of their more outgoing companions.

Adult feral cats can be adopted as outside shed-livers; it takes enormous effort and time to get a glimmer of response from them. Those who know about these things say that kittens who do not have any contact with humans after they are born will be feral, regardless of whether their mother is a stray domestic cat or a feral cat living in a colony. They will be frightened of people and demonstrate all of the signs of fear and anxiety that an adult cat would – spitting, hissing, and running from human contact.

To become pets, feral kittens will need to be socialised. If they are eight weeks or younger, it is straightforward enough; older than that and they will take much more time, although there have been success stories. Eleven to twelve weeks is the cut-off point.

If you have small children, some cats will suit you better than others. Rescue centres will be able to tell you whether a cat is used to a young family or not.

YOUR RESCUE CAT'S HEALTH

Many cats end up in shelters and adoption centres because they have medical problems. They may be deaf, blind, or have been abandoned by their owners because they suffer from Feline Immunodeficiency Virus (FIV), a virus which by lowering the number of white blood cells makes the animal less able to fight off infection. Because it is such a slow-acting virus, many FIV-positive cats can enjoy a normal lifespan with no obvious health issues. Crucially, FIV is species specific. It can only be transmitted from cat to cat, not to humans or other animals. It used to be thought that FIV-positive cats should be homed singly, but recent studies by Glasgow University's Companion Animal Diagnostics have found transmission rates of cats in the same household as low as 1–2 per cent. The main route to infection occurs through biting, as the virus is carried in blood and saliva, and does not survive very long outside the body. Although many people avoid FIV-positive cats for fear of the vet's bills which could follow, some rescue centres are prepared to help with bills even after the cat has been re-homed. Always seek advice from staff.

FIV is often confused with FeLV (Feline Leukaemia) – but they are two very different viruses, differing greatly in how they affect a cat, and its expected lifespan. FeLV is a serious risk to a cat's health and longevity, whereas FIV is not.

Like FIV, the Feline Leukaemia Virus belongs to a group of viruses called 'retroviruses', but to different families within the group. Both are long-term viruses which compromise a cat's immune system, leaving him more susceptible to other infections. In addition, FeLV also causes tumours in 20–30 per cent of infected cats.

NEUTERING

Neutering your rescue cat or kitten is essential in reducing the overall number of unwanted cats. Cats Protection recommends that this be done at approximately four months, or sometimes younger.

Some charities including CP offer vouchers towards the cost of having your cat neutered. Others will have already neutered the animal themselves prior to adoption, according to how old it is.

Micro-chipping your pet is also highly recommended and again may have already been done by the charity or rescue centre.

So anyone thinking of adopting a cat can be confident that their prospective pet's state of health has been thoroughly checked and the necessary neutering (where age-appropriate) and vaccinations have been done. Remember that this has been an expense for the shelter, who will be hoping for a donation or adoption fee to enable them to continue their work.

IS YOUR HOME SUITABLE?

Before adopting a cat, ask yourself whether you can provide the right environment for him. Do you have a garden? If you live in a flat, does your tenancy agreement allow you to keep a pet? In some cases, you simply have to seek the landlord's consent beforehand. Don't just get a cat and hope that everything will work out: it may not.

If you live in a flat with no access to a garden, look out for a rescuee who was previously used to living indoors. Any cat who is used to being allowed to roam free would find it very stressful to suddenly find himself restrained inside. Rescue-centre staff will advise you.

Make sure you find out as much as possible about the cat you are thinking of adopting. Don't make a rushed decision. Most shelters, including Cats Protection, will allow you to visit several times before taking your new pet home. Staff might also want to do follow-up checks afterwards to see how you and your rescuee are settling in together.

Before bringing him home for the first time, be sure you have all the necessary items: cat litter, food bowls and bedding, etc. Individual organisations will advise. A cat arriving in new surroundings will normally be a bit shy for a while before his natural curiosity takes over. Spend as much time with him as possible. Talk softly to him, and try not to make loud noises or sudden movements that might scare a nervous animal.

All cats are different. Some are very sociable and will come to you for a cuddle in no time; others will take longer. But the important thing is to let them make the first contact on their own terms.

Five years ago we adopted two beautiful rescue cats, just a few months old. We had them neutered and did the follow-up vaccinations and had them treated for ringworm and Chlamydia by our local vet, in consultation with the small shelter who had uplifted them from a farm colony in Ireland and brought them to London. After much advice-giving and a home inspection, we were judged to be suitable adoptees. That was the easy bit.

The younger one, Fergus, whose mother we were told had been truly feral, was so acutely nervous that it took him nearly two weeks to come out from under the cooker.

Seeking advice from our vet, we were warned that if Fergus had not been handled by several people in the first few weeks of his life – 'socialised' – he would never fully adapt to living with a family.

But we persisted in talking gently to him, not trying to pick him up too much or to handle him until he felt ready. And then, exactly two weeks after we had first brought him home, he slowly crept across the floor towards me one evening. I hardly dared to breathe as Fergus jumped up on to the sofa and crawled on to my lap, climbing up my jumper towards my face until his eyes were looking into mine. Then, for the first time, he started to purr loudly and contentedly, and I knew we were going to be OK.

Now every night at the same time Fergus climbs up on to my lap and we go through our now familiar ritual. Somehow, in spite of his initial terror, Fergus has managed to find security with us. But if anyone but family comes to the house, he is out of the cat flap and away into the garden in a heartbeat. Luis, on the other hand, who is a far more laid-back character, boxed my ears with his paws within hours of his first arrival, and now greets newcomers on our doorstep like long-lost friends.

So get to know your cat by observing his behaviour. Take your time. We can promise you that it really is worth the wait.

FOSTERING

If you really love cats and would like to help but don't want the responsibility of an adoption, you could also consider fostering. Many rescue centres need foster homes for cats, especially during the breeding season when they end up with lots of unwanted kittens.

As a fosterer you will provide a temporary home for a cat or kitten till they can be permanently re-homed. One of the difficulties with fostering is that you might get too attached to the cats in your care and face the stress of having to let your foster cat go.

But if you can cope with that, and you have a suitable home for fostering, why not give it a try? Expenses for fosterers are usually covered by the rescue centres, so you will be doing a lot of good at little or no cost to yourself. To find out more about fostering, contact your local rescue centre.

But whether you are fostering or adopting, you can feel more than a little pleased with yourself for joining the ranks of the re-homers. And that's before all the joy and love that a once-forsaken cat can bring. Good luck to all readers who take a rescue cat home.

Acknowledgements

The authors are indebted to the archivists, librarians, animal advocates, welfare professionals, rescuers and cat-lovers who kindly helped us to discover so much hidden information on cats – at home, astray and feral.

Thank you especially to Francesca Watson and Dr Maggie Roberts of Cats Protection, David Allen of the Royal Society for the Prevention of Cruelty to Animals, Clare Boulton, librarian of the Royal College of Veterinary Surgeons, Dr Jenny Remfry, Kate Horne of SNIP International, Christopher Russell of Rhodes Minnis Cat Sanctuary, and Sonya Brucciani at the Mayhew Animal Home.

Extracts from *The Cat* and Annual Reports are reproduced by permission of Cats Protection; extracts from the *Animal World*, Annual Reports, Animal Rescue League and working-party reports by permission of the RSPCA. Extracts from the published work of Roger Tabor are quoted by permission of the Random House Group.

Extracts from Crown Copyright documents in the National Archives at Kew appear by permission of the Controller of HM Stationery Office. Extracts from Charity Organising Society reports held in the London Metropolitan Archives appear by permission of Family Action, and Our Dumb Friends League reports by permission of The Blue Cross. Quotes from the peerless on-line cat-history resource, *Messybeast.com*, are with permission of its originator and curator, Sarah Hartwell. Every effort has been made to trace the copyright holders of further unpublished documents and published works in print or electronic form from which quotations have been made.

We would also like to thank our publisher, James Gurbutt, and agent Felicity Blunt for getting behind this book so enthusiastically from the start, Emma Herdman at Curtis Brown for her continual support, as well as editors Caroline Knight, Olivia Hutchings and Joan Deitch, and publicity dynamo Grace Vincent for all their help and enthusiasm.

Finally, we would like to thank our daughters, Maria and Katy, and son Joseph, for their patience with our feline obsession, but who meanwhile seem to have inherited their parents' passion for pets.

And we will remain forever grateful to our friends Victoria and Ann for introducing us to those two wonderful cats, Fergus and Luis.

Bibliography

Anon, *Domestic Animals and their Treatment* (Royal Society for the Prevention of Cruelty to Animals, London, 1857)

Anon, *The Kind Treatment of Domestic Animals* (Dublin, 1858)

Beeton, S. O., *The Book of Home Pets* (London, 1861)

Bowen, J., A Street Cat Named Bob (Hodder, London, 2012)

Bradshaw, John, *Cat Sense: The Feline Enigma Revealed* (Allen Lane, London, 2013)

Cottesloe, Gloria, *The Story of the Battersea Dogs' Home* (David and Charles, Newton Abbot, 1979)

Dickin, Maria Elisabeth, *The Cry of the Animal* (PDSA, London, 1950)

Douglas, Nina Mary Benita, Duchess of Hamilton and Brandon, *The Chronicles of Ferne* (Animal Defence Society, London, 1951)

Fairholme, Edward George, *A Century of Work for Animals* (RSPCA, London, 1924)

Flegel, Monica, *Pets and Domesticity in Victorian Literature and Culture* (Routledge, London, 2015)

Fudge, Erica, *Pets* (Acumen, London, 2008; Routledge, London, 2014)

Hall, Rebecca, *Voiceless Victims* (Wildwood House, Hounslow, 1984)

Howell, Philip, *At Home and Astray: The Domestic Dog in Victorian Britain* (University of Virginia Press, 2014)

Jenkins, Garry, *A Home of Their Own* (Bantam, London, 2011)

Kete, Kathleen, *The Beast in the Boudoir: Petkeeping in Nineteenth-Century Paris* (University of California Press, Berkeley, 1994)

Lind-af-Hageby, L., *The Shambles of Science*, Extracts from the diary of Two Students of Physiology (Animal Defence & Anti-Vivisection Society, London, 1913)

Lind-af-Hageby, Louise, ed., *The Animals' Cause, a selection of papers* (Animal Defence Society & Anti-Vivisection Society, London, 1911)

Lind-af-Hageby, Louise, *Bombed Animals–Rescued Animals–Animals Saved from Destruction* (Animal Defence Society & Anti-Vivisection Society Pamphlet, London, 1941)

Malle, Anny, ed., *A Cat in Hell's Chance: The Story of the Campaign Against Hill Grove Cat Farm* (Slingshot, London, 2002)

Montague, Frederick, *Let the Good Work Go On (On the Work of the People's Dispensary for Sick Animals of the Poor)* (Hutchinson, London, 1947)

Montgomery, John, *Arthur: the Television Cat* (W. H. Allen, London, 1975)

Moss, Arthur, *Valiant Crusade: The History of the RSPCA* (Cassell, London, 1961)

Nurse, Dr Angus and Ryland, Diane, *Cats and the Law* (published by International Cat Care on behalf of The Cat Group, 2014; see also *www.thecatgroup.org.uk*)

Remfry, Jenny, *Ruth Plant: A Pioneer in Animal Welfare* (J. Remfry, Barnet, 2001)

Simpson, Frances, *Cats and All About Them* (Isbister & Co., London, 1902)

——, *The Book of the Cat* (Cassell, London, 1903)

Singer, Peter, *Animal Liberation* (2nd ed., Pimlico, London, 1995)

Smith, Carmen, *The Blue Cross at War* (Blue Cross, Burford, 1990)

Stables, Gordon, *Cats: Their Points and Characteristics, with Curiosities of Cat Life* (London, 1876)

Tabor, Roger, *The Wild Life of the Domestic Cat* (Arrow, London, 1983)

UFAW, *The Ecology and Control of Feral Cats: Proceedings of a Symposium Held at Royal Holloway College, University of London, 23 and 24 September 1980* (Universities Federation for Animal Welfare)

Winograd, Nathan, *Redemption: The Myth of Pet Overpopulation and the No-Kill Revolution in America* (2nd ed., Almaden Books, Los Angeles, 2014)

Winslow, Helen Maria, *Concerning Cats: My Own and Some Others* (David Nutt, London, 1903)

Wintle, Frank, *Helena Sanders and the Cats of Venice* (Souvenir, London, 1989)

Woodham-Smith, Cecil, *Florence Nightingale 1820–1910* (Constable, London, 1950)

Source Notes

PART ONE: ONLY A STRAY 1850–1930

Chapter 1: In the Matter of Cats

p. 4   'Cats contribute . . .' Carlos A. Driscoll, 'The Evolution of House Cats', *Scientific American*, June 2009 *http://www.scientificamerican.com/article/the-taming-of-the-cat/*

p. 4   'Popular opinion may be . . .' Beeton, *Beeton's Book of Home Pets* (1860), p. 657

p. 5   fn 'It is a frequent occurrence . . .' *http://messybeast.com/1880-diphtheria.htm*

p. 7   '[T]he cats of shy neighbourhoods . . .' Dickens, *The Uncommercial Traveller ebooks.adelaide.edu.au/d/dickens/charles/d54ut/chapter10.html*

p. 10   'He knows now surely . . .' *Animal World*, March 1881, p. 53

Chapter 2: Humblest of Servants

p. 15   'humblest among . . .' *Domestic Animals and Their Treatment*, RSPCA (1857), p. 60

p. 18   'I used to go out . . .' *Our Cats*, 9 December 1911, p. 118

p. 19   'First then because she is a pet . . .' Stables, *Cats: Their Points and Characteristics, with Curiosities of Cat Life* (1879), p. 358 *https://archive.org/details/catstheirpointsc00stab*

p.20   'In the class for black cats . . .' 'The Crystal Palace Cat Show', *Morning Post*,17 October 1883, p. 5

p. 21   'The cat literature . . .' Simpson, *Book of the Cat*, p. 31 *https://archive.org/details/bookofcatsimpson00simprich*

p. 22   'Floss . . . sleek and well bred . . .' *Our Cats*, 2 August 1902, p. 523

p. 22   'smart society woman . . .' *Our Cats*, 19 July 1902, p. 496

p. 23   'Cats of good moral . . .' *Brooklyn Daily Eagle*, 5 April 1896, p. 18

p. 24   'If at [a] fortnight's . . .' 'A Summer Home for Pets', the *Northern Messenger*, 15 September 1893, p. 5

p. 24   'In 1869 I made . . .' 'The Painless Extinction of Life in the Lower Orders', Benjamin Ward Richardson *http://en.wikisource.org/wiki/Page:Popular_Science_Monthly_Volume_26.djvu/659*

Chapter 3: Forsaken Cats

p. 28   'PERSONS who . . .' *West London Observer*, 30 January 1864, p. 4
p. 29   'For this second dog show . . .' *All the Year Round*, 2 August 1862, vol. 7, p. 495
p. 30 'When we hear of . . .' *The Times*, 18 October 1860, p. 8
p. 31   'to a degree that . . .' the *Animal World*, November 1882, p. 178
p. 31   'The [Home's] Committee . . .' the *Animal World*, February 1914, p. 23
p. 32   'never hesitated . . .' the *Animal World*, October 1900, p. 159
p. 32   '"Bad Sharp!" . . .' the *Animal World*, May 1876, p. 66
p. 33   'Her Majesty detected . . .' the *Animal World*, June 1898, p. 86
p. 33   'which were generally . . .' Winslow, *Concerning Cats: My Own and Some Others* (1900), p. 196
p. 33   'She has induced . . .' 'The Queen and her Cats', *Edinburgh Evening News*, 13 August 1888, p. 3
p. 34   '[W]hen the Court . . .' Louis Wain, *Our Cats*, 23 February 1901, p. 295
p. 34   'Sir, Grant me space . . .' *The Times*, 8 September 1877, p. 4
p. 34   'A very benevolent . . .' the *Belfast News-Letter*, 24 July 1875, p. 4
p. 35   'sanguinary swells . . .' the *Animal World*, 1 July 1879, p. 105
p. 35   'Now he feels its ragged . . .' the *Animal World*, 1 July 1879, p. 103
p. 36   'During one evening's walk . . .' *The Times*, 14 September 1877, p. 4
p. 36   'I am sorry to state . . .' ibid.
p. 36   'Stray dogs are taken . . .' ibid.
p. 36   'No relief can be given . . .' the *Animal World*, July 1879, p. 105
p. 37   'I have myself lost . . .' *London Standard*, 4 December 1884, p. 2
p. 37   'Probably such provision . . .' *The Times*, 14 September 1877, p. 4
p. 38   '"Jack Cat", "Pussy" . . .' the *Animal World*, March 1881, p. 106
p. 38   'We once had sixteen rescued cats . . .' the *Animal World*, July 1879, p. 47
p. 39   'comforts consistent with . . .' the *Animal World*, March 1881, p. 47
p. 39   'Thousands of poor strays . . .' Jenkins, *A Home of Their Own* (2012), p. 114

Chapter 4: Stray Cat Blues

p. 42   'The testatrix leaves . . .' *London Daily News*, 20 October 1882, p. 3
p. 43   fn 'thousands of stray . . .' *St Leonards Observer*, 26 September 1931

p. 44   'institution receiving cats . . .' 'Starved, Forsaken or Outcast', the *Animal World*, December 1882, p. 178

p. 44   'It has always . . .' ibid.

p. 45   'At present Miss Swifte . . .' the *Animal World*, December 1882, p. 179

p. 45   'Richard Barlow Kennett . . .' the *Animal World*, December 1883, p. 189

p. 45   'should think twice . . .' the *Animal World*, May 1891, p. 78

p. 46   'kind-hearted persons . . .' the *Animal World*, May 1904, p. 78

p. 46   '[there was concern] that . . .' Jenkins, op. cit., p. 117

p. 46   'You doubtless know . . .' the *Press*, 17 August 1896, p. 3 *paperspast. natlib.govt.nz/cgi-bin/paperspast?a=d&d=CHP18960817*

Chapter 5: 'Every Cat Wants To Be Personally Useful'

p. 50   'ARRANGEMENTS FOR . . .' the *Animal World*, December 1883, p. 189

p. 50   'stray cats were being . . .' the *Animal World*, May 1884, p. 78

p. 51   'little short of . . .' ibid.

p. 51   'much academic effort . . .' fn see for example Howell, *At Home and Astray: The Domestic Dog in Victorian Britain* (2014), pp. 73–101

p. 52   'very tentatively . . .' the *Animal World*, April 1884, p. 58

p. 52   'the Committee could not . . .' Jenkins, op. cit., p. 115

p. 52   'Our new plan will . . .' the *Animal World*, April 1884, p. 57

p. 52   'Through the generosity . . .' *http://archive.org/stream/scientific-american-1884-09-06/scientific-american-v51-n10–1884-09-06_djvu.txt*

p. 53   'Cats lie asleep much . . .' *Popular Science Monthly*, March 1885, p. 645 *http://en.wikisource.org/wiki/Page:Popular_Science_Monthly_Volume_26. djvu/667*

p. 53   'plump and well fed but . . .' the *Animal World*, September 1884, p. 143

p. 54   'the happiest day . . .' the *Animal World*, January 1885, p. 4

p. 54   'Mr Mitchell's Farm . . .' *Gloucestershire Echo*, 1 April 1884, p. 3

p. 54   'We shall do neither . . .' Cottesloe, *Lost, Stolen or Strayed* (1971), p. 75

p. 55   'could not object to . . .' ibid.

p. 55   'The bodies of 200 dogs . . .' *Dundee Evening Telegraph*, 14 August 1895, p. 4

p. 55   'The time needed . . .' *London and Municipal Journal*, 27 February 1896, p. 196

p. 55   'unable to take care . . .' the *Animal World*, September 1896, p. 134

p. 55   'a growing appreciation . . .' ibid.

p. 55   'received without charge . . .' the *Animal World*, April 1905, p. 62

p. 56   'Cats don't trouble us much . . .' *Pall Mall Gazette*, August 1889, p. 3

p. 56   'stray cats, picked up in West-end . . .' 'The Home for Lost Dogs', *The Strand Magazine*, June 1891 *http://www.gutenberg.org/files/46596/46596.txt*

p. 56   'Just now, especially . . .' *Pall Mall Gazette*, 3 August 1889, p. 3

p. 56   fn 'Battersea has been . . .' *http://www.mimedia.co.uk/2013/09*

p. 56   fn 'We've taken in 235,715 . . .' via email from Battersea Dogs and Cats Home, Head of Press, 4 November 2015

p. 57   'If they have kittens . . .' *Pall Mall Gazette*,3 August 1889, p. 3.

p. 57   'peaceful expression . . .' ibid.

p. 57   'Herculean', *London and the Municipal Journal*, 27 February 1896, p. 195 *see also* the *English Illustrated Magazine*, August 1895, pp. 445–9

p. 57   'instructions   to   arrest   . . .'   *http://hansard.millbanksystems.com/commons/1889/jul/18/homeless-cats-in-the-metropolis*

p. 58   'A band of ladies who . . .' *Pall Mall Gazette*, 3 August 1889, p. 3

p. 58   'Miss M – earnestly begging' *http://archive.thetablet.co.uk/article17th-november-1888/9the-boarding-of-cats-by-lady-colin-campbell*

p. 59   'sanitary authorities . . .' the *Animal World*, May 1891, p. 78

p. 59   'The cats, the starving cats . . .' *Pall Mall Gazette*, 3 August 1889, p. 3

p. 59   'a sympathetic old lady . . .' the *Standard*, 16 July 1900, p. 4

Chapter 6: The Case of the Cat Contessa

p. 62   'Her executors found . . .' the *Gentleman's Magazine*, January 1792, p. 89

p. 62   'There was one woman . . .' 'Of Cats' and Dogs' Meat Dealers', Mayhew, *London Labour and the London Poor* (1851), Part 1, p. 182

p. 63   'cruelly starving . . .' Sarah Hartwell *http://messybeast.com/1856-cat-hoarder-2.htm*

p. 64   'a little kitten . . .' *http://hatchingcatnyc.com/2014/04/05/crazy-cat-lady-lower-east-side/*

p. 64   'Four tiger-like tortoise-shell . . .' the *New York Times*, 19 March 1876 *http://messybeast.com/retro-rescue-usa.htm*

p. 65   'I have tried to do . . .' ibid.

p. 66   'cats possess more sympathy . . .' Mark Bostridge, 'Mr. Bismarck and Big Pussie: The Special Friends of Miss Nightingale', the *Independent*, 15 June 2003, pp. 1–2

p. 67   'At the Hammersmith Police . . .' the *New Zealand Herald*, 6 October 1883, p. 2 *see also* LMA MJ/SP/1886/01/005

p. 68   'The floor was . . .' *Pall Mall Gazette*, 20 August 1884, pp. 10–12

p. 69   'I would not have sold . . .' ibid.

p. 70   'The door closed upon him . . .' ibid.

p. 70   'intemperance in cats . . .' the *New York Times*, 10 June 1885, p. 4

p. 71   'The Countess de la Torre . . .' 'The Countess and her Cats', *New Zealand Herald*, 2 July 1887, p. 2

p. 73   'The Ellen M. Gifford . . .' Winslow, op. cit., p. 193 *http://www.guten-berg.org/files/9501/old/8cats10h.htm*

p. 73   'All around the sides . . .' ibid.

p. 73   'when all inmates . . .' *Our Cats*, 3 January 1900, p. 83

p. 74   'to provide shelter and food . . .' *http://hatchingcatnyc.com/2014/07/01/crazy-cat-ladies-of-washington-heights/*

p. 74   'these cats are only . . .' the *Rock Island Argus*, 27 August 1890, p. 2

p. 75   'It became very heated . . .' the *Indianapolis Journal*, 12 April 1891, p. 7

p. 75   'His claws and teeth . . .' ibid.

p. 75   'feed strays at night . . .' the *New York Herald*, 7 May 1893, *http://hatchingcatnyc.com/2014/07/01/crazy-cat-ladies-of-washington-heights/*

p. 76   Several women compose . . .' ibid.

Chapter 7: A Charming Abode for Felines

p. 79   'The institution of . . .' Salt, *Animals' Rights: Considered in Relation to Social Progress* (1893), p. 42

p. 82   'It is usual to . . .' *Freeman's Journal* (Dublin), 25 June 1885, p. 6

p. 82   'the benefit of the lost . . .' Mayhew Animal Home archives

p. 83   'a compact and charming . . .' J. Woodroffe Hill, *The Diseases of the Cat* (1901), p. 2

p. 83   'Forsaken cats are taken in . . .' *London Standard*, 8 July 1892, p. 6

p. 83   'Mayhew. On the 7th . . .' *Middlesex Courier*, 13 August 1897, p. 1

p. 83   'provide shelter, food . . .' *Rules and Regulations*, 27 June 1906, Mayhew Animal Home archives

p. 83   'THE POOR CATS . . .' *London Standard* (Classifieds), 1 August 1894, p. 1

p. 84   'The policeman on the . . .' the *Westminster Budget*, 17 August 1894, p. 17

p. 85   'Yes, it's a disgrace to . . .' *Our Cats*, 23 August 1902, pp. 575–6

p. 85   'deal with the question . . .' advertisement in the *Cat Manual* (1902) *http://www.forgottenbooks.com/readbook/The_Cat_Manual_1000020892#13*

p. 85   'to find an immediate refuge . . .' *Our Cats*, 12 January 1901, p. 235

p. 85   'without contact . . .' the *Animal World*, February 1899, p. 18

p. 85   'the human qualities . . .' 'Are Cats Immortal?' *Dundee Evening Post*, 8 December 1900, p. 2

p. 86   'every care is [being] . . .' Jenkins, op. cit., p. 177

p. 86   'Twice during the past . . .' the *Animal World*, May 1898, p. 77

p. 86   'If more cats are brought . . .' the *Animal World*, May 1899, p. 78

p. 86   'homes were found . . .' the *Animal World*, May 1905, p. 62

Chapter 8: Posh Cats

p. 88   'fine sleek black . . .' *Our Cats*, 7 November 1903, p. 35

p. 88   'rescued a stray . . .' *Sheffield Daily Telegraph*, 2 July 1904, p. 11

p. 88   'Persian tom living. . .' *Our Cats*, 16 August 1902, p. 541

p. 89   'hosts of starving cats . . .' *Our Cats*, 3 August 1901, p. 584

p. 89   'did she know . . .' *Our Cats*, 5 October 1901, p. 697

p. 90   'large tabby on . . .' *Our Cats*, 7 November 1903, p. 29

p. 91   'a slight recognition . . .' *Our Cats*, 5 January 1901, p. 196

p. 92   'well wishes for . . .' ibid.

p. 92   'who warmly thanked . . .' *Our Cats*, 19 January 1901, p. 223

p. 92   'They were a . . .' *Black & White Budget*, 26 January 1901, pp. 514–15

p. 92   'I do not know . . .' *Our Cats*, 19 January 1901, p. 223

p. 93   'as a result of the . . .' *Our Cats*, 26 January 1901, p. 238

p. 93   'for a long-haired half-bred . . .' *Luton Times and Advertiser*, 15 March 1895

p. 93   'for where there stands . . .' ibid., 23 November 1906, p. 7

Chapter 9: The Midnight Band of Mercy

p. 95   'noisy tramp cats . . .' the *New York Times*, 16 March 1893, p. 5 *http:// messybeast.com/bookshelf/1893-bandofmercy.htm*

p. 95   'a perfect right to throw . . .' the *New York Times*, 20 July 1893, p. 9

p. 96   'An anti-cat crusade . . .' ibid.

p. 96   'Because they murder . . .' ibid.

p. 96   'dress in old clothes . . .' the *New York World*, 31 December 1893, p. 25 *http://www.nellieblyonline.com/images/uploads/1893-12-31_Nellie_Bly_ And_The_Band_Of_Mercy.pdf*

p. 97   'The basket would shake . . .' ibid.

p. 97   'veiled lady with a basket . . .' *New York Herald*, 14 September 1893 *https://www.amherst.edu/alumni/learn/bookclub/pastfeatures/scoundrelsin- law/excerpt*

p. 97   'the most to be pitied . . .' *New York World*, 8 October 1893, p. 27

p. 98   'No men are admitted . . .' *http://messybeast.com/bookshelf/1893-band- ofmercy.htm*

p. 98   'The work is too dirty . . .' the *New York Times*, 6 October 1893, p. 6

p. 98   'Holding it up, she instructed . . .' the *New York Sun*, 16 November 1893

p. 99   'cruel extermination of cats . . .' the *New York Times,* 21 November 1893, p. 5

p. 99   'Cats Home was only a shield . . .' the *New York World*, 31 December 1893, p. 25 *http://www.nellieblyonline.com/images/uploads/1893-12-31_ Nellie_Bly_And_The_Band_Of_Mercy.pdf*

p. 100   'She lives like a pauper . . .' ibid.

p. 101   'We had no intention . . .' ibid.

p. 102   'the paradise on earth of crack . . .' *Dundee Evening Telegraph*, 4 November 1893, p. 2

Chapter 10: The Queen of Cats

p. 106 'came in crowds . . .' 'Homeless Cats', *The Spectator*, 16 September 1911, p. 16

p. 106 '*Left Behind*', *Daily Mail*, 21 August 1902, p. 7

p. 106 'I wonder that more cat-lovers . . .' Simpson, *Cats and All About Them*, p. 105 *https://archive.org/details/catsallaboutthem00simprich*

p. 107 'It really is a home . . .' ODFL, Fifth Annual Report, 1901–2, p. 39

p. 107 'unfortunate cats . . .' *The Times*, 24 July 1902, p. 3

p. 108 'an entirely new . . .' the *Morning Post*, 19 July 1895, p. 6

p. 108 'Trouble resulted . . .' 'The Royal London Institution & Home for Lost and Starving Cats', Report of Ch. Insp. Charles Arrow in TNA HO 144/21418

p. 109 'Mrs Williams . . .' the *Westminster Budget*, 3 July 1896, p. 15

p. 109 'placing a cat in . . .' the *Westminster Budget*, 3 November 1899, p. 15

p. 110 'capricious, feather-headed . . .' Frank Prochaska, *Royal Bounty: The Making of a Welfare Monarchy* (New Haven, 1995), p. 124

p. 110 'Party of cat workers . . .' – Chief Insp. Charles Arrow report in TNA HO 144/21418

p. 111 'It is reported . . .' the *Animal World*, May 1898, p. 77

p. 111 'one of the poor pussies . . .' the *Animal World*, July 1898, p. 11

p. 111 'There can be no . . .' the *Animal World*, July 1898, p. 98

p. 112 'The work was first undertaken . . .' *RLIHL&SC Annual Report to January 1903*, p. 17, in TNA HO 144/21418

p. 112 'A large number of cats . . .' *Hampshire Telegraph*, 20 May 1899, p. 12

p. 113 'kind and useful work . . .' 'Royal Patronage for Pussies' Home', *Our Cats*, 16 February 1901, p. 3

p. 113 'The Yellow Tram from . . .' leaflet in TNA HO 144/21418

p. 114 'The primary aim . . .' ibid.

p. 114 'Pussy Cat League . . .' ibid.

p. 115 'fairly luxurious style . . .' Chief Insp. Charles Arrow report in TNA HO 144/21418

p. 115 'Built at a cost . . .' *Annual Report to January 1903*, p. 26

p. 115 'The Camden Town Institution . . .' Simpson, op. cit., p. 32–4 *https://archive.org/stream/bookofcatsimpson00simprich#page/34/mode/2up*

p. 116 'It is not a home for cats . . .' *Truth*, 20 August 1903, p. 481

p. 117 'Ours is a work of . . .' Mrs Z. C. Morgan, *Truth and the Cats* (1903), p. 12

p. 117 'There may occasionally . . .' *Truth*, 20 August 1903, p. 481

p. 118 'No account of numbers . . .' Chief Insp. Charles Arrow report in TNA HO 144/21418

p. 119 'in the catteries are kept . . .' Morgan, op. cit., p. 11

p. 120 'Cats are not kept . . .' ibid.

p. 120 'It would have required . . .' ibid.

p. 120 'I am not playing at a Cats' Home . . .' ibid., p. 14

p. 121 'A number of ladies . . .' *Daily Illustrated Mirror*, 7 March 1904, p. 6

p. 121 'Black Cat of Holborn . . .' *Portsmouth Evening News*, 22 August 1904, p. 4

p. 121 fn 'Six cats are . . .' 'Queen Alexandra's Cat Fancy', the *Illustrated Sporting News*, reprinted in the *Montreal Gazette*, 16 September 1904

p. 122 'entirely indifferent . . .' *Sheffield Evening Telegraph*, 16 May 1908, p. 5

p. 123 'As much danger . . .' *Jasper Weekly Courier*, 30 September 1910, p. 3

p. 124 'favourite cat would be . . .' *New York Times*, 10 April 1920, p. 15

Chapter 11: Waifs of a Great City

p. 125 'Does she belong . . .' the *Animal World*, August 1908, p. 190

p. 126 'a detached pavilion . . .' Letter from Clough Williams-Ellis in LCC Architects Department, General Minutes, Battersea Dogs and Cats Home LMA, GLC/AR/BR/17/30299

p. 127 'Cat Sub-Committee . . .' General Purposes Committee Minutes, November 1910, p. 117, RSPCA Archive

p. 128 'These shelters should . . .' ODFL Receiving Shelters for Stray Cats, *17th Annual Report* (1912), p. 61, London Metropolitan Archives A/FWA/C/D 256/002

p. 128 'married a lady . . .' COS correspondence, 12 March 1912 LMA A/FWA/C/D 256/002

p. 129 'People who are . . .' ibid.

p. 129 'You will remember the case . . .' ibid.

p. 129 'The Home is perfectly . . .' COS correspondence, 13 April 1905 LMA A/FWA/C/D 256/001

p. 129 'There is one point . . .' ibid.

p. 130 'Some people believe . . .', 'FDL's terms of reference', quoted in *The Cat*, June 1967, p. 426

p. 130 'Infants' Anti-Sausage . . .' *Punch*, 19 January 1910, p. 52

p. 131 'Cats suffer from . . .' *Nottingham Evening Post*, 18 July 1908, p. 5

p. 131 'I am a mission . . .' *Herald of the Golden Age*, September 1902, p. 100

p. 131 'A little Paradise . . .' ibid., p. 101

p. 132 'get up early in the morning . . .' ibid.

p. 132 'I was formerly . . .' *Our Cats*, 5 December 1903, pp. 118–20

p. 132 'a small house . . .' ibid.

p. 133 'mercy and justice . . .' ibid.

p. 133 'humane women now . . .' ibid.

p. 136 'It is ten minutes to two . . .' *Herald of the Golden Age*, December 1902, p. 143 *https://archive.org/stream/heraldofgoldendec1902exetuoft/heraldofgoldendec1902exetuoft_djvu.txt*

p. 136 'rescue the cats of Slumland . . .' Kate Cording, *Waifs of a Great City*, quoted in Harriet Ritvo, *The Animal Estate* (1987), pp. 145–6

p. 136 'Secrecy is usually . . .' 'Fishing for Cats', *Daily Mail*, 21 May 1907, p. 3

p. 137 'Miss Cording is always . . .' the *Brooklyn Eagle*, 2 August 1908, p. 2

p. 137 'rank socialism . . .' *Western Daily Press*, 4 November 1909, p. 9

p. 137 'support various cats' . . .' General Purposes Committee Minutes, November 1910, p. 118, RSPCA Archive

p. 134 'three occasions had . . .' *Nottingham Evening Post*, 26 November 1910, p. 3

p. 134 'we cannot afford . . .' *Our Cats*, 5 December 1903, p. 119

p. 138 'Ring the bell . . .' the *Daily News* reprinted in the *Queanbeyan Age*, New South Wales, 14 April 1911, p. 4

p. 139 'My hat was torn . . .' 'Fishing for Cats', *Daily Mail*, 21 May 1907, p. 3

p. 139 'for the purchase of . . .' General Purposes Committee, 11 December 1911, p. 231, RSPCA Archive

p. 139 'Of late, cats' skins . . .' the *Fur World*, June 1913, p. 24

p. 140 'the bodies were . . .' General Purposes Committee, 13 May 1912, p. 292, RSPCA Archive

p. 141 'Having given all . . .' 'The Late Miss Cording' the *Animal World*, May 1913, p. 86

p. 141 fn '40,000 dogs' teeth . . .' *Western Daily Press*, 21 January 1914, p. 3

p. 142 fn 'Collectors attached . . .' *Sunderland Daily Echo*, 8 November 1913, p. 1

p. 142 'directed that her body . . .' *Yorkshire Evening Post*, 17 November 1913, p. 21

p. 142 'New and larger . . .' the *Animal World*, May 1913, p. 86

p. 143 'Twenty-four hours . . .' the *Brooklyn Daily Eagle*, 14 December 1913, p. 15

p. 145 fn 'By her side was a stuffed cat . . .' TNA MEPO 2/1592

p. 145 'During the last year . . .' the *Brooklyn Daily Eagle*, 14 December 1913, p. 15

Chapter 12: Differences of Opinion

p. 147 'an entirely new . . .' *Folkestone Herald*, 30 May 1914, p. 10

p. 147 fn 'One very noteworthy . . .' W. F. Morse, 'The Disposal of Superfluous Animal Life', *American Journal of Public Health*, November 1913, pp. 1227–30

p. 149 'a vast army of cats . . .' the *Manchester Guardian*, 11 February 1904, p. 3

p. 149 'specially constructed tricycle . . .' the *London Journal*, 22 April 1911, p. 602

p. 150 'a large black cat . . .' *North Devon Journal*, 13 October 1898, p. 6

p. 150 'gave his life in . . .' *Western Daily Press*, 17 March 1916, p. 8

p. 150 'on behalf of the stray cats . . .' *Newcastle Journal*, 1 March 1915, p. 6

p. 150 '*Dear Christians* . . .' ODFL *Cats Receiving Shelters Report for 1914*, pp. 93–4

p. 151 'take stray dogs . . .' Letter from Capt. Edward Fairholme in the *Newcastle Journal*, 27 August 1914, p. 7

p. 151 'The Germans . . .' the *British Journal of Nursing*, 2 January 1915, p. 17

p. 151 'Told how his society . . .' 'CONTEST FOR $30,000 LEFT TO CATS HOME', the *New York Times*, 3 February 1915, p. 6

p. 152 'Miss Cording chloroformed . . .' ibid.

p. 152 'So many animals were . . .' ibid.

p. 153 'thirty-eight dogs . . .' the *Animal World*, December 1914, p. 114

p. 153 'a special weakness . . .' *Sunday Mirror*, 1 August 1915, p. 9

p. 153 'those cats whose owners . . .' 'The Suffering of Cats in Wartime', *Yorkshire Post and Leeds Intelligencer*, 28 July 1916, p. 3

p. 154 'The League neither . . .' Dr C. Reinhardt-Rutland, 'The Humane Killing of Cats', the *Animal World*, June 1916, pp. 71–2

p. 155 'new electrical killer . . .' ibid.

p. 155 '20,000 Unwanted Cats . . .' the *Animal World*, April 1915, p. vi

p. 155 'The Animal Rescue League . . .' *Hull Daily Mail*, 10 February 1917, p. 4

p. 156 'London's Starving Cats . . .' *http://messybeast.com/retro-wartime.htm*

p. 158 'If this is their life . . .' Dickin, *The Cry of the Animal* (1950), p. 17

p. 158 'Owners of animals . . .' Montague, *Let the Good Work Go On* (1947), p. 10

p. 159 'being a great . . .' Dickin, op. cit., p. 4

p. 159 'forthright woman . . .' ibid.

p. 159 'When drowning kittens . . .' *RSPCA Almanac*, July–August 1918

p. 160 'You will not see cats . . .' C. Rowland Johns, 'Cat and Dog Life', *Wonderful London* (1926), p. 357

p. 160 'all the cats that . . .' *Dundee Courier*, 4 November 1924, p. 5

p. 161 'The public seems . . .' ODFL *Receiving Shelters for Stray Cats 17th Annual Report*, 1920, p. 63

p. 161 'During the past . . .' *Nottingham Evening Post*, 20 July 1925, p. 4

p. 162 'RSPCA slaughterer . . .' 'Fatal Cat Scratch', *Chelmsford Chronicle*, 26 February 1932, p. 3

p. 162 'It is not generally realised . . .' *Taunton Courier and Western Advertiser*, 17 March 1926, p. 7

p. 162 'When the present . . .' ibid.

p. 164 'widow of Capt. John . . .' *Yorkshire Post and Leeds Intelligencer*, 22 May 1929, p. 5

Chapter 13: As Bad as a Funeral

p. 165 'seven or eight pounds . . .' *Yorkshire Post and Leeds Intelligencer*, 5 December 1935, p. 6

p. 166 'Two thousand cats and dogs . . .' *Dundee Evening Telegraph*, 9 January 1937, p. 8

p. 166 'Children who are naturally . . .' ibid.

p. 166 'As soon as we hear . . .' ibid.

p. 166 'In north and east London . . .' *The Times*, 2 January 1937, p. 7

p. 167 'perfectly humane . . .' *Western Daily Press*, 19 January 1933, p. 9

p. 167 'Many householders . . .' *The Times*, 17 September 1937, p.

p. 167 'It is stated that . . .' *Western Daily Press*, 20 October 1936, p. 8

p. 169 'offering free . . .' *The RSPCA: Its Position Explained* (1933), p. 3

p. 170 'heaven for sick pets . . .' the *Animal World*, September 1934, p. 133

p. 170 'The Society . . .' *The RSPCA: What It Is and What It Does* (1928), p. 11

p. 171 'National Feline . . .' *Western Morning News*, 14 July 1925, p. 9

p. 171 'lost cats will . . .' *Derby Daily Telegraph*, 10 July 1929, p. 5

p. 172 'Visitors to the Continent . . .' *Nottingham Evening Post*, 22 November 1928, p. 10

p. 173 'Those who may . . .' Evelyn Sharp, *Manchester Guardian*, 22 April 1925, p. 6

PART TWO: GOOD HOMES WANTED 1930–1970

Chapter 14: 'A Chance of Life and Happiness'

p. 177 'passing strange . . .' the *Animals' Friend*, April 1927, p. 1

p. 178 'Rescue leagues are not . . .' the *Animals' Friend*, October 1927, p. 8

p. 179 'I like to think that . . .' the *Animals' Friend*, October 1928, p. 5

p. 179 'the first time cats . . .' the *Animals' Friend*, August 1928, p. 129

p. 179 'The Cats' Protection League . . .' the *Cats' Mews-Sheet*, January 1931, p. 1

p. 180 'Fully to line up . . .' the *Cats' Mews-Sheet*, 8 August 1932, p. 31

p. 180 'There is too much risk . . .' ibid.

p. 180 'an army of hungry . . .' the *Animals' Friend*, November 1928, p. 22

p. 181 'What causes . . .' the *Cats' Mews-Sheet*, January 1932, p. 3

p. 181 'woman with a basket . . .' the *Cats' Mews-Sheet*, 2 February 1933, p. 7

p. 182 'Opinions differ . . .' Simpson, op. cit., p. 48

p. 182 'cruel, preferring to drown . . .' *http://messybeast.com/retro-1920.htm*

p. 183 'streets of shabby . . .' the *Cats' Mews-Sheet*, 7 July 1932, p. 28

p. 183 'If your cat is a female . . .' *The Cat*, February 1935, p. 21

p. 183 'an organisation has . . .' *Hastings and St Leonards Observer*, 21 March 1931, p. 8

p. 184 'save an army of . . .' the *Cats' Mews-Sheet*, 3 March 1931, p. 10

p. 184 'To anyone who is really fond . . .' the *Animal World*, July 1935, p. 99

p. 184 'holiday home for cats . . .' the *Animal World*, June 1931, p. 83

p. 185 'We don't pick up stray . . .' the *Animal World*, October 1934, p. 14

p. 186 'Custom has decreed . . .' *http://messybeast.com/retro-1920.htm*

p. 186 'there are not so . . .' *Yorkshire Evening Post*, 4 August 1933, p. 6

p. 187 'the increase of . . .' *Nottingham Evening Post*, 9 February 1937, p. 7

p. 187 'taken by force . . .' 'Oo-oo Case', *Sunderland Daily Echo*, 17 December 1937, p. 7

Chapter 15: Blitz Cats

p. 190 'stray cats are to be . . .' 'Pussy's Part in Four-Year Plan', *Nottingham Evening Post*, 22 October 1938, p. 7

p. 191 '*ARP Handbook No. 12* . . .' *Air Raid Precautions for Animals*, in TNA HO 186/2489, p. 24

p. 191 'cat and dog lethalling . . .' TNA MEPO 2/6478

p. 191 'contaminated hair on cats . . .' *ARP News*, October 1939, p. 23

p. 192 '*Measures to Meet* . . .' TNA HO 186/1417

p. 192 'the best thing for animals . . .' *Ilford Recorder*, 7 September 1939, p. 4

p. 193 'A widespread and . . .' *The Times*, 7 September 1939, p. 3

p. 193 'All estimates had . . .' TNA HO 186/1418

p. 194 'It is difficult . . .' *The Cat*, September 1939, p. 1

p. 194 'indifferent, bad and nervy . . .' *The Cat*, September 1939, p. 1

p. 194 'I have no doubt . . .' 'The Stray Cat', *The Cat*, April 1940, p. 75

p. 196 'scores of animals . . .' the *Animals' Defender*, November 1939, p. 57

p. 196 'Staff pleaded . . .' Smith, *The Blue Cross at War* (Blue Cross, Burford, 1990), p. 44.

p. 196 'imprisoned cats . . .' 'Cats Left in Empty Houses', *The Times*, 25 October 1939, p. 2

p. 196 'Letters offering homes . . .' Mary Golightly, the *Dog World*, 6 October 1939, p. 640

p. 197 'two hundred cats . . .' Noney Fleming, the *Dog World*, 27 December 1940, p. 1226

p. 197 'The evacuated cats . . .' Lind-af-Hageby, *Animals Saved from Destruction* (Animal Defence & Anti-Vivisection Society, London, 1941), p. 28

p. 198 'Whilst I can assure . . .' *The Cat*, October 1940, pp. 28–9

p. 198 'going out with . . .' ibid.

p. 199 'cat-lovers all . . .' ibid.

p. 199 'Although this Society's . . .' ibid.

p. 200 'New or temporary homes . . .' ibid.

p. 200 'The Weston-super-Mare . . .' *Western Daily Press*, 23 June 1941, p. 3

Chapter 16: Cats of National Importance

p. 201 'Many piteous tales . . .' *Our Dumb Friends' League Report for 1940*, p. 54

p. 202 'wild, starving cats . . .' *Manchester Guardian*, 11 January 1941, p. 10

p. 202 'Everywhere the . . .' ibid.

p. 203 'found alive but died . . .' *PDSA News*, January 1941, p. 2

p. 203 '1,400 pets, mostly cats . . .' *RSPCA Annual Report for 1941*, p. 16

p. 204 'I noticed a large . . .' Smith, op. cit., p. 49

p. 204 'Florence Nightingale . . .' *Daily Mirror*, 20 September 1943, p. 4

p. 204 'a friend in London . . .' *The Cat*, February 1941, p. 62

p. 204 'I have rescued . . .' *Daily Mirror*, 3 December 1940, p. 11

p. 204 'Someone asked me . . .' Lind-af-Hageby, op. cit., p. 24

p. 205 'has fed hundreds . . .' *Daily Mirror*, 2 November 1940, p. 3

p. 205 'In a case heard . . .' *The Cat*, August 1941, p. 122

p. 206 'The large numbers of . . .' *ODFL* 45th Annual Report Shelters Branch p. 57.

p. 206 fn 'They don't interact . . .' *http://www.kentnews.co.uk/home/the_feral_cats_descended_from_world_war_2_heroes_1_1374852 11 May 2012*

p. 207 'finding homes for strays'. . .' *Feeding of Non-Essential Animals* TNA MAF 84/61, 23 July 1941

p. 207 'is it antipatriotic . . .' *The Cat*, September 1940, p. 111

p. 207 'mice were over-running . . .' *Daily Mirror*, 8 January 1940, p. 7

p. 208 'There is a scarcity of cats . . .' the *Animal World*, February 1941, p. 12

p. 208 'The Dogs' Home van . . .' *Hull Daily Mail*, 17 November 1941, p. 3

p. 208 'After a severe blitz . . .' the *Veterinary Record*, 5 July 1941, p. 390

p. 209 'work of national importance . . .' *The Times*, 31 December 1941, p. 2

p. 209 'a lenient view . . .' 'Feeding Our Pets in War Time', the *Animal World*, December 1941, p. 1

Chapter 17: Consumer Cats

p. 212 'There is no statutory . . .' TNA MEPO 2/6597, 16 October 1945

p. 212 'The evidence showed . . .' J. B. Moore, *Charitable Trusts* (1950) *http://www.austlii.edu.au/au/journals/ResJud/1950/40.pdf*

p. 213 '[One] has to see . . .' ibid.

p. 215 '500,000 stray cats . . .' *Dundee Courier*, 1 July 1953, p. 4

p. 215 'The total has been variously . . .' *The Times*, 26 June 1953, p. 3

p. 216 'Not only are . . .' *Hull Daily Mail*, 15 October 1949, p. 1

p. 217 'Londoners may not know . . .' *The Times*, 10 April 1952, p. 8

p. 218 'underground movement . . .' Plant, *Sweet Cat Purr Softly, The Story of the Feral Cat* (unpublished manuscript, 1995), partly reproduced in Remfry, *Ruth Plant* (2001)

p. 219 'easier to find . . .' ibid.

p. 219 '[Cats] are attached . . .' *Dundee Courier*, 1 July 1953, p. 4

p. 219 'Maggie' and 'Rosie' . . .' Hamilton, op. cit., p. 65

p. 220 'Animal welfare societies . . .' *The Times*, 3 August 1957, p. 7

p. 220 'saw the small animal . . .' Gardiner, *The Dangerous Women of Animal Welfare: How British Veterinary Medicine Went to the Dogs* (2014) http://www.research.ed.ac.uk/portal/files/14593619/The_Dangerous_Women_of_Animal_Welfare.pdf

p. 220 fn 'Most cats show . . .' Nerea de Clifford, Obituary, *Daily Telegraph*, 16 December 1987, p.

p. 220 fn 'wearing suede . . .' Gardiner, op. cit. http://shm.oxfordjournals.org/content/early/2014/01/15/shm.hkt101.full

p. 221 'Many hardened . . .' *Pet Trade Journal*, March 1959, p. 80

p. 222 'the cat and the dog . . .' the Humane Society of the United States, *Special Report on Controlling America's Pet Population*, p. 3 http://animal-studiesrepository.org/sp_reps/11/

p. 224 'The grandest colony . . .'

p. 224 'warm, rabbit-warren . . .' 'British Museum: request for help to rid museum of a very large number of cats living in and around the basement' TNA WORK 17/512

p. 225 'Most of the cats . . .' *The Cat*, January 1963, p. 174

p. 225 'was controlled by a female . . .' *The Cat*, September 1962, p. 135

p. 225 'the shooting by a pest . . .' *The Cat*, September 1962, p. 134

Chapter 18: Cool Cats

p. 229 'stray facing destruction . . .' Montgomery, *Arthur the Television Cat* (1973), p. 14

p. 231 'Thousands of healthy kittens . . .'

p. 232 'Homeless Animals . . .' the *Animal World*, January 1958, p. 1

p. 233 'Unlike the dog . . .' the *Animal World*, May 1958, p. 50

p. 233 'The RSPCA do not believe . . .' ibid.

p. 233 '[These] unhappy and lonely . . .' ibid.

p. 233 '*No "Welfare State" for Him* . . .' *The Times*, 8 November 1957, p. 15

p. 234 'The RSPCA has recently . . .' 'Cats for Research', *The Times*, 14 March 1958, p. 11

p. 235 'In every large town . . .' the *Animal World*, November 1961, p. 161

p. 235 'A great number of legacies . . .' ibid.

p. 236 'Are we getting any . . .' *The Cat*, February–March 1960, p. 55

p. 236 'For years it has . . .' *The Cat*, February–March 1967, pp. 454–5

Chapter 19: Strays, Strays and More Strays!

p. 240 'willy-nilly passing on . . .'

p. 240 'To give away . . .' *Feline Advisory Bureau News Bulletin*, January 1967, pp. 22–4

p. 241 'Her owners were finally . . .' *The Cat*, March–April 1970, p. 23

p. 241 'I think the Neutering . . .' *The Cat*, November–December 1969, p. 104

p. 242 'During April . . .' *The Cat*, June 1968, p. 61

p. 242 'general exodus . . .' *The Cat*, February–March 1967, p. 456

p. 242 'Strays, strays and . . .' *The Cat*, February–March 1968, p. 25

p. 243 'Mrs Walledge . . .' *The Cat*, September–October 1969, pp. 80–1

p. 243 'The recent purchase tax . . .' ibid.

p. 243 'We recently have taken . . .' *The Cat*,

p. 244 'confusion, disappointment . . .' *The Cat*, January 1970, p. 4

p. 244 'It is a desperate . . .' *The Cat*, August 1967, p. 454

p. 244 'misguided people . . .' *The Cat*, October 1966, p. 309

p. 246 'Can anyone doubt . . .' *The Cat*, January 1969, p. 4

p. 246 'Should we be . . .' ibid., p. 5

Chapter 20: How To Market a Three-Legged Cat

p. 250 'notevenolder. . .'*http://www.thedailymews.com/information/charities-and-rescue-centres/680-north-shore-animal-league-america*

p. 250 'My wife adored animals . . .' *Animal People*, January–February 2013 *http://www.animalpeoplenews.org/anp/2013/02/22/babette-lewyt-rescuer-who-rescued-the-north-shore-animal-league/*

p. 250 'We have the same concept . . .' the *Wall Street Journal*, 6 March 1975, p. 1–2

p. 251 'These are not strays . . .' *http://www.thedailymews.com/information/charities-and-rescue-centres/680-north-shore-animal-league-america*

Chapter 21: Cats Have Rights Too

p. 254 'people came to think . . .' Singer, *Animal Liberation* (2009 edition), p. 219

p. 255 'We believe that . . .' *http://www.peta.org/about-peta/why-peta/pets*

p. 256 '[We are] often criticised . . .' *RSPCA Annual Report 1969*, p. 41

p. 256 'it was very easy . . .' *Homeless Animal Committee Minutes*, 24 November 1966, RSPCA Archives

p. 256 'The argument to destroy . . .' *Homeless Animal Committee Appendix A*, October 1971, RSPCA Archives

p. 256 'fast gaining the . . .' ibid.

p. 258 'Central guidelines . . .' Hall, *Voiceless Victims* (1982), p. 184

p. 258 'Of all the ideas . . .' *The Cat*, May–June 1976, p. 46

p. 259 'We make no money . . .' *The Times*, 8 April 1972, p. 2

p. 259 fn 'To use intravenous . . .' *The Spectator*, 20 September 1974, p. 3

p. 260 'In fact, the sum spent . . .' *The Times*, 22 January 1974, p. 16

p. 260 'Cat-lovers, who take . . .' ibid.

p. 261 'because the RSPCA need to know', *Christian Science Monitor*, 3 July 1980 *http://www.csmonitor.com/1980/0703/070304.html*

p. 261 'He was a very scared . . .' ibid.

p. 261 'The tremendous increase . . .' *The Times*, 26 June 1976, p. 2

p. 261 'New homes were . . .' ibid.

p. 262 'NECESSARY PUBLIC SERVICE . . .' *Battersea Dogs Home Annual Reports 1959–79*, Wandsworth Heritage Service

p. 262 'returns of cats and dogs . . .' ibid.

Chapter 22: 'Why We Must Euthanize'

p. 266 'the "miracle of birth" . . .' *http://www.all-creatures.org/aro/q-wright-phylis.html*

p. 267 'matriarch of catch . . .' *http://www.nathanwinograd.com/?p=7682*

p. 267 'Why We Must Euthanize', Phyllis Wright *Humane Society Journal*, Summer 1978, pp. 24–5 *http://animalstudiesrepository.org/cgi/viewcontent.cgi?article=1002&context=v23_news*

p. 268 'It is a problem, the solution . . .' *Journal of the American Veterinary Medical Association*, August 1974, pp. 363–70

p. 268 'With an estimated 80 . . .' the Humane Society of the United States, *Special Report on Controlling America's Pet Population* (1975), HSUS Special Reports Paper 11 *http://animalstudiesrepository.org/sp_reps/11 p. 1*

PART THREE: A WALK ON THE WILD SIDE

Chapter 23: The Third Estate

p. 274 'Trapping of semi-wild strays . . .' *The Cat*, May–June 1973, p. 45

p. 275 'a borough swarming . . .' *The Cat*, May–June 1974, p. 50

p. 277 'every alley in Florence . . .' *The Cat*, February–March 1966, p. 224

p. 278 'Not all of them are starving . . .' *The Cat*, May 1965, p. 98

p. 278 'The Cats of Venice . . .' *The Cat*, May 1965, p. 98

p. 278 'we went in January . . .' *The Cat*, February–March 1966, p. 221

p. 279 'Suffragettes of . . .' *The Cat*, February–March 1966, p. 224

p. 279 'It began two days ago . . .' *The Times*, 5 January 1966, p. 8

p. 280 'The Guardia . . .' Wintle, *Helena Sanders and the Cats of Venice* (1989), p. 167

p. 280 'Inglesi Go Home . . .' *Daily Mail*, 6 January 1966, pp. 1–2

p. 280 'The women are due . . .' *The Times*, 7 January 1966, p. 15
p. 281 'So far, only a very few badly . . .' *The Cat*, February–March 1966, p. 221
p. 281 'I have seen the cats of Venice . . .' ibid., p. 222
p. 281 'A stray cat which . . .' the *Guardian*, 12 October 1966, p. 4

Chapter 24: The Untouchables
p. 283 'For all those years . . .' Remfry, op. cit., p. 58
p. 283 'Sheila thus gained . . .' ibid., p. 59
p. 284 'Staff who feed . . .' *The Ecology and Control of Feral Cats: Proceedings of a Symposium Held at Royal Holloway College, University of London, 23 and 24 September 1980*, Universities Federation for Animal Welfare, p. 83
p. 284 'broke in with . . .' *Sussex Life*, October 1993, p. 4, RSPCA Archives
p. 285 'There are thousands of semi-wild cats . . .' *http://www.britishpathe.com/video/catching-cats-aka-model-catching-cats*
p. 287 'at how many trapped . . .' *The Cat*, November–December 1979, pp. 8–9
p. 288 'Little Wildie Kittens . . .' *The Cat*, January–February 1976, p. 2
p. 289 'Celia Hammond . . .' *The Times*, 11 April 1978, p. 16
p. 291 'CAT stepped in . . .' *The Times*, 19 May 1982, p. 16
p. 291 'CAT CONTROL . . .' interview with Jenny Remfry, London, April 2015
p. 291 'wait quietly for a cat . . .' Plant manuscript, op. cit.
p. 292 'She was the daughter . . .' ibid.
p. 293 'The strangest people . . .' ibid.
p. 294 'The cats in the station . . .' ibid.
p. 296 'where people boasted . . .' Hall, op. cit., p. 171
p. 296 'too much trouble . . .' ibid.
p. 296 'part of a big package . . .' *Willesden Observer*, 11 June 1982
p. 297 'For the first time . . .' Jenkins, op. cit., p. 313

Chapter 25: Feral Frenzy
p. 301 '"Domino", "Pickle" . . .' Colin Tudge, 'The Wild Cats of England', *New Scientist*, 16 April 1981, p. 154
p. 303 'Our familiar fireside cat . . .' Remfry, 'Feral Cats in Britain', *Bulletin of the Feline Advisory Bureau*, Winter 1979, p. 11
p. 304 'As I studied this enclosed . . .' *http://www.feralcats.org.uk/overview.html*
p. 304 'Unwanted kittens . . .' UFAW 1980, op. cit., p. 82
p. 305 'Before trapping . . .' ibid., p. 84
p. 305 'vermin fit only . . .' ibid., p. 91
p. 306 'We still use the chloroform . . .' ibid., p. 93
p. 306 'The feral cat is . . .' Tabor, op. cit., p. 179

p. 308 'kinder to have . . .' *The Times*, 25 January 1982, p. 6

p. 309 'Where I worked . . .' communication from Kate Horne, October 2015

p. 310 'few received veterinary care . . .' *http://messybeast.com/retro-rescue.htm*

Chapter 26: The Moral Maze

p. 313 'My understanding is . . .' *Hansard*, 9 June 1986

p. 314 'a bland, idealised story . . .' *The Times*, 8 May 1984, p. 16

p. 314 Old ladies, on . . .' *The Times*, 17 May 1984, p. 9

p. 315 'He seemed a . . .' ibid.

p. 316 'Veronica began . . .' Communication from Christopher Russell, October 2015

p. 318 'The vast number of . . .' Tabor, *The Wild Life of the Domestic Cat* (1983), p. 182

p. 319 'persons caring for barn . . .' *www.neighborhoodcats.org/. . ./California_-_San_Mateo_County.doc*

p. 320 'shocked to learn . . .' *http://www.nathanwinograd.com/?p=11902*

p. 320 'subsidized abandonment . . .' 'Animal Welfare Forum: 'Management of Abandoned and Feral Cats', *Journal of the American Veterinary Medical Association*, 1 November 2004, p. 1378

p. 320 'The [HSUS] view was that . . .' Sarah Hartwell *http://messybeast.com/usferal.htm*

p. 321 'the goal of any feral . . .' *http://zimmer foundation.org/MI/nl/pdf/071.pdf*

p. 321 'The elimination of . . .' *VICE News*, 16 July 2015

p. 323 'his food was paid for . . .' *http://www.purr-nfur.org.uk/famous/humphrey.html*

p. 324 'handling an angry . . .' Sarah Hartwell *http://messybeast.com/feralkit.htm*

Chapter 27: Asylum-Seeking Cats

p. 325 'He is a workaholic . . .' 'Humphrey – the Downing Street Dossier', David Millward, *Daily Telegraph*, 3 March 2005

p. 326 'As well as being treated . . .' ibid.

p. 326 'He was very thin . . .' *The Cat*, November–December 1995, p. 8

p. 327 'You could not have met . . .' *The Cat*, May–June 1996, p. 38

p. 328 'brutal murder . . .' *The Cat*, March–April 1986, p. 20

p. 328 'turned into a monster' *The Cat*, September–October 1986, p. 26

p. 328 'the privilege of . . .' *The Cat*, March–April 1986, p. 18

p. 329 'Rescue, Our . . .' Cats Protection League, 1995 *Annual Review*, p. 4

p. 332 fn 'The truth is . . .' Telephone interview with Maggie Roberts, Director of Veterinary Services at Cats Protection, May 2015

p. 333 'The little girl played . . .' *The Cat*, September–October 1997, p. 6

p. 333 'make us laugh again . . .' *The Cat*, September–October 1996, p. 8

p. 334 'When my wife, Wendy . . .' interview with Alfie Teale, May 2015

p. 335 'He was obviously a stray . . .' *The Cat*, November–December 1994, p. 37

p. 336 'daily medication for . . .' *http://www.pdsa.org.uk/press-releases/case-studies/poorly-puss-patch-is-feline-fine-thanks-to-pdsa*

p. 336 'Grisn . . .' *The Cat*, May–June 1996, p. 39

p. 337 'I wanted desperately . . .' *The Cat*, September–October 1996, p. 41

p. 337 'They were released . . .' *The Cat*

p. 338 'feed at the back door . . .' *The Cat*

PART FOUR:
RESCUE CATS ARE TOP CATS 1990–2020

Chapter 28: No-Kill

p. 342 '100 per cent . . .' Winograd, *Redemption: The Myth of Pet Overpopulation and the No-Kill Revolution in America* (2009), p. 180

p. 343 fn 'direct injection of sodium . . .' *http://www.humanesociety.org/about/policy_statements/statement_euthanasia.html*

p. 344 'not putting animals . . .' *https://www.arlboston.org/euthanasia-policy-qa/*

p. 345 'Typically shelter workers . . .' *http://www.researchgate.net/profile/Arnold_Arluke/publication/264943272_Managing_Emotions_in_an_Animal_Shelter/links/549b3a9f0cf2d6581ab2e287.pdf p. 146*

p. 347 'desperate, unhinged . . .' *http://www.animals24-7.org/2015/02/26/casualties-of-the-save-rate-40000-animals-at-failed-no-kill-shelters-rescues/*

p. 347 'There was justification . . .' *https://groups.yahoo.com/neo/groups/Animal_Rights_Debate/conversations/messages/9346*

p. 347 'We never put a healthy . . .' Telephone interview with Maggie Roberts, Director of Veterinary Services at Cats Protection, May 2015

p. 347 'air-conditioning . . .' 'Identity in Animal Shelters', Arnold Arluke Animal Sheltering, January/February 2007, p. 34 *http://www.animalsheltering.org/resources/magazine/jan_feb_2007/constructing_personal_identity.pdf*

p. 348: 'To be able to offer . . .' *http://www.peta.org/issues/companion-animal-issues/animal-shelters/*

p. 349 'far worse fate than . . .' *http://www.peta.org/issues/companion-animal-issues/cruel-practices/hoarding/*

p. 349 'cats who are let outdoors . . .' *http://www.peta.org/living/companion-animals/caring-animal-companions/caring-cats/indoor-cats/*

p. 349 Having witnessed first-hand . . .' *http://www.peta.org/issues/companion-animal-issues/companion-animals-factsheets/trap-neuter-return-monitor*

p. 349 'The international pastime . . .' *http://www.peta.org/about-peta/why-peta/pets/*

p. 350 'fantasy relationship . . .' Flegel, op. cit., p. 59

p. 350 'By virtue of their . . .' *http://www.mammal.org.uk/sites/default/files/Domestic%20Cat%20Predation%20on%20Wildlife.pdf*

Chapter 29: Love Me, Love My Rescue Cat

p. 355 'on the RSPCA website . . .' *http://www.people4chineseanimals.org/China-Cat-Cafe.html*

p. 357 'pro-cat faction . . .' 25 January 2011 *http://www.bbc.co.uk/news/uk-politics-12265112*

p. 357 'arrived [at Downing Street] . . .' *http://www.dailymail.co.uk/news/article-1357213/Downing-Street-cat-takes-Cabinet-seeing-ITV-reporter-Lucy-Manning.html*, 16 February 2011

Chapter 30: Celebrity Cats

p. 360 'The cat sat . . .' James Bowen, *A Street Cat Named Bob* (2012), p. 18

p. 360 'healthy stray . . .' *http://www.rspca.org.uk/adviceandwelfare/pets/cats/straycats*

p. 361 'Annie Mole . . .' *http://london-underground.blogspot.co.uk/2010/07/tube-photo-of-week-angel-tube-cat.html* *http://www.islingtontribune.com/news/2010/sep/two-cool-cats-big-issue-seller-and-stray-called-bob*

p. 363 'bearded musician . . .' *http://www.spin.com/lil-bub-indie-cat-mike-bridavsky/*

p. 364 'Lil BUB is a healthy . . .' *http://www.lilbub.com/about*

p. 364 'Being ferals . . .' *hamiltonthehipstercat.bigcartel.com/about-hamilton*

p. 365 'came tumbling out . . .' *http://www.buzzfeed.com/summeranne/the-future-is-here-and-her-name-is-princess-monster-truck#.hgvgNa5wN*

p. 365 'brands and charities . . .' *http://www.wired.co.uk/news/archive/2014-08/22/instagranimals-and-their-owners*

Chapter 31: Cat Crisis

p. 370 'nobody coming . . .' *http://www.nottinghampost.com/Number-cat-adoptions-plummets-rescue-centre/story-13170812-detail/story.html*

p. 370 'unwanted older cats . . .' *http://www.cats.org.uk/news/forgotten-feline-pensioners-left-on-the-shelf*

p. 370 'ever-growing cat crisis . . .' *http://www.cats.org.uk/news/unwanted-cat-numbers-hit-all-time-high*

p. 370 'The cat population . . .' *http://www.rspca.org.uk/getinvolved/campaign/catcrisis*

p. 371 'Usually it takes . . .' *Daily Mail*, 20 August 2009, p. 17

p. 371 'Many landlords will . . .' *http://www.persona.uk.com/nle/C-SoC/OBJ-046.pdf*

p. 372 'Intending to end . . .' *http://www.rspca.org.uk/utilities/aboutus/mission/pledges/pledge2*

p. 373 'The owners of independent . . .' *http://www.animals24-7. org/2014/02/14/rspca-of-england-wales-caught-in-a-crossfire/*

p. 373 'A no-kill policy . . .' *http://www.telegraph.co.uk/news/earth/wild-life/10422641/RSPCA-accused-of-persecuting-owners-of-animal-shelters. html*

p. 374 'Bruce and Eileen Gough . . .' *http://www.kentonline.co.uk/canterbury/ news/devil-cats-rampage-ends-thanks-19608/*

p. 375 'He was doing exactly . . .' *http://www.theguardian.com/environ-ment/2014/feb/25/rspca-chief-executive-gavin-grant-steps-down*

Chapter 32: Cat On–line

p. 378 'one of the internet's . . .' *http://www.forbes.com/sites/marcba-bej/2011/05/10/petfinder-com-arranges-17-million-adoptions-by-open-branding-technology/*

p. 379 'We had a lot of cats . . .' *The Cat.*

p. 379 'Houses with rooms full of cats . . .' *http://www.thecatgroup. org.uk/faq/ faqfind.html*

p. 380 'How Much Is That . . .' International Fund for Animal Welfare 2012 Report *http://www.ifaw.org/united-states/resource-centre/ how-much-doggie-my-browser*

Chapter 33: Cats Come Home

p. 384 'If we can increase . . .' Joint press release 12 November 2008 *http:// www.maddiesfund.org/ad-council.htm*

p. 385 'Among the most cherished . . .' *http://www.animals24-7. org/2014/03/12/why-we-cannot-adopt-our-way-out-of-shelter-killing/*

p. 385 'Since every pet . . .' ibid.

p. 386 'Please do not allow your . . .' *http://www.peta.org/issues/companion-animal-issues/overpopulation/euthanasia/*

p. 387 'so many younger, cuter . . .' *http://www.animals24-7.org/2014/03/12/ why-we-cannot-adopt-our-way-out-of-shelter-killing/*

p. 388 'PetSmart Charities® . . .'*https://www.petsmartcharities.org/adopt-a-pet/ adoption-centers*

p. 388 'Through a unique . . .' *http://www.petco.com/petco_Page_PC_founda-tionprograms.aspx*

p. 389 'Many animals may . . .' *http://www.petco.com/Content/ArticleList/ Article/32/1/7721/How-to-Find-the-Right-Pet-For-Your-Family-at-an-Animal-Shelter.aspx*

p. 390 'an appalling idea . . .' *http://www.dailymail.co.uk/news/article-2581881/ Anger-charities-sell-rescue-cats-giant-pet-superstores-years-campaigning-against-sale-animals-shops.html*

p. 391 'The thought of cats . . .' ibid.

p. 391 'The centre in Pets . . .' *http://www.cats.org.uk/news/media-statement-from-cats-protection-with-respect-to-pets-at-home*

p. 392 'popped into the . . .' *Your Cat*, 12 June 2014 *http://yourcat.co.uk/Your-Cat/pets-at-home-hail-new-cats-protection-centre-a-success.html*

p. 393 'all about the cats . . .' *http://www.dailymail.co.uk/sciencetech/article-3057484/Who-going-cat-call-Ratbusters-Animal-charity-lends-homeless-moggies-householders-scare-away-rodents.html#ixzz3arBY2SLP*

Postscript 1904

p. 395 'You talk of poor dumb . . .' the *Animal World*, 1904.

Postscript 2007

p. 400 'We are so concerned . . .' *http://www.celiahammond.org/index.php/about-us/olympic-rescue*